# TRANSFORMATIVE LEADER'S ROADMAP

*Systematically Actualize Your*
*School's Full Potential*

by JOHN SHINDLER

**Transformative Leader's Roadmap**

*Systematically Actualize Your School's Full Potential*

© 2021, John Shindler.

# TABLE OF CONTENTS

# Introduction

A transformative leader exists within every educator. And each school possesses the capacity for growth and excellence. This book will be your roadmap for actualizing your school's full potential. It is intended to be utilized by leaders in any role within a school – principals, directors, coordinators, chairs, coaches, team leaders, teacher leaders, and others.

The roadmap outlined in this book provides a theoretical foundation and practical steps to guide your institutional improvement work. It gives the reader a clear sense of where their school is currently and what would be required to move up the improvement "pathway" to more actualized roadmap locations. Each school's journey up the pathway represent growth toward a more effective, empowering, connected, and self-evidently fulfilling experience of teaching and learning.

The development of the roadmap represents 20 plus years of research into over 500 schools, countless interviews and conversations with transformative leaders, and involvement within multiple school improvement efforts.

The chapters of the book progress developmentally. In the initial chapters, the elements of the roadmap are built into a complete model. The chapters in section two provide clear insights and practical guidance in the following areas:

- Cultivating the quality of trust at the school.
- Facilitating a school-wide vision.
- Empowering instructional leadership for improved practice.
- A meaningful process for engaging strategic planning and decision-making.
- Examining your school climate with a comprehensive systems framework.
- Using classroom management and discipline to support your school's improvement process.

This foundational content is then synthesized into three culminating chapters. Chapters twelve provides a clear set of instructions for improving a school which is currently at a lower level on the roadmap by way of encouraging greater capacity, coherence, and intention. Chapter thirteen explores how to move a school currently in the middle to high range on the "pathway" to the highest realms on the roadmap, defined by trust, empowerment, and connection. Finally, Chapter fourteen engages you, the leader, in an exercise of self-reflection, and personal vision setting.

When we have a meaningful understanding of where we are, can clearly see where we are going, and recognize in practical operational terms what is required to improve, we can act effectively and trust our steps. This book is your roadmap for systematically actualizing your school's potential with confidence.

More Transformative Leader Resources can be found at:

- transformativeclassroom.com
- calstatela.edu/schoolclimate

## Author:

A passionate livelong educator, Dr. John Shindler is the Director of the Alliance for the Study of School Climate (ASSC) and a Professor of Education at California State University, Los Angeles. He is the author of *Transformative Classroom Management* and several articles related to teaching, leadership, and school change. He is the creator of the School Climate Assessment Instrument (SCAI) and the Paragon Learning Style Inventory (PLSI). He works with schools throughout the world to support more empowering, effective, healthy, and conscious school climates.

# Acknowledgements

I am deeply grateful for all the support I have received over the past twenty years in the creation of this book. I would first like to thank my family and friends for their eternal support and encouragement. I am blessed to have such positive and caring people in my life.

I am blessed to be able to work with my dear colleague Dr. Albert Jones who has been instrumental in the research, practical application, and idea featured in this book. The book contents reflect many hundreds of hours of our conversations and work together in the field.

Next, I cannot thank my editor Sheila Balk enough. She brought her experience as a teacher, leader, and master editor to the process and improved the quality of the book immensely.

I would also like to thank Dr. Martha Mutz who was instrumental in the early development of the book and helped structure many of the ideas.

I deeply appreciate my university, California State University, Los Angeles, and the community of educators – administrators, faculty, and students within the Charter College of Education for their ongoing support, opportunities for application of these principles, and the sabbatical time to write. Sabbaticals are invaluable to those of us at teaching universities. This book would not have been possible without one.

I would like to thank the many transformative leaders who have been profiled here. I am grateful they allowed me to observe them in action, discuss their methods, and in some cases work along-side them. They are an inspiration to me and make an invaluable contribution to their schools and the field in general.

I would like to thank everyone at the Alliance for the Study of School Climate for working as a team over the years and being committed to quality service to schools, and all those whom we have been privileged to serve.

Finally, I would like to thank all of those who have inspired the thinking of this book. There are too many to list, but I would like to name a few – Linda Inlay, Carol Dweck, Michael Fullan, Forest Parkay, Michael Beckwith, JoAnn Burkholder, Clint Taylor, Rob Ricciardelli, Bruce Brown, A.D. Williams, and all my teachers.

I hope this book honors their faith and support.

# EXPANDED
# TABLE OF CONTENTS

## Chapter 9: Meaningful Strategic Planning and Effective O/Outcome Data Usage ................................................. 214

## Chapter 10: Exploring the Eight Dimensions of School Climate and Function ........................................................ 257

## Chapter 11: Moving to the Next Level in the Area of Classroom Management and School Discipline. ...................... 271

# PART I:
## Building the
## Roadmap

---

# CHAPTER 1:

## Introduction to the Roadmap and School Improvement Pathway

Welcome to your guide to becoming a transformative leader and supporting your school's process of growth. Within every building lies the potential to be a high performing vision-driven school – a transformative school. What is commonly missing is a roadmap for actualizing that potential. In this book, we offer a clear, research-based roadmap for how to understand the process of school change, and a practical methodology for moving your institution up to higher levels on the roadmap. The benefits of that growth include improved performance, but also assume higher levels of function and climate quality, as well as a school which embodies a greater sense of ease, sanity, and satisfaction.

### Why Do We Need a Roadmap?

First, to initiate improvement, we need to have a conceptual as well as operational understanding of where we are currently. Without that knowledge we lack the ability to appreciate and define our existing situation clearly. Second, we need a roadmap to know where we are going, and what we mean when we refer to concepts such as "better" or "improved" or "higher performing." If we cannot define what we are about, or where we are going, in tangible terms which can be shared and understood by everyone, it will limit our ability to cultivate the qualities of *vision* and *trust* – which are essential factors to our growth.

The school effectiveness roadmap, laid out in the first portion of this book, will help illuminate the inner workings of schools and the process of change. Most readers will find that being able to explore the anatomy of their school will be empowering in and of itself. The following chapters will explain the practical steps required for elevating your school from its existing location on the roadmap to the next level. For some readers, that may imply a starting point at a lower location on the roadmap and the need to build a foundation of function and plant the seeds for future growth. For other readers, the roadmap will be helpful in supporting their process of going from "good" to "great" and breaking through to the next level. No matter where your starting point, the roadmap will be a useful aid in clarifying how to ascend to the next stage of growth along your journey.

## A Brief History of Our Work at ASSC and the Origins of the Effectiveness Roadmap

Over the course of the past 20 years, my colleagues and I have explored what makes schools effective. We began our journey by asking a basic question – "what is the most essential phenomenon within a school?" We concluded that the X-factor was the school's climate – that basic quality that defines each school and the totality of that which happens within it. We began our efforts (as the Alliance for the Study of School Climate, ASSC) with the goal of understanding schools and helping educators. We then created the School Climate Assessment Instrument (SCAI) and began to assess climate at schools using this very broad and inclusive eight- dimension survey. Our goal was to provide a mirror for educators so that they could accurately recognize their performance in the area of school climate. We were successful, and content with this as our function, but soon we found the SCAI also predicted student achievement (and other outcomes) almost perfectly – i.e., a 0.7 correlation (explained in more detail in chapter 2). While at the time most educators were still viewing social-emotional climate and academic achievement as separate, even competing consideration, our research demonstrated that they both had the same root – that basic X-factor. Near the same time, we had developed a classroom teacher style matrix we used in our teacher and administrator credential courses, and in our consulting to help make sense of the different intentions and practices within classrooms. What we realized was that the matrix provided an ideal topography for how the climate and achievement data could be mapped and understood. When we combined the two, the essence of the school effectiveness roadmap was born. Over the past decade or so we have revised and further validated the instrument and model with additional data and applied action research from use in the field. We have been able to see how powerful it can be as a means of prediction as well as explanation. We have presented it all over the country, to various groups of educators and the reaction has been the same – "Yes, that's it!" In addition, we have been engaged with hundreds of schools in their improvement processes, seeking out transformative leaders, and studying what they did. What we have found is that the process for moving forward varies somewhat from one situation to another, but the basic principles for affecting positive change will be similar. Those common principles can be explained and operationalized into the practical action that best activate an institution's potential. What we find it that for some educators the roadmap model may require a paradigm shift to appreciate, while for others it will connect with their vision and values immediately.

### Figure 1.1: School Effectiveness Roadmap

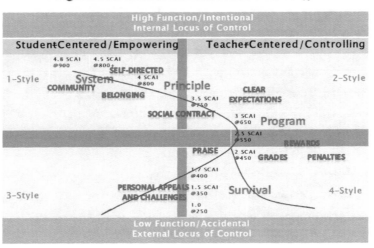

Figure 1.1 depicts the basic elements of the school effectiveness roadmap. The more productive, effective, and desirable locations on the roadmap are defined by higher levels of personal and collective function and empowerment. The **vertical axis** represents a continuum of *function* and *intention*. Moving up on this axis will imply creating more capacity, coherence, intention, and efficiency. The **horizontal axis** reflects a contrast between *empowerment*, *connection* and *trust* versus control, competition, and fear. Movement up typically implies a great deal of intention, effort, and the building of effective structures. Moving over to the highest levels on the roadmap most often implies a shift in the mindset guiding the vision. We call that "making the left-hand turn." Without it, the function and performance levels of a school will be limited.

## Using the Roadmap and the Book – The Journey is the Destination

Throughout the book, as well as your process of school improvement, it will be useful to keep in mind that both the nature of the more desirable locations on the roadmap and what it takes to progress there will be inter-related. When your school ultimately demonstrates the values and practices defined by higher levels of vision, trust, and empowerment, you will find yourself experiencing all the benefits and outcomes that correspond to those higher locations along the pathway. Concurrently, the nature of the qualities require for that growth movement will be the same as the qualities that reflect successful outcomes. We teach and lead who we are (collectively and individually). And who we are will manifest ultimately as our performance level. So, in a very real sense, the nature of the journey is the experience of the destination and vice versa.

While the school effectiveness roadmap is somewhat complex – it will take us the first five chapters to fully build – when entirely represented it provides a rather complete macro-theoretical foundation as well as an applied toolbox for unpacking the countless micro-practical implications required for leading your team in the process of meeting its full potential.

## Moving Up the "Pathway"

Within the overall roadmap, there is a typical theoretical *pathway* of phenomenon onto which most schools can be found. We do occasionally find schools operating off that common pathway, but for reasons we will explore in more detail, most schools exist and/or move in this predictable pattern. And yes, it is true that each entity along with its teachers and leaders exists within a physical and socio-cultural context that presents limits and challenges, however the capacity for substantive growth up the pathway exist within every school.

When we look at schools in general we find that most of their efforts to improve leave them at about same level over time. There reality is that meaningful improvement will require following a narrow path and accepting that real change will not be found in implenting short-cuts, quick fixes, or methods that would not imply real change. This is true for individuals, teams, companies, and schools. The process will be similar for all organisms. What we have found is that groups at different points along the pathway are not only doing very different things, they are trying to do very different things. Your location on the roadmap will be defined by three inter-related variables 1) what you value, think and feel (references), 2) what you do (practices and actions), and what occurs as a result of what you do (outcomes).

We have collected data from hundreds of schools over the past few years and interviewed several highly effective school leaders. What we have discovered is that where the school is located geographically tells us much

> "The means are implied in the ends."
> – *Gandhi*

less about it than where it is located on the effectiveness roadmap. The reason is that the location of the references, practices, and outcomes at any school will tend to be at the same location on the school effectiveness roadmap. Therefore, given the knowledge of either the common references/values, the common practices, or the common outcomes, the roadmap will be able to accurately predict the qualities or rating of the other two factors. Certain climates produce corresponding achievement levels, and certain practices produce corresponding kinds of climates. And most telling of all will be the references/values that inform the practice. So, moving up the pathway to higher levels on the roadmap implies consideration for each of these three factors, and addressing each of them within the growth process.

**Reflection 1.A.:** Recall the last effort that you were able to observe closely that was referred to as a "program implementation." What happened to the program goals in the long-term? What forces limited the program's effectiveness? Did staff buy in? Why or why not?

*NOTE: This is the first of many reflections that will be included in the chapters to encourage reflection on specific topics corresponding with the text.*

The starting point on our journey to becoming a more effective leader is to recognize that *everything is connected*. "Everything" at the school includes all the actions, methods, practices as well as all the thoughts, intentions, emotions, climate, and culture. Denial of this fact is responsible for a vast amount of wasted time, money, and effort, and why most improvement efforts fail (Kotter, 1995, Fullan, 1993). Often, we hear leaders lament, "We need to do something at this school to . . . "This seemingly proactive and well-intentioned sentiment is commendable. However, it is useful to recognize that we *are* doing something all day every day. While sometimes it is useful to add a strategy or program into the mix to promote a positive outcome, no strategy can fix a fundamentally problematic context by itself. And more often than not, what we tend to find is that implementing a series of add-ons into a school or classroom results in rather mediocre results overall. If the values/references within the context do not support the new practice it *will* be rejected or dissipate eventually. And if we survey teachers and leaders in high and low climate and/or performance schools, we find that each group is working hard. Yet a critical difference is whether those efforts feel like they are moving one forward and making a difference or just coping and treading water.

In examining what creates true improvement, higher levels of function and high-quality outcomes, success is dependent on a series of complex but rather explainable factors such as vision, trust, function, climate, and quality. These concepts can appear abstract and elusive, but in this book, we will operationalize them, and explore how to promote them as practical realities. An especially critical quality indispensable to any effort toward meaningful growth is vision. Too often we attach the vision in an organization to a person. Having leaders who possess visionary qualities will be useful indeed, but the quality of vision can be created within any group. Sustainable vision is an attitude, a set of practices and collective movement with confidence in a clear direction. Vision is part of the culture of great schools, and something any organization can cultivate.

---

**1.2: Axioms for School Improvement**

1. Everything is connected, everything is consequential.
2. We cannot solve problems at the same level of consciousness with which they were created. Form follows consciousness.
3. That which we place attention upon will grow.
4. We lead who are and we teach who we are.
5. The only person that we can control is ourselves.
6. If we (individually or collectively) do not believe it in our hearts, we do not truly believe it.
7. Actions predict outcomes.
8. Values predict Actions, so values predict outcomes.
9. Overall school performance will be a direct reflection of the typical practices being used on any given day at the school.
10. School improvement is possible only when both vision and trust exist.
11. Addressing symptoms (outcomes) will keep us stuck in our roadmap location. But solving real problems (values and actions) will encourage our growth upward.

---

The definition of school improvement today is dominated by the goal of raising student achievement scores. And the implied means is "whatever it takes." Yet, the fact is that how we get there *is* the key to obtaining and sustaining higher levels of achievement. As a result of the external pressures to improve, and the prevalence of heavy-handed external program "implementations," we may associate improvement and change with something unnatural and forced. The growth process, when approached with a sensitivity to how individuals and groups function, can be rather satisfying and rewarding. Creating a healthy, functional, and vision-driven school is more likely to improve student achievement scores (as well as real student achievement by any definition) than trying to attack student achievement scores directly, with "programs." The highest locations on the roadmap produce both high student achievement as well as high student achievement scores, but they are also defined by a healthy climate, an emotionally sane and satisfying environment, meaningful learning, and critical life lesson learning. There is no compartmentalization or compromise necessary. Every move up the pathway is innately more natural and enjoyable to those within the school. Figure 1.3 outlines some of the markers of successful movement up the pathway.

**Reflection 1.b** – What has your experience been with efforts characterized as "school improvement?" Was the focus internal or external? How do you associate the term? What are the feelings that come up when you think of the words "School Improvement?"

Figure 1.3: Frequency of Certain Phenomenon within Schools Successfully Moving up the Pathway

| More | Less |
| --- | --- |
| • Vision within the collective clarifies your work | • Need for telling, selling, bribing, and coercing people to get them to perform well. |
| • Integrity of the efforts from leaders, teachers, staff, and students in a direction leading to growth. | • Disconnected action from leaders, teachers, staff and students that tends to add up the "same old same old." |
| • Internal discovery of high-quality practice as a result of asking the right questions and looking in the right places. | • Need for administration to externally implement programs and policies onto others that are resisted, ignored and/or replaced later. |
| • A clear sense of the long-term and how today fits in. | • The feeling that coping and getting along in the short term is all that you can handle in a typical day. |
| • A solid context (school and classroom climate and function levels) allowing for qualities such as creativity, trust and innovation to emerge naturally. | • School and classroom environments that perpetually requires so much management and maintenance that creativity and innovation are viewed as luxuries or fantasies. |
| • A pervasive feeling of movement, growth and winning, and that something is being built. | • A familiar feeling related to the need to solve the same set of problems day in and day out. We are on a treadmill. |

### *Story of School A: Moving from a Low to a Higher Location on Pathway*

*School A began their process of growth lacking a guiding vision. It had historically experienced a negative climate including a poor self-perception. Its practices could best be characterized as incoherent at best and ineffective in many cases. After doing a complete school assessment, they recognized the essence of their "real problems" and set out to move from their lower-level performance on the effectiveness roadmap to the next level.*

*The focus was on creating more intention, coherence, and capacity. They created a school leadership team to process data, develop plans, and coordinate their professional development. They changed their schedule to include a professional development period once a week so teachers could process ideas and plan collaboratively. They used the idea of a psychology of success and growth mindset to guide their thinking in evaluating and selecting practices. After two years, school A has seen a significant change in how students and staff perceive the school. Outcome measures such as achievement are steadily improving. Their move up the pathway has been grounded in creating a more functional school and has had the effect of creating optimism among the students, teachers, and staff.*

### Progression of the Book Content

After building the school effectiveness roadmap in chapters two-five, in chapter six we examine how to cultivate trust among the leadership, teachers/staff and students within the school and the necessity to emphasize **process values** over **outcome values**. While trust is often associated with a feeling; operationally, trust in an organization will also require a clear sense that the ship is heading toward a direction that makes sense, and policies are in place that allow adults and students to feel a sense of confidence in the plan.

In chapter seven we explore how we can cultivate a guiding school vision and offer ideas for supporting this quality within the school. The roadmap offers an effective means of guiding your vision toward your desired growth destination. In chapter eight, we explore how to support and encourage high quality practices and how to act as an expert instructional leader. While vision is the most essential catalyst, the best indicator of success for any school will be the quality of the instructional practices and the capacity of the school to function as a professional learning community.

In chapter nine, we examine strategic planning and how to use outcome data effectively. We offer a vision-based process for strategic planning and how to use data to recognize and solve real problems rather than symptoms. In chapter ten, we take each of the eight dimensions of climate and examine their interdependence as well as their independent contributions to the overall climate of the school. For each dimension we offer guiding questions to support your school's investigation and processes of reflection. Often the most effective strategy for change is to change the internal guiding questions we are using to inform our strategic as well as daily actions.

## *Story of School B: moving from a middle to a high location on pathway*

*School B is a successful independent school with an excellent reputation. However, as they examined their SCAI survey results they realized students felt much less voice, power, belonging or pride in the school than would have been expected. As leadership explored more deeply, they realized that while rigor was emphasized, the same value was not placed on creating empowerment, connection, and other social and emotional values.*

*As a result, the leadership team set out a few goals. 1) make the school a more empowering place for students and adults, beginning with making the **1-Style classroom** the norm. 2) Use student input more effectively and commit in the future to valuing student voice. 3) Create a "what we do and what we don't do list" to help guide the evaluation and selection of* *practice. 4) Create the structures in the schedule to provide opportunities for teachers to collaborate, observe on another, and really understand ideas such as the 1-Style classroom, project-based learning, and inquiry.*

*The most immediate result was students feeling the intended empowerment and that they were listened to and responding with great appreciation, translating into increased motivation, better behavior, and innovative ideas for new clubs and school initiatives. The teachers became more of a team, and many teachers are breaking out of their teacher-centered comfort zones. Both leadership and the teachers can see a clear trajectory toward meeting their potential as a school.*

Because of the critical place of classroom management in the school improvement process, Chapter eleven is entirely devoted to how to move up the pathway in this area. Basic factors related to a sound social contract, sanity promoting policies, and clear, logical, and empowering practices make up a solid foundation at any school. As schools seek to move up in this area, the task will be to promote more student self-direction, community bonds, and social and emotional growth within the individuals and the collective – in other words the **1-Paradigm classroom** (Shindler, 2009).

Given that all schools are currently at different locations on the roadmap, the needs of leaders and schools will vary. Each school will ultimately need to enter the improvement process relative to where it is currently. Therefore, the next two chapters are devoted to schools at two distinct starting points. Chapter twelve outlines the process of moving a school from a lower performing location to higher levels of function, climate, and efficacy. The nature of this effort will be defined by developing a sound school vision, building the capacity for sustained growth, engaging in a process of self-evaluation. Goals here would include clarifying the requisite intentions moving forward, ensuring coherence, and encouraging sanity and efficiency.

Chapter thirteen explains how to go from "good" to "great." How a school that is currently performing well by most standards can move up the pathway and actualize more of its potential. While this trajectory requires a potential paradigm shift toward more empowerment and activation of the human capital, it implies a great many adjustments in practice from a more teacher-centered, and top-down structure to a more student-centered, and democratic structure. And for many schools, this transition will require as much letting go of attitudes, practices, and policies that define the lower/middle levels as adding more transformational attitudes, practices, and policies.

## The Leader's Journey

In the final chapter, the focus is you as the leader and your personal journey of vision-setting and growth which will inevitably mirror the broader school effort. Regardless of the location of your school, department, team, or institution geographically or on the improvement roadmap, you will need to cultivate your personal intention related to your role as a leader. This chapter will support your process of self-reflection and personal leadership development. No matter your current mindset or the state of your school, as you engage the process of reading this book and endeavoring to facilitate the improvement at your school, you are encouraged to consider adopting the following three basic personal values. They are:

1. **Willingness** to become an expert in the nature of the roadmap and the mechanics of the change process. Much of the book will resonate with your experience, and your instinctual sense of how things work, but there will also be some areas where your assumptions will be challenged, and it may imply the need to change your thinking or your practices. Included in that willingness will be the need for patience with yourself, others, and the process. If you are looking for quick fixed or clever strategies that you can use as short cuts to promoting meaningful and systemic change, you will not find many here. The effort here is to support your growth as an authentic leader not someone who is posing as one.

2. **Commitment** to a department, a school, or a district, team, institution, etc. This commitment will imply time and a real concern for the well-being of those of whom you are entrusted to work

and lead. It will require an attitude of service and an emergence of your sense of purpose as a leader.

3.  **Openness** to cultivating a vision. Your success will be dependent on your ability to see within the institution the highest good while nurturing a shared vision among the collective. You will need to develop the personal skills, knowledge, and dispositions to inspire others to see a more functional, empowered, and satisfying place that can emerge out of the current state-of-affairs. Appreciate the reality of where folks are but hold the vision of their potential as an even more accurate reality.

Within each school is the potential for excellence. As transformative leaders we need harness the power of "yet." We may not be where we could yet be but tapping into the vision of what can be brings hope and energy to our work and everyone at the school. Change is a team effort. When we look around, we see abundant evidence that improvement needs visionary leadership and a quality roadmap. In the next chapter, we will begin the process of building the school effectiveness roadmap which will function as a guide for your improvement process.

## REFERENCES

Fullan, M. (1993) *Change Forces: Probing the Depths of Educational Reform*. The Falmer Press.

Kotter, J (1995) Leading Change: Why Transformation Efforts Fail. *Harvard Business Review*. March 1995, p. 59-67.

Shindler, J. (2009) *Transformative Classroom Management*. Jossey-Bass, San Francisco, CA.

# CHAPTER 2:

## Assessing the Essential X-Factor within Schools, and Understanding the R-X-O Inter-Relationship

In this chapter, we explore the essence of school climate and why the School Climate Assessment Instrument (SCAI) is so strongly correlated to other school outcomes such as student achievement. This strong relationship will inform the development of the school effectiveness roadmap. At the heart of the roadmap is our finding from hundreds of school assessments that school effectiveness has an essence and can be represented in a somewhat predictable pattern, with explainable causes and pathways for growth.

### The X-Factor – And How it is All Connected

When we initiated our efforts as the Alliance for the Study of School Climate (ASSC) in 2001, we began by exploring what in our experience characterized the most essential factors in schools. As three educational generalists, we came to the determination it had something to do with climate and culture. As we examined the nature of schools more deeply, we realized that *it* was all connected. Everything within a school relates to everything else. This recognition is one of the reasons I have remained what could be called a "generalist" to this day. To me, the connectedness and what that implies *is* the point. While the best solutions are most often very practical and specific, the essence of the true problems can most often be found in the sub-text.

We began our work with an assumption that there was an essential X-factor in the process of school effectiveness and improvement. Our findings, after two decades, have proven we were on the right track. To begin the search for the nature of this X-factor, or basic DNA of a school, we explored the research into what made schools successful, and students healthy, happy, and achieving. When we boiled down the research and our experience, we found there were three key areas that defined a successful context and what could be characterized as psychological orientations toward school – learning, interacting, self, others, success, life goals, etc. We would refer to these three qualities as aspects of a "psychology of success" (POS). These three POS factors, or their opposites a "psychology of failure" (POF) can be seen as operating within both the individual and the institution. Therefore, they point to useful considerations for both micro and macro action and define the health of a school's ecosystem.

## Psychology of Success (POS)

Each of the following aspects of a school's psychological ecosystem are essential to the overall quality and health of the school. Yet, each can be defined and pursued independently as well.

- First, to be successful, an individual or group needs to feel a sense of personal agency and power. This factor is related to where one perceives the root cause of phenomenon to be. And internal causality recognizes it as being based in personal choices, a sense that there is a law of cause and effect principle at work, and that our thinking is an initiating source. We termed this critical factor **internal locus of control**, which has been an early label used in hundreds of studies over decades. It could be contrasted to an *external locus of control* defined by fatalism, blaming, and a victim orientation. Internal locus of control has been shown to be more predictive to future success than any other variable including socio-economic factors. (Auer, 1992; Bar-Tal, 1977; Klein and Keller, 1990)

- Second, to be successful, mentally healthy, and happy an individual or group needs to experience a sense that they are Ok, connected, and loved (Maslow,1954; Ostermann, 2000. We use the term *acceptance and belonging* to capture this general experience. Both aspects are related and necessary. To be fully ourselves and able to reach our potential, as well as experience peace of mind and sanity, we need to feel a sense that we are acceptable – to ourselves and others. Self-acceptance is much more likely in an environment in which we feel a sense of belonging from others. For the group, this means having a positive identity, common goals, caring and communal bonds, and feeling like we have a place and are welcome and valuable to the group. The experience of acceptance and belonging could be contrasted to feeling alienated, worthless, judged, compared, unloved, and/or not good enough.

- The third variable for success is related to how we view success itself. Borrowing from the excellent work of Carol Dweck (2006) and the distinction between a *growth vs fixed-ability mindset.* When we approach a task (or life generally) with a growth mindset, we are saying in essence, that we learn from our experience and everything that happens is good, because it leads to learning and growth. This approach is rather simple. And that mental and emotional simplicity and freedom leads to an ease of mind, a clear sight and a lack of fear. It also leads to better performance. In contrast, a fixed-ability mindset leads to an innately fearful affect, especially fear of failure. This causes an uneasy mind, and a vast and complicated emotional complex, which goes something like this "If I do well, I will feel Ok, but if I don't I will not feel Ok because it will show me that I am not very good at (whatever it is) and that will make me feel inadequate, and less good in comparison to others, which is unacceptable to my ego, and so I need to find a way to either win, quit, make an excuse, rationalize or something else to deal with the troubling thought of not doing this right." Each of us brings some amount of growth orientation and some amount of fixed-ability orientation into each action we take. Those who can learn to bring more growth orientation to their lives set a trajectory toward more happiness, success, and peace of mind. In schools, we create the conditions for more growth or fixed-ability mindsets with our policies, practices, and conscious and unconscious messages to students.

In chapter four, we will revisit the idea of a psychology of success, and how these three factors play out within the activity of a school. And we will show why at the heart of what it takes to move up to higher levels on the roadmap, encouraging these POS factors will be integral to our success.

## Creating the SCAI Climate Survey

One intent in creating a survey to measure school climate and, ultimately this essential X-factor, was to capture the POS/POF reality within a school. Other survey goals included ensuring its relatability, and the lived school experience, and structuring it in a way as to imply a range of levels of quality. Those goals have guided our thinking and revisions over 20 years.

One defining quality of the SCAI resulted from the choice to use an analytic trait (rubric) structure rather than a traditional Likert scale. The reasons that we made this choice were to 1) be able to describe levels of phenomenon in more concrete terms, 2) imply a range of quality and POS represented by three levels, 3) imply more or less desirable conditions including an upper level condition to guide thinking within the survey item analysis process, and 4) enhance validity and reliability levels. Below is an example of an item (5f) from the SCAI. Note the three levels.

**Figure 2A. Example Analytic Trait Instrument Item Example from the SCAI vS-G-9.4.0**

| 5.f. | | |
|---|---|---|
| Teacher-student interactions can be typically described as supportive and respectful. | Teacher-student interactions can be typically described as fair but teacher-dominated. | Teacher-student interactions are mostly teacher-dominated and reactive. |
| <----------O----------O----------O----------O----------O-------à | | |

# Defining School Climate

Given our broad and inclusive definition of school climate, we settled on eight sub-scales or dimensions for the SCAI. Each dimension includes a series of items related to how that dimension manifests in a school day. The eight dimensions are the following:

1. Physical Environment
2. Teacher Relations
3. Student Relations
4. Leadership and Decisions
5. Classroom Management and Discipline
6. Instruction and Assessment
7. Social-Emotional Climate
8. Community Relations

The initial goal for employing the survey was to help provide a reliable indicator for school personnel as to the level of quality of practice, psychology of success, and the extent to which the climate X-factor was present in both what they were doing as well as how people perceived what they were doing. That is, a clear sense of the health of the ecosystem. Even though the survey was a little odd looking to some, users quickly appreciated both its accuracy and ability to provide a clear mirror on their school as well as its efficacy in implying next steps for improvement.

After we had collected and analyzed data from our first several schools, we found information rich with implications (Shindler, Jones, Taylor, 2006). In fact, what was evident was that everything was, in fact, connected and there was an underlying X-factor rooted within the school phenomena. Specifically, some of the findings from that first data set (which still hold up to this day) include the following:

» There was a high inter-item correlation, which meant there was an essential phenomenon or theoretical construct operating below the surface.

» Dimensions were also correlated. Data from each school tended to have a trend at a particular level. In other words, if school A had one dimension at a 3.3 level, it was likely that most of the other dimensions would be in a narrow range near 3.3 as well. This consistency showed that there was an implicit DNA operating to define all aspects of the school.

» Both the overall climate mean as well as the dimension means were highly correlated to the school's California student achievement measure. We have since used the percentile rank of the student achievement scores within any state, and the high correlation (0.7) has remained a robust finding. We attribute this high correlation to 1) the ability of the instruments' content to capture the X-factor/DNA related to overall effectiveness, and 2) the design of the instrument to pinpoint the level of that X-factor/DNA accurately as a result of the anchoring quality of the analytic trait structure.

» We did not (and still do not) find many outliers where the SCAI score was high, and the achievement scores were low, or visa-versa (less than 1 in 20). Schools tend to fit the pattern in nearly all cases. (See scatter plot of ratings in figure 2B).

» Schools could be classified at being at one of three levels, or types of ecosystems – low, middle or high (See Figure 2.F below). These levels correspond to the three levels of items. Each level has its own unique nature and underlying DNA, and most all phenomena in the school will fit into a single level.

The strong relationship between school climate (SCAI) and student achievement percentile can be seen in the initial data set shown here as a correlation scatter plot distribution in Figure 2.B below.

# School Climate Score (SCAI)
# by Student Achievement (percentile)

SCAI Ratings by Achievement Percentile

When ASSC SCAI School Climate ratings at any school are correlated with the student achievement scores at that school, we find a very strong relationship. As you can see in the scatter plot figure from one data set, when the climate is high, the achievement is high, and when the climate is low the achievement is also low. This degree of correlation (+0.7) is only obtained with the SCAI.

This data-driven realization encouraged us to reflect on the nature of the relationships among values, practices, and results at a school. As we collected data from subsequent schools, we found this pattern between what leaders and teachers did in a school and the results they obtained was astonishingly consistent.

This relationship between any school's climate rating and its level of student achievement would become central to our efforts to make sense of the underlying principles governing school function and performance. And it informed the ongoing construction of the "school improvement roadmap and pathway." As this roadmap emerged, we found, after collecting data and spending time in subsequent schools, most all schools fit onto an explainable pattern. Soon we began to feel confident in the following assertion: if we knew one of the following variables at a school - a) the SCAI climate ratings, b) the student achievement scores, or c) the kinds of practices that were predominantly used - we could, with great certainty, predict the other two variables (After reading this book you will likely be able to predict each of those variables with similar accuracy).

One reason that our emerging roadmap became so predictive was that we found that there were three core aspects within any school phenomenon (the way the essential X-factor of a school plays out). Each was interdependent and, thus, all three would inherently define the location of the school on the roadmap. If one were affected or changed, we could assume the others would change as well (See Figure 2.C).

> "The end is inherent in the means."
> – Gandhi
>
> "In the final analysis, means and ends must cohere because the end is preexistent in the means."
> – Martin Luther King

The first of the variables is related to the kinds of mental processes, knowledge, and values which are held by the staff (and to a secondary extent by students) as individuals and as a collective. We decided to call that variable "references" or R's, for short, from the term in Perceptual Control Theory that characterizes what any organism uses to inform its processing as it engages the world (Powers, 1998). These references are our picture of "good schooling" and are, to a great extent, the guiding DNA of a school.

The second variable we termed the X's standing for all the various forms of actions at the school such as practices, pedagogy, interactions, and applied policies. The third variable are the outcomes or O's at the school (See Figure 2D). Outcomes are the results, perceptions and effects that occur – large and small. What we came to understand more intimately was that these three variables were aligned by their very nature, and therefore both interdependent as well inseparable. Moreover, how we prioritize each will ultimately define how we approach the process of improvement.

These interrelated variables are depicted in figure 2.C below in a triangular relationship. As you will notice, the arrows emanate from the R as it is the primary origin of cause - the R's intend/inform the X's and the X's result in the O's.

Figure 2.C R-X-O Inter-Relationship and Primary Direction of Influence

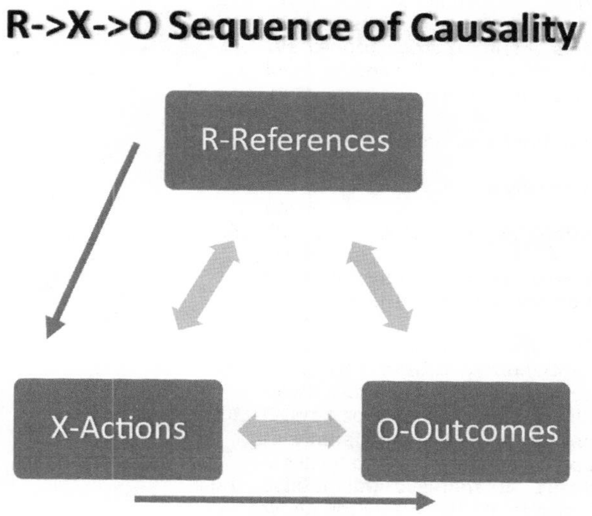

## R->X->O Sequence of Causality

Over time, we realized that the quantitative data supported the observational data as well as what wise thinkers have been saying for centuries: what we ultimately get in the end starts with our values, vision, and intention, by way of how we put those R's into action with our actions/X's. As Gandhi said, "the end is inherent in the means." In other words, depending on the X's utilized, we will inevitably get different O's. The implications of this inter-relationship between R, X and O will likely make progressively more sense as we continue to build the growth pathway/roadmap in the next few chapters.

| | R or Reference | X or Action/Practice | O or Outcome |
|---|---|---|---|
| | **We teach (or lead) who we R** | **X = What we Do** | **O's are our Results** |
| **Contents** | • Values<br>• Conditioning<br>• Perceptions<br>• Internal Picture of "Good School"<br>• Intuition<br>• Skills and Knowledge<br>• Beliefs and attitudes<br>• Personal narratives<br>• Identities<br>• And everything contained in the unconscious | • School staff Behaviors in general<br>• Pedagogical practices<br>• Applied Policy<br>• Interactions<br>• Routines and patterns of behavior<br>• Communication<br>• And all the unconscious modeling and messages we send | • Student Achievement Scores<br>• Student Behavior<br>• Learning levels and forms by students and staff<br>• Motivation levels and forms for students and staff<br>• Disposition and emotional states of being of students and staff<br>• Incidence of phenomena – i.e., tardiness, absences, violence, substance use, winning teams,<br>• School climate and culture (as experienced) |
| **Definition** | We will use the term reference (or R) to refer to everything in the minds and nervous systems of the individual or collective organism. The organism can be of any size – individual, classroom, school, or district. The R's are the DNA at the school. | We will use the term X to describe what the educators (or the members of any organization) do. Again, we need a larger term for all the active things which are done intentionally or unintentionally during a school day. | We will use the term O to represent all the countless specific outcomes and results of actions that we care about and that are meaningful to us in schools. The O's are the symptoms of the health of the ecosystem. |
| **Rationale** | So why the term reference? First, we need a term that is inclusive of all the kinds of mental processing listed above – the thinking and feeling that ultimately guides our actions. To deal with each of these mental processes separately, while potentially useful, would be create complexity which would not serve our purposes here. | While we typically spend a great deal of time thinking about our actions, most educators underestimate is influence. We will demonstrate in the next few chapters why X's predict almost everything else especially the O or Outcomes. The primary task of school improvement will be to encourage more high-quality X's and fewer low quality X's. | The outcomes resulting at the school or organization will give us insight. If we want to know what we are doing, we need to look at what we are getting. If our R's are defined by a desire for quality, those R's will guide X's, and the result will likely present as quality O's. |

# R's/DNA Translate into Quality of School Climate

Since the SCAI directly or indirectly measures the R's, X's, and O's at a school, our data has been useful in making sense of the relationships among the three. Over time, what became clear, in most cases, schools were at different locations on the roadmap were not only doing different things, they were *intending* to do different things and the R's, X's and O's at each school tended to align with one another almost perfectly – both conceptually and as measured qualitatively. Each school not only had different O's, but they used different X's, and as one observed more closely, one could hear, read, and infer very different R's running the show. In other words, different DNA produced different animals.

For those in a school whose members rated their overall climate and function on the SCAI at a 2.0/5, and for those who self-rated at a 4.0/5 SCAI level, the experience of school is very different. While educators in each school are likely doing what they think is best, the data showed that what that looked like varied significantly. And yes, there are often many external factors that contribute to the difference between the 20percentile achievement/2.0SCAI school versus the 80percentile achievement/4.0SCAI school. Yet, regardless of circumstances, these data suggest that where there are certain kinds of R's and X's, there will be corresponding O's. Moreover, most likely all schools that practice 2.0/5 SCAI level X's will look a lot like one another, regardless of their geographical location, and a lot more alike than they do when compared to a 4.0/5SCAI school nearby.

---

### 2.E. Axioms for School Improvement (revised from Ch.1)

12. Everything is connected, everything is consequential.
13. We cannot solve problems at the same level of consciousness with which they were created. Form follows consciousness.
14. That which we place attention upon will grow.
15. We lead who are/R and we teach who we are/R.
16. The only person we can control is ourselves.
17. If we (individually or collectively) do not believe it in our hearts, we do not truly believe it.
18. Actions/X's predict Outcomes/O's
19. Values/R's predict Actions/X's, so Values/R's predict outcomes/O's
20. Overall school performance will be a direct reflection of the typical practices being used on any given day at the school.
21. School improvement is possible only when both vision and trust exist.
22. Addressing symptoms (outcomes/O's) will keep us stuck in our roadmap location. But solving real problems (values/R's and actions/X's) will encourage our growth upward.

---

As we progress in the development of the school function roadmap, you will see different locations on the roadmap are not just defined by more or less of a particular set of practices but are in many ways about the *kind* of practices used. People are thinking about school in different ways at different points on the roadmap. Regardless of the amount of will, good intentions, or faithfulness of the implementation, the use of 2.0/5SCAI quality X's will not lead to high performance level outcomes. By their nature 2.0/5 X's cannot lead to 4.0/5 O's.

To make progress up the roadmap, R's and X's need to change in kind. DNA needs to change. And in our experience, schools at the lower levels of the roadmap often improve more as a result of what they stop doing, as opposed to what they add. As we will discuss throughout the book, the process of changing DNA will imply considering R's first, and then finding X's consistent with those values and vision. The results will follow. As we have witnessed over the past two decades, the well-intended but ultimately misguided over-emphasis on outcomes has had a detrimental influence on the quality of schools.

Yet, to be clear, among the assumptions informing this book and supported by our experience is that most educators in most schools work very hard and care sincerely about their students. It is likely that the schools currently operating at lower points of the roadmap will face uniquely challenging conditions. Therefore, just because the principles for understanding the nature of school performance are explainable, it does not imply that school improvement can be assumed to be a simple process. If it were, we could stop here at chapter two and assume readers who were interested in school improvement would simply adopt R's and X's from schools with high function (not that that is not a sound idea).

The take-away we hope the reader to glean at this point in the book is that to change an ecosystem, practices need to change, and for practices to change the references/DNA that are consistent with those improved practices need to exist in the consciousness of the organization. Form follows consciousness. Therefore, any meaningful school change will require an intentional process of reflection and self-evaluation. The following chapters develop a roadmap for supporting growth, improvement, and successful movement upward. Subsequent chapters will explain how to use the roadmap logic in action to create change. In Chapter three we will begin to build the theoretical roadmap of school function and effectiveness beginning with an examination of its vertical axis related to function and intention.

## Exercise 2.1: Levels of schools

When we examine the phenomenon within a school, we find various aspects of the school climate, culture, function level (as well as the achievement level as discussed earlier) tend to fit into a pattern. What happens at a school tends to be at one of three levels as depicted on Figure 2.F below. The qualities of a high-level school include a clear vision, clear guiding values, practices defined by empowerment, collaborative faculty, and staff, and mostly POS promoting practices. Schools in the middle level tend to rely on programs to a great extent, focus on doing what works, and reflect congenial relationships among the adults. Schools at the low level of the chart tend to be defined by lower achievement levels, a generally competitive attitude among the adults, and a common approach to pedagogy that could be best characterized as domesticating. Usually, we see the qualities from each column displayed together, and rare see them intermixed within any school.

### Reflection Questions:

1.  Do you recognize the level at your school? Which column does your school fit best? Does the SCAI accurately predict the column if you have such ratings?

2.  Why do you think school phenomenon fit into such a pattern?

3.  How does reflecting on the R-X-O sequence help explain the three-level pattern and the outcomes disparity between the levels?

4.  Most schools fit into the middle column, why do you think this is so?

## Figure 2.F: The Three Levels of School Climate and Their Characteristics

| | Level 3 | Level 2 | Level 1 |
|---|---|---|---|
| System | Intentional/Coherent | Semi-intentional | Accidental |
| Ethos | Sound vision translated into effective practice | Good intentions translated into practices that "work." | Practices defined by the relative self-interest of faculty and staff |
| PCT Level | System/Principle | Program | Sensory |
| Effect on Students | Liberating Experience changes students for the better | Perpetuating Experience has a mixed effect on students | Domesticating Experience has a net negative effect on students |
| Staff relations | Collaborative | Congenial | Competitive |
| Psychological Outcome | Promotes a Psychology of Success | Promotes a Mixed Psychology | Promotes a Psychology of Failure |
| Outcomes SCAI/%tile achievement | 3.8-4.7/80 %tile+ | 3.0-3.7/25-75%tile | 1.5-2.9/-20%tile |

# REFERENCES

Auer, C.J. (1992). A Comparison of the Locus of Control of First and Second Grade Students in Whole Language, Basal Reader, and Eclectic Instructional Approach Classrooms (Doctoral Dissertation, Northern Illinois University, 1992). *Dissertation Abstracts International, 53* (11), 3856.

Bar-Tal, D. B., and Bar-Zohar, Y. (1977). The Relationship between Perception of Locus of Control and Academic Achievement. *Contemporary Educational Psychology. 2*, 181-99.

Dweck, C (2006) Mindset: A new psychology of success.

Klein, J. D., and Keller, J. M. (1990). Influence of Student Ability, Locus of Control, and Type of Instructional Control on Performance and Confidence. *Journal of Educational Research, 83*(3) 140-46.

Maslow, A. H. (1954). *Motivation and personality.* New York: Harper and Row.

Osterman, K.F. (2000) Students' need for belonging in the school community. Review of Educational Research, 70(3), 323-367.

Powers, W.J. (1998) *Making Sense of Behavior: The Meaning of Control. Benchmark* Publishing Inc. Dallas TX.

Shindler, J., Jones, A., Taylor C., (2006, January*) Examining the School Climate Achievement Relationship: Research from 14 schools in one Urban School District.* Paper presentation at the Annual Meeting of the American Association of Colleges of Teacher Education, San Diego, CA.

# CHAPTER 3:

## The Vertical Axis – Building Greater Function Through Intention, Coherence, and Capacity

This chapter explores the vertical axis of the school paradigm matrix we will use to build the overall school effectiveness roadmap. This axis represents the level of intentionality and function for a school (and/or classroom and/or individual). It is the "how" to the horizontal axis's "what" and "why." This axis does not imply the kind of intentions that are guiding a school but does infer that the stronger and better defined those intentions are, the more effectively the school will function. Understanding what it takes to move up this vertical axis is critical to schools in all stages of an improvement process, but it is especially so for schools in the early process. The considerations introduced here will be central to our discussion of how to move up the references, practices, and outcomes (R-X-O's) from lower to higher levels of function in chapter eleven.

The essential elements making up the conceptual nature of the vertical axis are 1) intention, 2) capacity, 3) coherence, and 4) efficiency. The extent to which these qualities are addressed and operating effectively will define the overall function level of a school, and thus the height of its location on the school effectiveness roadmap. The essential qualities of this vertical axis are depicted in the center column of the school paradigm matrix in Figure 3.1.

**Figure 3.1 Vertical Axis Highlighted on the School Effectiveness Matrix**

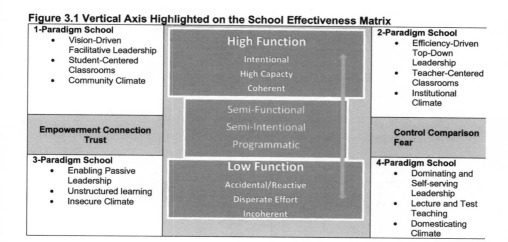

## What is Intention and Why is Growth so Dependent on it?

Intention is essentially having a picture of where you want to go and an awareness of what is good for everyone (individually and collectively), and then using that picture to guide your choices. We can call it a vision, a purpose, or goals. But if we want to improve our school and move up the pathway, we will need a vision to pull us upward. In identifying some of the ways the most intentional institutions operate, we would see some of the following elements.

- A set of guiding values (R/references) operate both implicitly and explicitly. People know them, understand them, and appreciate why they are valuable.

- A vision. People have a clear idea of "a good school" and what people do in one. What would our school look like if it were meeting its full potential?

- A definition of quality and success. Good X/Actions/practices are operationalized — including an intentional definition of "the way we do things around here."

- A shared understanding of how we are going to get from point A (current state) and point B (our vision). *Process values* are emphasized over *product values*.

- A well-defined picture of the school's intended product. What should a student have learned in their time at the school? What qualities define our graduates? How we need to orient new students so they understand what the school is about and how they can succeed?

## Capacity and Encouraging Structures that Maximize Potential

An institution will be able to move up the function continuum to the extent that it takes advantage of and/or builds its capacity. Capacity relates mostly to the extent to which the human capital is harnessed for the benefit of quality systems and outcomes for the whole. A simple analogy would be the foundational structure of a building that allows it to bear weight. A more human analogy would be the utilization of the individual skills and use of teamwork among the players on a team that supports their ability to perform well.

There is a vast array of variables that will influence the extent to which an institution or classroom is maximizing its potential – many of them related to complex people skills, but for an examination related to the vertical axis we will focus mostly on organizational structures. Ways schools are effective at optimizing the capacity of human and organizational elements at the school include.

### Inquiry teams as PLCs

In one high performing school, leadership examined their structures and realized the quality of their collaboration could be better supported by remodeling their PLC thinking. So, they created "Inquiry Teams" with team leaders who were chosen based on their expertise as lead teachers and facilitators. The teams were given one period to accomplish their goals and were primarily responsible for setting their own objectives and agenda.

At a nearby school, the decision was made to embed 3 collaborative periods a week. The school's guiding principle as "structures in support of the vision."

- Structures in place providing a means for individual teachers and students to share expertise and collaborate. One of the most effective structural elements for the school to embrace relates to what it means to be a true "professional learning community." Another is developing expertise related to cooperative learning skills within the classroom.

- Structures in place to make informed decisions. Ideally, schools are best served when there is a committee of committed individuals who possess solid expertise, who digest key data and insights relevant to the school's purpose and performance, process that data, and uses it to inform the school's agenda, strategic planning, and improvement efforts.

- Structures are in place to include student voice in decisions most affecting them, both in and out of the classroom.

- Creativity, new ideas and growth are encouraged, and a systemic process of self-reflection is structurally embedded.

- Professional development (coherently aligned to the school's intention) is cultivated that includes both external expertise and perspective as well as internal expertise.

## Coherence – It All Needs to Work in Harmony

What our research says is that everything is connected and consequential. Therefore, attaining higher levels of function require coherence among the elements in the school. Keeping in mind the R->X->O sequence, it is essential that the references (values, visions, missions, beliefs, narratives, etc.) that drive the actions at the school are congruent, and that the actions/X's/ practices are congruent with both the references and one another. What our experience tells us is that initially most school leaders assume there is an acceptable level of coherence among the practices and policies at their schools, but in most cases, when they examine their climate and function data related to this area more closely, they find that it not the case. Incoherence is the norm and has become increasingly so given the ever-expanding number of imposed external values, policies and competing public and professional demands.

In the book *Coherence,* Fullan and Quinn (2016) outline a series of what they term "drivers" (consistent with what we call R/references) that lead to either more or less coherence (See Figure 3.2). The list will be useful as we build a pathway up the effectiveness roadmap. But what we find is that these author's drivers are quite challenging to the current way many schools are run, so what they identify as the right drivers are less commonly used as guiding references than those they suggest are the wrong drivers.

Table 3.2 Fullan and Quinn's Right and Wrong Drivers from the book *Coherence*

| Right Drivers | Wrong Drivers |
|---|---|
| 1. Focused Direction | 1. External Accountability |
| 2. Collaborative Culture | 2. Individualism |
| 3. Deep Learning | 3. Technology |
| 4. Internal Accountability | 4. Ad hoc policies |

Too often, schools can be working faithfully at applying these wrong drivers. As a result, many schools exert great effort applying practices that keep them stuck in a low or middle level of function. The problem is not their level of effort or sincerity, but the extent to which their guiding references are sound and/or coherent. In our examination of schools, we find that most schools will improve more by 1) rethinking their guiding references and 2) stopping the use of certain X's/practices, rather than adding new programs or working harder at their current R's and X's. As we build the complete school effectiveness roadmap and pathway, you will see that emphasizing the right drivers and de-emphasizing the wrong drivers will be necessary to move to higher levels of effectiveness.

We might think of coherence as harmony and congruence. In its most powerful application, it looks like a well-functioning team's internalized systems, shared vision, high levels of intrapersonal confidence and trust, the micro and the macro being aligned, and the absence of the feeling that you are asked to violate one value to meet another value or use practices which feel wrong. In its more common and pragmatic application, coherence in a school or classroom appears as consistency of policy, alignment of curriculum, program fidelity, quality control, and uniform standards of practice (See Table 3.3). Some of the ways to encourage coherence as a school include:

- Creating a list of practices that "one should see" and a list of those that "one should not see" at the school based on a high-quality intention/R (I recommend using the construct "psychology of success." POS)
- Aligning professional development with the mission of the school.
- Aligning the teacher evaluation process with the highest values/R's of the school.
- Making decisions about the physical environments in the classrooms based on the highest learning values/R's at the school.
- Regularly auditing practices and policies for congruence with one another and the highest values/R's at the school.
- Checking in on how everyone feels about using certain practices or policies.

## Efficiency – Everything Works on a Practical Level

A school could be considered more or less functional to the extent that what occurs there reflects order, quality and efficiency (See Figure 3.3). In other words, things are working to get them where they want to go. But we have to be careful when we conceive what we mean by "what works." In a technical sense, everything works. Every action/X works to produce some outcome/O. What has been done at a school has worked to produce what exists there currently. Instead, we must consider not just if things are working, but if they are working to encourage our highest R's, desirable long-term results, and sustainability.

On a practical level, if the procedural, day-to-day policies, routines, bureaucratic and housekeeping issues are not in order, things will feel off and people will be frustrated. We have all seen a little thing become a significant thing when it interferes with the well-being of either the students or the adults at the school. For example, it is difficult to plan a sequence of learning activities when the schedule is interrupted by unscheduled assemblies and students being pulled out to other locations without notice.

Our ability to enjoy the sense of ease and comfort to be able to think creatively, feel secure, trust one another, etc., are all dependent on things running smoothly on a practical level. The following are some of the ways we can encourage our schools (or classrooms) level of efficiency include the following.

- Recognize when the small stuff is significant and when it is not. If you want a no-cell phone policy, it will only work if everyone is consistent. But if you are tired of nagging students about hats and few adults really cares anyway, then maybe it is time to lose the policy. Likewise, hearing a student's put-down of another student in the hall within your earshot, or seeing the nets on the basketball hoops being ripped or missing may be perceived as being small things. Yet, they have huge symbolic significance. Your actions represent a concrete reflection of your values. However, a lot of other small things are better ignored. Don't maintain policies which are not consistently applied, either because they are not critical, or no one has the courage to follow through on them

- Have sound reasons (and input from stakeholders) if you are going to change a long-held routine. Most teachers have a concrete-sequential cognitive type, and changing routines is especially troubling for that group (Lawrence, 2009).

- If a sound structure is not in place which encourages a desired practice, the responsibility for poor execution is on the leadership. For instance, the schools schedule will have an enormous impact on such things as your ability to encourage collaboration, professional development, teachers feeling like they are valued and appreciated, as well as your ability to deliver various kinds of instructional practices. Effective leadership will imply creating a schedule that encourages the kinds of instructional practices/X's outcomes that are valued and being assessed.

- Have those who are most concerned about and impacted by a policy or procedure develop it and be responsible for periodically re-evaluating it.

## Why is a School More or Less Functional?

In Figure 3.3, the differences between the R's and X's at high, middle, and low functioning schools are outlined. As you explore the dimensional differences represented, you can see that function is more than just "things working." Of course, things working is usually a byproduct of functional R's and X's, but high functioning organizations have other common qualities as well. When some of these qualities are missing, function level will be limited. When many are missing, a complete reboot is likely required before improvement will be possible.

**Figure 3.3. Defining Three Levels of the Vertical Axis by its Primary Qualities.**

|  | Intention | Coherence/ Alignment | Capacity | Function/ Efficiency |
|---|---|---|---|---|
| **High/ Target** | The school has a clear vision that is shared by most. Quality instruction is operationalized and expected. The mission is seen in the actions of the adults. Excellence is valued. | The school tends to be principle and system-driven. So, all practice and policy decisions are made based on the integrity of ideas in relation to the mission. One can see the big picture in the micro practices and vice versa. | Structures are mission-driven. Data is used by teams to inform growth. The school is actively evolving the structures necessary to be a PLC. | Actions are purposeful and things work effectively based on a clear standard for quality. Efficiency is taken on as a collective duty. |
| **Common/ Middle** | The school has a vision statement. There is a shared expectation that the adults are accountable for the success of students. Good behavior and academic standards are spelled out. | The school tends to be program-driven. Attention is given to making sure practice reflects fidelity to the plan. The school implements a great deal of what is assumed to "work" to maintain order and keep students on task. | Structures are in place which promote effective management of the school. Data informs decisions. Teachers are given time to collaborate within departments. | "Things working" is the primary goal, so this level is usually mostly effective when it comes to practical day-to-day matters. What works is the primary R at the school. Efficiency is primarily the domain of the administration. |
| **Low/ Problematic** | Vision and mission are in writing only. The intention is to find ways to get through the week and avert risks related to non-compliance. The over-abundance of attention goes to students who are not behaving properly. | The school tends to be reactive and incoherent in its policy development. Policies and programs are brought in to deal with discrete issues and perceived deficiencies. | Structures are mostly related to contractual obligations and fulfilling district level mandated professional development. | There is a great deal of what could be defined as dysfunctional. On many levels there are things that do not work and frustrate stakeholders. There is a lot of blame that is generated as a result. |

When the four factors of intention, capacity, coherence, and efficiency are given attention, a school will tend to move up the vertical axis. But it is useful to understand the kinds of policies and practices limiting movement upward – we can call them vertical axis roadblocks. They include

- Expecting the use of lower-level intentions/R's and practices/X's to somehow achieve higher level results/O's. Without changes in X's, O's will not change, no matter how faithfully we implement any of them. Chapters eleven, twelve, and thirteen explore the process of facilitating the necessary changes in detail.
- Placing too much attention on *outcome values* versus *process values*. Being outcome-driven will tend to keep us stuck at the middle level.
- Emphasizing what Fullan and Quinn (2016) call the "wrong drivers."

    ○ External accountability tends to encourage "doing what it takes" values. These are typically incoherent and individualistic or imposed in a disempowering manner.

    ○ Individualism, competition, and comparisons will lead to long-term social dysfunction and work against the goals of collaboration, trust, and making the left-hand turn on the pathway.

    ○ Technology in the service of high-quality references is valuable. But when it is a goal in and of itself, it tends to keep us stuck in the middle of the roadmap.

    ○ Adding programs based on good reasons seems sensible, but if they lack coherence with other values or practices, the result is frustration and shifting attention away from building capacity to becoming an excellent level school.

The components of the vertical axis are presented in this chapter in a mostly value-neutral fashion. They represent the "how" of moving upward on the roadmap. But for a school to achieve its full potential, we need to include the "what" – the content of chapter four. What is our intention? Not all intentions are created equal, and each will imply a different set of R's, X's, and O's and thus a different location on the roadmap. Likewise, our capacity for maximizing our human and structural potential will be best accomplished if we consider our efforts through the lens of what human beings need to thrive. And creating a school reflecting a high level of coherence includes using leadership and pedagogical principles and practices consistent with sound socio-emotional and human development principles. Even the notion of efficiency will look different depending on the goals we use to pursue it.

In the next two chapters, we will complete the construction of the full school effectiveness roadmap. And as we explore the practical and applied process of moving up the roadmap later in the book the essential components outlined here will play a vital role.

## REFERENCES

Fullan, M & Quinn, J. (2016) *Coherence: The Right drivers in action for schools, districts and systems*. Corwin, Thousand Oaks, CA.

Lawrence, G (2009). *People Types and Tiger Stripes. Using psychological type to help students discover their potential*. Center for Application of Psychological Types, Gainesville, Fl.

**Exercise: 3.1**

**Examining Related Items from the ASSC SCAI (staff secondary version 7.4)**

Below are three survey items from the ASSC SCAI secondary climate instrument. First, as you examine the items, you will see that the emphasis of the descriptors for each item relate to the level of function and coherence at the school. These are good examples of items that will bring some awareness to where a particular school is on the vertical axis of the roadmap.

**4. Leadership/Decisions**

| Level - 3 | | Level - 2 | | Level – 1 | |
|---|---|---|---|---|---|
| **High** | **high-middle** | **middle** | **middle-low** | **low** | |
| 4.a——O————————— O ————————————— O ———————————— O ———————————— O ——————— | | | | | |
| School has a sense of vision and a mission that is shared by all staff. | | School has a set of policies, a written mission, but no cohesive vision. | | School has policies that are used inconsistently. | |

**5. Discipline Environment**

| Level – 3 | | Level - 2 | | Level – 1 | |
|---|---|---|---|---|---|
| **High** | **high-middle** | **middle** | **middle-low** | **low** | |
| 5.a————O————————— O ————————————— O ———————————— O ———————————— O ——————— | | | | | |
| School-wide discipline policy is consistently applied. | | School-wide discipline policy is used by some staff. | | School-wide discipline policy exists in writing only. | |
| 5.b————O————————— O ————————————— O ———————————— O ———————————— O ——————— | | | | | |
| It is evident from student behavior that there are clear expectations and consistency in the discipline policy. | | In many classes, there are clear expectations, and most teachers are fair and unbiased. | | Students must determine what each teacher expects, and behavioral interventions are defined by a high level of subjectivity. | |

---

**Reflection 3.2:** How did the items help you in the processes of representing your school on the vertical axis of the roadmap?

# CHAPTER 4:

## The Horizontal Axis –
## Promoting Empowerment and
## a Psychology of Success

> "Management is doing things right; leadership is doing the right things."
> — *Peter F. Drucker, Educator*
>
> "Never believe a few caring can't change the world. For indeed, that is all who ever have."
> — *Margaret Mead, Educator*

This chapter examines the horizontal axis of the school effectiveness road-map. In the previous chapter we examined the vertical axis and the nature of some of the *how's* to moving up the roadmap (i.e., promoting intention, capacity, coherence and efficiency). Here we will explore how different kinds of intentions will produce very different kinds of outcomes. *What* are our intentions? *Why* are we doing what we are doing? And *who* are we trying to be as we do it?

The horizontal axis implies a continuum of intentions/R's and actions/X's from more trusting and empowering to more fearful and controlling. When we put the two axes together, a matrix is produced with four quadrants and four distinct "school paradigms."

**Figure 4.1 Depicting the Horizontal Axis of the School Paradigm Matrix and Improvement Roadmap**

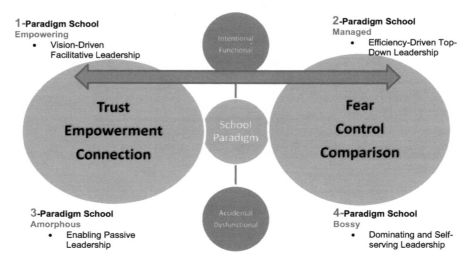

1-**Paradigm School**
Empowering
- Vision-Driven Facilitative Leadership

2-**Paradigm School**
Managed
- Efficiency-Driven Top-Down Leadership

**Trust**

**Empowerment**

**Connection**

**Fear**

**Control**

**Comparison**

3-**Paradigm School**
Amorphous
- Enabling Passive Leadership

4-**Paradigm School**
Bossy
- Dominating and Self-serving Leadership

These four paradigms will provide the topographical layout of the school effectiveness roadmap throughout the book. Each represents distinct R's, and X's and as a result will lead to distinct and predictable O/outcomes which can be seen in both classrooms and school-wide. The 4-Paradigm school is characterized by low function and intention, driven by fear and controlling R's. The 3-paradigm school attempts to allow freedom and autonomy but is characterized by low function and accidental quality, producing unreliable results. The most common school is the 2-Paradigm school reflecting adequate levels of function and is defined by mostly control-based R's and X's. Finally, when high quality intention is combined with high trust and empowerment, the result is the 1-Paradigm school. These four paradigms will be synthesized in the next chapter and explored in depth in the remaining chapters. A clear pathway from where your school is now to where you want it to be should emerge as your understanding of the roadmap and the nature of each paradigm develops.

## What Questions Guild Our Intentions and Practices?

To a great degree the intentions guiding our actions in both the large and small things will be driven by the internal questions we are asking and answering. We are constantly asking and answering questions internally and interpersonally. Asking the right questions keeps us focused on what is most important. Some questions such as "how can we promote more self-responsibility in our students?" will pull us up the roadmap. Focusing our attention on the 1-paradigm location. Other questions such as "why don't the students follow the rules?" will tend to keep us stuck at a lower level as it is external and encourages us to go into a victim mindset. Appendix X of the book offers examples of both empowering questions as well as limiting questions. And as you will see in both the content and the recommendations of the book, inquiry questions are used as often as advice in helping facilitate understanding of what it takes to move up the roadmap, and your use of them is strongly encouraged in the process of facilitating growth at your school.

The qualities that define the horizontal axis represent a synthesis of interrelated factors. The primary factor in this axis is related to the guiding intentions/R's at the school. Is the goal of the X's to create more empowering environment for faculty, staff and students or a more confining environment based in an effort to control? When we examine our motivations related to this question more closely, what we will recognize is that efforts to control largely come from a fear-based mindset, and the desire to empower is actually more natural and productive. Empowering R's are based in trust of – our abilities, our school's level of function, and the potential of the students themselves. What we see in the field is that without an explicit and shared commitment to this side of this axis, the X's at most schools tend to be defined by the 2- and 4-Paradigm side of the continuum.

On the trusting side of the axis are R's based in "connection." The fear-based end of the continuum will inherently be defined by a sense of separateness, competition, and comparison. Connection is empowering both emotionally and practically. A world defined by separateness and competition is a fearful place. In the classroom, this contrast appears as either student-center or teacher-centered R's and X's. These contrasting school R's are represented in Figure 4.2 below.

Figure 4.2: The Elements of the Horizontal Axis of the School Paradigm Matrix

| | Toward Empowerment | Mixed Motivation | Toward Control |
|---|---|---|---|
| **Ethic** | **Empowerment** – Foremost in the intention of the school is to empower teachers to be excellent and facilitate classrooms defined by self-responsible and self-reflective students. | Occasional Messages of empowerment undermined by practices that project mistrust. | **Control** - The message is that people basically cannot be trusted, so they need to be controlled by others and/or external mechanisms. |
| **Motive** | **Trust** – The emotion motivating action is the desire to build the capacity in each individual, class, and school which is defined by faith and trust in human potential. | Verbal messages of trust, but most actions imply that others are not ready to be trusted. | **Fear** – While the word fear is not often used explicitly, the feeling that pervades the school is "we better not ___ (trust students) or else _____ (something bad will happen." |
| **Who is it about?** | **Those I serve** – Leaders thinks about what is best for teachers and students. Teachers intend to create **student-centered environments.** | The goal is to be more student-centered, but we are not sure how, or if it would even work at this school. | **Me** – Leaders try to create a convenient world, for leaders that involves limiting teacher power. In the classroom that looks like **teacher-centered environments.** |
| **Relationships** | **Connection** – There is a basic sense that people are connected, we are an entity as a school, and what each of us does matters to the rest of us. | People are left mostly on their own and find connectedness where they can. | **Comparison** – Everyone is on their own, and rules and policies operate to catch those that exhibit misconduct and leave the rest alone. |
| **Psychology promoted by R's and X's** | **Psychology of Success (POS)** – Internal LOC, Belonging and Acceptance, Growth-Orientation. | Mixture of both POS and POF R's and X's. | **Psychology of Failure (POF)** – External LOC, alienation, and Fixed Ability-Orientation. |

## Refection Check in – "I am not sure I do trust what happens when I give up control."

As you become more acquainted with the roadmap, you will better recognize that many of the choices we have assumed in our time as educators have been false dichotomies. One of those false choices is order vs. trust. The 3-paradigm location represents blind faith and an absence of a clear intention. Commonly, leaders operate under the assumption that they have to choose between the 2-paradigm (control) and the 3-paradigm (amorphous). The better option – the 1-paradigm is not as easy to produce, but it represents the highest level of effectiveness in the end. So, let's examine a few ideas which distinguish a trusting and empowering world from a "let folks do whatever" world.

- In a high function context trust is earned. Therefore, trusting someone who has not shown they deserve to be given the freedom and responsibility to do the task is not wise or effective.

- Safety is job one. But the R's which guide one's pursuit of safety will be different in each paradigm. Our guiding questions might include - Do students really feel safe if they don't trust their peers' intentions, and their teachers' ability to create a healthy environment? If safety is all about adult supervision, would we expect it to promote self-responsibility or simply compliance?

- What if I give up control to someone else and they mess it up? This is where leadership in the classroom or school comes in. Building a growth-orientation requires allowing others to make mistakes, learn from them, and break free of a fear of failure. But high stakes outcomes need to be attended to by competent people who will own the outcomes. Leadership requires countless judgment calls. But if someone else can do it and wants to do it, why are you holding onto control?

- In the final chapter of the book, we encourage you to explore your own personal vision and growth journey. Many times, in the job of school leader, what seems like a simple practical matter is really more of an indicator of who we are being at that moment. Usually developing a trusting culture in a school will start with the leader's self-exploration of themselves (including their fears and insecurities).

As we undertake the process of supporting the movement of a group of faculty and staff up and over to the highest levels of growth, performance, and personal satisfaction, one of the challenges is to make the process operational and as practical as possible. Most teachers appreciate, once they are shown the roadmap, that a move up and over will enable them to be more successful. However, making that move can feel scary and uncertain if there is not a supportive process for change and a clear set of X's operationalizing and empowering that move. Moving up the roadmap implies *embracing change*: meaning both new understandings (R's) and new practices (X's), both in the classroom and as a school team.

Change is difficult for the most daring, but for the average teacher it represents a substantive challenge. Chapters six through twelve will operationalize the process of changing both intentions and practices and effective ways to facilitate the change process. We all recognize personal and/or institutional change is impossible in the absence of trust, so what is required to develop that trusting culture is outlined in Chapter six. In Chapter seven, we will examine in more detail how to effectively facilitate the process of supporting more effective R's at the school, and in chapter eight we will explore instructional leadership and what it takes to support more effective X's in detail. Chapter thirteen will explore the process of moving a school from 2-Paradigm to a 1-Paradigm R's and X's. Making this shift is both the most challenging and most rewarding job a leader can undertake – as a person, for the institution, and for the students.

## Psychology of Success – An exceptionally Useful and Powerful Construct

When we boil down the research related to those factors which define such essential qualities as self-esteem, achievement orientation, persistence, grit, confidence, ease and well-being, agency and others, some common themes emerge (Auer, 1992; Benham, 1993; Dweck, 2006, 2006; Klein & Keller, 1990; Joseph, 1992; Rennie, 199; Shindler, 2009; 2016).

These themes can be reduced to three basic psychological orientations that operate within individuals, classrooms, and schools as a whole. The three factors are distinct but inter-related and serve as a useful definition for what constitutes a "psychology of success" (POS). They are:

- **Internal vs. External Locus of Control**
- **Belonging and Acceptance vs, Alienation and Inferiority**
- **Growth vs. Fixed-Ability Orientation**

First, we want to promote an **internal versus external locus of control (LOC).** This means we see our R's and our X's as the cause of our O's – we have cause and effect. An internal LOC helps us feel our power and choices within each situation. Internal LOC is found to be the most predictive variable for student achievement – even higher than SES or ethnicity (Rennie, 1991; Shindler et al, 2016).

Second, we feel more confident, safe, and expressive in situations in which we have **a sense of self-acceptance and belonging** within a group, which helps us feel connected to others. We are better able to feel into our true potential and trust our natural instincts to make a positive contribution and share our gifts. Belonging and self-acceptance among students is at the essence of any effort to promote social and emotional learning (SEL, Osterman, 2000), and also critical in the effort to encourage student achievement and teacher effectiveness (Shindler, et al, 2016).

Third, when our confidence comes from a **growth orientation** rather than a fixed-ability orientation we see all things as opportunities for growth rather than a threat to our self-esteem Dweck 2006; Shindler, 2009). Within a school, this looks like a place where people are finding ways to express their potential and improve who they are, as opposed to a place where people are playing it safe and avoiding being judged. Figure 4.4 outlines how these three qualities appear when examined within an individual, classroom, and school.

In our work within schools, we find the concept of a "psychology of success" (POS) to be a powerful and useful tool for many reasons. Using the lens of these three qualities helps illuminate and clarify so much of what is happening both in terms of the R's and X's at a school. A few of the ways that we see POS being useful include:

1. The R's that define a POS are easily recognizable as valid both theoretically, but also within our beings. Most of us desire to live in a world defined by those three qualities, and we are mostly miserable in one defined by their opposites.

2. Decades of research support the relationship of each of these three POS components to student achievement and self-esteem among other desired outcomes (the references listed in this chapter represent a small sample of the research in these areas).

3. *Transformative Classroom Management* (Shindler, 2009) outlines the practical steps for creating a POS in the classroom. Carol Dweck's book *Mindset* (2006) explains the Growth-Mindset in detail.

4. POS is a highly useful tool to use for faculty vision clarification. We have incorporated it in countless faculty trainings, leadership trainings, school retreats and within our education courses. Often this has been in the form of a powerful and clarifying exercise in the classifying X's at the school (See Appendix A – the Process of Leading a POS Classification Exercise).

5. Students are able to understand these factors as well. Using the components for student self-reflection is effective.

6. Movement up and over on the roadmap requires teachers to internalize the concepts of a psychology of success and embrace them as desirable goals.

7. POS is built into the structure of the ASSC SCAI and can be integrated into a potential assessment, data analysis, and school improvement process.

## Figure 4.3: Psychology of Success – Each Element Characterized at the Personal, Classroom and School Levels

| Element/ Psychological Principles | Personal Application | Classroom Application | School-wide Level |
|---|---|---|---|
| **Internal Locus of Control**<br><br>Life is in our hands.<br><br>We are the authors of our own fate.<br><br>There is cause and effect in the world, and the first cause is our attitude.<br><br>We are responsible for own success or failure. | I move through the day feeling responsible for how things go and for my level of happiness.<br><br>**Leader**: I take responsibility for the state of the union. I am secure in my power, so I am comfortable empowering and giving credit to others.<br><br>**Teacher**: I hold the belief that my student's welfare depends mostly on things I can control. I look for ways to help my students grow. | Promote a clear and consistent cause and effect world in the classroom – actions have positive and negative consequences. Encourage increasing levels of freedom and wise choices. Promote student ownership and voice. Create clear learning goals and assessment outcomes students can attain with full application. | What strikes one first is that there is a high level of order at the school. The clarity of expectations, norms and TRUST empowers others to be ultimately capable of being self-responsible. There is minimal supervision, but immediate follow-through by adults when students violate the school's social contract. Evidence of student ownership is all over the school from the walls to the student self-led activities. Students feel a sense of power and are not afraid to question the authority at the school. Teachers feel validated and empowered by leadership and they in turn empower their students. |
| **External LOC**<br><br>External events are the cause of what happens to *us*.<br><br>Life is an accident.<br><br>It is someone else's fault. Things just happen. | I experience an underlying feeling there is little I can do to improve things. I see mostly evidence that no matter what I do, not much gets better. Parents, the system, and students are too much to overcome.<br><br>**Leader**: I spend a lot of energy trying to exert power over others. I often feel defensive. I trust very few people.<br><br>**Teacher**: I like to keep students feeling dependent on my approval. I like to give rewards and praise to control my students. | Create vague and shifting rules and be inconsistent in applying them. Be autocratic and ignore students need for power. Compare students to one another on variables over which they have no control. | What strikes one first is the substantial amount of adult effort expended in nagging, corralling, and supervising students. Policies are constantly being generated to stop non-compliance from happening, or to bribe or coerce students into more desired behavior and effort level. Adults seek obedience and are continuously offended by the students' lack of respect for their authority. Students assume that random acts of abuse are around the corner when there are no adults around. Most student complaints are met with annoyance from adults. Students learn to make good excuses. Teachers learn to make lots of calls home. |

| Acceptance and Belonging | In a basic sense, I like and respect myself. I have others I actually like and respect too. I feel like at least some people are supportive of me and what I am trying to do. | Create an emotionally safe class defined by intolerance for putdowns and abuse. Encourage students to work together and support one another toward personal and collective growth. Focus on strengths of each student and the idea that we all have different gifts. Find ways for the class to win together. | The school puts a lot of attention into creating rituals and celebrations. Students are celebrated for a wide range of efforts and gifts. Collaborative projects in and out of classes are frequent. School-wide expectations exist related to appreciating and showing respect for one another, and adults take that job seriously starting with no tolerance for verbal abuse on campus. Faculty is given time to collaborate and make plans for both classroom and whole school initiatives. Students are included in leadership meetings when possible. Parents are welcomed at the school. The school takes its identity seriously and seeks to connect membership with the values of excellence, positive character, and service to others. |
|---|---|---|---|
| We are unique and wonderful the way we are. | **Leader**: Believe the school team has its heart in the right place even if it is not perfect. I let others know that I am a fan of their effort and who we are. | | |
| We have necessary and valuable gifts to share. | | | |
| We are part of a supportive collective. | **Teacher**: When I look at my students, I see human potential and young people who need to be shown unconditional positive regard. I trust they appreciate what I do for them even if they don't always show it. | | |
| Others appreciate us and are interested in helping us thrive. | | | |
| **Alienation and Inadequacy** | I am not sure that I am doing very well, and I spend a lot of time feeling defensive. When I walk into a room, I wonder what others are thinking and I suspect that they say negative things about me when I am not around. | Create a competitive class where students struggle against one another for recognition, grades, and approval. Define ability in a single way. Grade only what you can count. Make it about you and demand obedience as you ignore student-student mistreatment. | The school puts most of its attention on grades and test scores. There is a subtle or not so subtle message to students that they are as valuable to the school as their test scores or athletic ability. Teachers and administrators regularly make student-student comparisons. Traditions, school spirit and non-sports extra-curricular activities are an afterthought. In class students do a lot of independent work and traditional assessment, out of class there is mostly a focus on a desire for sports success and individual student academic awards. Adults do not know many of the students who are walking in the halls. The school's culture is tolerant of casual putdowns between its members. |
| We experience mostly our inadequacies and perceived weaknesses. | **Leader**: I have a difficult time respecting the faculty and I do not disguise it well. I feel like faculty members see me as either critical or incompetent. | | |
| We feel separate from the group and not appreciated. | | | |
| We do not feel able to trust others and do not perceive the world as a supportive place. | **Teacher**: When I look out at my students all I can see is how much they lack. I have a hard time getting my heart into building a positive classroom culture, it just seems like a pretense for how we all really feel. | | |

| | | | |
|---|---|---|---|
| **Growth Orientation**<br><br><br>We accurately perceive that if we apply ourselves, we improve in anything we attempt.<br><br>We trust the process to get us results. We focus on growth and the journey and not so much on temporary relative abilities. We use mistakes as opportunities to learn and grow. | I feel quite free and trusting of myself to take risks and try things. I am not too worried if things don't go perfectly.<br><br>**Leader:** It is easy for me to sell the idea that the school is improving because I really believe it. Promoting growth is what I am about, and I try to help others self-reflect. I support and encourage innovation and risk taking.<br><br>**Teacher:** In my class, we are free to make mistakes and I conspicuously include myself. I see my growth as a teacher and follow my vision of becoming more effective all the time. | Value the process over the product. Encourage a system of self-reflection and feedback. Encourage a climate where it is ok to make mistakes and taking risks is encouraged. Focus on growth and learning and not on relative attainment. Project high expectations for all students, especially in the area of investment and quality of effort level. | Throughout the school there is a distinct message (conspicuous R) that it is about growth, rather than relative performance. Teachers are encouraged to try innovative practices, and students are encouraged to take risks and attempt new things. Bringing in a negative attitude in any form is discouraged. Quality in every area of school life is defined and discussed, and students are asked to continuously self-assess based on those criteria. Student-student comparisons are avoided, and tests are de-emphasized. Students who have overcome challenges are celebrated. As a school, there is a feeling life is getting better all the time and adults find regular opportunities to support that notion with evidence. |
| **Fixed Ability Orientation**<br><br><br>We inaccurately perceive our abilities as a fixed quantity. So, we do not see the need to persist if things do not go well initially. We eventually learn to fear failure and are crushed by mistakes and unfavorable comparison. | I see that I have some gifts in this job, but I know others are much more gifted in some areas, and so I stick to what I am good at. When things don't go well in a day, I feel crummy and stupid, and a part of me just wants to quit and do something that is less brutal to my ego.<br><br>**Leader:** I tend to focus my attention on how we are doing relative to other schools and I find great comfort in finding schools doing worse than us.<br><br>**Teacher:** I find it very difficult to teach students with so many limitations. I grade on a curve to prepare them for real life. | Value just the final product. Focus on who is able at this or that and compare student's work and aptitude. Use destructive criticism or subtle judgment for mistakes. Encourage and/or allow students to connect their grades to their self-worth. Promote a fear of failure motivational mindset. | Very quickly in the school, one will hear about the limits and challenges of the students and the neighborhood, then the percentages of students who did not pass various tests. The "haves and the have not's" at the school are clear to everyone, and people know their place. Innovation is seen as a waste of time because "those students" will just make a mess of it. Students learn to stay out of trouble and avoid being criticized by peers and adults. In the teachers' perceptions, the students are their grades, and so they try to motivate students by using the promise of a good grade, public shame, and comparison as motivators. |

As you can see from Figure 4.3, the construct of a POS proves insight and consciousness raising on virtually all levels. We can use it from the most personal and micro to the most macro and organizational. Asking guiding questions based in the qualities of a POS is a highly empowering exercise, inherently implying movement up the roadmap. So, on a personal level, we might ask ourselves if our unconscious R's (such as our beliefs) are more guided by the principles of POS or POF?" (If you are honest with yourself, you might be really surprised by the answer). We can ask a group of teachers or students if they are using more POS or POF thinking at any moment to help ground a situation. As a leader, teacher, or even a student, we can ask ourselves, "Is this action going to lead to more POS or POF in the situation?" We can look around at the school, the nature of the relationships, the level of effort, and the overall climate and ask if our O's are reflecting more POS or POF (This idea is expanded in Exercise Two at the end of this chapter).

---

**Figure 4.5: Growth vs. Fixed-Ability Orientation.**

Throughout their research over 30 years, Carol Dweck (2000; 2006) and her colleagues have developed a very useful paradigm with which to examine academic self-concept, achievement, and motivation. They have demonstrated in a series of studies with students (Dweck, 2000; 2006) that future success is not as much the result of talent (i.e., fixed ability factors) or current level of ability, as it is the result of the orientation/cognitive strategy one uses to approach learning tasks (i.e., a growth mindset). Dweck presents these useful lens for distinguishing two contrasting cognitive strategies for feeling competent and how, over time, they have dramatically different results. When a student uses a growth orientation they view a situation as an opportunity to learn and grow. They do not see their performance within a situation as a measure of their innate ability as much as a measure of their investment – better results requires more practice. Students who approach tasks with a fixed-ability orientation view the context as a reflection of how much ability they innately possess in that area. The result is a student who is looking for situations which will not challenge their fragile self-image or make them feel "dumb." Dweck (2000, 2006) found that students with a growth mindset pattern were more likely to persist in the face of failure and experience higher levels of academic achievement.

Revisiting our principles from the previous chapter related to the qualities necessary for moving up, it is good to keep in mind that our intentions related to the horizontal axis will manifest differently depending on how well we are doing with the vertical axis related to function, and vice versa. *A bottom-line principle for success will be that promoting a POS (in some form) within and out of the classroom needs to be fundamental to the R's at the school, as it serves both causes.* A POS can help clarify our intentions/R's (moving us up) and pull us toward the more empowering regions of the roadmap. Secondly, the better we understand the form and nature of these qualities, the better we will recognize how much they facilitate our capacity to improve our effectiveness in all areas. And finally, because the qualities of a POS are sound and help focus our intention, they can encourage coherence. In fact, when you view the current practices/X's at your school within the lens of either promoting more POS or more POF, you can see that a) the level of incoherence was probably much higher than you assumed, and b) you can see clearly what is holding you back from moving up.

Why intention and coherence are so critical to success can be seen when we examine three schools intending some effort to apply POS promoting practices into the overall mix.

- A low to middle performing high school had the admirable idea of having their students self-reflect their level of growth mindset. But this self-reflection practice was an isolated event and largely inconsistent the mostly POF promoting practices used at the school. The intent was good, but the result was an X that was incongruent with most other things within the students' experience (as well as the school's R's). The net result was that it was ineffectual and quickly forgotten.

- A middle performing high school implemented a peer tutoring program in which 11th graders worked with 9th graders in a structured setting. The result was a bump in the climate and achievement scores at the school. But because the program was an isolated X (and existed only at the program level) and only semi-consistent with the guiding R's other X's at the school, it had a limited effect. In addition, there were other X's at the school that promoted opposing values and dispositions, thus, undermining its power. Capacity was enhanced, but coherence was not.

- A high performing school had students self-reflect their process investment based loosely on their level of POS. Because the X was intentional, consistently applied, and congruent with the other X's and R messages students encountered in their classes, the X became part of the system – "the way we do things around here." The result was enhanced capacity, because of the coherence between the existing R's and X's. In addition, the efficiency (i.e., buy-in versus resistance and confusion) of doing something like this in the classroom will be highly dependent on whether it is familiar and comfortable. This application is an effective representation of how the 1-quadrant is not the 3-quadrant as well as showing why this 1-Paradigm school performs so well.

## CONCLUSION

In the coming chapters, you will be encouraged to consider how you can facilitate the movement of your school across the horizontal axis of the roadmap and incorporate more POS and less POF into your school's R's, X's and O's. When we examine the notion of vision, you will likely recognize the value of including a more POS-promoting element into your school's guiding direction. When we explore the nature of the critical element of trust among all members of the school community, POS provides a practical set of instructions for making that quality actualized. As we examine our school and attempt to identify our "real problems" rather than just the symptoms, what we find is that the real problems almost always have something to do with not enough POS based X's and/or too many POF X's. In the next chapter, we combine the vertical and horizontal axis to create a complete matrix and what functions effectively as a roadmap for school diagnosis and improvement.

## Exercise 4:1: Classifying POS as a formal exercise

See Appendix A at the end of the book.


## Exercise 4.2: Assessing Your R's by Your O's

As you examine each of these lists. Where would you currently assess your school in relation to whether the O's at your school reflect more the POS side on the left, or the POF side on the right?


**How a Psychology of Success (POS) or Psychology of Failure (POF) Reference Appears in the Individual Level Outcomes.**

| POS | POF |
| --- | --- |
| Persistence in the face of challenging situations. | Give up to save face and protect ego. |
| Being OK with mistakes | Fearing criticism, unfavorable comparison, or feeling inadequate. |
| Feeling trusting of others and supported by the group. | Feeling as if you can't trust others, and/or students don't trust the adults to create a safe environment |
| Feeling as if you have a way to contribute and your work has meaning. | Feeling as if your work is done for an external reward or out of a sense of obligation. |
| Feeling empowered. | Feeling Domesticated. |

## How a Psychology of Success (POS) or Psychology of Failure (POF) R appears in the classroom level O's.

| POS | POF |
|---|---|
| Students feel encouraged to and encourage others to take risks and make mistakes. | Students play it safe. |
| Students think and talk about what is good for the health and function of the collective. | Students think and talk in terms of their personal comfort. |
| Students trust the collaborative process. | Students feel either uneasy with collaborative effort or take advantage of it to waste time. |
| Students feel empowered to suggest changes to policy or rules when they need to be changed to serve the collective good. | Students assume they have little voice or power. |
| Everyone is rooting for everyone else because each of our "goods" is to the benefit of the others. | Students default to the assumption that they need to take care of themselves because the environment can be hostile and competitive. |

## How a Psychology of Success (POS) or Psychology of Failure (POF) R appears in the school level O's.

| POS | POF |
|---|---|
| School feels welcoming and safe. | Students brace themselves when they come in the door. |
| Mostly one hears positive recognitions. | Mostly one hears negative recognitions |
| Students trust that a POS R is "the way it is" so anything else appears odd. They complain when they do not see adults using POS creating X's. | Students are confused when teachers use POS promoting X's as they are not familiar. |
| Students ask process quality questions such as "When we are doing this, should we focus more on. . .or. . .?" "If we want to do it this way, would that work?"<br><br>"We need more time. May we have 5 more minutes?" | Students ask for praise or comment related to completion, for example,<br><br>"Teacher I am done,"<br><br>"teacher, did I do it right?"<br><br>Teacher, do I get my points?"<br><br>"We didn't get it, so we just stopped." |
| Students seek ways to start groups which satisfy their interests and assume that is encouraged. | Students avoid being at school or assume that any request that they make of adults regarding new ideas will be met with resistance. |

**Exercise 4.3: Horizontal Axis and POS/POF reflected in the SCAI items**

All items in the SCAI imply location on the roadmap and therefore higher rated items will reflect more intention as well as more empowerment and connection. Items all reflect more POS in the high end and POF at the low end. For some items, the use of POS language and concepts is more explicit. The following are a sample of items in the SCAI representing where the POS element(s) are very evident. In items 2a and 2b related to faculty interactions, faculty collaboration corresponds with the high rating options and competition on the low option. In item 5a, related to the discipline and management used, student power and ownership is represented on the high end, and teacher dogmatism is reflected on the low end. In item 6h, related to instruction and assessment, the use of assessment data to promote a growth-orientation corresponds to the high end and the use to reinforce a fixed-ability orientation is characterized at the low end.

### 2. Faculty Relations

| | Level – 2 (middle) | | Level –1 (low) |
|---|---|---|---|
| Level – 3 (high) | | | |

| High | high-middle | middle | middle-low | low |
|---|---|---|---|---|
| **2.a** ----O---------------- O ------------------- O ---------------------- O ----------------------- O ---------------- | | | | |
| Faculty members commonly collaborate on matters of teaching. | Most faculty members are congenial to one another and occasionally collaborate. | | Typically, faculty members view one another competitively. | |
| **2.b** ----O---------------- O ------------------- O ---------------------- O ----------------------- O ---------------- | | | | |
| Faculty members approach problems as a team/collective. | Faculty members attend to problems as related to their own interests. | | Faculty members expect someone else to solve problems. | |
| **5.e** ----O---------------- O ------------------- O ---------------------- O ----------------------- O ---------------- | | | | |
| Maximum use of student-generated ideas and input. | Occasional use of student-generated ideas. | | Teachers make the rules and students should follow them. | |
| **6.h** ----O---------------- O ------------------- O ---------------------- O ----------------------- O ---------------- | | | | |
| Students are seen as the primary users of assessment information, and assessment is used for the purpose of informing the learning process and is never used to punish or shame. | Assessment is seen as something that occurs at the end of assignments. Grades are used primarily for student-to-student comparison. | | Assessment is used to compare students to one another and/or to send a message to lazy students. | |

## REFERENCES

Auer, C.J. (1992). A Comparison of the Locus of Control of First and Second Grade Students in Whole Language, Basal Reader, and Eclectic Instructional Approach Classrooms (Doctoral Dissertation, Northern Illinois University, 1992). *Dissertation Abstracts International, 53* (11), 3856.

Bar-Tal, D. B., and Bar-Zohar, Y. (1977). The Relationship between Perception of Locus of Control and Academic Achievement. *Contemporary Educational Psychology. 2*, 181-99.

Benham, M.J. (1993). *Fostering Self- Motivated Behavior, Personal Responsibility, and Internal Locus of Control*, Eugene, Oregon.. Office of Educational Research and Improvement (ERIC Document Reproduction No. ED 386 621).

Csikszentmihalyi, M (1991) Flow: The Psychology of Optimal Experience. Harpers. New York.

Davis, L.E., and Peck, H.I. (1992). *Outcome Measures--School Climate: Curriculum and Instruction*. Paper presented at the Annual Meeting of the Mid-South

Educational Research Association (ERIC Document Reproduction No. ED 353 335).

Dembrowsky, C.H. (1990). *Developing Self-Esteem and Internal Motivation in At Risk Youth.* Practicum Paper (ERIC Document Reproduction No. ED 332 130).

Dweck, C. (2000) *Self-Theories; Their Role in Motivation, Personality and Development.* Lillington, NC: Psychologists Press.

Dweck, C (2006) Mindset: A new psychology of success. New York, Random House.

Fitch, G. (1970). Effects of Self-Esteem, Perceived Performance and Choice on Causal Attributions. *Journal of Personality and Social Psychology. 44,* 419-427.

Hagborg, W.J. (1996) Self-Concept and Middle School Students with Learning Disabilities: A Comparison of Scholastic Competence Subgroups. *Learning Disability Quarterly. 19,*(2 ) 117-26.

Huberman, M., & Middleton, S. (2000). The dilution of inquiry: A qualitative study. *International Journal of Qualitative Studies in Education, 13,* 281-304.

Hunter, J., Csikszentmihalyi, M., (2003) Positive Psychology of interested adolescents. *Journal of Youth and Adolescence, 32,* 27-35.

Inderbitzen, H. M., and Clark, M. L. (1986). The Relationship between Adolescent Loneliness and Perceptions of Controllability and Stability. *Paper presented at the Annual Meeting of the Southeastern Psychological Association,* Orlando, Fl. April.

Klein, J. D., and Keller, J. M. (1990). Influence of Student Ability, Locus of Control, and Type of Instructional Control on Performance and Confidence. *Journal of Educational Research, 83*(3) 140-46.

Meaney MJ.(2001) Maternal care, gene expression and the transmission of individual differences in stress reactivity across generations. *Annu Rev Neurosci* 4,1161-1192.

Osterman, K.F. (2000) Students' need for belonging in the school community. Review of Educational Research, 70(3), 323-367.

Rennie, L.J. (1991). The Relationship between Affect and Achievement in Science. *Journal of Research in Science Teaching,* 28 (2) 193-09.

Sharidan, M. K. (1991). Self-Esteem and Competence in Children. *International Journal of Early Childhood, 23,* (1) 28-35.

Shindler, J. (2003) *Creating a Psychology of Success in the Classroom: Enhancing Academic Achievement by Systematically Promoting Student Self-Esteem.* Classroom Management Resource Site, CSULA. Retrieved on 10/11/08 from www.calstatela.edu/faculty/jshindl/cm.

Shindler, J. (2009) *Transformative Classroom Management: Positive Strategies to engage all learners and promote a psychology of success*. Jossey Bass. San Francisco, CA.

Shindler, J., Jones, A., Williams, A. (2016) Examining the School Climate – Student Achievement Connection: And Making Sense of Why the First Precedes the Second. *Journal of School Administration Research and Development, Summer 2106 v.1.*n.1. pp7-16.

Tanksley, M. D. (1994). *Building Good Self-Esteem for Certain Fifth Grade Children through Cooperative Learning, Individualized Learning Techniques, Parental Involvement, and Student Counseling*. Practicum Paper (ERIC Document Reproduction No. ED 367 095)

Wang, M. and Stiles, B. (1976). An Investigation of Children's Concept of Self-Responsibility for their Learning. *American Educational Research Journal. 13,* 159-79.

# CHAPTER 5:

## Where are You Currently? and Where are You Going? Building and Exploring the School Effectiveness Roadmap

> "A clear vision, backed by definite plans, gives you a tremendous feeling of confidence and personal power."
> – *Brian Tracy, Motivational Author*
>
> "All you need is the plan, the roadmap, and the courage to press on to your destination."
> – *Earl Nightingale, Motivational Author*

When setting out on any journey, it is useful to have a roadmap. When engaging in the process of school improvement it is no different. If we do not have a defined sense of where we are currently, and a clear sense of the direction and location of where we are going, then what are we using to guide our choices and actions?

In this chapter, we guide you to construct and explore the school effectiveness roadmap. The purpose of this roadmap is to represent where the different intentions and performance levels of any school are located in relation to all possibilities. We will also identify the locations representing a common "pathway" onto which most schools typically fall. This roadmap provides the school and/or classroom leader a means of locating where they are in terms of intent (References/R's) and actuality (Actions/X's and Outcomes/O's), offers depictions of other possible destinations, and provides routes to get from one's current location to other chosen destinations. While the reader may be tempted, as they gain understanding of the roadmap, to think in terms of comparisons, we encourage a focus on growth and what would be needed for setting out on a journey of improvement.

In the following chapters, we will explore the various requirements and processes necessary for any school to move up the pathway depicted within the school effectiveness roadmap. First, we will put together the building blocks of the roadmap and then introduce some of its implications for uses.

## Building Block One: Combining the Two Axes into One Matrix

The first step in constructing the school improvement roadmap is to define our geography. In this case, by combining the basic foundations of the roadmap – the vertical and horizontal axes. The vertical axis as described in Chapter three is defined by higher or lower levels of intention, capacity, coherence, and efficiency, or "how well" our school functions. The horizontal axis as described in Chapter four is defined by the "what" and "why" of our intentions, values and practices related to the degree to which they are inspired by – trust vs. fear, connection vs. comparison, and empowerment vs. control. The result of combining the two axes is a four-quadrant matrix which will function as the latitude and longitude of the roadmap and is depicted in Figure 5.1 below.

Figure 5.1: Combining the Two Axes into One Matrix – the Four Leadership Styles/ School Paradigms

| | Empowerment Connection Trust | Control Comparison Fear |
|---|---|---|
| **High Function**<br>**Intentional**<br>**Leadership** | **1-Paradigm School**<br><br>**Empowering**<br><br>• Vision-Driven Facilitative Leadership<br>• Student-Centered Classrooms<br>• Community Climate<br>• Mostly 1-style teaching<br>How can we systematically promote the growth and human potential of all individually and collectively? | **2-Paradigm School**<br><br>**Managed**<br><br>• Efficiency-Driven Top-Down Leadership<br>• Teacher-Centered Classrooms<br>• Institutional Climate<br>• Mostly 2-style teaching<br>How can we effectively implement our chosen programs and practices consistently? |
| **Low Function**<br>**Reactive**<br>**Leadership** | **3-Paradigm School**<br><br>**Amorphous**<br><br>• Enabling Passive Leadership<br>• Unstructured Learning<br>• Insecure Climate<br>• Primarily 3-style teaching (but also a random combo of others)<br>How can we provide enriching learning opportunities based on student interests? | **4-Paradigm School**<br><br>**Bossy**<br><br>• Dominating and Self-serving Leadership<br>• Lecture and Test Teaching<br>• Domesticating Climate<br>• Mostly 4-style teaching<br>How can we keep students on task and performing given the many issues we have to deal with? |

Each of the four resulting quadrants characterizes a conceptual and practical nature or "paradigm," with each defined by a somewhat predicable set of inter-related R's, X's, and O's. Each paradigm will be guided by a somewhat different set of macro-guiding questions which will define its agenda.

Combining a reactive/dysfunctional structure with a control-based value results in what can be termed a **Coercive/Bossy 4-Paradigm** school environment. When an accidental/dysfunctional structure is combined with a trusting value, the result is a somewhat permissive and **amorphous 3-Paradigm environment**. When there is a high level of function and a control-based value the result is **2-Paradigm** school which is defined by structure and organization. Finally, a **1-Paradigm school** combining both high intention and a trusting and connecting climate can best be characterized as empowering. All school performance quality locations tend to fall somewhere into one of these four paradigms.

> **Reflection:** Bring to mind a school with which you are familiar. Can you place its R's and X's into one of these quadrants?

## Building Block Two: Adding in the R/X to O correlation onto the Roadmap

The next step in our synthesis process is to overlay predicted quantitative performance levels onto each point on the two axes of the roadmap. To do this we need to recall the relationship between the values/R's and practices/X's at the school and the outcomes/O's (explained in chapter 2). In any school there will be a strong relationship between the R's, X's (as measured by the School Climate Assessment Instrument (SCAI) and the resulting O's, as measured by student achievement and other indicators of school performance - illustrated in the correlation scatter plot of climate score and student achievement and depicted below in Figure 5.2

# Figure 5.2/2.1: School Climate Score (SCAI) by Student Achievement (percentile)

SCAI Ratings by Achievement Percentile

Student Achievement Score Percentile StateRatings

If we plot the most common location of those intersections from the scatterplot scores onto the School Paradigm Matrix, we find that most school's climate and performance levels fall into a common pattern. In other words, schools could be located hypothetically anywhere on the roadmap, but the vast majority of schools fall on a narrow "pathway" depicted below in figure 5.3 by the blue line. Along the line are shown points defined by first an SCAI rating between 1.0 and 5.0 and a corresponding student achievement rating between 10%tile (low) and 100%tile (high).

**Figure 5.3: Theoretical Pathway of School Performance Levels Using SCAI and student achievement correlation data.**

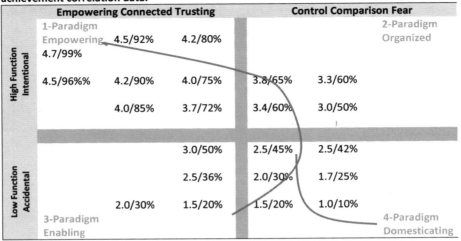

It should be noted that no matter where a school is on the roadmap the correlation between R's/references and X's/actions and O's/outcomes will be demonstrated. A school's performance may be an outlier from this curved theoretical pathway (the blue line), but not from the interdependent relationship between the R's and X's and its O's/outcomes which include student achievement as well as other effects such as attendance, discipline referrals, and teacher retention, etc.

As we plot the R-X to O correlation onto the School Paradigm Matrix, those schools defined by less intention and function tend to demonstrate lower performance. Those schools demonstrating the 3-Style or 4-Style paradigm tend to score lower in both achievement and climate/effectiveness ratings. While these schools can be very different in many regards, they will share the result of low performance indicators. Schools that demonstrate middle levels of performance tend to inhabit the 2-Style classroom and school paradigm. There are rare exceptions, but when the school achievement and climate levels are in the average-range they tend to be a 2-Paradigm school. The reason for this will be explored in more detail throughout the book.

# Adding a Few Final Building Blocks to the Roadmap

In the final synthesis of the roadmap, we add some more descriptors to help define each location (see figure 5.5). First, terms representing common X's (taken from the SCAI data and conceptual framework) are plotted on the roadmap. These terms such as praise, reward, social contract, and community represent both what is commonly valued as well as what is commonly practiced at schools located at that particular region of the roadmap.

Second, the levels of perception (LOPs, Figure 5.4) are included and located at points that represent where the dominance of a particular quality of thinking tends to lead. Sensory/reactive thinking is found in the lower region, and system and principle thinking is reflected in the higher region.

---

### Figure 5.4: Levels of Perception

The field of Perceptual Control Theory offers us a useful window into how any organism organizes its thinking. At any one time, we are using higher or lower thinking mechanisms or levels of perception (LOPs). The basic four levels are:

- System
- Principle
- Program
- Sensory/Reactive

A school, like any organism, can be seen as using higher or lower LOPs more regularly. Higher LOPs, such as being systemic and principle-driven, relate to higher levels of awareness and expanded use of one's perceptual capacity. Moreover, we are able to relate the dominant use of each of the LOPs to various locations on the roadmap. These are revisited in Chapter fourteen.

---

Finally, a low (L), middle (M) and high (H) location are identified reflecting the curve of the pathway and three general level locations which can be used as short-hand for the infinite points on the roadmap.

**Figure 5.5: Complete School Improvement Theoretical Roadmap with Pathway pattern reflected**

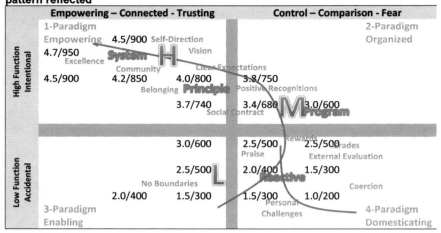

The overall synthesis of all building blocks produces a theoretical as well as practical roadmap with which to locate the function and performance level of any school. We will refer to this model throughout the remainder of the book as we operationalize the practical process of school improvement or "moving up the pathway."

---

**Reflection** - Given you current understanding, where would you place your school's level of function and performance on the school effectiveness roadmap - based on Figure 5.5?

---

### Some Implications of the Roadmap to Consider Going Forward

1. If we threw a conceptual dart onto the map above, we could reliably infer the likely R's, X's, and O's for a school from that location – i.e., what they are doing and trying to do.

2.  There are an infinite number of locations on the roadmap and each school is unique. But any two schools that share a particular location on the conceptual map will share many fundamental similarities.

3.  Schools at two distinct locations are inherently going to be using different R's and X's.

4.  The move up the pathway to the highest levels requires a "left-hand turn" toward the 1-Paradigm quadrant of the matrix.

5.  No amount of R's and X's defining the lower quadrants will result in higher quadrant O's. For example, no amount of program fidelity, 2-Paradigm leadership, and/or teacher centered teaching will result in 1-Paradigm results.

## Exploring Schools at Three Common Levels Along the Pathway

Schools at each of the different regions along the pathway – low, middle, and high – will be defined by common qualities (See Appendix B). The primary reason for this is that the R's/references that characterize each level reflect intentions and guiding questions specific to that level. As a result, the X's and O's will reflect those dominant intentions as well. As we explore each broad level, consider the ways in which the "how well" of the vertical axis, and the "what" and "why" of the horizontal axis define each level.

### Schools that Exhibit Low Function and Performance

When we examine schools that function and perform at the lower levels (below 2.6/5 SCAI ratings and below 30%tile academic performance) we see common qualities. First, there is typically a lack of function. Function is when things operate the way we intend. In low performing schools, there tends to be an accidental and/or reactive quality to the R's and the X's. Elements such as capacity, coherence and shared values tend to be less evidenced.

As we have discussed, we can accomplish low function with either a 3-Paradigm enabling/reactive or a 4-Paradigm dominating/domesticating brand of operations. In the 3-Paradigm school, students are usually on their own to navigate a chaotic and amorphous environment. Given this lack of structure students learn to cope and adapt to the "social Darwinism" and low expectation with a short-term self-interest mindset. Leadership in the 3-Paradigm school tends toward the laissez faire. In contrast, the 4-Paradigm schools, which have many prison-like qualities, place a great deal of attention on promoting compliance from students who are perceived to be untrustworthy. In these schools, students view the adults as the opposition and must choose between conformity and rebellion.

Four-Paradigm leadership tends to be top-down and authoritarian. However, most of the time a low functioning school will be a combination of the R's and X's of both the 3- and 4-Paradigm to create a very uneven and accidental set of R's and X's. The net effect being a set of R's defined by an absence of vision, X's defined by convenience for the adults, and O's that reflect very little psychology of success. Leadership tends to be defined by the "putting out of fires" and risk prevention strategies. A process for moving up from this low level of performance will be explored in detail in chapter twelve of this book.

## Examining the Common Middle Function and Performance School

Most schools function at the middle level on the pathway (between 2.7/5-3.5/5 SCAI ratings and 30%tile-70%tile academic performance). Why is this? The short answer seems to be that it is the easiest location on the map to operationalize, execute, and to defend to others. We will devote a great deal of attention to why this is as we explore how to move up and over on the pathway from this location throughout the remaining chapters and specifically in Chapter thirteen. Most of us attended middle functioning schools and we bring those references into our assumptions about what is both necessary as well as possible. For most educators it is easier to translate R's into X's in a teacher-centered 2- Paradigm school than in a school with student-centered approach. The 2-Paradigm school destination appears less risky, and more predictable, and while it is somewhat complicated, it does not require complex thinking. Therefore, we tend to solve the same old questions with the same old answers.

Most middle function schools contain teachers whose classrooms could be characterized by each of the 4 styles - with the majority falling into a 2- Paradigm teacher-centered approach.

The middle function school tends to value consistency, classroom order, and common standards. Solutions usually imply the implementation of a program. Most often guiding R's are well-articulated, and capacity is promoted through an effective use of standards-based planning and data-driven decisions. But consistency is not always coherence. And organizational standards are not sufficient when building human capacity.

In the classroom, the focus on applied behavioral strategies and external accountability tend to limit the growth of both teachers and students beyond this moderate level (Shindler, 2018). When control is the goal, anything that "works" is usually deemed acceptable. Therefore, all manner of X's are endorsed as long as they get results, no matter their underlying and/or long-term R's. Therefore, those who are attempting to be 1-Paradigm teachers find it a challenge when their peers are (in many cases) undermining their efforts and the administration does not value what they are trying to build. Two-Paradigm teaching, on the other hand, is affirmed and so there is no incentive in the system to grow beyond that approach. Nevertheless, this level of function is usually characterized by a solid level of order and instruction which is aligned with standards and assessments, producing satisfactory results.

Other default tendencies of a middle level of function include relatively collegial relationships (low capacity, but high comfort), and a compliance-based authority in and out of the classroom (low capacity, low empowerment, but high coherence) providing a source of organizational stability. The focus of the middle level school tends to be much more on the positive side and possesses higher expectations for students than the lower function school. As a result of those more clear and positive R's, the X's tend to promote more student engagement and skill development than the lower performing locations. Consequently, the O/outcomes reflect that higher level of function and focus on the positive.

As we have discussed, one of the findings of our research (Shindler et al, 2016; 2018) and an implication of the R-X-O roadmap (school improvement axiom #6, Figure 2.E)) is that actions or X's predict outcomes or O's. One of the ways we see this manifest itself is the case of the 2-Paradigm school improvement trajectory. If a school had been in the lower quadrants, we see the implementation of 2-Paradigm R's and X's improving the various outcome measures including SCAI and achievement. This is usually due to the school doing a better job with vertical axis qualities (capacity, efficiency, intention, and coherence). But once the school reaches that level on the roadmap, it tends to hit a ceiling and plateau. If improvement efforts began at the 2-Paradigm (and more 2-Paradigm solutions were implemented), the school finds that it tends to have flat results on indicators of improvement. The reason for this ceiling is complex in many ways but boils down to the laws of organizational improvement. Paraphrasing Albert Einstein – a school cannot solve its problems on the same level of consciousness at which they were created. In the terminology of the roadmap – a school cannot expect to obtain 1-Paradigm outcomes using 2-Paradigm R's and X's. Being part of a school that runs into this ceiling is frustrating for everyone involved. A school in the lower region of the roadmap may need to aim for the middle location on its path to improvement. And a 2-Paradigm may be the goal for some schools. But as we explore the various paths up the roadmap, it is possible to set out a trajectory that "cuts the corner" and embraces 1-Paradigm R's early on and seeks to cultivate "plateau-free" X's which can be developed without limiting the school's, teachers', and students' growth.

## High Level Function and Performance Schools and Why We Need to Make the Shift Left to Reach that Location

Much of the remaining discussion of the book will explore how schools can move up to the highest levels of function and performance (above 3.6/5 SCAI ratings and above 70%tile academic performance). The high functioning 1-Paradigm school represents the most natural and satisfying condition for working and learning. Hence, while it is not simple to create, it is very easy to appreciate once we have experienced it first-hand. It represents a "natural human condition." (Figure 5.6). And in reality, all schools have high function and performance potential innately within them. Yet, almost all schools function far below their potential.

On the one hand, it is true there are enormous challenges and factors in place which keep schools from moving higher. On the other hand, most of what is limiting the growth of schools involves self-limiting R's resulting in a long list of X's that seem necessary in a narrow view, but when viewed more broadly are not effectively leading to the outcomes we most desire.

### Figure 5.6. 1-Paradigm as the "Natural Condition."

The 1-Paradigm School and the 1-Style classroom are inherently more satisfying because they allow us to function in a condition that is natural and satisfying. We can feel a condition as more or less natural in our bodies. In those that are natural we feel ease and joy. Yet, in most normal situations we spend a lot of effort contorting ourselves into the perceived demands of the situation.

| Natural Condition | Normal Condition |
|---|---|
| Our basic needs for Power, Freedom, Belonging, Fun are met. | We cope and manage our day so that we can find satisfaction in other ways |

High functioning schools by nature will always be vision-driven. Most of the time that means a purposeful effort made by leadership to cultivate collective R's including an alive vision. An alive collective vision means there is systematic collaboration among members of the school (high levels of intention, capacity, and coherence). Questions of how to best execute this R/vision guide the development of the X's. The resulting "professional learning community" represents the intersection of high capacity, trust, and connection. A climate of trust is foundational to the high functioning school. Leadership trusts that teachers will find a way to operationalize the R's into high quality practices, and teachers trust that students will actualize their potentials if they are given the contexts for doing so.

In the highest performing schools, classrooms are defined by mostly 1-Paradigm teachers who are trying to create communities of self-responsible learners. Instruction is defined by inquiry, cooperation, and active learning. As you examine the notion of a success psychology, you will recognize that a school will be high functioning to the degree that it is intentional about creating a psychology of success (POS) within the school generally, in each classroom, and for each individual within its walls.

Creating the 1-Paradigm school requires embracing the complexity of an evolving system. The leadership skills and practices required to facilitate a vision-driven empowering organism are vast and challenging, so the goal of this book is to identify and operationalize them as well as possible. The success of any effort to create the 1-Paradigm school will relate mostly to how well the adults ask and are guided by the right questions and references. The most effective factor in becoming a 1-Paradigm school is to fundamentally want to be a 1-Paradigm school.

---

**Reflection** – Take part in the activity in Appendix A, either on your own or as a faculty. Here you will be creating lists of those practices (X's) that either promote or undermine a psychology of success (POS). Afterward, use that list to rate your school. Note how predictive it is. If what you are doing currently is mostly from the POS promoting column, you will likely have a high functioning school. If what you do is mostly from the POS undermining (i.e., psychology of failure promoting) your level of function and performance will reflect it.

---

## "But what about my school? It's the exception to the model."

Upon seeing this theoretical roadmap presented, most educators recognize its validity as well as its usefulness to explain schools. But we do encounter those who question the validity and soundness of the model or believe their school proves that there are exceptions. Possibly, but not very likely.

First, there are those educators who feel inclined to defend the need for their school to operate from the right side of the quadrant. However, through our research, we have not found a high performing school which did not score highly on the SCAI. A high score reflects a student-centered, high trust, high collaboration environment. All schools that take a very teacher-centered stimulus and response, external, programmatic approach fall in the middle levels on the SCAI and in all other areas of performance, and therefore on the roadmap. The reason for this will be explored more fully as we discuss how to move from a middle to high functioning in the remaining chapters of the book.

Second, we hear people say that their school has a certain set of R's/intentions and their achievement does not match on this conceptual model. What we can say to this assertion is that again, the SCAI rating (i.e., R and X) and O's like student achievement always correlate. Neighborhood income level will affect that relationship somewhat, but much less than one would expect. Therefore, what we usually find is that once data are collected from the school the person finds that the correlation is present. What made things appear misaligned usually comes from the reputation of the school being an inaccurate depiction of the true R's and X's at the school. In the school that is high performing and has a reputation for being very teacher-centered and hierarchical, what we find when we survey the students is that most often their actual perceptions are that the school does have a clear vision, they feel respected by their teachers, the faculty collaborates, there is a sense of community, students engage in cooperative projects and are given substantial ownership of their learning.

They *are* demonstrating 1-Paradigm X's, so the reality is that they really do value 1-Paradigm R's.

The other example is the very uncommon school which perceives itself as a 1-Paradigm school, but scores in the average range on the SCAI. And when they look on the roadmap, they see their student achievement scores are not near where they would be predicted. These schools tend to be project-based and emphasize collaboration and self-discovery and have a 1-Paradigm mission statement. But, again, the problem is not the model. When those folks survey their school what they commonly find is a lack of vision, students do not feel challenged, students are not given the skills to work together, and typically the assessment X's in place are very weak and lack intention. In contrast, all of these qualities are positively present in the high functioning 1-Paradigm school. While this school sees itself as a 1-Paradigm school, what they have created is in fact somewhat of a 3-paradigm school.

## CONCLUSION

All schools in our experience speak of improvement, yet most change little from year to year. Much of the explanation for why schools experience stagnant growth is that when asked what they are trying to improve they offer mostly O's. Outcomes are not typically the real problem, references and practices are. If R's and X's don't change neither will the O's. And when we talk about getting better, what does "better" mean? To get somewhere more desirable than where we are, we first need to have a meaningful understanding of where we are and why. We need to understand the reasons why we are at our current location. Next, we need to have a meaningful understanding of what it will take to get to where we want to be. We need a roadmap. In the next two chapters, we will explore how we can use the roadmap to promote two indispensable qualities – trust and vision. No effort can succeed without them.

# Exercise 5.1:

In your group or on your own, reflect on why these various elements tend to occur together at various points in the effectiveness continuum.

| | Empowerment Connection Trust | Control Comparison Fear |
|---|---|---|
| **High Function**<br><br>**Intentional**<br><br>**Leadership** | **1-Paradigm School**<br><br>**Empowering**<br><br>• Vision-Driven Facilitative Leadership<br>• Student-Centered Classrooms<br>• Community Climate<br>• Mostly 1-style teaching<br>How can we systematically promote the growth and human potential of all individually and collectively? | **2-Paradigm School**<br><br>**Managed**<br><br>• Efficiency-Driven Top-Down Leadership<br>• Teacher-Centered Classrooms<br>• Institutional Climate<br>• Mostly 2-style teaching<br>How can we effectively implement our chosen programs and practices consistently? |
| **Low Function**<br><br>**Reactive**<br><br>**Leadership** | **3-Paradigm School**<br><br>**Amorphous**<br><br>• Enabling Passive Leadership<br>• Unstructured Learning<br>• Insecure Climate<br>• Primarily 3-style teaching (but also a random combo of others)<br>How can we provide enriching learning opportunities based on student interests? | **4-Paradigm School**<br><br>**Bossy**<br><br>• Dominating and Self-serving Leadership<br>• Lecture and Test Teaching<br>• Domesticating Climate<br>• Mostly 4-style teaching<br>How can we keep students on task and performing given the many issues we have to deal with? |

## Exercise 5.2: Roadmap Locations Reflected in SCAI items

As you examine the items from any of the versions of the SCAI, you will see at least some reflection of the high, middle, and low levels of the improvement roadmap. Below are three survey item examples. In the first, a high-level response represents a school which has an R related to showing physical evidence of whose school it is – the students. At lower levels, walls tend to include more comparative material. In the next item, from the teacher relations scale, the simple act of collaboration indicates both an intention for high function as well as a value for connecting personally and professionally. In lower function schools, teachers are more on their own and see one another within the lens of comparison, and adequacy and inadequacy. In the final example, from the discipline and management scale, in high level schools, practice is intended to lead to increased levels of self-direction. In lower-level schools, the goal is usually defined by domestication in some form.

You are encouraged to access the SCAI full survey examples from the ASSC website and complete the entire inventory informally as a leadership team. Discuss your ratings.

| 1. Physical Appearance | | | | |
|---|---|---|---|---|
| **High** | **high-middle** | **middle** | **middle-low** | **low** |
| 1.e--------5------------ | ----4------------- | -----3--------- | -----2------------ | 1------------- |
| Current student work is displayed to show pride and ownership by students. | Few and/or only top performances are displayed. | | Decades-old trophies and athleti records in dusty cases. | |

| 2. Faculty Relations | | | | |
|---|---|---|---|---|
| **High** | **high-middle** | **middle** | **middle-low** | **low** |
| 2.a--------5------------ | ----4------------- | -----3--------- | -----2------------ | 1------------- |
| Faculty members commonly collaborate on matters of teaching. | Most faculty members are congenial to one another and occasionally collaborate. | | Typically, faculty members view one another competitively. | |

| | | | | |
|---|---|---|---|---|
| 5.i--------5------------ | ----4------------- | -----3--------- | -----2------------ | 1------------- |
| Management strategies consistently promote increased student self-direction over time. | Management strategies promote acceptable levels of classroom control over time but are mostly teacher-centered. | | Management strategies result in mixed results: some classes seem t improve over time, while others seem to decline. | |

Where would you rate your school? Do your ratings correspond to your previous assessment of your current location on the overall roadmap?

# REFERENCES

Shindler, J. (2009) *Transformative Classroom Management: Positive Strategies to engage all learners and promote a psychology of success.* Jossey Bass. San Francisco, CA.

Shindler, J., Jones, A., Williams, A. (2016) Examining the School Climate – Student Achievement Connection: And Making Sense of Why the First Precedes the Second. *Journal of School Administration Research and Development, Summer 2106 v.1.*n.1. pp7-16.

Shindler, J. Limiting Influence of PBIS on the Growth of Schools and Students. Alliance for the Study of School Climate. Retrieved from https://www.academia.edu/37267399/Limiting_Influence_of_Using_PBIS_Strategies_on_the_Growth_of_Students_and_Schools

# PART II:

# Leadership Skill and Process Development for Moving Our School Up the Roadmap

---

- Building Trust

- Cultivating a School-wide Vision

- Effective Instructional Leadership

- Meaningful Strategic Planning

- Assessing School Climate Dimensions

- Moving Up the Pathway in the Domain of Classroom Management

# CHAPTER 6:

## Cultivating Trust and Encouraging Process Values

> "Trust is the glue of life. It's the most essential ingredient in effective communication. It's the foundational principle that holds all relationships."
> — *Stephen R. Covey*

In this chapter, we will explore the area of trust. Reflecting upon the last two chapters, we have seen that the quality of trust is vital for both the capacity to move our school upward on the roadmap and is the essence of our movement over to the highest locations. If we were to identify the two most essential qualities for our school improvement effort to actualize, they would be vision and trust. When both exist, almost anything is possible. When either is missing, our success will be limited. Trust without vision will appear as aimlessness and/or complacency. Vision without trust will play out as apprehension, stalled efforts, power struggles and active or passive resistance. When neither trust nor vision exist, improvement is virtually impossible. Therefore, taking a very intentional approach to cultivating the quality of trust will be critical to our success.

As we envision our journey up the pathway, the quality of trust will define the nature of both our desired location, as well as the processes it will take to encourage our progress. The 1-Paradigm location is defined by a climate of trust in and out of the classroom. Movement up the pathway will involve learning how to cultivate the qualities of trust in our 1-Style classrooms, and the organizational practices which guide the school.

---

**Reflection 6.1.** Begin by examining your answers to the following questions

Why do we trust others? Why do we trust a collectively cultivated Vision? Why do we trust that better things will happen if we change?

---

There are countless factors affecting the level of trust in a school with the stated intention of getting better. For the purposes of this chapter, we can identify five areas where trust is built and examine each in detail. If we effectively addressing these five factors, we will be on solid footing. As we have touched upon previously, much of the quality of trust is removing the existence of limiting fear. Therefore, we will want to examine some of the fears that are addressed when we promote the presence of a corresponding trusting quality. Yet, it is important to keep in mind that trust as it relates to our improvement process is not just about allaying fears; it is about engendering the existence of confidence and courage moving forward.

First, trust will be present when the leaders of the effort are seen as competent and worthy of trust. Are they up to the task and are they made of the kind of "stuff" which gives us confidence? The potential fear here is the leader is not up the task, and/or the kind of person who can be respected. We offer a series of qualities for assessing the degree to which a leader can be seen as trustworthy. Second, if one is to head down a path, it is important that the destination is clear and desirable. The fear is that the destination is a mirage, a waste of time and effort, and/or a half-baked idea, not well understood. Therefore, having a roadmap to our goal and the appreciation that it is a "good" place to go is necessary to trust that the journey is worth the effort. Likewise, we need to trust that the efforts in which we are engaged will result in getting us to our desired goal. Third, we will trust to the extent that we are on the same page, and we have a clear process to rely upon. Fear comes from feeling like we do not have the know-how and/ or the faith in the know-how of others to make it on our journey. Focusing on process actions/X's and process-based outcomes/O's rather than product-based outcomes/O's will promote more trust. Fourth, a group will trust to the degree it sees there are rules and expectations making things feel safe and encouraging responsibility. The fear is that once things get going, people will drop the ball, flake-out, or be selfish. Therefore, a functioning social contract and solid social bonds need to be in place for each of us to feel safe and solid. Fifth, it is of great value if we feel like we care enough about the group and its members to do what it takes to succeed. The fear is that it can feel meaningless if we do not feel connected to the collective and/or the cause is not engaging to us or what we think is best for everyone. In many respects trusting comes from liking. Consequently, we need to encourage communal bonds and a felt experience of moving up the pathway as a team, where WE will create a better place to work for all members of the school family.

---

**Reflection 6.2** – Take a moment to reflect on the level of trust you have for your colleagues and institution. Rate it between 1 and 10. Does your rating roughly correspond to your SCAI location on the roadmap?

---

As you pondered the reflection question above, was it difficult to rate your level of trust? My guess would be that it was not. Each of us can feel our level of trust. Its existence or absence is palpable.

Our movement and improvement are contingent on our ability to infuse our school with the qualities of trust and vision. Therefore, in a global sense, we are trying to make our institution a more trusting place by nature – i.e., more trusting references/R's, practices/X's and outcomes/O's. In other words, we believe in the value of trust, and do what it takes to create it. In the end, students, teachers, and staff all experience a more trusting life at the school. Our research and that of others finds that it is nearly impossible to find a school in which trust and vision exists without leaders who embody and promote those qualities.

## 1. Trust in the Leader as a Person

Scan your experience with groups, teams, committees, projects, organizations, and collectives of any kind. In those cases, whereas we grew to know a person in a leader role and found them to be up to the task, it is likely our level of faith and trust in the possibility of the group's success increased as well. Conversely, when we found the leader to be significantly flawed, it was likely that we had difficulty trusting that the whole venture would be able to achieve success.

This book and all the many leadership books and sources of advice can support growth and skill development (Covey, 1989; Fullan, 1993; Agular, 2013). And in the end, we will be judged across many criteria. However, who we are, and how we are perceived will be the single most significant factor in whether those in the school are able to trust engaging with us in a process of improvement. Who we are/R and what we do/X will always be inter-related. But call it our animal-instinct, people want to know your relevant R's before they will feel safe following you down the road.

In Figure 6.1, nine personal leadership qualities are outlined, and they characterize what we tend to require of a trustworthy leader. We might assess how we personally rate in each area. Some qualities might be more natural for you, while some might require a need for growth or support. For areas where you can improve, sometimes improvement comes from simply having a more intentional focus on that quality. However, sometimes the area reflects a quality that is not one of our gifts. For those aspects, we offer some ideas for supplementing and enlisting support from others.

Figure 6.1. Nine Essential Personal Leadership Qualities, what they look like, and what we can do if we are not strong in one of them.

| Needed Leadership Quality | What is looks like | Ways to supplement it |
|---|---|---|
| Has a Vision | Can see a better school emerging from the current state.<br><br>Comfort in the role as leader.<br><br>Listens with a sense of purpose.<br><br>Shares their picture with others regularly.<br><br>Possesses insight into new possibilities. | Formal vision setting process (see chapter 7).<br><br>Including visionary thinkers on the leadership teams.<br><br>Staying connected and involved.<br><br>Undertake a personal visioning process (see chapter 14). |
| Has Integrity | Is honest with themselves and others.<br><br>Can give a direct straightforward answer<br><br>Clear about their intentions for taking the job and expectations about how long they plan to stay.<br><br>Does not play games or get too unnerved by a crisis.<br><br>Character stands up to scrutiny. | Know not everyone will be pleased.<br><br>Stop seeing yourself as a victim.<br><br>Ask others for an honest assessment of your performance and how you are perceived. |
| Can move between Big and Small picture easily | Understands the essential/macro/general problem or issue and can see what it implies in the micro/concrete and applied level, and visa-versa. | Engages in discussions with a leadership team to flesh out what is essential. |
| In touch with Humanity | Has a heart for others<br><br>Is in touch with their own heart and feelings<br><br>Sincerely cares about the students in the school. | Spending more time with students in informal settings learning about their lives in and out of school. |
| Has Ego under control | See leader role as of profound importance, but he/she does not see it being about them.<br><br>They see their role as being a servant and can keep perspective about their importance.<br><br>Tends to be humble and gives credit to others. | Having an occasional reality check and asking if you have felt the need to inflate your importance.<br><br>Attempting to be humble and a servant leader until it becomes more natural and authentic. |

| Has her/his finger on the pulse | Leader is in touch with what is happening at the school.<br><br>And when they talk about the school, it tends to ring true as a valid interpretation.<br><br>Understands what others are going through. | Get out and talk to people.<br><br>Give useful surveys<br><br>Ask for clarification from others |
|---|---|---|
| Doer not just talker | Tends to find ways to "make it happen," rather than finding any reason why it cannot.<br><br>Following through on what they said they would do or give clear explanations for delays.<br><br>Has a sense of priority and can communicate what is essential to do now and what will be nice to do but will need to wait. | Don't make commitments to things that you know you do not really want to follow-through on.<br><br>Make lists of priority action<br><br>Sets goals<br><br>Use strategic plans in a meaningful way. |
| Good with Money | Have a healthy perspective on money – not afraid of it, nor obsessed by it.<br><br>Can see costs and budget in an accurate perspective. | Finds someone who is good with money to rely upon, even if you are too.<br><br>Prints out budgets and keep them in mind.<br><br>Is transparent.<br><br>Enlists development personnel. |
| Possesses a Sense of Moral Purpose | Takes a stand for or against something because it is right and/or for the good of the whole.<br><br>Understands the job is not just managing an entity but implies moral leadership.<br><br>Refrains from inappropriate use of power in actuality and appearance. | Moral leadership is intrinsic. This aspect of your role needs to be authentic. It may require some personal self-reflection and self-development. |

**Reflection 6.3:** We might validate this list in our own experience by reflecting on a few questions:

- What if I dropped the ball, ignored or neglected that area, what would happen?

- What price do we pay, in terms of trust, if any one of these areas is perceived as a weakness?

- Am I willing to accept the consequences of being accidental with any of these areas?

As you survey the list above, you may be inclined to be self-critical of past actions or defensive or even overwhelmed by the magnitude of your job. Yet, remember you can only control one person – you. Do your best and make a commitment to these qualities as intentions to grow in the future. Move beyond the past and simply focus on your level of integrity moving forward. As you become more familiar with the next four areas, you should gain more confidence in what it takes to promote greater overall trust at your school.

## 2. Trust in the Vision Location

**Refection 6.4**: Imagine that you are child, and your mother asks you if you want to go with her on her errands (and you have memories of previous trips that took forever, were tedious and went nowhere you desired). In an effort to assess this current trip, you ask her, "Where are we going specifically?" and "How long will it take?" In response, she says she is not sure in response to both of your questions. Given these responses and your history with these kinds of trips, what is your interest level for getting in the car? And if you did get in the car, what would your attitude be?

The reflection above may or may not resonate with your personal experiences, but it is a useful metaphor for what we are doing when we ask a group of people to engage in an improvement effort without being clear as to where it is headed. On some level, we each want to know where things are going and how much effort is going to be required. "To a better place," and "It depends" are not answers that engender a lot of trust. Having a target location that is clear and standing still is necessary to promote that trust. Clear, as in the R's, X's and O's that define the destination can be explained and concretized in detail. Standing still, as in there is a stable commitment to this effort and this location. In the classroom, students can most likely meet assessment targets that are clear and standing still, so providing them is critical to the 1-Style empowered classroom. In the process of school change the value of clear targets is no less essential. When targets are vague, we struggle to trust that what ourselves and others are doing is right.

# Growth "Pathway" on the School Effectiveness Roadmap

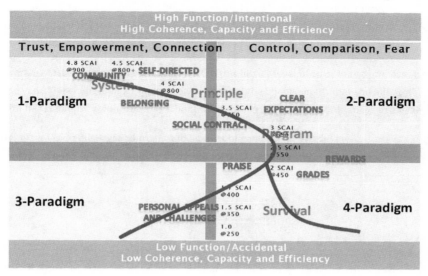

When the intended location on the roadmap is clear and operational, we perceive the process in the following manner:

- We are on the right path to a definable better place.

- The destination location is a target that is clearly defined and standing still. The group may choose to change direction because of new information or factors. But we are clear about where all possible potential directions would lead.

- The X's and O's implied by the location are well understood and appreciated as valuable and an improvement over the current X's and O's by the majority.

- The value of the better location is worth some discomfort, need for persistence, and growing pains to get there.

**Marshmallow Test:** – In a study over 30 years, Walter Mischel (2016) has asked thousands of students to choose between taking a single marshmallow immediately or waiting for a time in which case they can have 2 marshmallows. What the researchers have found is that those students who were able to delay their gratification and wait for the opportunity to have the 2 marshmallows rated higher on a number of traits including success, decision-making, self-worth, and cognitive functions, health and SAT score. This is a quality we can encourage in the classroom. The more POS the more students learn to delay gratification and use self-discipline. In addition, this research implies, within the change process, we can embrace the idea that it is worth some momentary effort or forbearance so that we can get a payoff in the future – i.e., moving up the pathway to a more functional and satisfying location.

To make the destination of our effort clear and standing still, we will first need to make it conceptually clear. Perhaps including a presentation to the faculty in which they can see the roadmap and are provided an explanation of the R's, X's, and O's that are implied in that desired location. The next chapter, related to the vision setting process, will provide a practical set of ideas and strategies for creating a clear, theoretical direction. Next, to make our destination tangible, we will need to discuss all the concrete implications of what we will be doing once we get there.

## Story of Lori

Lori was a new principal who inherited a 2.9/5 climate school (lower to middle level 2). Most of the teachers at the school had been at the school for a long time and had had largely top-down leaders. In past years, teachers had little faith in change initiatives as they seemed to be selected capriciously and were incoherent from one year to the next. So, when she began her work, the level of openness to being able to trust was low,

She began by setting the example of being absolute in her determination to make the school excellent. She communicated with all the teachers and staff on a regular basis and projected confidence that the school could, in fact, be excellent. Lori assembled a team of committed administrators and partners. The team set

out a vision of where things should ideally head. She also made a strong commitment to trusting students as leaders and capable of being responsible. Previously, few all-school events were held due to the fear students would be unruly.
She challenged the students to change that perception and her trust was reward-
ed with successful events where students showed a high level of maturity.

Overall, most aspects of the school reflected this higher level of trust in the process after
one year. The changes in X's lagged slightly behind the change in R's that she initiated
with her steadfast vision. Yet, the school went from a 2.9 to a 3.6 SCAI ratings in a year.

Her clear vision encouraged trust. And as trust began to emerge, the level of motivation and self-esteem of the school grew significantly.

Seeing the new location abstractly is an essential first step. And yes, most
members of the school will probably appreciate the idea of a school defined
by empowerment and vision-driven practices. But to arrive at a compre-
hensible location, we will need to change how we think and plan. First, we
need to talk about our desired reality, and allow others to talk about it like it
is an eventuality. Second, we need to let the naysayers and the complainers
complain, but we can't let that define the narrative. The narrative needs to
be "We are heading toward (blank) and most people are on board, and we
assume the others will appreciate it once we create that new normal." Third,
we need to validate the notion that the payoff is worth the effort. We can do
that by promoting pride in the progress and helping people see the results
they are achieving from the endeavor to move up the pathway. Just like in
the 1-Style classroom, growth toward more trust and self-direction may
not be readily recognized because it happens incrementally, so it requires
leaders to bring the new skills, abilities, and levels of trust and function to
the awareness of the group. Fourth, we need to find examples of schools
which have made similar efforts toward growth and have developed in positive ways and have experienced desirable O's. As we will discuss throughout
the next few chapters, honesty, integrity and listening need to ground our
process. So be wary of over-stating or over-selling progress.

You might be saying to yourself, doesn't moving up the pathway imply cultivating a more trusting entity by definition? Yes, it does. Therefore, while it

takes more trust to move further into the 1-Paradigm location, it also means we have become more trusting in general – in our classrooms with students, and with each other. So, the more we trust each other and practice trusting R's and X's, the further we move along up the pathway. Thus, the journey is the destination, and a winning journey will inevitably lead us to where we want to go. We need to learn to see ourselves as a high function 1-Paradigm entity along the way so that we can fully actualize as one.

## 3. Trust and Process vs. Outcome Values

The closer we get to the 1-Paradigm location we will increasingly appreciate how a primarily *process focus* will be more effective than a primarily *product focus*. One of the main reasons why this makes sense and is so critical to our effort is that a focus on the process inherently builds trust.

What do we mean by processes? In the 1-Style classroom, this means encouraging students to focus on the quality of their work, how they work together, reflecting on the operations they are using, self-evaluating their skills, etc. Among the faculty and staff members intending to operate in a 1-Paradigm fashion, processes are those R's in the form of "what we are trying to do," and X's in the form of "what we do." Consequently, it implies adopting high quality practices and trusting the buy-in and commitment of others. We can contrast this focus to an emphasis on product or Outcome/O values such as test scores and other symptoms of our results.

As we explore more deeply into the relationship between a process focus and the 1-Style classroom and the 1-Paradigm school operation, we find that a process focus is critical to promoting a psychology of success (POS) in each domain. A process focus builds internal locus of control, as it helps both students and teachers see the connection between their R's, X's and their eventual O's, i.e., "I am in control of my level of process investment, and I see that my invest level (cause), leads to the quality of my outcomes (effect)." Moreover, a process focus is at the heart of promoting a growth orientation - as a student, "I am not a fixed set of abilities," and as a school we are not determined by our exterior context or history, we are what we do today. The better we do, the better we will be.

Figure 6.2 Contrasting Effects of Process vs. Outcome Values in School Practice

|  | Process | Outcome |
|---|---|---|
| **Goal** | Quality process leading to quality outcomes. | Quality outcome by any means necessary. |
| **Common Effect** | Building teams that are on the same page. | Building collections of individuals who are concerned about how they are performing relative to others. |
| **Long-term result** | Focusing on a longer-range sense of efficacy of the practice, as defined by a quality application. | Focusing on the short-term, and whatever is working today in the perception of the individual |
| **Ability Assess & Improve** | Providing a focus for thinking about improvement. "Can I do a better job with the process?" "Can I improve on the process?" "Are my students getting better at the process?" | Providing a bench-mark for knowing where the progress is in relation to the desired outcome, but what is working and what is not are difficult to judge. Many factors could be contributing to my progress or lack of it. |

| | | |
|---|---|---|
| **Ability to Replicate** | As the processes becomes more familiar, the means for improving them in practice become better known and the ability to replicate or teach the quality processes are increased. | Any effort to teach what has worked to achieve an outcome will inherently lead to the analysis of the process. An outcome focus is inherently process neutral and un-teachable. |
| **Levels of Perception** | Processes values can exist at all levels of perception. But processes operate well at the system and principle level. So as higher-level perceptions tend to guide lower-level functions, process values tend to inform and improve the quality of programs and sensory interventions. | Outcome level values tend to lead to relative processes – i.e., whatever works. This orientation is by definition un-systematic and un-principled beyond what any individual decides to do. While there will be higher-level perceptions involved in the individual action, the collective R will tend to default to a program level when values are defined by outcomes. |

| Communication and Sharing | A value defined by a process is by definition operational, so can be communicated, explained and shared between members with a reasonable understanding of the goal. Different group members can share their own experiences as they practice applying the process, so the group can in essence learn from one another's experiences. | Communicating an outcome is easy on the surface. Group members can share their progress toward achieving the outcome, but it is more difficult to share how they are trying to reach that outcome with language and concepts others can understand. Constructive sharing will tend to be about the processes used to move toward that outcome. |
|---|---|---|

When our collective effort emphasizes quality processes, several positive effects are encouraged (See Figure 6.2). Among these effects is that we know not only what to expect from one another, but we can share, reflect, and grow in our R's and X's together. When the emphasis relates to outcome values, the assumption is that we are instructed to "do whatever it takes." This may not sound that undesirable on the surface, but upon closer examination, we are able to recognize that "doing whatever it takes" leads to low quality, short cuts, misunderstandings, an accidental climate, and a fundamental lack of trust. The scenarios below should help illustrate these effects.

## Compare Two Scenarios

**Basic situation:** Jessie and Maria are departmental colleagues. They have worked together for a few years. They are committed to the relationship, but they realize that they have a real problem with arguing. Neither of them really likes to argue or is trying to cause trouble, they just find themselves in arguments much of the time over both big and small matters.

**Scenario 1** – Jessie and Maria decide they want to stop arguing. So, they decide that they will commit to not arguing ever again. They shake hands and wish each other the best. (i.e., they make a commitment to an O value)

*Reflection*: How much faith do you have that these colleagues will change their behavior related to arguing?

Most people would not bet too much that the arguing would stop. It may stop for a while, but while there were good intentions, nothing of substance changed in the equation. They did not obtain any new R's or X's to solve their problem. Therefore, when the triggers that caused arguing in the past come up again, the likelihood will be that gradually they will find their old pattern and be back falling into the habit of unconscious arguing. But now, since they have made a commitment and broken it, they will feel even worse. They may feel guilty, resentful, blame, feel like the relationship is a lost cause, or helpless. Now they have added a feeling of being flawed to the problem of arguing. And where is their level of trust?

**Scenario 2** – Jessie and Maria decide to read a book on conflict resolution together. They agree to such things as to use "I" messages, and not to make things personal, and to pull back and look at things from the other's point of view and keep asking themselves what the larger R is in the big picture, and other helpful process X's that lead to more effective communication when the heat gets turned up. And they also commit to reflecting how their buttons get pushed and to respond to feeling of defensiveness more effectively.

*Reflection*: How much faith do you have that these two departmental colleagues will change their behavior related to arguing?

I am guessing that you have more faith in them in scenario 2 as they have process tools to use to address problems as they arise.

Reflecting on the scenario above, how much faith do we have when we hear of a school which commits to raising its scores or becoming a drug-free zone, or reducing their suspensions but plans to use essentially the same X's they were using in the past? Even if they add a program X to their existing X's, do we trust that their results will be significantly better? One school committed to improving their reading scores. Their conclusion after an intense three-year effort was that they realized they had to "change everything they did" to change their reading scores. We could say this was a school that met its outcome goal, but it would be more accurate to say that this was a school that learned it had to change its processes X's and make them organic to what they did (i.e., changed R's). As a result, what they experienced was a change in their O's.

If we are collectively trying to move to a location on the roadmap, we are, in essence, agreeing on the kinds of process X's we will use to get there. In fact, we can only get there using particular X's, while other X's may lead us to an entirely different location. When we share X's, we share the opportunity to discuss them as artists can discuss their art, or craftsman can share their craft. We can consider ways in which we have improved, insights we have gained, and results that have come from our growth and modification of our processes.

When we share simple O's, such as better test scores, or even the goal of better "classroom management," we have almost no idea the X's that the other person intends to use. Better test scores are much like the goal of winning (see sports analogy below). What is your first reaction when someone tells you the goal of the school is a 30-point gain? Or your team needs an undefeated season? What is your emotional reaction as a member of the team? My guess is a fear of failure arose almost immediately. In the short-term, that may create some energy, but eventually it will tend to encourage short cuts, cheating in various forms, losing consideration for others who are in the way of the goal, and in the long-term it can create lower quality process X's. In chapter nine, we will explore in more detail how a disproportionate focus on the outcome encourages us to make direct interventions to the symptoms of the problem while ignoring the real problem. Our data would suggest that for many schools this "doing whatever it takes" approach is the reason they are performing at a lower than desired level on the pathway.

> "It's that preparation that goes into each week. We have a term: 'Trust your training, trust your teammate, and trust yourself.'
> – Dan Quinn, NFL Coach

We will want to have some O goals as they are related to how we are doing with our R's and X's, but they should always be secondary.

## A Sports Analogy.

The well-known coach John Wooden was the master of creating process values as collective R's for his basketball teams at UCLA. The X's that he expected from his team included making a total effort, executing and applied the processes they had practiced, and playing as a team. All of these values are processes focused. He never told his team the goal was to win, nor provided them much if any feedback related to results. But he provided vast feedback related to the quality of their process investment and execution. We know that not only did his teams win, but they experienced great personal and athletic growth in the process of playing.

Contrastingly, there was a team in the NFL recently whose coach made a bold proclamation that their goal and expectation was to win the Super bowl. The team was talented, confident, and motivated. In the end, the team missed the playoffs, and underperformed relative to what they seemed capable of. Of course, this is only one team and one example, but it is worth examining these events from the lens of the collective R's that are created on a team with an exaggerated outcome value. The first question we can ask is, "If the goal is to win, how will we achieve that goal?" No matter what we say, if the goal is the O of winning on the scoreboard, we are implicitly directed to "do whatever it takes."

Which mindset would you assume led to – More trust and less fear of failure? More trust in one another? More enjoyment of playing?

## 4. Social Contract: Trust Requires Structures, a Sense of Safety, and Accountability

By definition, all groups have a social contract. Some are more intentional and conspicuous, others more accidental and neglected. Some promote function, others simply promote status quo. At the core of any social contract are social bonds. This level of bonds relates to such questions as:

- What is my job? And what is your job?
- What are the rules and what happens if we break them?
- What can I expect of you and what can you expect from me?

> "If the people cannot trust their government to do the job for which it exists - to protect them and to promote their common welfare - all else is lost."
> – *Barack Obama*

When we examine the idea of trust and the bonds creating it, it is useful to consider that the same mechanics producing these bonds it in a classroom are much the same for the school as a collective. In Figure 6.3, we examine the foundational bonds that hold a group together as a side-by-side comparison – classroom and school.

Social contract and social bonds are pre-requisites to the ability to trust communal bonds. When we think of creating a trusting collective, it can seem an overwhelming task. But it is not about perfection or an either/or situation, as much as it is about doing as well as we can.

At this point, reflect upon a few questions about the current state of the collective at your school, and recognize potential areas where you may have concern:

- Do faculty and staff feel like things are fair?
- Are those who are doing their part feeling supported?
- Are those who contribute less held accountable?
- Do the structures and policies encourage a sense of fairness?
- Are there comfortable mechanisms for communicating concerns?
- Do meetings have protocols for encouraging broad and respectful contribution?
- Does the school feel like a democracy?
- Are independent responsibilities clearly defined?

**Figure 6.3: Comparing Elements of the Social Contract/Social Bonds in the 1-Style Classroom and the 1-Paradigm School**

|  | 1-Style Classroom | 1-Paradigm School |
|---|---|---|
| **Rules and Expectations** | Rules and expectations exist in the minds of the students; they know the rules and assume others do, too. Students expect functionality as a result of the clear expectations in the class. The teacher takes responsible for following through when students violate rules. | Rules and expectations exist and are discussed periodically. People take the time to clarify rather than allowing misunderstanding. Rather than getting personal about what should have happened, people use experiences to clarify the expectations and codify them if it is useful. |
| **Accountability** | Students do what helps the collective run smoothly, partly because they appreciate why it is important and partly because they have seen first-hand that the teacher follows through on consequences. | Faculty and staff appreciate the rules and duties at the school involve them. Staff ensure that the policies in place encourage fairness and penalties for those who do not demonstrate the effort of the quality or the consideration that is expected. |
| **Sharing the Load** | Students work in collaborative situations and understand that the group outcome depends on the collective effort of each individual member. With practice, students become masters at contributing. Teacher grading, modeling and clarifications help support this growth. | As professionals and colleagues they feel it is their duty to do their part. Everyone tries to contribute in a way which fits their gifts or the pressing needs of the collective. Everyone appreciates that, once in a while, teammates need to sacrifice for the team. |
| **Count on Each Other** | Students count on their classmates to do what they have committed to in the social contract. When they don't, students call each other on it. Students also trust their teacher will do his/her job and provide support to those who are doing their best and consequences for those who are undermining the efforts of the group. | Faculty and staff members rely on one another to maintain standards and expectations at the school, as well as policies requiring ALL members to do their part. Faculty members trust leadership to interview with those who are letting down the group. |

## Resentment and History

We cannot deny that any collective has "history." Therefore, we need to be patient and accept that that history playing itself out as present behavior. We can move beyond this past baggage, but it will take as long as it takes, and it will take a little intention and attention.

If the faculty and staff have been around for a while, it is inevitable that some resentments have accumulated over the years. It is a cynical, but somewhat valid adage that "familiarity breeds contempt." We have all trusted and gotten burned. Maybe we were let down by a leader, maybe by a current colleague, or had negative things said about us which hurt. We have likely felt like we were part of the small group holding some aspect of the school together or doing what was required while others dropped the ball. Not to mention all the possible personal offenses that we have experienced over the years that we still are holding on to.

Groups do get past their histories and move on, and you can too.

Directly addressing hurts and history can be effective. But it can also keep us stuck focusing backward. Does your group need a professional to come in and help them heal? Maybe. Assuming your sense is that momentum and trust can be built now, here are some transformative intentions to help you encourage the members of the collective to move forward and get beyond the past:

- You are essential to my ability to move toward a goal that I really would like to accomplish for me and/or for the school (even if I still feel some residual hurt from the past).

- I realize resentment is not healthy or helpful, so I will stop being a victim and grow and mature.

- Moving forward is the right thing to do for the students.

- In the present day, we are in the process of building more trust and respect.

- You acknowledged what happened in the past and we came to an understanding.

- Things have changed and what made me feel untrusting is not there now, so I can approach things in a new light.

- Time has passed.

There is no simple global advice to be given in this kind of area. Rather than getting too clever and attempting to manipulate perceptions, relationships, and healing, consider treating others as adults who are ready to be their best selves.

## 5. Communal bonds

Communal bonds are those perceptions that imply we are part a connected human collective, such as a family, close-nit team, or a group of friends. Social bonds ask, "What is my job?" "What is expected of me?" and "What can I expect from you and the institution?" Whereas, communal bonds ask, "How can I help?" and "Who am I and what is my role in this group?" and "What does the group need from me, and what do I need from the group?" My feelings are important to others and others' feelings are important to me.

> "Because you believed I was capable of behaving decently, I did."
> — Paulo Coelho

If social bonds are not in place, the level of trust will not be sufficient to effectively sustain communal bonds. We have all experienced feeling let down, underappreciated, unfairly treated, or as if there was no adult in the room and have likely responded with a decrease in our level of trust. That may have taken many forms, but it usually includes an emotional withdrawal and a decrease in our level of investment in the effort.

Because communal bonds and the existence of "community" look similar across context, we can again compare them within the classroom and the school setting. And this is just one more place to remind ourselves that a 1-Paradigm school requires mostly 1-Style classrooms to succeed. Both solid social and communal bonds are critical in moving steadily toward our pathway goal.

**Reflection 6.5;** Which kind of school has more structure – a 2-Paradigm school based on organization and external enforcement or a 1-Paradigm school? Common sense may tell us that in the real world the 2-Paradigm school will be more structured because the 1-Paradigm school and the 1-Style classroom are just less predictable. But as you look closer, this rarely true. Real structure comes from quality of the existing bonds. Social and communal bonds are real. They exist in the minds and hearts of the students and members of the school community. Where do rules and external authorities exist? Externally. So, the real structure and forces which lead to order are much more present in the 1-Paradigm location than the 2- or 4-Paradigm.

Check your assumption. What would the students do in any school if all the adults left for 20 minutes? Or with the teachers if the leadership all disappeared? In a self-directed, empowered school community, not much would expect to change; that is real structure and order.

**Figure 6.4: Comparing Elements of a Communal Connection in the 1-Style Classroom and the 1-Paradigm School**

| | 1-Style Classroom | 1-Paradigm School |
|---|---|---|
| **Team Bonds** | In the high functioning classroom, there is the feeling, "We are in this together." The success of each of us is dependent on the success of what we can do together. Therefore, students tap into their need for being part of something larger and the intrinsic need to contribute and learn to trust each other and trust the enjoyment of that feeling. | In the high function school, faculty and staff members feel a sense of collective purpose and so enjoy the feeling of being part of a team effort. The feeling of trust, purpose and accomplishment feels good, so members of the collective feel an intrinsic motivation to promote more of those qualities over time. |
| **Feeling and Human Bonds** | Students learn to know and appreciate each other as individuals. They learn about who one another are and what each values and cares about. Knowing breads liking. Getting past the superficial and have others really know you and accepted for who you are is deeply rewarding. | Faculty and staff members relate on a human level and share about their lives in and out of school. They trust that others assume they have noble intentions and are committed to the cause, so they do not have to worry about being too cautious about how they act when they let down their guard. |
| **Identity and "We"** | The classroom has a strong sense of identity. That identity is forged through developing and experiencing a sense of shared purpose and a "we": Over time, we feel like the other members of the class "have our backs" and are on our side. We share more history and more team wins all the time. | The faculty and staff feel like this is their school. The location, the building, the students – it is all part of a place they feel a loyalty toward. They do both superficial things such as wearing school colors or insignia, and more profound things like reaching out to one another even when it is not convenient. |

| Team Wins | In the class, students work together on collective efforts and see positive results and feel positive about what the group has created. And over time, as the class feels and functions more effectively, each day they feel more like they are part of a winning effort and are lucky to be a member. Wining breads liking and trust. | The faculty and staff members work together to make improvements to the school and move toward a desired location on the roadmap and appreciate the efforts of others. That positive feeling breeds more optimism. The more successes they experience, the more the feeling of winning occurs, and the more energy there is for the next effort. Overall, no matter where the school started on the roadmap, adults feel great being part of a collective which is making a difference and fulfilling the potential of what it can be. |
|---|---|---|

One of the qualities which is inextricably connected to the level of trust and that needs to be cultivated to make the "left-hand turn" from the middle location on the roadmap to the higher levels is honesty. We need to be honest with ourselves, we need to be honest with each other, and we need to be able to make honest assessments without fear of penalty. If we examine the level of honesty at our school currently, it is likely we see a tendency to repress honesty. Because the level of trust is lacking, we lack the courage to be honest, leading to the tendency for middle level schools to be cordial but not genuinely collaborative. At this level, we can function as a polite group, but not as a team that can count on one another.

The growth toward the higher levels usually involves some uncomfortable work related to promoting greater levels of honesty. But as faith in each member

> "Trust starts with truth and ends with truth."
> — Santosh Kalwar

of the community's confidence to be able to express themselves honestly increases, our level of institutional trust grows along with it. When our R's are more transparent, we can work with our growth related to X's with more confidence and specificity. In the lower quadrants, the implicit principle related to R's is "don't ask, don't tell." In the 1-Paradigm school, the expectation includes a value for honest conversations about what we do and why we do it. Therefore, repeating a fundamental principle for moving to the 1-Paradigm, the implication here is that the nature of the journey and the nature of the destination are the same. In other words, if our goal is to become a trusting 1-Paradigm school which is defined by honesty, we need to trust that we can be honest today about what we need to do to move up.

After examining the idea of trust in more detail in this chapter, it should have become clear that it is an essential quality in our progress. There is no substitute for trust and no way to avoid creating it if we want to encourage growth at our school. Trust will be a core component of our ability to create the capacity to move upward on the roadmap to higher levels of function. And it will characterize the essence of our transition across to the highest locations. Therefore, each of the five factors determining the level of trust need to be given conscious attention and made part of our collective intention. Trustworthy personal qualities, a direction which is clear and standing still, a process-focus, social structures, and communal bonds will all be vital elements to the level of trust, and thus, our ability to progress up the pathway. Now we can shift our attention to building the other core ingredient required for our success – vision. Both trust and vision are fragile, need to be built over a period of time, and can be destroyed in an instant. It will be essential to keep the lessons from this chapter in mind as we work to promote the quality of vision at our school in the next chapter.

**Exercise 6.1:**
You are given each of the five trust factors explained about in a table. In each line of the chart one of the five trust factors is assumed to be absent. In your group (or on your own), determine in your own estimation and experience what would happen if that particular trust factor was missing from the process at the school. See the suggested answers below.

Factor is present = o
Factor is absent = x

| Leader personal Qualities | Location of the Vision | Process vs. Outcome emphasis | Social Contract/ Accountability | Communal bonds/We | Likely Result (if X is not present in the process) |
|---|---|---|---|---|---|
| X | o | o | o | o | Anxiety and political confusion. Most meaningful conversations occur outside of formal meetings and forums. |
| o | X | o | o | o | Uncertainty of purpose, lack of confidence that effort is worth investing in. |
| o | o | X | o | o | A feeling of pressure and a fear of failure. A sense that individuals and the school as a whole are being judged. |
| o | o | o | X | o | People feeling offended and reacting with anger and resentment or finding passive ways around the formal process to get their way. |
| o | o | o | o | X | A feeling that the effort has no heart and stays just a job and/or an exercise in organizational housekeeping. |

# REFERENCES

Agular, E. (2013) The Art of Coaching. Jossey Bass, San Francisco, CA

Covey, S (1989) Seven Habits of Highly Effective People. Free Press.

Fullan, M. (1993) *Change Forces: Probing the Depths of Educational Reform*. The Falmer Press.

Mischel, W (2016) The Marshmallow Test: Mastering Self Control. Webinar Presentation. Retrieved from http://longnow.org/seminars/02016/may/02/marshmallow-test-mastering-self-control/

# CHAPTER 7:

## Promoting a Vision and Elevating and Connecting the References/R's at the School

> "The world as we have created it is a process of our thinking. It cannot be changed without changing our thinking."
> — *Albert Einstein*
>
> "Change the way you look at things and the things you look at change."
> — *Wayne W. Dyer*

In this chapter, we explore vision and how to encourage a quality "living vision" at our schools. The starting point for this examination is the critical and determining role of "references" in shaping what happens within a school, a classroom, and each individual. We use the term reference or R's as a broad umbrella for the values, beliefs, intentions, conditioned mindsets, guiding principles, operative narratives, and perceptions of the world generally which are used to guide actions. Simply put, any school, classroom, or individual will only be as effective as the references it is using. For those in the role of school leader, the place to start is simply appreciating this reality. Next, remember that the only person you can control is yourself. But among our most important jobs will be to draw out of others their appreciation for the highest quality references and cultivate a process of growth and reflection.

**Figure 7.1/8.1/9.1. Improved X's/Action Represented in the Overall Improvement Sequence**

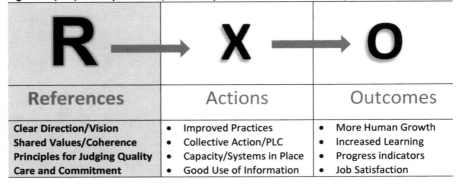

| References | Actions | Outcomes |
|---|---|---|
| **Clear Direction/Vision** | • Improved Practices | • More Human Growth |
| **Shared Values/Coherence** | • Collective Action/PLC | • Increased Learning |
| **Principles for Judging Quality** | • Capacity/Systems in Place | • Progress indicators |
| **Care and Commitment** | • Good Use of Information | • Job Satisfaction |

We cannot change R's directly, but we can encourage the process of change. We cannot unite the references of a group directly, but we can create the capacity within the system to support connection and the sense of purpose and team. A bottom line will be that our school's collective actions/X's will determine where we are on the roadmap, and our R's will determine our X's. Therefore, moving up the roadmap will mean raising the R's at the school. To that end, in this chapter we will explore the idea of supporting the process of raising the common references at the school from lower to higher levels. While our success depends on our ability to demonstrate sound human growth and learning principles in action; in all aspects of our job, we will likely want to make two forms of collective reference our highest priority – trust and vision.

In the previous chapter, we examined the idea of trust and how it can be inspired as a collectively held set of R's within a school and its classrooms. In this chapter, we begin with an examination of the nature and importance of the vision within the school. And we will set out practical school-wide procedures and leadership actions which will lead to promoting a vision that moves our school up the improvement pathway. Like trust, vision implies a direction and purpose. To be able to embody and facilitate that direction, a leader must be able to conceive it. Achieving requires conceiving first. Like with the foxes in the story, you will need to be able to see the better version of your school existing within the current one, to cultivate a shared living vision. Therefore, this chapter will devote a great deal of focus on the various forms that R's take and examining how leadership can support more 1-Paradigm R's.

Vision and mission are terms used regularly in educational contexts. Most schools have a vision statement, but fewer have an effective and true "vision" – the school's DNA which operates to guide everything else. So, developing a purposeful vision statement is just the start. We also

---

### The Hounds and the Fox

*There is a story of a group of hounds who were laying down in a wood. One of the hounds then saw a fox and gave chase, as a result, the other hounds joined in. But the fox was very fast and over time, one by one the hounds began to tire and quit the hunt. Except that is, the hound that saw the fox originally. That hound stayed with it.*

*The moral of the story is that we will tend to give up our pursuit of a vision unless we can see it clearly and concretely in our minds and know that it does exist.*

---

need to embrace the reality that effective leadership includes stewardship of the living vision at the school, which is a continuous process and involves most everything we do.

## Growth "Pathway" on the School Effectiveness Roadmap

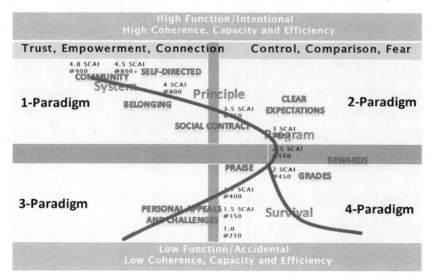

Every brand of vision can be found conceptually at some location on the school effectiveness roadmap laid out in the earlier chapters. The good news is the most effective location on the map is also the easiest to conceive. The less functional locations require significantly more work to maintain. A 1-Paradigm vision implies rather simple characteristics such as encouraging trust, empowerment, and self-regulation. It feels natural and inherently coherent. As individuals, we experience operating within this mindset as a sense of alignment, flow, and integrity. And on an affective level it will represent what our best selves desire to bring about. A 2-Paradigm vision requires a great deal more maintenance as it needs to be imposed externally. It typically involves cobbling together several disparate programs and features at the school level. This usually necessitates implementing several inherently high-maintenance, teacher-centered, and extrinsically based practices at the classroom level. For individuals, a 2-Paragidm is commonly experienced as internal competing interests: we want one thing but feel we should be doing another, and so we adopt internal games and coping mechanisms to make it through the day. We may be productive, but it takes a great deal of struggle and stress to keep it together.

All schools inherently have an "operating" vision, whether they have created an intentional vision statement or not. Each school's operating vision will be characterized by the intentions and references/R's of all its members played out as being and doing/X's. In other words, we teach and lead (i.e., X) who we R. In most schools there is little connection among the various individual R's. We could call this the "default vision" because it is what happens by accident (See Figure 7.2). The result of this default disconnection of R's is a corresponding disconnection of actions/X's and as a result outcomes/O's reflecting this somewhat accidental level of function and achievement – i.e., somewhere in the middle to lower part of the roadmap.

## Vision Requires Leadership

While a true vision exists as a set of R's or mindset at the school, it requires leaders to translate it into a functional, practical, and operational state. When we think of institutions that we consider "vision-driven" or "visionary," we inevitably find within them effective leaders with visions of what is best for the collective. Conversely, when we hear people within a school claim, "This school has no vision" what they are usually talking about is the current leadership lacks a discernable vision and/or has not created operating vision-driven principles at the school. While there may appear to be an apparent contradiction between 1) the need to be both non-authoritarian/facilitative and 2) actively leading and defining the process - you will find that this seeming paradox is largely superficial, and the reality is that both our efforts to empower others and our ability to trust our own calling to steer the ship in a positive direction can be integrated and feel quite natural. The key to integrity will be the desired goal/R for it to not be about either our will or theirs. It is about recognizing and cultivating the best qualities in the adults and students at the school. Potential wants to emerge. We just need to illuminate and then nurture it.

---

**Figure 7.2: The Forms of Vision – Defined**

**Intentional Vision** – A set of guiding values, principles, and beliefs (R's/references) and a corresponding set of selected practices (X's) which are developed and embraced by the collective, representing the way community members would like their school to be.

**Operating Vision** – The guiding R's/references which are collectively held and inform the X's/practices at the school currently.

**Default Vision** – The guiding R's/references of a school that operate unintentionally.

**Vision Statement** – A written document which outlines the vision and guiding R's at a school.

**Living Vision** – The personally accepted and appreciated R's/references and internalized processes (X's) those within a school use to execute their duties and guide their daily choices and actions.

---

When considering the vision development process, it may be useful to keep a few things in mind. First, and most importantly, where are you going on the roadmap? The path should be clear to you and the rest of the school community members. Second, change takes time. A vision implies a future state that is emerging as a present time reality. It is a journey to somewhere, but it is also how we act along the way and our attitude about being on a journey. Therefore, we need to accept where we are today on the roadmap, the current players we have on the team, and all the realities implicit within that location (See Figure 7.3). We need to therefore do what must be done today and keep our eyes on the prize with a long-term perspective.

Finally, it is useful to consider the unique leadership demands at each location on the pathway (Hershey & Blanchard, 1970, 1980, 2000). The needs of a school existing mostly in the lower quadrants will vary from one which is already poised for a strong "left hand turn." Over time, and as the school becomes more functional and faculty and students become more comfortable with 1-Paradigm R's and X's, leadership will want to give away increasing amounts of power and direction. In general, our mindset needs to be that each day the school is becoming more defined by higher function, is more principle vs. program driven, and uses higher quality R's and X's defined by more POS and less POF. And each day we look for ways to empower others and project trust.

---

**Figure 7.3: Vision – Things to consider**

- The cultivation of trust is a co-requisite to building a vision.

- A school vision will be functional and effective to the degree that it operates to connect the references/R's of the members of the school community

- For a vision to lead to change it needs to be aimed in a direction on the roadmap.

- Just as important to the vision will be a clear sense of who we are not and where we are not going.

- A vision needs to ultimately be operationalized by a coherent set of R's, X's, and O's.

- Ideally a vision should imply a destination which is naturally satisfying and empowering – as in the 1- Paradigm school characterized by 1-Style teaching.

- Vision to be effective requires leadership or at least stewardship. Leadership can come from anywhere on the staff, but in practice, unless an administrator takes on the role of vision steward, vision will become diffused or stale.

- Visions need to be given life with attention, commitment and application or they will lose efficacy. To be effective, a vision needs to be part of the regular conversation, intentional, and represented in the faculty development process.

---

Being a visionary leader requires a great deal of skill. Modelling 1-Paradigm R's and X's and doing the internal work to "Be the Change" requires much discipline, commitment, and a personal intention. As we will examine in the last chapter of the book, the leader's personal process is both essential to the success of the school as well as an invaluable opportunity to use the role of leader to develop as a person. In most cases, the personal and pro-fessional vision development processes will mirror one another.

The genesis of a vision and the initiation of a change process can begin with anyone and can happen immediately. If the leadership, teachers, and staff all think with 1-Paradigm R's and act with 1-Paragigm X's tomorrow, at some point the school will take on those qualities and will increasingly experience 1-Paradigm outcomes. It may be wise to approach the change process incrementally, but either way – moving up will imply a belief that this higher location on the roadmap is what is right and where you belong (i.e., you are the hound which saw the fox). Conversely, if you are not per-sonally convinced the higher location is better (or that the fox is real), you will likely find conscious and unconscious ways to keep your leadership actions/X's and your school where it is.

We see this "instant 1-Paradigm School" scenario played out in both likely as well as unlikely contexts. An example of an unlikely context was at a local alternative school. The students had mostly been removed from or felt unwelcome by the regular system for both behavioral and academic reasons. However, the leaders and teachers at this school embraced a set of empowering R's – connect with the students, help them develop their own goals and gifts, and make school a place people want to be. The X's at the school were guided by those R's so there were no formal programs just practices supporting more psychology of success (POS). The result within a couple of years was that the SCAI climate ratings were around 4 out of 5 and the achievement scores were above those of the local schools. The key to this success was that everyone bought into the vision of the school and the R's that defined it. R->X->O – they committed to being a 1-Paradigm and the outcomes followed. In part, what made this success possible was that the school received little attention and there were low expectations for a "last chance" school. Therefore, they could do what they intrinsically believed to be best – i.e., create the natural learning condition in which people want to teach and learn.

## Facilitating the Emergence of Both a Formal and Informal School Vision

Promoting the emergence of vision at the school will entail both a formal written vision as well as an ongoing, organic living vision. Both are critical and they will each support the other over time. The formal written vision statement will bring concreteness, solidness and will represent a symbolic act of unity. The ongoing process of vision growth development will make the written product more operational and actualized. Both formal and informal vision development represent the highest level of priority in our job as leader. It is advised to engage in the formal vision creation or revision process as soon as you feel comfortable and confident that the group is ready. Later in this chapter, we will explore creating a living organic vision. Engaging in the strategic planning process explained in Chapter nine will act synchronistically to enhance the soundness of your vision.

---

**Reflection 7.a**: If you have observed or been involved in the process of an institution constructing a vision or mission statement, recall the results of each of those processes.

- How did the actions/X's that took place in the classrooms and school reflect the words in the formal vision statement?

- How did the vision statement act as a guiding force for those in the school?

- If there was inconsistency between the vision (guiding R) and the regular actions (common X's), were the leaders, teachers and staff aware of the incongruity between stated R's and actual X's?

---

## Facilitative a Formal Process for Vision Statement Creation

Engaging in the formal process of creating a guiding vision statement is essential to your ability to function in the higher locations on the roadmap. This statement should provide the most conceptual and essential language defining our collective R's. Therefore, it is a critical part of the process. What we commit to on paper is part of our public face and a very concrete social contract. It will be fundamental to our institutional assessment, strategic planning, and report creation process.

Leading the faculty in a formal process of creating a vision will be a defining act, so treat it carefully. Be deliberate.

While all faculties can benefit from a vision formation process eventually, some are not ready immediately. We want the process to result in a good outcome, not just *any* outcome. Are those in leadership and all the members of the faculty ready to move past the cordial and comfortable to the possibly disharmonious and the real? You might ask them. See what they say. Possible conflict and hurt feeling should not scare us away, but if we see a civil war as a likely result, we may want to ease into this process more slowly and cautiously. And keep in mind we cannot move up the pathway unless we can develop the kind of trust it takes to be honest with one another.

## Pre: Formal Vision Creation Activity

Every school is in a different situation, has a distinct history, and has likely done vision setting in the past. Therefore, you will have to determine what makes the most sense for you in this process - what activities in what order. We might ask ourselves a few questions:

- If we engaged in a whole faculty vision setting activity today, what would the most likely outcome be? Am I Ok with that outcome considering that what we put in writing may be in place for a long time?

- Do we as a group have enough context or information to engage in this currently? Will the necessary quality R's be present in our conversation?

- Do the relationships and politics among the faculty reflect the degree of respect and openness necessary to do this at this time? Are we ready for the possibility of latent disagreements becoming overtly displayed, with all the feelings and fall out which may follow?

Preparation may be enhanced by a few capacity building activities. First, we may want to include the information data provide. The ASSC School Climate Assessment Instrument (SCAI) or other measures of organizational function can be useful to help the faculty recognize the current state of the school. Second, having the faculty assess where they are on the school function roadmap, depicted in chapter 5, helps structure the analysis and narrows the discussion. Third, having the whole faculty engage in an activity in which they classify common X's into either promoting more psychology of success (POS) or psychology of failure (POF) gives a definition to quality and makes the process less random and subjective. This preparation should be done before the formal vision setting activity.

### Activity A: Survey participation and analysis.

Data has a way of focusing the discussion so there is more clarity in the cause and effect for why things are the way they are at the school. Most data can function to do this, but comprehensive data related to organizational function and/or climate can be especially helpful. When the faculty and staff are shown that they rated an area 3 out of 5 (and possibly the students did as well), the questions related to how the school is doing related to a particular area can take on a more objective perception. We are less in the realm of guessing and conjecture. Typically, what we find is that there are few surprises in the data - mostly just confirmation. Add to that what the data imply about the school's location on the roadmap, and we have a common set of R's/references for what might be next.

## Activity B: Locating the school on the pathway in a whole faculty meeting

Before faculties are shown the pathway depiction, they very rarely recognize what they had been doing as defining a "location." They tend to see what they are doing as the best they can, given the situation. But when they do see the pathway, they come to recognize that they are *somewhere*. And as a result, members of the faculty have a clarity and language that they did not have previously. They also tend to experience an inner challenge which feels positive but implies some insecurity - motivated to make a change, but appreciating that change is defined by unknowns. It is common after faculty members engage in a self-assessment and situate themselves related to the roadmap, they begin to adopt the phrases "moving up the pathway" and "making the left-hand turn (toward more student-centered practices)" more frequently.

Any group of people who knows what they want, can agree on their R's, and is committed to matching X's will be vision-driven. But where are they going? At some point if the vision does not feel right, it will break-down, followed by the initiative and motivational level of the group. Moving up the pathway implies an inherently more satisfying and authentic way of being. We are moving to more trust, more consistency, less maintenance of gimmicks and programs, and less need for cleverness, coping, and survival thinking. Moreover, the roadmap implies operational applications – X's for each location including the 1-paradigm school and the 1-style classroom. This concreteness provides an opportunity to create an even more vivid vision – as well as one that is more satisfying and produces the highest-level outcomes.

## Activity C: Taking part in an activity classifying X's into more POS or POF

If we were to examine how any of us justifies the X's we use in a day, it would be with a somewhat amorphous criteria which is defined by what works and gets results and is doable in our experience and given our needs. That is fine for the most part. But the net result of using subjective criteria for judging value of X's is that basically *anything* can be justified. Take a simple concept like "what are good ideas for motivating students?" A wide range of suggestions would be offered in response, and likely many would seem to diametrically oppose one another. Conversations about topics where individuals tried to convince one another of the efficacy of their perspective typically lead to little change in opinion. Therefore, to achieve an optimal result from any such values clarification process we need to include more than just a discussion.

What we have found to be very effective is to have faculty engage in an activity in which they classify teaching practices into those that promote more **POS** – as in locus of control, acceptance and belonging, and growth orientation or more **POF** as in external locus of control, fragmentation and worthlessness, and fixed ability orientation. What we find time and again, is that there are several members who have previously proudly defended what are essentially POF promoting X's, but after engaging in the activity there is no one who will. Once any educator sees lists of practices displayed within this dichotomy, they better recognize the relationship between practices and their psychological effects. So, spend an effective hour creating a clear taxonomy of self-evidently desirable X's, vs. self-evidently undesirable X's. This process encourages the connecting of R's (for the better) as well as defining concrete solutions to moving up (Facilitating this exercise is explained in Appendix A of the book).

### Vision-Statement Formation Process

The formal vision statement creation process needs to begin with a clear sense of what we want to accomplish. We will want to have produced the following (as much as possible):

1.  A document that reflects a vision which works both externally as a formal display of what you are about and works internally to guide your work. An effective vision will be defined by the following characteristics:

a. Includes both R's (who we are and what we value) and X's (the kinds of practices defining us and to the use of which we are committed) so that it is meaningful. O's are fine too but are not sufficient on their own (see reflection below).

b. Implies the kinds of things the school stands for, and what observers would and would not see as a result.

c. Implies a location on the roadmap.

d. Intends to guide the work and decision-making at the school as well as promote accountability of all its members.

2. The perception and the reality that the process was democratic and reflected the input of most if not all members of the collective.

3. Distinguishes the school's R's and X's from the other school in the area. (Optional, but recommended)

4. A supplemental document that outlines "what we do" and "what we don't do" at this school. (Optional, but recommended)

A vision statement is a concept implying examples and non-examples – like any concept. Therefore, the concept attainment process used in the classroom or elsewhere is essentially what we are doing here. The stakes are just higher. This process is also like the social contract process used to create the agreements within a class of students, or the faculty as a group. The result is, in as few words as possible, what we are about and can be unpacked to imply an infinite number of practical applications. For example, if we used the phrase, "self-responsible leaders" in our vision, the words are only abstractions. Therefore, we would need to be able to identify in practical terms what a self-responsible leader looked like and/or what it would take to produce one.

In the end, there must be both a reality as well as the perception that the vision statement was developed by the collective as a whole. Either the perception, "this was done by a few" or the reality that it was, will more than likely result in a vision statement seen to be superficial or top-down. Therefore, rushing, being impatient with dissent, or being too heavy-handed will undermine faith in the sincerity of the process.

Some motivated faculty groups may be capable of undertaking a process in which everyone is in the same room, completes the task, and leaves with a product. This will be true if your faculty is small, highly cohesive, and implicitly trusts you and one another.

If you want to be more deliberate you may want to envision the process happening in the following stages:

1.  Set out the task and have a discussion to determine the level of cohesion and to put the idea into the heads of the faculty and staff to process.
2.  Create a committee to process the ideas of the whole.
3.  Engage in the brainstorming process as a whole faculty.
4.  Process the whole group's ideas into a product in the committee.
5.  Bring the synthesis product back to the faculty for review and revisions.
6.  Formal vision product should be reviewed and revised by the committee.

## Introductory Conversation

To begin, we will want to make it clear to everyone that we want to create or improve the vision statement at the school. Some of the important considerations at this early stage will include

1.  Help everyone understand how the process will unfold.
2.  Encourage the conversation to begin before the formal process begins.
3.  Leadership should have prepared by exploring the idea of what an "improved" vision means to them, including corresponding R's, X's, and O's.

4.  Allow for divergent voices. Disagreements and competing visions are not necessarily negatives. Contentious conversation – while maybe not fun do not necessarily suggest the process should not proceed.

5.  If we anticipate an impending low-quality outcome (i.e., currently, low quality R's have the most appeal), we may want to put off the next steps until conditions are more conducive.

6.  If we have not incorporated any of the pre-vision activities, we may want to do those first, and/or find ways to bring high quality (i.e., 1-Paradigm) R's into the conversation.

---

**Figure 7.4: Rules to Use in Whole Faculty Brainstorming Discussions**

- Use I-statements, not you-statements.

- Commit to sincere effort.

- Be specific and avoid sweeping unsupported generalizations.

- Be honest but be respectful of others' feelings.

- Use active listening skills.

- Focus on realistic possibilities and use growth mindset informed language

- Wait your turn and don't interrupt.

- Remember we are all on the same team/side and in this undertaking together.

---

## Vision Committee Composition

We can use an existing committee which is charged with similar tasks to take on the vision committee role. Or we can create one. Either way we need some visionary members – those you trust to guide the conversation to higher levels. Also include members who relate to the less visionary element of the faculty. Having support staff, students and parents on the committee is encouraged. You will want them to know up front what documents will ultimately be created from the overall process and may have peripheral functions (such as a "we do," and "we don't do" list and even a mission statement, or a conceptual framework). Those are all useful in and of themselves. They all have different purposes and functions. But make the aim one quality product at a time.

### Formal Brainstorming and Idea Generation

Before the engaging the whole faculty in the process, prepare a clear plan for the group that includes enough time for rich brainstorming. Provide a picture of a quality work product and set time marks for each element of the task. It is essential that the vision committee take on the role of representatives and engage their work throughout with the interests of the whole in mind.

In a whole faculty and staff gathering, place the members into smaller table teams of 3 or 4. No matter how cohesive, the overall group of teachers and staff will be dominated by some who will talk more. Having smaller groups allows those who are more introverted to have their voices heard. Allow enough time for people to relax, discuss and reflect. The instructions should be clear and visible. Give examples of phrases that imply values/R's and practices/X's as well as outcomes. Instruct table teams to create a few phrases that they feel reflect the essential vision of the school. Optionally, you may have groups read their ideas aloud and allow others to ask them judgement-free questions. In the end, you will want each group to have generated a few phrases they believe succeed in reflecting an ideal school vision – including R's, X's, and O's.

### Synthesis and Processing within Vision Committee

The vision committee should then look for commonalities within the what the whole school teams created and reconcile ideas into a single document. Using their own conceptual paradigms and concept attainment skills the committee will review all the specific ideas and capture the essence of a school vision.

The concept attainment process of the committee should include both elements related to references/R's – such as values, beliefs, narratives, identities, etc., as well as some implication of desired practices/X's. Synthesizing them down to components defining a few qualities:

- What makes the school unique?
- What is the educational philosophy of the school (here is a useful place to imply a quadrant from the roadmap)?
- What is really important to those at the school?
- What defines a graduate of the school?

In the end, the product should be general enough to be able to be used as a definition, but specific enough to imply the special qualities of the school, what it is about, and even infer what it is not about. For example, the committee may take dozens of ideas suggested and pare them down to a vision statement such as:

> *"At Jefferson Middle School, we create an environment in which all students are empowered and supported in meeting their potential and develop into self-responsible contributing members of the school community, in a student-centered, active learning environment."*

In addition, the committee should consider including a second expanded component of the vision outlining the kinds of Actions/X's – the practices, strategies, programs, policies, and ways people act that define the school. For example, the committee, using the content from the small group brainstorming, might create a list of defining practices at the school, such as:

- At Jefferson Middle School, we believe:
  - Students learn best in an active, hands-on setting.
  - Our goal in the area of classroom management is to create greater levels of self-responsibility over time. Therefore, we encourage students to learn from their choices, reflect, and find ways to contribute, and we avoid using rewards or punishments.
  - Assessment is a tool to help students understand their progress toward their learning goals, and not an agent of

comparison or related to personal value. We encourage self-assessment and matching our teaching methods and assessment targets.

- ○ (This list can be as long as necessary to fully operationalize the desired practices for the school).

Finally, the committee should compile the desired outcomes/O's gathered from their peers in the brainstorming portion of the exercise into a third piece of the process. This list can include any type of outcome which is perceived as important to the members of the school community and can include affective and experiential qualities as well as success indicators. For example, the list for Jefferson Middle School might include the following.

If we at Jefferson Middle School are successful in our mission as outlined in our vision statement, some of the outcomes we expect are:

- Students will love coming to school, and teachers will love working here.
- Students will appreciate why JMS is different from other middle schools.
- Students will reach their potential as learners.
- Students will obtain the resources they need to achieve their goals.
- Students will be prepared to show their success to their parents during their student-led conferences.
- Etc....

The vision document should ideally include three parts – sections related to R's, X's, and O's. Longer or shorter versions will likely be needed for different purposes as the situation requires, and different parts may or may not always be included. For the teachers and staff, the complete, three-part vision document should be understood and used by everyone.

## Whole Faculty Review and Approval

Once the vision committee has created a product, it should be shown to the faculty for discussion and a vote of approval. Amendments can be suggested. Especially if there are certain words causing an issue with some faculty members. Alternate words may be suggested and voted on. If most of the members of the faculty seem to be happy with what is ultimately proposed, it is time for a vote.

There is no magic threshold when it comes to how much dissent is acceptable for the product to be viewed as legitimate. Everyone needs to be given a chance to voice their thoughts and feelings and contribute within the formal process. In a democratic process, not everyone's opinions need to be reflected in the final product. The result will reflect the best and most true and noble R's, X's, and O's of the school community. Nevertheless, erring on the side of aspirational is preferred, so if leadership recognizes the product becoming largely defined by convenience, an over-representation of teacher authority or is simply too innocuous, suggestions for revisions should be made and the committee needs to go back to the table.

If the content of the document is not acceptable at any stage, the process may need to be restarted with a greater level of input and guidance the second time. It does not have to be a work of art, but if some part of your being is not inspired by the words on the page, there is a need for improvement.

Yet, most likely, this process will feel energizing as it taps into the best parts of ourselves and brings us together and engenders a sense of "team." So, the document creation process is a great start and indispensable to your success. But where is that vision six months later? If it is just words on paper or on a wall, it is not worth much. If the process went well, we should have a highly useful product to anchor our improvement efforts, giving us common language for our journey, and useful to everything from our school promotion to our strategic planning. If we want the process to translate our vision into results, we need to think of our vison as something alive – a "living vision."

## Highly Recommended Companion Document – the "What We Do and Don't Do" List

The intention of the formal vision statement is to create a concept of who you are and what you do with the fewest number of words. Once that is done successfully, consider a secondary process and resulting document clarifying in more detail "what one should see" and "what one should not see," at the school related to practice. This is an extension and expansion of part two of our vision process related to the school's X's. In essence, the document should depict the result of a concept attainment exercise representing examples and non-examples of X's/practices/actions that reflect the desired R's and vision at the school.

Abstractions tend to be easier to agree upon than specifics, so it may require more patience than the process of creating our abstract vision. You will need to engage a structured process, similar to the one used to create your vision statement.

It is best to organize the content of the document into categories, such as instruction, assessment, classroom management, technology, social and emotional, community, etc. There will be two columns; one for those X's/practices an observer should see used within the school, and one for those X's that an observer should not see used at the school. It is recommended that it is extensive, but not exhaustive list (4-9 items per category). The content should be specific enough that one would recognize it when they saw it. The final product should be suitable for sharing with all school stakeholders, including parents and students. You are encouraged to tailor the process to fit the needs of your school.

Operationalizing the specific practices/X's that characterize your vision will build capacity (for becoming a professional learning community) and coherence among the X's, from classroom to classroom. In addition, it generates practical conversations around what constitutes quality practice, and encourages a culture of internal accountability and self-reflection.

Very often we use pedagogical terms which have relative meanings. Examples include concepts such as positive, engagement, student-centered, praise, rewards, high standards, responsibility, cooperation, etc. Too often we know little about what any individual teacher means when they use these terms, or what it would look like in their teaching. For example, we may all agree our school's vision should include "high expectations" as a value. But we may potentially have individual teachers who perceive that concept in very different ways. For instance, one teacher may seek to create "high expectations" with the use of a 4-Style approach including grading on a norm-referenced curve, and making success rare, resulting in few students receiving higher grades (this is not recommended practice). Another teacher, employing a 1-Style logic may use the term "high expectations" to imply being warm but demanding, and providing clear and well-defined learning targets (Shindler, 2020). The goal for this teacher is for all students to be able to hit the learning and behavioral targets (highly recommended practice for moving up).

Disagreements, challenges, and insecurities will undoubtedly arise as we move up the roadmap from being congenial (but less honest) with one another, to being truly collaborative. But to grow as a community, faculty members need to feel comfortable talking about practice with their peers. Therefore, leadership will require encouraging emotional safety through policy and practice. Throughout the process, we will want to help faculty members remember a) conflict is healthy, b) we can be respectful and even loving, and still disagree, c) growth is the goal, not conformity, and d) no one is expected to be perfect, but we do want to be as aspirational as possible. Tap into the feeling that the process work itself is leading to a brighter tomorrow, no matter how much of a grind or a challenge it may seem today.

**What about those faculty members whose input is problematic?** Often after being shown the roadmap, and engaging in the POS classification activity, there are teachers on the faculty who are still attached to their 4-style and/or a low functioning 2-style. We have a couple of choices to move the process forward. Option one, we could remove all language that is met by majority disapproval. Option two, we agree the document will include all items that are agreed to by 2/3 vote. In this case, some grumbling may occur. For the leaders reading this, you will need to decide which is more desirable, either a) setting out a clear vision which you and most members of the staff like, yet some members are not thrilled about, or b) representing all perspectives as valid and worthy of inclusion. While ownership, voice, and representation are utmost values, the preeminent value must be moving the school to a level of function making it a better place to work and be a student.

## Leadership: Facilitating a Living Vision and Moving the Collective R's Up the Pathway

When we bring to mind a school, team, organization, classroom, or committee we would characterize as "visionary" or vision-driven, it likely involved a person or people who stewarded or facilitated that vision. Survey stakeholders at any school about their perception of the level of vision at the school, and what we find is that most of the time, they are talking about what their leadership/administration does – its X's. One definition of vision would be X's which connect R's and point them in a direction. Perceptions are an important reality. The general perception that the school has vision is an important R to have in the process of promoting a living, organic, evolving, school vision.

It is beneficial for those who find themselves in a leadership role to have the gift of seeing the big picture, but it is not essential. Anyone can facilitate a living, organic, evolving vision process. To understand the nature of effective stewardship, it might be useful at this point to define the terms in our phrase "living, organic, evolving vision process." We could use the term living to reflect that an effective vision needs to be practical and operational and imply X's as much as R's. We can define organic as the degree to which the vision reflects the true and real R's in the hearts, nervous systems, and minds of the community. Finally, an effective vision needs to evolve. We can define a school's evolution as the process of becoming more of its highest nature and purpose and reaching more of its potential as an entity.

There are three primary means the facilitator will use to encourage the vision:

- Listening and observing

- Asking guiding questions

- Articulating and reflecting the movement of the group

## Listening and Observing

There is an item in our elementary student climate survey which asks about how often the student sees the principal around the school. The item is very predictive. In high performing schools the principal is visible. As important as any aspect of the vision creation process the leader must 1) make it clear they want to listen and know what is going on, and 2) actually listen and be in meetings, classrooms, and talking to students. The reason this is so important is that in a concrete operational sense, it is not what we say about what we do, but what we actually

> **Figure 7.5: Some Challenges to Improving Our School's Vision**
>
> - We each bring in different sets of R's and it is difficult to connect R's
>
> - Being the facilitator of a vision requires skills and intention.
>
> - Our students' R's may influence us and challenge our ability to apply a collective R that is different from the one that they are used to from their homes and/or their previous school experiences
>
> - The human need to fit in and/or avoid conflict can act to encourage a tendency to cling to our more mediocre R's, so we do not lose friends.
>
> - R's will tend to become diffused or stale without attention, intention, and regular processing. Without momentum in the vision cultivation process, it will perish.

do. Moreover, there is no way to know how people feel sometimes if we do not ask them. Surveys are valuable, but personal conversations are both symbolically important – they show we care and are listening, and practically important - we learn so much from informal interactions. Therefore, we need to be clear about when we are in the role of formal evaluator and when we are in the role of "curious and supportive colleague." We will examine this distinction further in the next chapter.

---

**Doing Listening Right**: John is an experienced principal who took a position at a new school. He made it a point to ensure his new staff knew that he wanted to hear what they had to say. He set aside time in his daily schedule for one-on-one meetings with faculty who came in on their free periods. He also devoted time in faculty meetings to hearing concerns from faculty about how the school could be better.

**Doing Listening Not So Well:** Principal Charlotte wants to be out on the school campus, and so has committed to being in many of the classrooms during the day. However, teachers are not sure what her intentions are as she sits in their class, and she does not often follow up. For many, it seems more like she is just checking up on them, which for some feels invasive and not supportive or useful.

---

## Asking Guiding Questions

The skill of asking reflective question is an invaluable art when applied to clarify the living vision and connect R's. But doing it sincerely and with a mindset based in service is essential. Therefore, first, we need to project support and non-judgment. Second, we need to assess our colleague's level of openness and trust in the perspective we are offering. If there is a sense we are trusted, we can act as an agent of reflection. In many cases, this process implies asking our colleagues to reflect on recent X's, in relation to their own R's and the R's implied by the school's vision.

Some of the broad question themes can come from ideas in this book such as:

- "How are you doing aligning your X's with your intended R's?
- "Are your X's more POS or POF promoting and/or consistent with the school's practices we do/don't do lists?

- "What is the dominant level of perception/LOP with which you are operating right now?

We will be most effective asking questions that imply larger constructs such as POS, yet within the context of the immediate situation and the most relevant concerns of those to whom we are speaking.

The process of asking reflective questions about the X's being used in and out of the classroom is critical to our job as an instructional leader and will be discussed in more detail in the next chapter.

## Articulating and Reflecting the Movement of the Group

No matter how much progress the collective is making up the pathway, it only becomes real and noticeable to the members when they recognize a) there is progress and b) that progress is headed in the direction of our vision. Without a sense of momentum, the collective will have a weak sense of vision efficacy. So, the vision leader or facilitator needs to provide an additional sense of the "We." *We* are making it happen. *We* are becoming what we envisioned. *We* are becoming a more functional team all the time. There is no need for dishonesty or deception, and there is also no need to hold back on projecting the energy that "*we* are winning." Collective success is a powerful motivator (the power of "team wins"). We need the fuel of feeling successful and connected as we do our work. Therefore, no matter the personalities of the facilitators of the vision, the actions need to encourage both a sense of "We" and of concrete, practical progress.

Find examples of the school's vision in action – the R as X's. These X's may be actions within a classroom you have observed. They may be reflected as outcomes that have changed. Maybe fewer students are being sent to the office as

| Figure 7.6: Trust Killers |
| --- |
| - Judgment |
| - Shame |
| - Blame |
| - Superiority |
| - Unfavorable comparisons |
| - Deceit |
| - Hidden agendas |
| - No follow-through |

a result of improved practice. If you hear a student say something positive which reflects the essence of the vision, share it. Maybe a student says, "I like coming to school, I am doing cool projects in all of my classes" or "in my other school the teachers did not care as much." These O's reflect a collective improvement of X's or a "team win."

Other effective strategies are to simply use language from the vision statement or the "things we do and don't do" list in conversation and presentations. We might take a minute at the end of a faculty meeting to give teachers the chance to recognize the positive accomplishments or growth of their colleagues. We could use the vision statement to reflect on an event or a new proposal. One way or another, we need to hold the vision in the front of our minds. It is living to the degree that it is practical and current and reflects what we truly care about.

What an organization or school comes to realize is the more progress they make, the more progress they are motivated to make. Winning breeds liking and liking breeds winning.

---

**Figure 7.7: Trust Builders**

- Sincere listening

- Empathy

- Self-deprecation

- Humility

- Compassion

- Consistency

- Honesty

---

**Doing Articulating Team Wins Right**: Sarah is the AP for students at her school. The school took part in a survey from the year before, and the data showed students did not feel a sense of voice. The faculty spent a lot of energy for the next year working to improve this. After the faculty took the survey again, Sarah was able to show the faculty the data and lead them in an activity in which they shared with one another what they had done. The mood was one of celebration, but also excitement to do even better in the future as a team.

**Doing Articulating Team Wins Not So Well**: Paul has been principal for two years and has mandated a new program that is well-received by some, but many are not sold on its efficacy or fit for this school. Paul takes every opportunity to show faculty selective data he feels proves the program is working. Those who like the program tend to be somewhat more convinced by the data presentations, but those who are not supportive feel like the data do not answer the right questions, and in many respects do not fit their own experience. Reflecting on the three aspects of the vision process outlined in this section, Paul may have done an adequate job of the third part of the process – articulating the success, but he did not do an effective job in either listening or asking questions. We could also infer that it is best if the conclusion that the team has been successful comes from the members of the team and is not a hard-sell of the leadership's own agenda.

---

### Figure 7.8: A Story of a 1-Paradigm Leader

A very useful example of a leader who used a R->X->O approach rather than simply trying to remediate (X) his problems (O's) is that of Dewey, an experienced principal who took a new position in an elementary school in Kentucky. He inherited the lowest performing school in the district, located in a neighborhood that others would assume would produce an intractably low performance level. Dewey could have focused on the problems and the circumstances of the students at the school. In other words, he could have taken an approach that was defined by a reaction to the current O's, and no one would have questioned him if he had spent the next year talking about all of the excuses for the low performance, and all the remedial programs he would add into the school to deal with those problems. No one would have questioned him because that is the normal route with the normal result being a school mired at the lower levels. So, if he had taken that route, he would be just another leader who assumed he was doing the best he could in a challenging situation. However, he did not take the normal route.

Dewey recognized that the school needed to change its self-perception/R's along with most of their other R's. First, they needed to stop thinking about all the reasons that it could not happen, and they needed to think about what they wanted. What was their picture of a great school? Then they needed to adopt only practices/X's that were consistent with that picture. He did have the benefit of a majority of his faculty members being mostly interested in taking on the challenge.

Dewey inherited test scores that were far below the districts norm and about a 15% passing rate relative to the state standard. They also had a yearly average of over 400 office behavioral referrals, twice the amount of any other school in the district. What they quickly created was a 1-Paradigm school, with 1-Style teaching in their classrooms. In other words, high level X's as a consistent manifestation of their high-level R's. After the first year, the test scores went up to a 30% passing rate and the referrals dropped to about 100. The next year, the test scores went up to a 40% passing rate and the referrals went to 60. After four years of committing to a 1-Paradigm approach, their X's and O's reflected that level on the pathway. Collectively Dewey and his team saw the pass rate soar to 75% which was better than the local private school, and their discipline referrals decreased to approximately 15, lowest in the district.

Dewey's story is not very common in terms of how often it happens, but it is common to schools who approach improvement with an R->X->O orientation, starting with a commitment to 1-Paradigm R's and X's. The reason it is not common is that in most challenged schools they try to solve symptoms, which is noble, but in a broader sense mostly futile. We will explore why solving symptoms is ineffective later in Chapter nine.

## Assessing Perceptions of Vision Level in the SCAI Survey

In the ASSC School Climate Assessment Instrument (SCAI) there are a few items relating to the level of vision at the school. Figure 7.9 represents two of the most directly worded examples. It is no accident that the first two items on the Leadership Sub-Scale are related to vision. As you examine the content, you will recognize how the descriptions of the low, middle, and high levels represent the corresponding locations on the roadmap. It should be noted that these items function very effectively (over 0.7 total item correlation) to predict both overall function/climate as well as O/ outcomes such as student achievement levels.

**Figure 7.9: Two SCAI Items Related to School Vision**

| 4. Leadership/Decisions | | | | |
|---|---|---|---|---|
| Level - 3 | | Level - 2 | | Level – 1 |
| **High** | **high-middle** | **middle** | **middle-low** | **low** |
| 4.a------O------------------- O ----------------- O ----------------- O ----------------- O ----------- | | | | |
| School has a sense of vision and a mission that is shared by all staff. | | School has a set of policies, a written mission, but no cohesive vision. | | School has policies that are used inconsistently. |
| 4.b------O------------------- O ----------------- O ----------------- O ----------------- O ----------- | | | | |
| Vision comes from the collective will of the school community. | | Vision comes from leadership. | | Vision is absent. |

## Meeting the Needs of Different Cognitive Styles Among the Staff

In the process of connecting references and creating a "We" among the collective, it is critical to have in mind that members of the faculty, staff, and administration learn and process differently and, as a result, will feel connected and trusting for somewhat different reasons. Certain of the members of the faculty will process their world more concretely, while others will process more abstractly. Some members will like it when there is order and structure, whereas others will be more comfortable with less structure, or even resist the idea of structure. Some portion of the members of the faculty will process more with their feelings and be motivated to harmonize, while others will be more logic-driven and be motivated to dissect the situation and make sure it all adds up.

When we include many of the processes for connecting references and building a collective set of R's and X's described here, we will satisfy the needs of each of these different kinds of cognitive styles. Yet, in addition, maintaining awareness of how the respective members of the school community process will be useful. Figure 7.10 characterize the way different adults process. Keep in mind those differences as we explore the remaining processes for connecting R's in this chapter.

| | Concrete/Practical Types | Abstract/Intuitive Types |
|---|---|---|
| **Feeling/ Harmony Types** | **Harmonizers** **Practical-Feelers** I am the most loyal of all the types. I like harmony and people working together. Unless I feel like a practice is harmful, I will likely be okay with adopting it, if it is required and it is demonstrated to me. I have a soft heart for students and like to be a peacemaker. I will put the team first in many cases and prefer leaders who are inspiring and lead with heart. | **Connecters** **Abstract-Feelers** I trust my intuition. I have a good sense for what is good for people and will create long-term benefit. I like to understand why I am being asked to do something. I really like working in groups and contributing my gifts. I can be very passionate about a cause, and equally passionate about things I do not like. I prefer leaders who are empathetic and have their finger on the pulse of the group. |
| **Thinking/ Logical Types** | **Technicians** **Practical-Thinkers** I am the most structured and organized of the types. I like things that work and are efficient. I will mostly be critical of what I see as unnecessary effort. Theory does not tend to persuade me but seeing results will. I like evidence, and I trust my experience and that of others. I am loyal to mentors who have good track records and leaders who are straightforward and organized. | **Scientists** **Abstract-Thinkers** I need to see the logical consistency of what I am doing. If it does not make sense to me, I will struggle to be able to implement a policy. I tend to want to break things down and find the flaws, but I am also the most gifted of all types in building plans, models, or diagrams. I will have strong feelings which may emerge as leadership and vision, or as being a skeptic and critic. I prefer leaders who have a big-picture/vision. |

It is essential as a leader to appreciate that we learn and process differently (Lawrence, 2009). What leads one person to make a change may not be what leads another to the same conclusion. The 40% or so of your faculty who are more abstract will likely embrace the vision creation process and for them, when an abstraction makes sense, they will look for ways to make their X's fit the new R. For the more practical-minded members of the staff, what will convince them is their experience and X's that work to achieve results. For the more abstract group, if an X violates their R's, they will have difficulty employing it, no matter the price. For the concrete group, no matter now elegant and theoretically sound an explanation is, an idea is only valid if it works in practice. Therefore, we will want to keep the needs of each group in mind as we explore the following processes for changing R's. Engaging the faculty in an exercise where they realize their own learning style/personality is highly recommended. It is enlightening for each individual, the group as a whole, and provides you with a resource to better understand those whom you lead individually and collectively. The Paragon Learning Style Inventory (PLSI) is available on the book website.

## Why Do We Change our R's?

To change our practices/X's, we need to first change our R's (i.e., values, beliefs, attitudes, self-perceptions, worldview, educational philosophy, assumptions about people, etc.). In the long-term, any person's X's will be a display of their R's played out in action. Therefore, as we engage in leading the process of change, we will want to take an honest and informed look at why those who we are leading would be willing or able to change their R's.

If we simply tell people what they have to do, without some alignment between that person's R's and the X we are requiring, there will be resistance in some form. In schools, that resistance manifests in ways such as uneven application of a policy, misuse of a program, or even complete disregard for an agreed upon X. And yes, performing an X because one would rather do it than live with an undesired consequence does technically represent a change in R's, but we can probably agree that this is a last resort and represents a low-quality motivation (and level on the roadmap).

As we consider why anyone adopts new values, appreciations, beliefs – new R's, we need to appreciate everyone's differences. We all have different forms of intelligence (Gardner, 1993). A good place to start is some of the organic ways people vary like those in the personality research (e.g., Figure 7.10, and Appendix D). Often differences are not simply random subjectivity. In fact, they can be largely understandable if we recognize how different cognitive preferences process new ideas, make change and are motivated. Therefore, as we examine some of the most common reasons why any of us changes our R's, it will be useful to consider that some reasons will be more prominent given certain types of human intelligence.

As we set out to raise the quality of the R's at the school, we will want to continuously ask ourselves the question, "Why would anyone adopt what others believe to be better R's in exchange for the ones they had previously?" Below are a few of the reasons why people will ultimately replace or adopt an R.

- Because the new R makes so more sense.
- Because I have seen it work.
- Because I want to be a team player and part of the cause.
- Because people I trust are including and encouraging me.
- Because I have new information and/or conditions have changed.
- Because I have to change, so I can avoid something undesirable.
- Because something inside (instinct, intuition, inner voice, conscience, sense of purpose, etc.) is telling me that it is intrinsically right.

As we explore each of the reasons, it will likely bring to mind how each might be more useful for various individuals and/or contexts. Implications are offered for each of the reasons.

## Because the New R Makes More Sense.

When we go through the process of showing the staff the roadmap and engaging in the POS/POF classification exercise, the conceptual picture of what "better" looks like becomes much more vivid and appealing. In our experience, we find all types recognize the validity of the model presented; however, some types will react with a stronger sense of connection. Those who "see the light" so to speak, will likely come more from your abstract group as well as those who are on a personal journey of growth. Sometimes we call these the "early adopter" group because they have less of a need to see what it would all look like in application before appreciating and ideas validity. It typically just makes so much sense to them that moving up and making the "left hand turn" are reasonable and desirable.

**Implication**: Include these people on the planning and vision setting committees. We will want to later have them explain how their R/vision is being actualized in the X's in their classes. This may be simple anecdotes, full presentation, or even peer support. It is very important to keep in mind that this group is always in jeopardy of being labeled the "insiders" or the favorites and, as a result, marginalized. Therefore, all committees need to reflect representatives from several groups within the school.

**Reflection 7.b** – What are other's perceptions of the early adopters and the insiders at your school?

## Because I Have Seen it Work

While most every faculty and staff member will leave the POS classification exercise with clarity and a strong intention to stick to POS R's and X's, that determination can gradually fade This is especially true for the more practical-minded and routinized teachers on your faculty. For these teachers, we need to assume that their R's will be persuaded by X's in practice – theirs or those of others they can see firsthand. They desire results that they judge as desirable and are within their capability to persuade them to make a change.

**Implication:** The first implication is that we, as the instructional leader, need to be patient, especially if we are more abstract-minded and our tendency is to believe a compelling argument and/or an elegant theoretical design is reason enough to have faith in a method or strategy. Second, we need to find every manner to make the conceptual concretized, which usually involves examples, modelling, demonstrations, data, and talking about what "it looks like when we do it." Finally, sharing the O's with this group will help too – what are the benefits that are being experienced as a result of a particular R being put into X.

## Because I Want to Be a Team Player and Part of the Cause

Some of the members of the staff will be motivated by being part of a collective noble effort. This may or may not be a distinct group. But for some, sharing in an effort intended to make the school better involving working as a team will be inspiring. Just engaging in creating something collectively will make anyone more likely to support it.

**Implication:** Situating what you are doing within a team concept and speaking of the effort to move toward your vision in inspiration language will aid your level of success. Mostly because that is exactly what you are doing in meaningful school improvement. It must be a team effort. And what is more noble than changing the trajectory of a whole group of students' lives for the better? We are encouraging teachers to meet their potential as a human for the good of everyone.

## Because People I Trust are Including and Encouraging Me

Being included in the leadership and planning of the effort will increase a sense of ownership and commitment greatly. For some though, they are not eager to support a new idea unless someone whom they trust is there to encourage them. This is especially true for those who might be classified as the extroverted feelers.

**Implication:** No matter your current R's related to self-reliance which may include letting everyone make up their own minds or sink or swim independently, accept that this will probably back-fire with some teachers. While our interactions with this group (and our instructions to other early adopters to check in and encourage them) may at times feel high maintenance, they are likely critical to keeping those in this group connected and feeling supported.

## Because I Have New Information and/or Conditions Have Changed

For everyone in the effort, we will need to project our commitment and sincerity. For any teacher who has been at the school longer, they have seen things come and go. So, what is different about this change effort? They have seen new ideas be sold to them and, as time goes on, leaders eventually shift attention to something else. And they have heard that the new program or initiative is essential to the school's success until it is replaced with a new focus, new research, or a new flavor of the month in schools. So, all that said, what is it that you are about and what is the stable, consistent agenda that is worth really understanding and cultivating a collective expertise around?

**Implication:** We need to communicate that this is not a new initiative as much as the new normal. Having the whole faculty and staff take part in self-assessing with the SCAI provides them information in the form of data. Data takes us out of the role of "telling" and lets us show significant findings. Because we really value learning and take on the mindset of a lifelong learner, we are constantly gaining wisdom and knowledge to improve what we do.

## Because I Have to Change so That I Can Avoid Something Undesirable

In some cases, we may have teachers on the staff who regrettably have become so attached to POF (psychology of failure) R's and X's that they will tend to resist or ignore the ideas offered by others in the school's improvement effort. Other teachers simply play by their own rules.

**Implication**: As we will discuss in the next section (and in chapter 8 related to instructional leadership), we will need policies and structures which make better teaching an expectation as an employee of the school. We will want to use any and all methods to support the awakening of these members of the staff, but in the end, they do not have the option to work against the growth of the school. Dissonance makes everyone else's job more difficult, and it is not good for students.

## Because Something Inside (Instinct, Intuition, Inner Voice, Conscience, Sense of purpose, Etc.) is Telling Me That It is Intrinsically Right.

When we first begin our work in education our motivations usually involve making a difference and making the world a better place. Over time, that tends to get suppressed, partly because our sense of inspiration is replaced by the mundane reality of the day-to-day job. Too often colleagues feel welcome to share thoughts related to the mundane, but not those related to their sense of purpose.

**Implication:** As the leader help the inner voice in your teachers saying it is OK to be proud to empower students, face your fears, accept your moral purpose as a person, and embrace the journey. If you diminish the value of the effort, they will too. Feel into your own sense of empowerment, as we will discuss in the final chapter. And finally, aide each member of the staff in recognizing their instinct is telling them the truth – moving up the pathway will be more rewarding, more satisfying, and feel internally "right."

We might characterize this area of our work within the domain of the "art of leadership." When to employ which kind of influence requires some thought and sensitivity to the needs of others. Yet, if we are attentive, patient, and considerate of how challenging teaching is even on a regular day, we will be able to find the most organic ways to lead others in doing better things for themselves and their students. But it is important to try our best to keep our egos out of it, and see others as human being, and not as cogs in a machine. Winning in the long-term is about creating a winning culture and cultivating effective high-quality processes. Short-term improvements stemming from intimidation or reluctant compliance are usually long-term losses.

## Examining Vision Leadership Related to a Range of Unconscious and Semiconscious R's that Are Operating at the School

Finally, let's turn our attention to all the implicit and subterranean references operating at the school. For some of us, we are more naturally tuned in to this dimension of the school phenomenon. For others this more affective realm can seem rather mysterious and obtuse. But if we are to support the movement at the school beyond simply the practical inefficiencies, we will need to place at least some attention on this realm of our school.

Starting with ourselves, we will need to reflect upon our underlying assumptions about the school before we can consider how the assumptions of others may be limiting our growth. We might ask ourselves "What is our honest attitude about the school?" How would we rate our own X's on the POS vs POF dimensions? Do we take responsibility for doing what we can, given what we control, or do we make excuses and/or get fatalistic? Do we take a growth orientation and embrace the journey of self-improvement, or do we slip into a fixed mindset? Our process of self-reflection will likely need to be ongoing. Growth is not an exercise, but a lifetime commitment. Engaging the processes in Chapter fourteen will be helpful here as well.

If we were to name the forms of R's representing the subconscious and semiconscious realms at the school, we might arrive at the following list:

- Beliefs and Values
- Narratives
- Knowledge
- Unconscious R's

As we explore each area, we gain a better sense of how each of these underlying areas have power over our ability to improve. In fact, since they are the most subterranean R's they are the most solid and true, and thus, are the most defining. What that means is they will be the most challenging to alter, but also represent the most powerful source of potential change.

## Beliefs and Values

What are the values at your school? What are the beliefs about learning and children or adolescents? How much consistency is there around these questions? When you look out at the X's/practices of the adults at the school, what values/R's do they imply? As you examine the belief statements in Figure 7.11 below, consider which description best defines the common beliefs at the school today.

Figure 7.11: Beliefs of Adults at a School Encouraging either Growth or Limitation

| R's in the form of values and beliefs leading us up the function continuum | R's in the form of values and beliefs leading us down the function continuum |
|---|---|
| The Modus Operandi at the school is defined by the process: R -> X -> O (i.e., references lead to actions which lead to outcomes). | The modus operandi at the school is defined by the sequence: Circumstances-> reaction -> rationalization |
| When we look at students and other adults in the school, we see individuals who are growing and basically good and in need of a supportive context to help them grow and learn. | When we look at the students and other adults in the school, we see individuals who will do the minimum and/or misbehave if they are not controlled, bribed, or punished. |
| Primary Focus on quality processes | Primary Focus on quantitative outcomes |

| | |
|---|---|
| The "Real World" is what we make it. We have compassion for the challenges of this career and the lives of our students, but we are making the future by the X's we use today. | In the "Real World" you need to accept that you just have to do what it takes to survive and cope, and there is not that much that really makes a difference anyway. |
| Doing "what is right" values = integrity, with a recognition that everything is connected. | Doing "what works" values = cleverness and convenience. |
| Value for a process of reflection which does not shy from discussions about the state of the collectively held R's. | Vague expectations of "adequate" or "inadequate" performance that are left unexamined. |
| Critique of the school is encouraged to be constructive, open, and done purposefully | Critique of the school is usually passive aggressive, in closed quarters, and/or avoided entirely. |
| Improvement efforts seek to find answers to the "real problems," and address root causes. | Improvement efforts attempt to respond to the "symptoms" of the real problems directly. |
| Those in the school find ways to build trust in one another and the collective and seek to become "trustworthy" members of the collective. | Those in the school allow fear and mistrust to become normal and seek ways to protect their self-interest from the "others" |
| Goal for students is liberation. | Goal for students is domestication. |

After reading this list, the implications for a leader might seem overwhelming on first glance. Yet, any successful journey is one of a thousand small steps. So, accept where you are today and take a few steps in a quality direction. First, we need to understand and recognize the presence of as many of these counter-productive beliefs as possible.

Second, we want to look for opportunities to bring clarity to any situation we can. We need to be the most conscious presence in the room. Frustration, fear, and fatigue make the list on the right look valid, but in actuality represent a flawed perception. Therefore, without being oppositional, we want to gently help those in the school recognize that they really do desire those values on the left no matter what they may be saying today. If it were the case that by espousing the values on the left, we were being self-serving, we could be accused of being manipulative. But the reality is we are acting in the service of what is good for everyone – teachers, staff, students, and parents.

Third, we want to find ways to promote the principles on the left as inspiring the true reality of "the way it is here" or at least the way "it is becoming here." The use of mantras can seem corny, but they are effective and show we are not afraid to lead, by defining the reality. We might say, "I know everyone here puts their students first." Is this completely true? Maybe not absolutely, but it will be truer the more we say it. Consider using some of the ideas on the left in your regular mantras. Another powerful tool is to acknowledge the high function R's when we hear them and simply validate them as "the way we all think here." Much of our success will come from having our radar out for all evidence that these quality producing R's are operating and finding ways to validate their use.

## Formal Documents Reflecting the School's Purpose

In the next chapter, we will discuss the idea of policy in more detail. For now, ask yourselves the following questions about the R's defining the written documents used at the school.

- How well are the principles outlined in your school's vision reflected in your documents?

- Are procedures consistent with the vision and with one another?

- If a stranger read your action plans, accreditation documents, curriculum documents, and discipline policy, what would it say to them about your actual vision and true collective R's?

---

**Reflection 7.c** - As you review your policy documents, what are some of the phrases you see operationalizing what you are about? For example, at one 1-Paradigm school they created a poster that said, "the reward at this school is we do not use rewards." What would you put on a poster to define the R's at your school?

---

## Narratives

The more we examine why schools are the way they are, the more we recognize the power of the conscious and unconscious narratives we use to talk about ourselves, our colleagues, our school, and our students. A narrative is simply the story we tell ourselves and others about our perceived realities. We hear them best when we and the teachers are speaking off the record. No matter what our formal or public message is about our school, the private narrative we use in our inner dialogue, our lunchroom conversations, or the way we talk about our school to friends and family are our true R's. How closely do private R's match our stated vision? As we have discussed earlier, engaging a formal vision development process and maintaining an intention to improve can bring more hope and positive expectancy into the narratives expressed in private. Shifting the narrative language into greater alignment with the school's growth trajectory will be essential to our job as vision facilitator.

Keep in mind that narratives are entirely invented in our heads. The story we choose to tell ourselves or others about any particular topic, event, or condition is just one of an infinite number of stories that we can tell ourselves about it. It may seem like it is "the way things are," but we know we do not have to look far to find others who tell a very different story about the same condition. Sometimes that person with an entirely different perspective was us a few years ago (or less).

Figure 7.H offers a partial list of possible narratives – toxic on one side and life affirming on the other. Among the toxic narratives the most common is a victim mentality. There is nothing that will kill our growth up the pathway like a recalcitrant victim narrative. It should be public enemy #1 on your list of things to run out of town. While toxic narratives appear mostly in a few recognizable forms, true and life-affirming narratives are limitless. All the ways in which we can grow, all the ways we can unleash potential, and all the wonderful gifts and talents of staff and students are endless. Therefore, here we selected some of the most useful life affirming counter narratives to the five most common toxic narratives that we have come across.

Figure 7.12: Toxic Versus Life Affirming Narratives

| Toxic and Dysfunction promoting narrative concepts | Life-affirming and function promoting narrative concepts |
| --- | --- |
| **Victimhood:** "This job would be better if it were not for. . ." Or "Because of the (students, parents, location, budget, etc.) I am not capable of being happy or doing a good job or producing certain results." | (derived from a psychology of success)<br><br>"I do my best and accept myself."<br><br>"Everything is an opportunity for growth."<br><br>"it all in my attitude."<br><br>"I am responsible." |
| **Entitlement:** "I didn't get into this job to ___ ." Or "These students should know ___ by now." | Our job is to take who walks in the door and help them grow and mature. If they need to develop some skills before they are ready to function like they are ultimately capable, I need to teach those skills. |

| | |
|---|---|
| **Cynicism:** "I've been around, I've seen it all, and none of it makes a difference." Or "Good luck trying that with our students." | There are no guarantees for how anything will result, but my job is to do my best and control what I can control – my R's and my X's. My question is "how do I need to change to be the kind of teacher or leader that it will take to get the results I believe are possible?" |
| **Guilt:** "I am doing the best I can, but no one appreciates me." "How can we. . " "I don't care." (when, in reality, one is just in a state of denial as a result of feeling judged and criticized. So, they project rationalization for giving up." | I know there are an infinite number of ways to be unhappy right now, but to be happy I have 3 choices, 1) acceptance of what is, 2) enjoyment of what is and what I need to do, or 3) enthusiasm in what I do. Which one am I capable of right now? |
| **Inadequacy:** It was better when..... I can't until.... | What's Important Now – W.I.N. |

Anyone can find support for both life-affirming narratives as well as toxic life-denying narratives. If we took 10 seconds to look at any student or colleague in the school, we could find many ways to perceive them as flawed, threatening, problematic, incomplete, bothersome, or ignorant. But what did we gain by creating that narrative? The answer is usually self-protection or some other type of ego defense. We tell ourselves that story to avoid feeling responsible or judged ourselves, so we create a reason to outwardly project judgment or apathy. We can also do this with whole faculties, classrooms, or schools. Like all toxic narratives, this one is entirely invented, and by holding on to it, we make it feel valid, solid, and necessary.

The best way to change a narrative is bring it out in the open and investigate it honestly. We can find subjective observations to support either the negative and surface (toxic narrative) story or the life affirming and fundamentally true story. What if we looked at that same student or colleague and saw potential: a beautiful being emerging, a whole series of gifts and talents, strengths, and ways to contribute, and someone from whom to learn? Same person, new narrative. How does that new narrative change the way you think about your next action related to that person? (Another case where our X's will evolve as our R's become more evolved) Recall the story of Dewey the 1-Paradigm leader described above. The narrative at his new school was that the kids from this neighborhood were losers and would always be losers, so it would be best to approach school with that attitude. Dewey believed and projected the narrative that the students had vast unmet potential waiting to be untapped. He was effective in changing the narrative and as a result was able to build new school phenomena, we could rightly call life-affirming.

---

**Two incoming Teachers-Two incoming R's**

During a break in a summer workshop a teacher who had transferred to the school was walking by an elderly janitor. Making conversation, the teacher said hello, and seeing that the janitor was very friendly, ask him, "So tell me, what are the students like at this school?" The janitor replied, "What were they like at the school you came from?" The teacher said that the students there were especially immature, unmotivated, and needed to be constantly reprimanded or they would not do any work and misbehave. The janitor said to the teacher, "I think you will find them the same here." The teacher said "thanks" and walked on. A bit later, another new teacher transfer came by and engaged the janitor and asked about the students at the school. Again, the janitor simply asked the teacher what the students were like at her other school. The teacher said that the students were enjoyable people, really blossomed over the year, and responded to being given increasing opportunities by doing wonderful work. The janitor looked at the teacher and said, "I think you will find them the same here."

## Skills and Knowledge

Not all knowledge will lead us up the function continuum. As you examine where you want to go, align your leadership skills, pedagogy, school communication, policy, to your desired R's. This is especially essential for the school's professional development. We see schools spend a great deal of time and money to train their teachers to do low level X's. In the next chapter, we will examine the X's which will move you up, and those keeping you stuck or even moving you down. More knowledge does not mean better knowledge. 2-Paradigm X's by way of 2-Paradigm R's will get 2-Paradigm results, no matter how well we execute those X's.

## Unconscious Beliefs, assumptions, fears, desires and baggage

This area is vast, yet, rarely explored. Nonetheless, we should not hide from the fact that *we teach who we R*, and likewise, *we lead who we R*. So, what is in our unconscious, in the form of the following, will play out as X's and ultimately as O's.

- Scripts
- World views
- Fears
- Desires
- Associations
- Biases
- Prejudices
- Energy – open or closed

Our job as leader is to provide opportunities for the teachers and staff to reflect, share, feel supported, be honest with themselves and others, and trust the school's efforts are about growth. Judgment and/or the appearance of preaching will almost always be counterproductive. Growth and change here needs to be a personal journey. But we can provide venues for those self-examinations, and we can model self-assessment.

Sharing your own stories of how you changed can be effective, for instance when you overcame a fear, or used a different narrative after realizing that the one you were using was based in a flawed perception. In addition, throwing out a reflective question that is not attached to anything evaluative can offer a safe place for individuals to process. For example, you might muse, "You know, I was just thinking of how during my second year of teaching, my energy used to change when I taught one period compared to another. In the first, where I liked all the students, they came in and I had such a positive expectancy that I felt like my energy went out into the room and affirmed them all, and in the second, I was so discouraged that when they walked in I would lean back and give them a cold affect. I wonder, if I had done better sending an encouraging energy out to that second class, and if it would have gotten them on my side more effectively. What do you all think? Can you relate?"

Every teacher has a basic underlying desire to contribute, effectively serve their students, and feel proud of their work. For some that desire is hidden by fears and toxic internal narratives, but it is there. Empowering, collaborative, and supportive climates bring out the best in people. Put yourself in the shoes of your teachers and staff. If you were them, what would you need from a leader to feel safe and supported to be able to work past your fears, insecurities, and defenses, and access more of your potential as an educator?

In the next chapter, we will examine the process of supporting the growth of the X's at the school with a special emphasis on instructional leadership. Put simply, the X's at the school are our vision/R's played out in action. Encouraging better practice is the inseparable companion to the process of cultivating and improving our living vision at our school.

## REFERENCES

Gardner, H. (1993) Multiple Intelligences: New Horizons. Basic Books, New York, NY.

Lawrence, G (2009). *People Types and Tiger Stripes. Using psychological type to help students discover their potential.* Center for Application of Psychological Types, Gainesville, Fl.

Shindler, J (2020) "I Have High Expectations" But What Does that Mean in Practice. Retrieved from www.transformativeclassroom.com

# CHAPTER 8:

## Instructional Leadership and Facilitating Growth in the X's

> "In the final analysis, means and ends must cohere because the end is preexistent in the means."
> — *Martin Luther King Jr.*

Transformative Leadership involves the process of supporting the movement of the quality of the practices or X's at the school up the effectiveness roadmap to ever higher levels. The best representation of where a school is on the pathway is the typical X's being used throughout the building each day. More success equals better X's and vice versa. To create the necessary leadership culture, we need to include the content and lessons of the preceding chapters. Meaningful change is best encouraged in a context of trust, the use of an intentional "meta" by way of a guiding vision, and shared quality references/R's. As we pursue the goal of improving practice, building increased capacity, and promoting coherence are requisites to our ultimate effectiveness. And to define what we mean by "improved practice," we will need to conceive our work within the logic of the effectiveness roadmap.

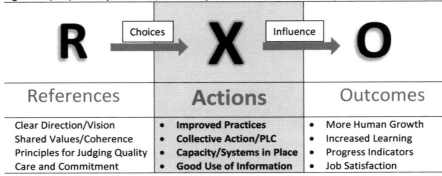

**Figure 7.1/8.1/9.1. Improved X's/Action Represented in the Overall Improvement Sequence**

| References | Actions | Outcomes |
|---|---|---|
| Clear Direction/Vision | • **Improved Practices** | • More Human Growth |
| Shared Values/Coherence | • **Collective Action/PLC** | • Increased Learning |
| Principles for Judging Quality | • **Capacity/Systems in Place** | • Progress Indicators |
| Care and Commitment | • **Good Use of Information** | • Job Satisfaction |

In this chapter, we will explore the idea of improving and evolving practice broadly. Much of the chapter is devoted to the critical area of instructional leadership and setting our intention and leadership style in this area. This growth and change process inherently involves both a collective and sub-jective aspect. It will need to involve both the "We" and each individual "I." As much as possible, we want to conceive change within the context of creating a change culture – a community of growers. The process of encouraging building-wide better practices and instructional leadership is more about creating the structures of self-direction, capacity for collective growth, and coherence - in other words, a 1-Paradigm intention applied to improvement. Yet we each will need to engage this process relative to our present location on the roadmap. The goals of excellence and personal growth are the same, but the methods used may need to be differentiated based on our personal needs and context.

> **Observation:** When we visit a school, after listening to a few teachers, observing the practices, looking at the walls, and noting how we were interacted with by those in the office, we can (with a little practice) predict, with great accuracy, the school climate and achievement levels of the school. Just like R's, X's will be an accurate way to classify the paradigm defining a school.

## Some Important Principles to Keep in Mind about X's?

- This book uses the symbol X to represent all actions and/or behaviors exhibited at the school, in and out of the classroom, including instructional practices, methods and strategies in the classroom, as well as routines, patterns, policies, programs, communication, structures, and in general, how people act and the dispositions they project into the environment as a whole.

- All X's are interconnected and affect one another.

- X's are actions and exhibitions resulting from our R's by way of our choices, they include both what we intend and/or are aware of, and what we do not intend and/or are not aware we are doing. More self-awareness and intentionality related to our R's will translate into higher level X's.

- Some X's will lead the school or classroom up the pathway to higher levels of function and others will lead it down. By definition, everything "works," so the phrases "well it is working" or "that will not work" are essentially pointless. Every X in every context can be said to work in some logic, so the more valid question to be asked is "what is it (the X) working to produce?" – we might add "in the long-term, to get us where we want to go?"

- We can only control ourselves – our R's and our X's. Our X's will create conditions which influence others' R's, X's, and O's, but we cannot directly control them.

- Students have experienced X's from their previous years, previous schools, homes and elsewhere. They will become accustomed to some X's more than others. Therefore, initially, in some cases, they will desire more of the same no matter how functional or dysfunctional the previous X's were. Yet, over time ALL students come to appreciate functional and life-affirming X's no matter what they have experienced in the past. And once a student become accustomed to a world of high-level X's, they tend to no longer want to tolerate lower-level X's.

- Each of the X's an individual uses affects the whole. If one person exhibits/practices higher level X's then our school gets better, our students adopt more of a "psychology of success," and when others of us try to use higher level 1-style practices in our classes, they work more efficiently. When one of us uses lower functioning practices (see those that promote a "psychology of failure") then it makes all of our jobs more difficult and our school less functional.

- R's are the leading indicators of X's, and X's are leading indicators of O/outcomes. Therefore, be patient and focus on the process and trust that the results will follow.

- The quote from MLK (listed at the beginning of the chapter) accurately describes the results of our research into school improvement (Shindler et al, 2018). The full quote is "In the final analysis, means and ends must cohere because the end is preexistent in the means, and, ultimately, destructive means cannot bring about constructive ends." Translated into the terminology of this book – *Lower-level X's will never get you higher level O/outcomes* (no matter how expertly we use them).

## Co-requisites for Changing X's: Trust, Vision, and a Firm Understanding of the Roadmap

The process of change will, by its nature, elicit insecurity, suspicion, rationalization, fear, comparison, mistrust, and frustration. Change is possible, but the necessary conditions must be in place, or it is unlikely. Just providing what we judge to be valuable information or quality training in a professional development workshop, rarely translates into sustained improved practice. If we expect improvement without considering all the other factors needed to be present for X's to change, we will be disappointed. Recalling the discussions in the previous three chapters, we might reflect on how trust, vision, and a firm understanding of the roadmap apply to the process of instructional leadership and improving the X's at the school.

**Trust:** What most of us learn rather quickly when we enter the field of K-12 education is that, in the average school, communication is usually indirect, and resistance takes on a passive form. Few openly question ideas which make them uncomfortable, or they see as problematic. But when people leave the public context and reconnect in private, the honest sharing begins. One reason for this is that schools have not been historically structured to be empowering places, and teachers learn not to trust. Too often they feel worried – that the new program this year won't be replaced by another next year, the leader will not lose the optimism reflected in the opening day speech as time goes on, or that the system is designed to fully consider their needs and support them.

Developing trust in a 1-Paradigm empowering cultural reality will mean working through some trust issues. We can put ourselves in the shoes of those we are tasked to lead and ask "Why should I trust you (me)? And "Why should I trust changing my X's will be a good thing for me (them)?" Our earlier discussion on trust (Chapter six) should be a helpful place to start. But simply asking ourselves what we would need to risk changing can be a useful source of insight. Most educators need a sense of reliability from leadership and the process generally, as well as a sense of safety to take chances and make mistakes.

**Vision:** Recall the story of the fox and the hounds in the last chapter. If the school's vision is "your vision," others may not appreciate it, value it, or understand it. But if it is "our vision – in the metaphor, we have all seen the fox (i.e., the higher location on the roadmap), we will approach reflecting upon and improving our practices/X's with a more willing attitude. Trust, vision, and motivation will always be interdependent. That being said, everyone is unique, and every situation is unique. Depending on where we are on the roadmap, we may need to support the school's growth process with more or less pushing and/or pulling. Growing the "we," the "meta," and the shared vision at the school, unit, classroom, unit, team, department, PLC, SLC, will always be vital to the cause.

**Effectiveness Roadmap**. "Where would you locate that practice/X on the school effectiveness roadmap?" This question can be asked in a thousand forms, by any member of the school community – leaders, teachers, staff, students, parents, consultants, etc. This question represents a commitment to being an active member of a professional learning community, the rejection of the status quo, and a sign that the community has the will to be better and the courage to grow. It represents a disposition Fullan and Quinn (2016) refer to as internal accountability - one of the qualities characterized as the "right drivers." This self-reflective orientation implies both internal locus of control as well as a growth orientation. It assumes our relationships are built on love and are not so fragile that we would be threatened by a challenging question from someone who cares about us. This question needs to asked with respect (for each individual as well as the school as a community) from those with the most power, with the goal of having it be a commonly accepted practice in all realms of the school. When we hear students holding their peers and teacher to high standards, we know we have come a long way on our growth journey.

Examples of this question in other forms:

- Are you being the best version of yourself?
- How is that practice working for you?
- What outcomes would you predict that X will lead in the long-run?
- Would you call that X more of a psychology of success (POS) or psychology of failure (POF) promoting practice?
- What evidence do you see that this X is moving your class to the next level?

---

**Exercise 8.1:** Consider engaging teachers and staff in an exercise in which they take the question "Where would you locate that practice/X on the school effectiveness roadmap?" and reflect upon how to apply it to their work within their professional learning communities. We might ask the teachers and staff to generate both 1) a few different ways of saying it that they feel are respectful and they themselves would respond to positively, and 2) what else needs to be included in the interaction to help support the growth and reflection process and honor feelings and relationships.

---

# Growth "Pathway" on the School Effectiveness Roadmap

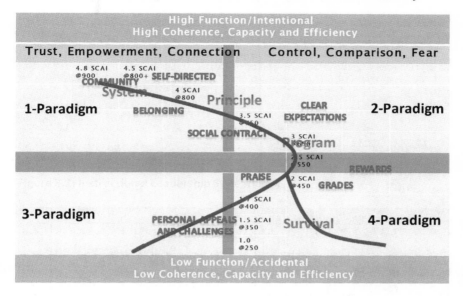

Cultivating the qualities of trust, vision, and an operational understanding of the roadmap will encourage an environment which is conducive to progress. Moreover, efforts to promote these qualities will also enhance efforts in the area of instructional leadership. If we are not, as yet, where we would like to be with one of the three, we will not want to wait on moving forward to improve the instruction at the school. In the world of sports, we see that while interpersonal trust and liking breeds winning, winning also breeds interpersonal trust and liking. Therefore, applying that phenomenon to our school, we might consider the experience of attaining positive results and of being in a trusting and harmonious condition as co-requisites.

In the following sections we will examine four areas where leadership is critical to the growth related to the X's at the school.

1. Instructional leadership and improving the quality of pedagogical practices

2. Applied organization and policy actions

3. Manifested culture, routines, and rituals

4. Display of dispositions and emotional climate

As you explore each area, the need to be grounded in your vision and the big picture will be clear. Yet, be sure to be attentive to the micro level as well. Sometimes your macro success comes largely from the care you take with the little things. And remember every time you personally make the choice to engage in a high quality/1-Paradigm leadership act, your school has just moved an increment up the roadmap.

## Instructional Leadership

If our school improvement process were a vehicle, the vision cultivation process at the school could be considered the steering wheel, and instructional leadership would be the engine. All parts of our vehicle will need to work in concert, but the effort will have no power without quality instructional leadership. Over time, we want the nature of the instructional leadership to be defined increasingly by personal growth by way of self-reflection. Ultimately, we want to function as a collective professional learning community – a teacher power school. But assuming this reality prematurely can lead to a location in the 3-Paradigm quadrant of the roadmap and everything that entails. Therefore, we need to ground ourselves firmly in the realities and needs of our current context, and the forms of instructional leadership supports they imply, with our eyes set clearly on our desired destination.

In order to create a solid foundation in the qualities of the vertical axis of the effectiveness roadmap, first we need to ground all efforts to improve X's in the big picture intention/R's. Second, we need to build capacity – that means putting functional, empowering, and connecting structures in place, and giving more ownership and decision making to those who are in the best situation to do so. Third, committing to placing a high value on coherence – that means leaders ask themselves and others if policies, programs, and common practices are congruent with one another and consistent with the vision. Finally, can we make the growth and change process as streamlined and efficient as possible? Burn out is a real threat to the success of the effort. There is such a thing as too much of a good thing.

# Our Leadership Style

Being an effective instructional leader will mean embracing the R's and X's of the location on the roadmap we are seeking to achieve. Along with the question, "What do I need to do?" We also need to periodically ask, "How do I need to grow?" As you examine Figure 8.2 and the rest of this chapter, you might ask yourself, "If my school is going to reach the destination we desire, how will I need to change and grow to be the leader who will facilitate the journey?" and "What do I need to learn to do, and what do I need to stop doing?"

Figure 8.2: Instructional Leadership Style Matrix

| | Empowerment – Connection | Control - Comparison |
|---|---|---|
| **High Function – High Capacity - Intentional** | **1- Paradigm – Empowering**<br><br>**Narrative** – Every day we are moving up the roadmap to a more solid manifestation of the 1-Paradigm and we are building the capacity through the development of the strengths and efforts of our community.<br><br>**Hearts and Minds** – We build community and team structures, high trust levels are intentionally cultivated, growth is the goal for both teachers and students, and we see knowledge as a continuous construction.<br><br>**Skills** – Developing 1-Style classrooms, Project-Based Learning, Inquiry, active engagement of PLC structure, and POS promoting practices in all areas of the school.<br><br>**Policy and Organization** – Policy is regularly re-aligned and coherent with the evolving school vision to move the school forward. Structures are put in place to build capacity and support a teacher-powered school, reinforce commitments, and to meet students' fullest potential. | **2-Paradigm – Managing**<br><br>**Narrative** – Every day we are becoming more skilled at the implementing the programs and professional development we have chosen, and we have systems in place to make sure our efforts are consistent and evidence-based.<br><br>**Hearts and Minds** – We build an efficient school that feels sane and solid, we take pride in our school and are committed to all students.<br><br>**Skills** – Developing 2-Style Classrooms, Direct Instruction, implementing programs with fidelity, and using data to make decisions.<br><br>**Policy and Organization** – Policy is in place to create function and order and to keep everyone on track. Structures support function and consistency. |
| **Low Function – Low Capacity - Accidental** | **3- Paradigm – Enabling**<br><br>**Narrative** – We are all engaged each day in practices that are for students and take into consideration who they are. Good teaching is difficult to define.<br><br>**Hearts and Minds** – We really care about our students. We have pride in our school.<br><br>**Skills** – Uneven application of teaching skills, common result is characterized by good intentions which translate into little and/or inconsistent student growth and/or positive climate.<br><br>**Policy and Organization** – Few policies are in place. The idea that policies are needed is subtly resisted. Policies adopted are treated as suggestions by most. | **4-Paradigm – Coercing**<br><br>**Narrative** – I will be making sure everyone implements the programs with fidelity like those whom I favor.<br><br>**Hearts and Minds** – One day the morale at the school will be better when everyone finally starts doing what he/she is supposed to do.<br><br>**Skills** – Taking control of your classroom, Direct Instruction, focus on directly improving test scores, and whatever works to keep students on task.<br><br>**Policy and Organization** – Policies are created in response to an existing problem area and are intended to limit liability to risk. Policies are defined by mistrust. |

A critical factor in our success will be the extent to which we embrace our role as a true leader and coach, as compared to simply a manager, evaluator, coordinator, chair, or administrator. Embrace the importance of individual and collective growth as the key to why our school will improve. Like the successful athletic coach, theatrical director, or business leader, we need to know what "good" looks, feels, and sounds like and be systematic about how we lead others to higher quality performance. As we become experts in knowing which X's are consistent or not consistent with our desired destination, we grow in the capacity to be effective instructional leaders. Appendix 8.1 outlines the qualities of classrooms in each of the 4 paradigm quadrants. The book *Transformative Classroom Management* (Shindler, 2009) provides a practical explanation of the different paradigms and explains how to create the 1-Paradigm classroom in detail. We will also examine practice more specifically in Chapters 11-13. In many ways, the degree to which colleagues will listen to and respect us will be strongly related to our interest level in understanding the intricacies of their jobs.

**Attitude toward working with Students with difficult homelives**. Assuming the same students; represented are four different approaches.

| | |
|---|---|
| **1–Paradigm** We need to stick with our processes and keep our eyes on where we are going, so the students learn to trust a 1 Paradigm class. | **2–Paradigm** We need to use extrinsic reinforcements and comparisons, so students learn how to stay on task to learn. |
| **3–Paradigm** There is not a lot we can change, so it is best we just give students independent work and let them do the best they can. | **4–Paradigm** Since many students are used to being talked to roughly, shamed, and punished, we will need to do that if we are to get results. |

## #1 Roadblock to Improved X's – The Force of Mediocrity and Gravity Toward the Mean

Before we explore a series of instructional leadership strategies for moving the X's to higher levels, we need to examine the primary roadblock or antagonistic force discouraging our efforts. This force is the quality of mediocrity and the tendency for things to find their way back to the status quo.

We have assessed the climate and function level of over 500 schools to date. The most common profile is the low 2 bordering on the 4-Paradigm location on the roadmap. The reason that this location is so common is because it does not take much courage or vision to exist there. Change starts with an internal and courageous personal "Yes" to something better. If you and the others at the school do not feel compelled to create an empowered 1-Paradigm school, it is likely not going to happen. If you are fine with mostly "doing whatever works" (i.e., making an internal R/agreement that mediocrity is acceptable) and 2-Paradigm teacher-centered teaching, you will most likely land at that location as time goes by.

---

**Reflection 8.a:** Check in on where you are today when it comes to what you love to see and hate to see in a classroom. What does great instruction look like to you? When you see a 2-Style teacher-centered class, do you a) admire the control and order or b) recognize the limitations to the students' potential and lack of empowerment? Do you love the idea of a self-motivated learner, or are you fine seeing compliant students?

---

As much as possible, we will want to pull the process toward the positive vision of "better." In any situation there will be those who are attached to dysfunctional X's and in the words of Don Miguel Ruiz (1997), an inspirational author, have made a lot of "agreements with mediocrity." Our agreements with mediocrity are places where our best selves know that we could do better, but we rationalize to ourselves and others why we need to maintain the dysfunctional pattern. When someone suggests a better set of X's are possible, the agreements with mediocrity in the room hear criticism of who they are and what they do currently, and their egos experience it as an attack.

Therefore, when you sense the desire of others to pull things back down to "what works for me," the status quo, and what is necessary in the "real world" – and all the other rationalizations for mediocrity, you will need to activate your most effective inner resources and skills and work with it constructively. You will need to recognize that person or group for who they are - fearful and insecure and probably at least a little ashamed, even as they may sound outwardly confident and be projecting that you and your ideas are the problem.

Expect resistance. But also appreciate that moving to a higher level on the roadmap is what each person's best self ultimately desires. Therefore, in various forms and contexts our respectful but unapologetic message is - we validate their feelings, understand that change is difficult, and will support their growth. Moreover, we should communicate that the school is moving on a path to better (for their good and good of all members of the school community), and the expectation is that each teacher embraces growth and excellence. That person's best selves will be inspired by this message. As time goes on, those best selves will patiently and compassionately need to help their agreements with mediocrity stop running the show.

## Guiding our X's with Higher Level R's and Guiding Questions

One of our most important jobs as an instructional leader is to help practitioners elevate the R's they use to make decisions about their X's. Higher level R's will translate into more effective X's. When we analyze our thinking, we will recognize that, to a great extent, it is driven by guiding internal questions. Being more intentional about the quality of internal questions we are asking (which direct our thinking and choices which become our actions) is very useful. If we stop at any point in time and ask a few questions, the answers will tell us a great deal.

- Are the questions I am asking myself pulling me up to the higher levels of perception (who I want to be, and what principles I want to live by)?
- Are they bringing my down to lower levels of thinking (getting by, coping, and survival)?
- Are my questions playing into my ego's desire to be a victim and see life as happening to me, or are they empowering me to transcend my circumstances?

When we ask different questions, we solve different problems, make different choices, take different actions, and ultimately produce significantly different outcomes. That which we place attention upon will grow. Our intentions direct our attention.

Now, let's explore the thinking of a teacher with a high functioning classroom. In this classroom, the teacher's X's are a result of a vision and a picture of a quality environment. High functioning classrooms are driven by questions related to what actions need to be taken to create that high functioning picture such as, "How is this practice going to promote more self-responsibility or community?", or "What are the skills required to do effective inquiry, or self-evaluation of one's learning, etc.)?" In other words, higher forms of thinking, such as quality principles and systems are operating to raise the level of the X's. If the answer to those questions is affirmative then the practice is assessed as useful to continue, if the answer is negative the practice is judged to be in need of change or to discarded.

For example, A teacher wants cooperative learning to be fundamental to her/his class and, at the start of the year, engages the class in a cooperative activity. In a possible scenario, the teacher attempts to build the necessary teamwork skills at the same time as trying to have the class process some new content. The outcome is that the results are mixed at best. Some students get the idea of cooperative group skills and collaboration while others were too focused on the content to internalize the cooperative skills involved. So, what is the take-away? If we are asking ourselves 1-Paradigm classroom R level questions, we might ask, "Is this a worthy practice to pursue?" "Will it get better with more skill development?" "Do I need to focus on simpler content for a couple of iterations of the process before I use such challenging content?" Given our answers to these questions, our conclusion may be that we need build skills within a new process before applying it to new content. We may determine it would be useful to add ongoing self-reflection and debriefing activities to help facilitate the cooperative learning skill development process.

In contrast, in the low functioning classroom, the mindset for selecting X's is related to whether the X "works" or not. That may sound rather sensible. However, the R's for what works are usually something related to cleverness, trying to control others and convenience for the teacher – reflecting lower quality thinking. The "what works" R's are essentially unrelated to the creation of high-quality results, or a psychology of success, so it does not promote much quality control for making choices about the best X's. Often teachers use the terms "well it works" to refer to something that they have gotten used to doing or is convenient. The outcomes that this X produces do not reflect high quality, but somehow this teacher has created a mental justification (i.e., probably an unconscious or ill-conceived R/agreement with mediocrity) which helps them feel okay about doing something that the evidence says is not getting them great results.

A common guiding question in a low or middle functioning class would be "Are my students on task and doing what I want them to do?" That sounds practical, but the answer to that question can lead virtually anywhere. Often it leads to the next even lower quality thought question, "What can I do to my students to make they behave?" Usually answers to this question lead to direct interventions that miss the point, deal with symptoms, apply cleverness instead of intelligence, and get long-term results which lead down the roadmap. Examples of these kinds of interventions would include the use of colored card charts, student comparisons, busy work, negative recognitions, and the regular expressions of disappointment to name a few. The evidence shows these strategies create an ever more dysfunctional climate and a greater perceived need for more of the dysfunctional strategy/X. Like extrinsic rewards, the apparent cure is the problem, and so in this vicious (addiction to mediocrity) cycle more of the problem is needed to create what appears to be desired results such as acceptable levels of control. Sometimes a lot of effective X's are mixed in with these techniques, so it is difficult to recognize that they are making the teacher's job more difficult and moving the O's down the function pathway.

In fact, what is taking place in most classrooms is characterized by both X's which are leading the results down and X's which are leading the results up the pathway. This is why a sound set of R's is required and a corresponding set of high quality promoting guiding questions is needed to discern the quality of any potential X. If we do not make intentional use of high-quality R's, old habits, the grind of the job, and mental gravity will tend to default to the use of lower-level guiding questions like "is this working?"

## Building Growth Capacity and Structures to Encourage Self-Improvement

Moving up the roadmap means building ever more effective structural capacity to make growth, self-improvement, and collaboration more normal and natural. In the 1-Paradigm location, the working assumption is that we have an innate desire to be excellent, grow, and contribute to something larger than ourselves. Having this goal alone will guide us to sensible thinking toward this target. But this section offers a few ideas for building such capacity.

### Personal Goal setting

In a very tangible sense, we need to move together as a school on our growth journey. Our vision, our target X's, and our collective success mindset will be the tide to raise all boats. We also need to create a mechanism for all members of the school community, administrators, teachers, and staff to engage in empowered individual self-improvement. A powerful tool to promote the capacity and growth trajectory within the process is to have everyone set personal improvement goals each year. Making the process of goal setting formal implies that, as a school, we place growth and an internal locus of control as priority R's for ourselves (just like we do for our students).

When engaging the process of individual faculty and staff goal setting, here are a few suggestions to consider:

- The goal setting process needs to be engaged sincerely. If it is seen as a formality, then it will have limited benefit and indication issues with buy-in to the vision.

- Goals should be challenging – encourage the focus to be on the process not the outcome. Include an emphasis on the amount of care, effort, and sincerity one puts into creating their picture of success. We want them to reach for excellence, so will need to take the element of failure out of the equation.
- An effective goal setting format produces the best results (See example below). The focus should be on solving real problems, stating them in present tense, and making them concrete.
- Identify a number of categories for goals reflecting a range of priorities at the school. For example:
  - Classroom management
  - Motivation or climate
  - Instructional methods and strategies
  - Content area or technological expertise development,
  - Special Needs and or ELL student success
  - Personal or professional growth and development
- Have teachers set goals for two time points in the year. First point, about 6 weeks into the year with a focus on procedures and initial implementation of structures. Second point, Spring when there will be more evidence that our efforts have shown results.
- Make the goals operational – i.e., specific, measurable, assessable, assign responsibility and have a timeline. We suggest the following process – for each goal:
  - State it in an effective goal setting format.
  - Define the starting point, the problem being addressed, or the current intermediate location of your progress.
  - Potential roadblocks and hurdles.
  - How you plan to reach your goal – specific practical steps and strategies that imply actions over time (not lists of techniques).

- Indicators you will have met your goal – as many forms of evidence as possible.
- Why this goal is a priority focus area for you at this time.
- What supports you will need or would request from the school.
- (Optional – note the area of state teacher standards for as many of the goals as possible).

Each year, each member of the school community should have a formal meeting to discuss 1) his/her assessment of their success in relation to their goals for that year (spring is best), and 2) early Ideas for goals for the coming year (summer or fall is best).

**Field Example:** One very effective leader in her second year of a turn-around effort had all the teachers in her school create goals. She met with each teacher to review their goals and offer support and ideas. One of the teachers brought to the meeting goals that reflected a minimal interest in self-growth. The principal politely asked the teacher to think about a more meaningful set of goals and rescheduled a meeting for 2 weeks in the future to discuss the new goals.

**Reflection 8.b:** What would you have done upon seeing the teacher's initial set of insincerely produced goals?

What message did this leader send by being polite, but firm in her requirement for a sincere effort?

## Leadership as Coaching and Growth Encouragement

The role of leader means we need to accept that we need to exhibit a higher level of courage and integrity when it comes to working with others. We are not just leading a process, we are leading people. Therefore, clarifying our own references and confronting our fears and hesitancies will be essential.

What principles/R's are we using when we interact person to person? Are we taking on the mantle of "Servant Leader?" Do we see ourselves as a coach? In any case, 1-Paradigm results will require us to embody our role as the facilitator of something larger than ourselves. Therefore, we need to be able to authentically believe and communicate that we are performing our work in the service of the collective's journey and not our own needs for power, compliance, or personal gain. Keeping that reference in mind will go a long way to quiet the voices inside us leading to fear of confrontation, unworthiness, defensiveness, and other ways we limit our potential effectiveness.

A useful lens for thinking about building emotional capital among the members of any collective is the concept of 'social frames" (Haralambos, 1991). These are unspoken, but assumed, implicitly operating two-way agreements that help structure any social body. For teachers in the classroom, remaining aware of one's role in the unspoken adult-child agreements is critical for helping students feel solid, secure, and motivated (Shindler, 2009). At the institutional level, when we take on the role of leader, we also step into a similar dynamic.

There are a series of unspoken social frames defining a sense of function, solidness, and rightness for adults (See Figure 8.3). The nature of social frames is that they work as a two-way street, each side will implicitly or explicitly expect to receive a response from the other party when they perceive they have demonstrated their side of the unspoken agreement. There are three of these frames which are most pertinent to our work as change leader. First, when a member of the school community makes a *contribution* to the cause, they expect some *gratitude* from those in the role of leader. Second, when a member is making a substantive *effort*, they expect *recognition*. Third, when a member has shown a significant level of *commitment*, they expect to be given more *responsibility and freedom*. Conversely, when these qualities have not been demonstrated by a member of the collective, the other members of the team might expect the corresponding response would logically reflect less of the positive reaction. Similar to our students, we can assume the adults in the school are very sensitive to what they perceive as unfairness and logical inconsistency. Figure 8.3 outlines the three social frames and explores the likely result in the case each were violated.

Figure 8.3 Adult-Adult Leader Social Frames

| Member Action or Attitude | Leader Response/ Disposition | Byproducts of Disequilibrium |
|---|---|---|
| Contribution | Gratitude/ Appreciation | If one feels as if they are making a contribution, but not being appreciated by the leader, they are likely to reduce their motivation to contribute and/or feel conflicted when they feel inspired to share. |
| Effort | Recognition/ Reward | If one feels as if they are making a substantive effort and the leader is dismissive, they may be disinclined to maintain their high level of effort or shift their effort into other venues. |
| Commitment | Responsibility/ Freedom | If one shows commitment and is not given more freedom, it implies that the system is not fair or respectful. Giving freedom to those who have not shown the commitment reflects a betrayal of the social contract to the other members. |

Being deliberate about building these frames will be essential to our effort to move the school upward. We want the members of the school community to feel like they can express their best selves, share their gifts, and know they are working in an environment defined by appreciation and love. Our goal should be to grow each of these qualities within the individuals and the collective continuously. As you likely recognize, building these qualities is consistent with all of the other efforts that we will want to make as we facilitate the journey of the school up the roadmap. Looking for ways to trust and give away power and be excited about the contributions of others should become the normal condition.

**Reflection 8.c**: When have you been in a situation where one of these frames was not operating congruently? How did you feel? What did you do to compensate for how you felt?

## #2 Roadblock – Unfair Conditions

Just as we will need to cultivate the implicit collective experience of functional social frames, we will also need to facilitate a sense of fairness and a dynamic balance within the relationship between increased responsibility and the requisite increased support. Our movement up the roadmap will involve all members of the community raising their games. The active intention on behalf of those in leadership roles is to encourage transferring increased levels of power, agency, and trust as much as possible/earned. This means all administration, coordinators, teacher leaders, directors, chairs, department heads, directors finding ways to empower those in their charge, and everyone finding ways to empower the students. But empowerment often means more work, more creative and intentional teaching, and more time spent collaborating, planning, and in professional development. Therefore, to balance out the equation and encourage the desirable experience of being given more responsibility, leaders, especially those in the role of administrator need to support the practical realities associated with what it takes for teachers to accommodate and sustain a higher level of performance. These supports will likely include:

- Smallest class sizes possible.
- Optimal number of adults in the classroom.
- Sufficient time for those adults to plan and fulfill their potential as a professional learning community.

- Special Education teachers in adequate numbers (and in the classroom if the commitment of the school is to inclusion, and/or with adequate ratios in pull out situations).

- Having an adequate number of counselors and mental health support staff who have enough time to work with the social and emotional, community building, personal crisis, and school climate issues of the school as well as other duties such as scheduling or case management.

- A discipline system that encourages teachers to develop the skills to solve their own classroom issues, but also recognizes that for the good of the whole, students who choose to cross "the line" may, as a last resort, need to be removed or given consequences to encourage them to be accountable for the school's social contract. And leadership supports the teacher when they have acted based on wise, justifiable, and good faith reasoning, consistent with the collectively agreed upon policies.

- Leaders having the backs of teachers and staff who have done their jobs in the face of criticism by parents, public, students, staff, or others.

- Raising funds to pay for support, specialist, and counselor positions, and partnering with agencies which provide extra support personnel for priority initiatives.

## Supportive Personal Interactions

Much of our success facilitating the movement of the collective up the roadmap will be our ability to connect personally with each individual teacher and support her/his distinct growth process. We all need to find our style based on our gifts and personalities. For some of us personal interactions come more naturally, but there are common skill-based/X elements to being successful in our human interactions with others. Some may come more easily, and others may require us to stretch. If we appreciate these skill's value and recognize them as helpful to our overall success, we need to make an effort to make them habitual parts of our job. The following is a list of leadership skills and practices to aspire to when working with others.

- **Be transparent.** Being honest and let others know where you are coming from is essential. So, let your agenda be as clear and open as possible. Honesty breeds more honesty and hidden agendas breed more hidden agendas.

- **Ask don't tell.** In the 1-Paradigm, our job is to encourage a process of reflection and growth. High quality reflection questions give others a chance to take control of their own growth process, and they send a message of respect.

- **It's OK to be straightforward**. Questions are better in most cases, but if there is a direct message needing to be sent, it should be sent without the need to apologize. If the school needs something to happen (i.e., people to be on time, certain words to not be used, responsibilities to be met, etc.) we do not need to either add unhelpful emotion (i.e., enabling or shaming), or any more explanation than is necessary. We can simply provide information to others in the name of the collective.

- **I-Messages**. Owning and sharing our feelings can reduce the need for others to be oppositional or defensive. If we personally are not good with what someone else is doing, we might employ what Thomas Gordon (1974) refers to as I-messages. We can simply state that we want or need something, are not Ok with something, or are having a reaction to something. Here we are speaking for ourselves, trusting the other person will appreciate our experience and consider it respectfully as we would if they shared such a message. Examples include: "I am not OK with everyone focused on their cell phones during meetings, I feel like it is … Would it be OK if we put away all cell phone for the hour? Or "I am feeling like I am trying to be fair, but I feel frustrated, so help me understand what else I can do to help …."

- **Be Generous with "Put-Ups."**. Find places to positively recognize others in public and private. Become an expert in understanding the difference between positive recognitions and personal praise (See Figure 8.4 below). It will be the same both in the classroom, between teacher and student, and between adults. Where one is in the role of encouraging growth, positive recognitions are better in many ways than praise. Where praise says, "I like you because you are doing what I like," positive recognitions say, "I see you are choosing excellence and I want to let you know I see your success in that effort." You may want to give yourself a target for how many put ups you share in a day.

Figure 8.4 Comparison of Positive Recognition vs. Praise with Examples of Each

|  | **Positive Recognitions (Use)** | **Personal Praise (Avoid)** |
|---|---|---|
| **Characteristics** | • Focuses on the actions, effort, and/or choices not the person <br> • About the other's goals <br> • Criterion referenced/quality-focus <br> • Concrete informational <br> • 1-Paradigm practice | • Focus on the person more than action or the effort <br> • About what we liked <br> • Norm Referenced/comparison-focus <br> • General and abstract <br> • 2-Paradigm practice |
| **Examples** | "I am seeing so many of your students …." <br> "It was cool how you stayed with that student and helped them …." <br> "I see so much evidence of student voice on your walls." <br> "You are so expert at …." | "You are one of our best teachers" <br> "I like how you are following our school's policy for …." <br> "Your progress makes me so happy" <br> "You're ___ is better than ___'s" |
| **Effects** | • Encourages intrinsic motivation <br> • Encourages growth mindset <br> • Empowers and creates agency and self-confidence. | • Encourages extrinsic motivation <br> • Encourages fixed-ability mindset <br> • Manipulates and creates dependency and insecurity |

- **Go Door-to-door, Get out there**. Some leaders walk into the room, and everyone stiffens. Others walk in and everyone smiles. Here are ideas to help you be the more charismatic.

  - Come in with a smile and easy energy. Blend in.

  - Have your hands free. Put anything that you were carrying down near the door.

- When possible (and it is not disruptive) get involved in what the students are doing. Ask them about their work or assist them if that is what makes sense.

- Start looking for ways to be curious, encourage students, connect personally with the students and the teacher.

- There is no need to always find things to positively recognize, but when opportunities present themselves find things to positively recognize (evidence of 1-Paradigm teaching or student work) in the moment or later in an email or future conversation.

- Say "goodbye" and "thank you" (even if it is silently) with an affirming smile.

- **Critique face to face.** Try to never share bad news or be personally critical in public or impersonally. We need to share evaluative and corrective feedback face to face when possible. A recent study found that 70% of administrators feared talking to teachers about their performance. It is understandable, but it is a hurdle leaders need to get past. And if we get used to creating and projecting "safe honesty" the potential causes of the common fear should be diminished. This is a great place to practice trusting (rather than fearful) leadership X's, and a big step in our overall movement up the roadmap. Here are some ideas for creating "safe honesty" and making the difficult talks more effective.

  - Start with connection. Send the message you are on the person's side.

  - Lead with positives. End on a hopeful note.

  - Guide the conversation as much as possible with questions, i.e., ask don't tell.

  - Keep the subtext that both of you are part of the team, and the job is for the team to grow and get better every day – i.e., "What is good for students?"

- Listen attentively and acknowledge feelings and perceptions - even victim stories and excuses. But steer things back to what is important now. What will it take to get good results for everyone?
- Listen from a place of gratitude for all this person does each day, the effort they make and the difficulty of the job. And know that their best self longs to be excellent and to experience self-respect.
- Ask how you can be supportive and of service.
- Say "thank you" from your heart and not as a formality or a strategy.

- **Consider the Other Side.** Actions which can seem to make sense to us from our side, can often be experienced negatively for others. We may have a good reason such as expediency, or noble intentions, however, it is important to ask, "What if I was on the other end of that interaction, how would I feel?" Figure 8.E outlines some of the strategies to avoid and better alternatives.

Figure 8.5. Interactive Strategies to Avoid and Better Alternatives

| Strategies to Avoid | Better Alternatives |
| --- | --- |
| Hit and run emails. Where we load up a lot of demands or criticisms and send it without notice. | Let others know you are going to send loaded emails and explain why you are doing it. Or communicate directly. |
| Using superficial and/or manipulative techniques when communicating. Saying one thing with words and another with non-verbal messages. | Be authentic. Express congruence between what are saying and your intention. Share how you feel. |

| Passive aggressiveness. For example, showing false approval in a face-to-face interaction and then later bashing the person or punishing them indirectly. | Be honest. It will be necessary to make distinctions between the person and the words. Honor the person, express solidarity with them, be a friend, empathize, but also let them know you cannot agree with or support what they said or did. |
| --- | --- |

## Structures that Encourage Maximum Capacity - Collaboration, Reflection, Intentional Practice, and a Professional Learning Community

The term *professional learning community* (PLC) is gaining wider use. Becoming a 1-Paradigm institution will require that we embrace this idea in both a practical as well as ideological sense. To encourage higher quality X's, we will need to use multiple means to promote higher level and collectively shared R's. The PLC structure can be a powerful contributor. Moreover, to create the sense of community and team among our faculty and staff the PLC format can encourage meaningful ways to accomplish a valuable quality – team wins. When a group collaborates on a task and feels a sense of success and pride, it bonds in a powerful way. The experience of collective success creates greater incentive and confidence to collaborate on other tasks in the future.

In the research into school change and restructuring the factor that tends to come up as the number one contributor to successful change is *time* – teachers having formal opportunities to learn, collaborate, share, and plan outside their regular planning time (Mujis & Harris, 2003). Without the reflective phase in our work, our efforts become stale and repetitive, and we are set up for burn out. Moving up the roadmap implies building in time for teachers and staff to collaborate.

Recall our discussion of process vs outcome values in chapter seven. Understanding where we are in our progress toward a target product outcome (i.e., suspension rates, or meeting proficiency on a test, etc.) will have some value, but it will not necessarily encourage growth or excellence. Yet, when we have a clear set of *valued processes* that we are attempting to cultivate into our practice (i.e., instructional skills, problems to solve, implementing a high-quality strategy, etc.), we have material we can share, analyze, learn from one another, recognize our growth, and incorporate into our classrooms. Not only does the regular opportunity to share and process our progress toward "better" lead to better, it is hugely satisfying.

Becoming a true "professional learning community," required both a formal structural element as well as being a fundamental part of the nature of the X's in the school. It needs to be in the DNA/R's. Teachers and staff need to embrace being a community of practice and members of a vision-driven team. When that vision has a definable nature, such as becoming a 1-Paradigm location, the work of team is given clarity and focus.

The structural element of being a PLC should promote the capacity for the overall process to function effectively. Some of the practical elements for creating function within the formal PLC sub-unit structure include:

- Select at least one sub-unit for the primary location for collaboration. If you want to foster integration across grade levels, you may want to use grade level as your unit. If you want to promote subject matter continuity as your unit, you may want to use the subject matter or department the unit. Using both can work but select one as the primary.

- PLC meetings are well-planned and have a leader with an agenda and objectives for the meeting. But the

> **Team Wins/Successes**
> Among the most powerful events that can occur at a school for encouraging the movement up the improvement pathway are "team wins." These are times when two or more teachers or students do something collaboratively showing evidence that they have grown in essential skills, understandings and/or awareness. Team wins promote the essence of the 1-Paradigm – connection, mutual trust, and a sense of self-efficacy. Moreover, team wins are intrinsically satisfying in ways that external rewards or praise can never be.

rule is that the highest priority content is processed at some point, so encourage faculty to articulate their concerns as formal agenda items.

- Urge evidence-based thinking. But apply a broad and holistic definition of evidence. In addition to any quantitative data, include informal surveys, student input, teacher observations. As importantly, include the group's consensus evidence of current levels of students' knowledge, skills, and dispositions, especially as they relate to the school's core R's/values (such as the building internal locus of control, a growth orientation and community). In a very real sense, the unit is an action research team, using data to improve its practice. Figure 8.6 represents a potentially useful structure to chart PLC unit values/R's and corresponding evidence/indicators of success related to each value.

- Collaboration is much more impactful if teachers in the same unit can have the same planning period (such as all 6th grade teachers have 5th period PLC meeting, or all 3rd grade teachers have a recess and a special once a week for their PLC meeting).

- Build in substantive time in professional development days to be devoted to planning and innovation, and if applicable applying the ideas from any workshop or presentation.

- Encourage teachers to create interactive presentations for their PLCs.

- Provide substitutes or release time for the use of peer-peer observation. These events should be well-planned and include a pre-conference, post conference, and a defined set of foci. They should be non-evaluative, mutually supportive, and focus on the exchange of quality processes and practices.

Figure 8.6 Example Evidence of Progress toward Our Process Values

| Specific Collectively Agreed up Process Value | Evidence-Based Progress Indicators |
|---|---|
| Students feel empowered and value asking questions | We are holding the line on our strategy to ask them to restate.<br><br>They are asking more clarifying questions before the task.<br><br>We are having to answer fewer procedural questions once activities have begun.<br><br>Etc. |
| Students feel a sense of community and belonging. | We are using less competitive structures in our class.<br><br>Students are less concerned with who they are assigned to work with.<br><br>Students are more attentive to one another when they are sharing.<br><br>Etc. |
| ..... | .... |

Promoting a true professional learning community includes both a clear grounding in the mission, principles and defining practices of the target roadmap location, as well as the continual effort to grow in that mission. Our foundational and ongoing guiding task as a school will be to cultivate the collectively held R - "We are a community of learners taking pride in being innovative and honing our expertise through a process of reflective practice and collaborative examination." Therefore, leadership needs to build in the structural capacity making those ingredients likely. When the everyday normal X's at the school include teachers striving to achieve the goals, they have set for themselves, and trusting that they have a mechanism to innovate and share, we have an empowered faculty. Yet, recalling our discussion of trust earlier, another important piece is to make sure teachers are able to contribute in ways which make the most sense and they have a sense of fairness. We are all in this together. Each improved X by one member improves the whole and conversely, those team members who neglect their responsibilities to the whole undermine the integrity of the social contract and can potentially pull things downward. Therefore, each member of the faculty and PLC sub-unit needs to feel internally responsible to grow and hold one another accountable.

## Working with Teachers at Different Levels of Skill and Disposition

Teachers vary widely in terms of who they are and where they are in their professional journey. They have unique personalities and learning style needs (See Table 7.10 related to learning style differences). They have different intentions for what they are trying to create in their classrooms (See Appendix 8.1 – teaching style matrix). Depending on where they went to school or have worked previously, educators will have a wide range of conceptions of "school." Yet, given everything, our job is to encourage a growth culture. We need to provide opportunities for collective and individual learning for all of those we are asked to support, so that each educator meets their full potential.

We know from decades of research into teacher development and situational leadership (Hershey & Blanchard, 1996) when it comes to instructional coaching, we need to consider where each educator is presently and adjust our leadership style based on his/her levels of 1) commitment and effort, and 2) knowledge and skills. Table 8.7 outlines a range of levels (A-F) for where any teacher at any given time could be classified on those two continua.

Caution: If we feel solid in our belief that all humans have equal value and no one is inherently better than anyone else, we will not confuse our task here. The intention of classifying levels is to provide a lens to help educators become more effective. We want all teachers to reach their full potential and be excellent. Therefore, it should not be used as a taxonomy for judging other's worth. There is an AA level teacher within everyone.

Figure 8.7 Descriptions of 5 Levels of Commitment/R's and Skills/X's

| | Commitment/ Effort related R's | Skills/ Knowledge related X's |
|---|---|---|
| A Level Exemplar | C-R:A – Committed to creating a high functioning, student-centered 1-Style classroom community, and being a contributing teammate and leader in the school. | S-X:A – Confident in the use of 1-Style classroom practices, cooperative and project-based learning, inquiry. Can explain what they do as well as how and why they do it. |
| B Level Contributor | C-R:B – Motivated to be a good teacher and be part of the solution. | S-X:B – Has facility with lots of sound practices which engage students and promote real learnings and a positive classroom. |
| C Level Under the radar | C-R:C – Open to ideas for improvement. Congenial with students and the other members of the faculty. | S-X:C – Uses many strategies that "work" in some reasonable sense. Keeps students engaged. |
| D Level Limiting Movement Up | C-R:D – Set in their not very effective ways. Sees students as the cause of their problems. Prefer to work on their own. | S-X:D – Uses a lot of ineffective, reactive, or randomly related strategies which occasionally produce some learning or order, including many 3 and 4-Style practices. |
| E Level Red Flag | C-R:E – Resistant to change. Low self-awareness. Stuck in victim mode. | S-X:E – Most practices are an attempt to get through the day and cope or react to external issues. Mostly 4-Style or 3-Style practices. |

C-R:A = Disposition Reference Level A, S-X:B = Skill Practice Level B, etc.

We may be in a school with mostly A and B level teachers, or one where they are mostly C and D. We start from where we are, and where they are. Just like our teachers, what we can do today will likely be different based on with whom we are working, but the basic roadmap and the pathway will be the same. We are just on different places on the pathway. Our goal is always moving up: individually and collectively.

Table 8.8 Differential Leadership Needs for Teachers at Different Levels of Commitment/R and Skill/X

| | Higher Commitment and Effort<br><br>(C-R: A's and B's) | Lower Commitment and Effort<br><br>(C-R: C's, D's, and E's) |
|---|---|---|
| **Higher Skills and Knowledge X's**<br><br>(S-X: A's and B's) | ✓ Trust and Responsibility<br>✓ A chance to share what they do and coach others – teacher leadership roles.<br>✓ Encouraged to take risks and stretch.<br>✓ Seek out new initiatives to bring to the school.<br>✓ Enlist this group in data analysis and change efforts. | ✓ Sincere use of the goal setting process.<br>✓ A structure to share skill expertise.<br>✓ Sell them on the vision. |
| **Lower Skill and Knowledge X's**<br><br>(S-X: C's, D's, and E's) | ✓ Information<br>✓ Access to training<br>✓ Focus on growth and progress<br>✓ A mentor teacher<br>✓ Opportunities to observe in high-functioning classrooms | ✓ An individualized improvement plan, including goals and resources<br>✓ A mentor teacher<br>✓ A few practical strategies at a time to focus upon with support.<br>✓ Observation in high-functioning classrooms<br>✓ Reasonable plateaus/ stages for growth and self-assessment. |

Participation and accountability to the school-wide social contract and collective policies need to be uniform for all members of the school community. Likewise, messages from those in positions of leadership should encourage the sense of team, the collective journey, and the value of interdependence – we all need each other to achieve our vision. But within the school community, individuals will have their own personal and professional growth requirements. As a leader recognizing those needs and determining the best support for each individual teacher and staff member will lead to the most desirable results and feel the most fair and congruent to those involved.

- If we were to create a short-hand process for providing each teacher the support best suited to his/her growth, we could assign teachers as being either high or low skilled and being either high or low dispositions and effort level. The result is a 2x2 matrix resulting in four combinations as shown in figure 8.8. For each of the four possible combinations, a corresponding set of distinct individualized leadership supports would be implied.

- Teachers who are high (A's and B's) in both commitment and skill levels need to feel valued and have their effort and dedication recognized by leadership. If it is, their efforts are validated and their need to grow and emerge is met. If this need is not met, they may be inclined to reduce their effort levels and find other venues to expand their talents. They also need to be given copious opportunities to share what they know and what they do, both for their personal benefit and for the benefit of everyone else. It is also recommended that your school vision, school leadership, and/or strategic planning committees include a strong representation of teachers who have bought into and can operationalize the 1-Style classroom values/R's and strategies/X's.

- Teachers with a relatively high level of skill and a low level of commitment need a reason to join the cause. This can be accomplished by enlisting them into vital committees or having them share within their PLC. Often it will require a member of the leadership team to sell them on the value and opportunities inherent in being more invested. In some cases, this person has lost faith in the leadership or the school. Reaching out to them and finding out how they could have their faith renewed is often useful.

- Teachers with a relatively low level of skill and a high level of commitment need resources for growth. They should be given a mentor who can model the kinds of practices that define the school's desired effectiveness roadmap destination. It is better to have the same 1-Paradigm mentor for all of these teachers than to assume that any experienced teacher will be an effective mentor/model. Provide this teacher with written resources that explain the kind of pedagogy that characterizes the target. Send them to trainings related to high quality practices. Ask this teacher what would help them to grow in confidence with 1-Paradigm teaching.

- Teachers who currently demonstrate relatively low levels of both skill and commitment will benefit from all the school-wide growth structures (i.e., goal setting, professional development, PLC structure, etc.) but will require an additional level of support as well. It will be advisable to provide these teachers a devoted mentor, and/or instructional leader. Advice that is broad and general will likely be ineffective. When working with the low D/low S profile we will want to see our job as "teacher building." That means we want to operationalize both the "what to do" and "why we do it" part of the job. Scheduling opportunities for these teachers to observe high performing teachers will be valuable, but the process should include as much as possible 1) an explanation by the mentor teacher what she/he was intending and why, and 2) the opportunity for the emerging teacher to ask questions about what she/he observed. Things need to be broken down so the improvement process can be engaged in pieces, stages, and steps and then brought back to the big picture such as moving up on the roadmap, creating more POS, and/or building toward a project-based classroom. Change for the teachers in this quadrant will represent a challenge for the school community. Letting go of well-worn agreements with mediocrity/R's and the ineffective habits/X's will take time.

**From Chapter 7: Why Do We Change our R's and X's**

- Because the new R makes so more sense.

- Because I have seen it work.

- Because I want to be a team player and part of the cause.

- Because people I trust are including and encouraging me.

- Because I have new information and/or conditions have changed.

- Because I have to change, so I can avoid something undesirable.

- Because something inside (instinct, intuition, inner voice, conscience, sense of purpose, etc.) is telling me that it is intrinsically right.

Reasons and paths to improving X's will vary with each individual. Recall our list from Chapter seven related to the reasons that people change. Insights and revelations can come in all sorts of forms. In many cases just trying something new can lead to liking a practice that we did not believe would work. So, we should trust that humans will eventually come to appreciate better for both the good of others as well as their own job satisfaction. Over time, when we are able to make our vision/roadmap destination concrete, operational and attractive, we should feel the movement and buy-in.

As discussed in the previous chapter, it is vital that we encourage trust in our process values and evolve a deeper understanding of what leading and teaching look like at our desired destination. We might use the reflective lens, "is what I am doing consistent with 1) who I want to be, 2) how I want to teach, and 3) where our school is going." If we have created and disseminated a written list that helps make the progress and growth promoting, versus growth limiting X's, classification process operational and concrete it will be highly useful. It may take the form of our school's "things we do" and "things we don't do," list, or a chart classifying practices that promote a psychology of success and those which undermine it. Figure 8.9 below includes a sample of some of the practices that would fall on either side of our chart.

Figure 8.9 A Sample of X's That Lead Us Either Up or Down the Pathway

| Pedagogy leading us up the function pathway | Pedagogy leading us down the function pathway |
|---|---|
| • Process assessment<br>• Inquiry, project-based learning or direct instruction depending on the target area (matching methods to targets)<br>• Skill building in cooperative learning<br>• Social contracts<br>• Community building activities<br>• Creating conditions for learning<br>• Liberating practices | • Comparison in assessment<br>• Lecture and test<br>• Worksheets without clear intentions<br>• Colored card behavioral charts<br>• Gimmicks<br>• Reward systems<br>• Trying to directly control others with external means.<br>• Domesticating practices |

## Applied Organizational Policy

In a high functioning school, policy is applied as a useful, practical set of rules that are generally agreed upon which help the school reach its goals and is grounded in its guiding vision. When you find your policies taking on a reactive or punitive character they need to be re-examined. It is probably most efficient to consider effective policy within the lens of the vertical axis qualities. Five questions to ask ourselves when creating or evaluating a policy:

1.  Is the policy a reflection of our "meta"/intention and highest quality R's and the roadmap destination we desire?

2.   Is the policy coherent with both your vision and all the other desirable X's including other policies, programs, and practices?

3.   Does the policy address a real problem or just a symptom?

4.   Does the policy encourage the capacity for continued growth in the long-term?

5.   Does evidence suggest that the policy is encouraging the outcomes intended in the near and long-term future?

**1. Vision and Destination Driven**. Do we see our mission in our policy? For example, if our vision implies a value for student empowerment, our policies need to encourage student empowerment. Operationally defining phrases such as "global citizen," "21st century learner," "college-ready," or "student-centered environment," or other indeterminate terms can be necessary.

> *We witnessed a positive example of putting this principle into action a few years ago. A principal of an Inland Empire HS was committed to being a 1-Paradigm school. When it was time to make a policy around gum chewing, he used the mission of the school to develop the policy. The core of the school's mission was for students to be self-responsible (at this school it meant acting like college students). So, he made them a deal: if he saw gum around the school, he would make a "no gum" on campus policy. However, if they exhibited responsibility, reflected in the absence of any gum, no policy would be necessary. As time went on there was no gum being discarded around the school, so the policy remained chew gum responsibly.*

**2. Coherent with Other R's and X's.** Upon closer examination, you may find what most schools realize and that is many of your policies are in conflict. The realization usually goes something like this "we are used to (blank) because it makes sense, but we are supposed to (blank) based on our policy." If the policy is mandated by a district or state and is not optional then work with it as a given as you work toward your own vision. What appears as hypocrisy or insensitivity will quickly dissipate your efforts toward trust and shared values.

> **Reflection 8.d**: Examine the following X's at the school – teacher evaluation and retention system, professional development agenda, discipline system, strategic planning process, student evaluation and assessment practices, and budget allocations. Do they reflect alignment with your school's mission and vision? Are they congruent with one another and your desired destination?

**3. Real Problem or Symptom**. Solving real problems is fundamentally related to a process of evaluating the operating R's within the problem context and then examining how well the currently used X's are working to meet the needs of the situation. Solving real problems is almost always about changing what we do. But trying to solve symptoms with a policy usually results in an ineffective policy that causes a whole new set of unintended problems.

> *One example: Adopting a no-suspension policy is well intended but can exacerbate and compound the discipline issues it was intended to solve. Another example: The principal who is unhappy with how some teachers were getting to school late, so implemented a policy where all teachers needed to clock in and out whenever they left the building. The R sent was that teachers were not professionals and could not be trusted. The pathway location of the school dropped down a notch, but fewer teachers were late. Would you judge it was worth it?* In the next chapter we will explore more fully the problems with solving symptoms as opposed to the real problems

**4. Does the Policy Build Capacity?** Many policies and X's can "work" in the short-term and effect the movement of a lower performing school up the roadmap to the middle location. In many cases, these X's have a limiting effect on the growth potential of the school, its staff, and its students. The X's which are encouraged in our discipline system are especially defining to our growth potential. We will explore these "plateau" producing practices when we discuss moving up from the lower locations of the roadmap in Chapters 11 and 12.

**5. Long-Term Results**. A vision-driven school is patient. The logic in the 1-Paradigm is to trust the process and eventually the results will follow. Some policies are simply about efficiency or procedural expediency. All schools require policies for program-level matters. A lack of efficiency is a limitation to the school's movement potential. But it is also possible to overload the system with too many policies. Likewise, when we commit to a more trusting and aspirational policy, it may initially appear to be a failure. However, if a policy is not performing perfecting today, it does not necessarily mean it is not ultimately the best policy. Sometimes a school needs to grow into a new location on the roadmap by way of some messiness and a few growing pains, because the destination is worth the trouble.

*Examples of this patience and faith in a vision are the schools that commit to implementing student-led conferences for the first time. In nearly every case we have observed, initially the practice did not go very well. Many people questioned the policy and typically the school's students were not ready for something requiring this level of self-responsibility. But when the school stayed committed to the practice, within a couple iterations their results were exciting. Students and parents both were much more engaged in the conference process and students developed more self-responsibility for their learning. Dedication to the use of the policy eventually reflected the intended results, enhanced the school, and moved them further up the roadmap. In all cases, the ultimate pay-off required commitment through the early stages.*

**Figure 8.10: Policies Creation Principles on the Function Continuum.**

| Policy leading us up the function pathway | Policy leading us down the function pathway |
|---|---|
| • Policy (primarily) driven by school vision<br>• Process-oriented performance evaluation based on school values.<br>• Systematic teachers' collaboration process<br>• Parent role = resource in school and consumer of information.<br>• Standards = a reflection of an intention curriculum integrity, benchmarking, sequencing process. | • Policy (primarily) driven by external mandates or reactions to negative events.<br>• Product-oriented performance evaluation based on external criteria<br>• Programs implement onto the school<br>• Parent role = outsourcing of discipline (i.e., phone calls intended to appeal to their authority over student).<br>• Standards = adoption is an end in itself, and following standards will, in itself, lead to quality learning. |

## Program Coherence and Purpose

Like policies, determining the fit or efficacy of a program entails asking ourselves a few essential questions:

- Will this program support our movement up the effectiveness roadmap to our desired location? In other words, is the program aligned with our meta/vision?

- Does the program fit with the best X's we are encouraging stakeholders to use currently? In other words, is it congruent and coherent?

- Does the program imply a long-term and plateau-free trajectory? Or is it a quick fix?

- Does the program solve a real problem, meet a fundamental need, and/or support the work of adults in a way that they will appreciate?

- Will the program be good for the high/high teachers as well as everyone else? Or will some teachers have to suppress their best instincts to be able to execute the program?

Programs should be resources to help adult professionals be more effective in ways that encourage excellence and growth. Yes, some teachers for some reasons will be better with a script. But that should not be the rule. The 2-Paradigm is defined by program fidelity. If this is your goal, encouraging the faithful implementation of your chosen programs will be important. If a 1-Paradigm location and school culture is your goal, programs need to be given their place – programs serve the people and their vision. People are the authority, and programs are among their tools.

All programs were created by humans with some expertise as well as some limited understanding. Some are excellent, others are not. All include assumptions about human nature. Some have a 1-Paradigm location end implied within them. Others portend other roadmap destinations. It is helpful to keep in mind that the content in some programs could have a limiting influence on your growth. Moreover, programs that may benefit one teacher may limit another. Program selection is an area where the role of leader requires the mindset of skeptic and protector and requires research, consultation, and discernment.

## Professional Development

When approaching the idea of professional development (PD), as with considering programs, we need to begin with the idea that some PD can help us move upward on the pathway and some can actually lead us down and introduce disruptive or limiting R's and X's. As we become more aware of what is required to move our school up the pathway, we will become increasingly astute in our assessment of the kinds of influences we introduce into our school.

Consistent with being a 1-Paradigm, teacher-powered school will be a substantial reliance on tapping the existing pedagogical capital within the building. Therefore, we should empower our teacher leaders to run the PD in many cases. This sharing may take the form of a teacher demonstrating their use of a practice or reteaching information they learned in an external workshop.

As a professional learning community, the school may embrace a PD "value for the month," i.e., "how I created higher levels of student engagement without bribes." Afterward, during an all-school meeting or within sub-PLC units, faculty can share what they did in their classes to promote the value. Nothing will cement in an X like teaching it! Reading or hearing about an X is good, seeing it is better and teaching it is the best.

Part of a 1-Paradigm culture is to see PD as an ongoing organic process. A high quantity of it should be structured into the PLC or departmental activities. For teachers with the most enthusiasm for growth, PD should be something they own for themselves. Sharing ideas should be promoted as the norm. Focusing activities such as classifying by effect on POS will help support quality control and movement in the right direction on the road-map but taking ownership of one's growth is what excellent professionals do and is expected in a 1-Paradigm culture. The job of leadership is to bring resources to the school and support and compensate the willingness to learn and grow.

## Facilitating Connected R's and X's by How We Evaluate

The faculty evaluation process is a profound opportunity to "walk the walk" with our R's. If we are using an evaluation framework which does not imply a 1-Paradigm form of practice and/or we are not engaging faculty members in self-reflection and real personal goal setting based on individual needs for growth we are missing a golden opportunity.

Optimally, creating criteria for teacher evaluation consistent with our vision, our quality X's list, and the development of a psychology of success, is beneficial. This is a useful place to take advantage of the benefits of a committee.

If we have been mandated by the district to use a certain framework, we may want to find a way to supplement it. The framework developed by Charlotte Danielson (1996) provides a solid alignment with 1-Paradigm R's and X's.

## Selecting Shared R's by Who is Hired

When we have an opportunity to hire a new member of the school community, we will want to be sure that their R's are a good match from the start. Ask yourself throughout the hiring process, "If this person stayed in their job for the rest of their career, would I feel good about this hire?" Given your vision statement, are they able to communicate why the school is a good fit? If you have a "things that we do" and "things we don't do" at the school list, how do they react to it?

Beware of investigating the R's of a potential new hire with broad general terms. Words like positive, best practices, effective, responsible, engagement, rigorous, and others are vague and can mean vastly different things to different people. Listen first to how they talk about their ideal classroom, especially what they would *do* on a typical day? If they have dispositions/R's that are a good fit but have worked in contexts which endorsed X's that do not reflect your target X's, do not necessarily disqualify them — R's trump X's, usually. But they should understand what you are about and what good/desirable/acceptable X's look like at your school. But hire mis-aligned R's at your peril.

## Culture, Routine and Rituals

The culture in a school will be defined by the tens of thousands of little things that people do each day — all of the X's. There is rarely one person powerful or charismatic enough in a school to prescribe or convince everyone to create a high-functioning culture, if it had not previously existed or was not in the DNA of the current teachers. The only way that it will happen is systematically cultivating a clear set of R's that we share and guide us. Routines and rituals have both a symbolic as well as practical function in cultivating our shared R's, by way of shared X's.

Symbolically, our routines and rituals define the "the kinds of things we do here." They tell us what is most important and by extension imply our priorities. Do we intentionally put time into bonding and team building? Most schools wanting to embody the 1-Paradigm create multiple ways of bonding the students into teams and giving teachers ways to build connections. Including planned activities, systems, structures, and rituals which bond members make the statement that connection and community are intentional priorities.

On a practical level, rituals (i.e., assemblies, celebrations, the use of school phrases, theme days, and traditions) create habits and patterns of action. So, as we have discussed with other areas of the change process and how R's and X's are related, just doing something regularly can help us appreciate and like it more because we get more confident in the practice and have something to share with others who engage in the same activity. So just doing 1-Paradigm activities can encourage the growth of 1-Paradigm references. Take the example of the school that is committed to having their students take part in service learning. That starts with an R, but once the students experience the activity (service learning), they see that X as a part of what defines the school – "because I regularly take part in activity X, I appreciate that it reflects an R for the school."

Rituals bring us together and connect our individual R's. They define who we "R" to a great degree. For some faculty, just being given the informal opportunity to bond can promote more community. For other faculties, bonding will require intentional team building. Therefore, efforts to bond faculty and students needs to be systematic and encourage folks out of their comfort zones. Leadership means pushing past comfort to access hearts.

Routines help us with the programmatic level of function. We want to routinize those things which will make our lives less complicated and awkward. Where can we bring in efficiency to promote ease? In the classroom, it pays to ask ourselves the question, "What can I routinize with the students' taking charge and ownership?" This is a question leading to higher level R's and X's. We want efficiency and we want students to get in the habit of and feel the enjoyment of contributing.

**Case Example:** At one higher performing urban public school, team building takes place early and often. There are numerous student team competitions that are ongoing. These activities bring a lively energy to the school day and provide opportunities for that precious "team win" experience for all students and adults. But do consider the necessary features of a "healthy competition." (Shindler, 2009). Essentially, we need to keep the hype high and the rewards insignificant. The point is doing something healthy in teams (making a poster, or plan, or finding the most ___, or having the most participation in ___, etc.) and bonding together (advisory group, period 3 class, graduation class, etc.). The goal of the competition should be fun, belonging, contribution, highlighting multiple gifts, showing spirit, bonding student-student and student-teacher). When the prize is substantive or the competition rewards the most advantaged students, it will undermine the desired goals.

Class meetings and ongoing support groups are a potentially powerful practice. Class meetings should be used for specific purposes, have very defined rules, and be led by someone who is well trained. However, once expertise is developed, even students can run their own meetings. But it is suggested that students are introduced to the idea by way of quick collective decision-making activities in the classroom. Processing feelings, concerns and grievances needs to come after the group has developed a skill base for being able to actively listen, share and act respectfully with the collective good in mind. Those skills will likely require several iterations of the process to cultivate.

The content and quality of faculty meetings are a routine part of the year which must be considered carefully. Consider both the symbolic as well as the practical implications of how these meetings are conducted.

- What is the best use of time for (the busy adults attending) this meeting?
- What does the content of your faculty meeting say about you and what your school is about? Do members get a chance to connect?
- Do members get a chance to share and highlight contributions?

- Are team wins highlighted?
- Are the real problems exposed or are they brushed under the rug?
- Is the content something that could be put online or an email?
- Does it make sense to stay together for the whole meeting, or break into smaller units at some point?
- Will we all leave the meeting with something having been created, or a new idea?

What we find is that schools where the quality of faculty meetings has been rated with a low score on the SCAI, a substantive improvement in the rating will occur simply by setting the intention to guide better meetings. This aspect of our school is one of the easiest to improve, and we send a powerful symbolic message when we do so.

Figure 8.11: Routines and Rituals that will Either Move us Up or Down.

| Routines, Rituals and other X's that lead to a higher functioning school culture | Routines, Rituals and other X's that lead to a higher functioning school culture |
|---|---|
| • Practices promoting students feeling like they are part of the school and have importance.<br>• Norms that are "virtually absolute" related to emotional safety, especially in the area of refraining from verbal abuse and put-downs.<br>• Regular use of conflict resolution instruction, modeling and reflection, and a systematic use of peer mediators.<br>• Practices allowing every student to see a pathway to winning, and a deliberate effort to validate a diverse range of gifts. | • Practices that have the effect of making students feel like there are winners and losers at the school, and some students have an advantage.<br>• Practices isolating students and leave them on their own<br>• Practices promoting competition or comparison.<br>• Lack of clarity and a perception among students that penalties come out of left field or because staff are personally offended. |

## CONCLUSION

Fundamental to our job as leader is facilitation of the process of growth related to the use of X's at the school. The most accurate evidence of our progress on the roadmap will be the actions we observe being demonstrated in and out of the classrooms each day. Embracing the role of instructional leader is essential. Our job will be to support the growth of each member the faculty toward more 1-Paradigm practices and the collective in becoming an ever more effective professional learning community. Moreover, we will want to promote coherence among the practices, policies, and procedures at the school, informed and guided by our vision.

In the next chapter, we will explore the place of O's/outcomes in our process of school improvement and present a model for strategic planning which will support our vison-driven efforts.

## REFERENCES

Blanchard, K., and Hersey P. (1996) Great ideas revisited. *Training & Development*, v.50, n. 1.

Danielson, C. (1996). *Enhancing professional practice: A framework for teaching*. Alexandria, Va: Association for Supervision and Curriculum Development.

Fullan, M & Quinn, J. (2016) *Coherence: The Right drivers in action for schools, districts and systems*. Corwin, Thousand Oaks, CA.

Gordon, T., & Burch, N. (1974). *T.E.T., teacher effectiveness training*. New York: P.H.

Haralambos, M. (1991) *Sociology: Themes and Perspectives*. London: Collins Press.

Mujis, D., and Harris, A. (2003) Teacher Leadership – Improvement Through Empowerment. An Overview of the Literature. *Educational Management & Administration*, v. 31, n. 4, pp. 437-448

Ruiz, M., & Mills, J. (1997). *The four agreements: A practical guide to personal freedom*.

Shindler, John (2009) *Transformative Classroom Management*. San Francisco, CA. Jossey-Bass/Wiley Press.

Shindler, J., Jones, A., Williams, A. (2016) Examining the School Climate – Student Achievement Connection: And Making Sense of Why the First Precedes the Second. *Journal of School Administration Research and Development, Summer 2106 v.1.*n.1. pp7-16.

## Exercise 8.1: Classify Teacher R's and X's

Examine Appendix 8.1 below and the four distinct teaching style classifications represented.

1.  As you reflect on the practices/X's at your school, identify the style that reflects the most common X's used.

2.  Reflect on the R's/references that are associated with each quadrant/style in the figure. Do you recognize the relationship between the R's of each of the teachers at the school and the resultant X's they are using currently?

3.  If you were to have teachers self-assess and classify themselves into one of the four styles, would they assess themselves accurately? Would it encourage insight?

# Appendix 8.1.: Teaching Style Classification

| | Student-Centered | Teacher-Centered |
|---|---|---|
| **Effective/internal LOC** | **1-Paradigm Teacher**<br>• **Facilitator**<br>• Relationship-driven<br>• Goal = self-directed students, community<br>• Motivation = internal/ build sense of self-efficacy<br>• Clear boundaries<br>• Build students' collective responsibility<br>• Answers "why we are doing this?"<br>• Long-term goals: the management may be messy at first, but auto-pilot by end.<br>• Primarily project-based learning, cooperative learning, authentic assessment, criteria-based self-reflection, and peer evaluation.<br>• Psychology of Success (POS) promoting practices/X's<br>• "Our" class | **2-Paradigm Teacher**<br>• **Orchestrator**<br>• Structure-driven<br>• Goal = on task behavior, orderly class<br>• Motivation = external/ positive reinforcement<br>• Clear consequences<br>• Build students' collective efficiency<br>• Answers "what is expected?"<br>• Short-term goals: the management will be in good shape by the second week.<br>• Primarily Direct instruction, tests, papers, homework, worksheets with some cooperative work.<br>• Practice promotes a mixed of POS/POF<br>• "My" Class |
| **Ineffective/external LOC** | **3- Paradigm Teacher**<br>• **Enabler**<br>• Reaction-driven<br>• Goal = keep students happy<br>• Motivation = student interests<br>• Unclear boundaries<br>• Students - increasingly self-centered<br>• Chaotic energy<br>• Goals are vague (management problems happen early and are still happening by end of the term)<br>• Primarily open-ended tasks based on student interests. Subjective quality criteria, independent projects, and project-based learning with little or no quality control.<br>• Verbal support for nurturing POS, but actual environment/X's produces a mix of POS and POF<br>• "The" students | **4- Paradigm Teacher**<br>• **Dominator**<br>• Obedience-driven<br>• Goal = let students know who is boss<br>• Motivation = to avoid punishment<br>• Arbitrary punishments<br>• Students – increasingly immune to coercion<br>• Negative energy<br>• Goals are to break students will (students respond out of fear, but slowly increase hostility and rebellion).<br>• Primarily lecture and test. Worksheets defined by repetitive knowledge-based task, independent work graded by the teacher.<br>• Psychology of Failure promoting practices/X's<br>• "Those" students |

# CHAPTER 9:

## Meaningful Strategic Planning and Effective O/Outcome Data Usage

In this chapter, we will explore the variable we term outcomes or O's and outline a model for engaging meaningful strategic planning. Outcomes range from indicators we can count like scores on tests, to more contextual phenomena such as how people feel, as well as everything else resulting from what we do at our school. O's are, in essence, the "evidence" of the previous seeds we have sown. Since everything at the school is connected, every outcome is evidence of the cumulative references/R's and actions/X's which preceded it.

Figure 7.1/8.1/9.1. Improved X's/Action Represented in the Overall Improvement Sequence

| R | Choices → X | Influence → O |
|---|---|---|
| References | Actions | Outcomes |
| Clear Direction/Vision | • Improved Practices | • **More Human Growth** |
| Shared Values/coherence | • Collective Action/PLC | • **Increased Learning** |
| Principles for judging quality | • Capacity/Systems in place | • **Progress indicators** |
| Care and Commitment | • Good Use of Information | • **Job Satisfaction** |

Periodically engaging in a process of meaningful strategic planning will be vital to supporting the actualization of our school's vision and our journey toward our desired roadmap destination. Effectively situating our outcome values in that work will be essential.

In this chapter, we will explore how outcomes best fit into our school improvement planning and examine two of the most critical considerations. First, we will want to emphasize process related outcome indicators and de-emphasize product measures. Second, in our strategic planning and data-driven decision making, we will want to address the "real problems" and avoid trying to directly solve symptoms.

As one in the role of leader, it is difficult not to place a great deal of attention on the O/Outcomes. Especially those that are quantitative such as test scores and other mandated reporting measures. These are often how we are judged by others to a great degree. Nonetheless, as a leader of a team, we need to emphasize that success will be more likely if we focus on processes rather than products. Therefore, we need to discourage our own and others' human tendency to put too much emphasis on the quantitative and product related outcomes and to focus more attention on the O's that relate to elements of quality as well as the R's and the X's they reflect.

## Outcome Changes will Lag Behind Reference and Practice Changes

It is important to keep in mind that changes in the O's will lag behind the changes in the R's and X's. Therefore, encourage patience within the process and trust in the vision. A quick fix mindset is typically detrimental to our success. A clear target destination and a quality vision will lead to better choices of actions and that will then influence outcomes eventually. Yet we will still have to live through the influence of all the X's of the past working their way through the system. It is just part of the growth process. Most notably, we will see this lagging influence of the past in teachers and students struggling to adjust to higher quality instructional and management practices/X's as they accommodate more aspirational R's.

**Figure 9.2: Principles to Apply Related to the Use of O's/Outcome Data**

- Everything at your school is connected, so all O's are related (e.g., in our research we find between a 0.7 and 0.9 correlation of each of the climate areas to one another and to achievement overall).

- O's are evidence (lagging indicators) of the aggregate R's and X's at the school and will eventually reflect them. O's will inevitably shift in a positive direction when high functioning R's and X's are consistently implemented.

- O's (like R's and X's) can be located onto the effectiveness roadmap. Therefore, there are typical O's that will be found in each of the 1, 2, 3 and 4 school and classroom paradigms (see Figures 9.3 and 9.4)

- Placing value on processes (X's) will encourage growth more effectively than placing emphasis on outcomes (O's). Process values tend to encourage shared learning and the growth of a professional learning community. They imply a value for quality over expediency and are consistent with development of a psychology of success. Outcome values tend to encourage a focus on the ends, imply at least a little competition, encourage doing "whatever works" to achieve the goal, and promote an anxious climate (See Figure 6.2).

- Some outcome data represent symptoms of the real problem, while some outcome data can represent evidence of the real problem. It is important to make the distinction. Moreover, addressing outcomes directly is discouraged. It typically leads to a focus on trying to solve symptoms and usually misses the real cause and/or the real problem (See Figure 9.5).

- Comparisons internally or externally are almost always an unhealthy and detrimental ingredient. Comparisons tend to imply the question "are we doing OK, versus others?" This usually leads to complacency given a favorable comparison or dejection when the comparison is unfavorable. It tends to shift the focus away from quality, growth, and self-reflection. So, a relatively high score does not necessarily mean you are succeeding, and a relatively lower score does not mean you are failing.

## Locating O's onto the Roadmap

As with R's and X's, discussed in the previous two chapters, we can locate the O's of a school on the effectiveness roadmap (See Figure 9.3). Our O's (scores, rates, student experiences, perceptions, defining qualities, etc.) typically correspond to theoretical roadmap locations. The R's, X's and O's at a school will be inter-related and as a result most often fit a combined location profile. The R's and X's at a school that has a climate of 1.5 out of 5 will be very different than those at a school where there is a 4.5/5. Likewise, when we find a 1.5/5 climate and function level, we almost always see a corresponding low level of student achievement and other outcomes. In the same way, when we see a SCAI climate rating above 4 out of 5, we can be quite certain that the achievement is going to be at a matching high level. Figure 9.3 below highlights four theoretical locations on the roadmap.

Figure 9.3 Locating Four Theoretical School Performance Levels on the School Effectiveness Roadmap

## Growth "Pathway" on the School Effectiveness Roadmap

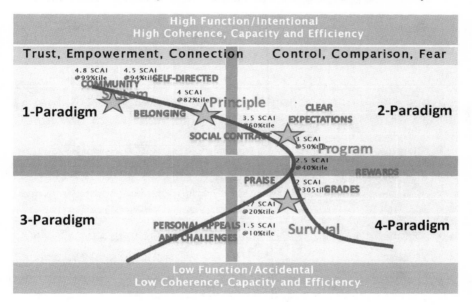

Each of the four locations in Figure 9.3 implies a corresponding series of R's, X's and ultimately O's. The nature of these four locations is outlined briefly in Figure 9.4. We could also characterize them quite accurately by their dominant quality (i.e., level of perception) – system-based (highest), principle-based, program-based, reactive (lowest), or the relative amount of psychology of success (POS) or failure (POF) practiced. Therefore, if we have a solid sense of any one of the essential qualities of a school – the R's, X's, or the O's, we would be able to confidently infer the level of the other two qualities.

**Reflection 9.1:** As mentioned earlier, if any member of our team at ASSC is given one of three pieces of data – 1) student achievement scores, 2) SCAI climate survey ratings, or 3) observations of the practices at the school, we can then predict with great accuracy the other two variables. How is it that we can do this? What is your explanation?

Figure 9.4. Descriptions of R's, X's and O's at schools at Four School Effectiveness Roadmap Locations

| Climate/Function Location on the Roadmap | Common R's | Common X's | Common O's |
|---|---|---|---|
| **1.5 Climate Location** | R's defined by POF – external LOC, fragmentation, fixed ability orientation. Coping. Plentiful excuse-making about the students, parents, and conditions (the context). Competitive survival. Sensory/Survival level of perception (LOP). | 3- and 4-Paradigm teaching. A great deal of lecture and test. Worksheets and low critical thinking. Rote learning and homework-driven. Either dominant or passive classroom management. Effort to domesticate students. | Below 30 percentile test scores. Low student motivation. High discipline referrals. Low teacher morale. Low collaboration. Low trust and hope for improvement. Student's main goal is self-preservation. |
| **2.5 Climate Location** | POS is mixed with much POF defined R's. Cleverness, coping and making it through the day is the goal. The value is control and responding to problem situations. Orderly management and institutional coherence is the goal. Program and Sensory LOP. | Programs are implemented to improve function and coherence. 2-Paradigm management and Direct Instruction used by the model teachers. Upper track students receive a higher quality of instruction. | 30- 50 percentile test scores. Students in the upper tracks feel served, but most others feel as if they are just passing time. Students look to meet basic needs for power, fun, and belonging outside the system. Teachers are cordial to other another. A sense that this is the best that can be done. |
| **3.5 Climate Location** | R's are defined by more POS with some POF. Goal of helping students be successful is norm. Mostly attitude of competence and shared expectations. Faith in best practices. Vision of effectiveness is present. Principle and Program LOP. | Some 1-Paradigm teaching, but mostly effective 2-Paradigm. More cooperative learning and inquiry. Mostly still rely on well-executed direct instruction. Many programs are used faithfully to coordinate X's. Teachers share X's. | 50 – 80 percentile test scores. Sense that the school is functioning adequately. Most students feel as if they are able to find a path to success if they apply themselves. Teachers are more cohesive than not. Trust level is very high. |
| **4.5 Climate Location** | R's are intentionally defined by POS. Principles drive how macro and micro choices are made. The school has a clear vision of excellence and empowerment. Principle and System LOP | More 1-Paradigm teaching than 2-Paradigm. High amounts of inquiry, project-based learning, and student ownership. Self-reflection in daily activities. Teachers collaborate on how to do better with 1-Style X's and leadership supports that effort. | 80-100 percentile test scores and highly recognized performance. Overall sense that school provides the best route to life-time success. Teachers trust one another and leadership. Students trust what they are doing at school is meaningful and will lead to their growth. |

## How Does Our Context Influence Our O's?

Many readers are likely questioning how the school's context factors into one's ability to move up the roadmap. You may be asking "what about where my school is located, the demographics and socio-economic issues with my students and parents, as well as the influence of all the schooling which has come before?" All of these realities are important to consider in our work in general and our efforts to move up the pathway. Knowing who we are teaching – their needs, their knowledge, skills and dispositions, their cultural backgrounds, what we can and cannot count on from parents – is vital to our success. Therefore, it is true that what we need to do to move up the pathway will depend to some degree on those factors. However, considering that, the R's and X's that will keep us in the low quadrants of the roadmap are going to be essentially the same no matter who are students are, and those that are going elevate us to the higher quadrants will be the same no matter who our students are.

Our current circumstances are simply part of what constitutes "the job" at any particular school - whether our job is to run a school, teach a class, coach a team, coordinate parent involvement, advise other teachers, or counsel students. All students have needs and characteristics – because of their age, gender, circumstances, learning style, home lives, previous experiences of schooling, and so on. Our job is to take all of that into account and find the best ways to help that student learn and grow. Their individual and collective characteristics are helpful to know, consider, and use to influence the choices we make in our work, but they are not ultimately determining. They may define our starting point, but they do not present finite limits to where we can go, only the challenge level of the task. For the most part, our context factors will influence us in three basic ways:

1.  Where we are today and our starting location on the pathway.

2.  How quickly we are able to move up.

3.  The type and quantity of effort that it will take to move up.

The most important implication of our context factors is that it may require us to help our students become accustomed to different higher functioning R's and X's. For example, transitioning a group of students who have been used to being taught in a 4-Paradigm into becoming a functioning 1-Paradigm class will take much longer, require much more skill, and represent many more challenges when compared to inheriting students who are used to a high functioning 2-Paradigm when it comes to supporting students toward becoming 1-Paradigm self-directed community of learners. In the situation where we are faced with moving from a 4-Paradigm location, it is a bit more work? It is a bit more complicated task? It will require more school-wide coherence in the effort? Nevertheless, the persistent question is always "do we want to do what it takes to move up, or not?" It is possible. But we must appreciate and embrace the challenge.

**Looking Ahead:** Chapters twelve and thirteen will go into more detail in explaining how to move from specific locations. Chapter twelve outlines the path starting from the lower quadrants, and chapter thirteen explains the pathway from middle to high functioning quadrants.

No matter our current roadmap location, growth will require leaders of any effort to support a healthy and sane mindset. We need to be clear about the relative importance of the various outcome indicators at the school. That clarity starts with us not sending mixed messages. We cannot say in one breath that the school needs do whatever it takes to improve test scores and with the next to say trust the process of movement up the pathway. The dominant message that will register will be the fear-based outcome message. When we do send mixed messages, we inadvertently cause people to lose faith in the process of growing in their use of quality X's and to revert to coping and convenience-based X's with which they have felt safe (i.e., agreements with mediocrity), familiar and perceive as having "worked."

## Examining Some of the Most Critical O's/Outcomes

Why do any of us give importance to a particular outcome? Frequently it is because others use them to judge our performance. Sometimes it is because they attract attention to us or our school. In addition, we will consistently find that they provide us with useful data related to our progress. Yet, regardless of the reasons why we attend to any outcome measure, it is helpful to view it as the effect of an antecedent cause. Let's examine a few of the O's that are likely to be of interest to those in leadership roles. For each, we will examine how it would evidence as a 1-Paradigm phenomenon (effect), and the most essential R's and X's (causes) that would contribute to its demonstration (See Figure 9.5).

Figure 9.5: Target Outcomes/O's and Contributing R's and X's

| O's of Interest | Target Appearance as 1-Paradigm Evidence (What we desire) | Primary Contributing R's and X's (How we get there) |
|---|---|---|
| Overall Learning Level | In the 1-Paradigm location — learning is viewed from the perspective of the whole student and whole community. Evidence of knowledge, skills and dispositions are important. Students are self-reflective and self-directed. They can work in teams and solve problems. They feel empowered to have a voice and be given ownership over their learning. | 1-Paradigm X's which are motivated by 1-Paradigm R's. Teachers commit to promoting high functioning classrooms and intentionally moving their students to more self-direction and community-building. Increasingly more inquiry and project-based learning is used. Assessment promotes clarity of the skills and dispositions necessary to accomplish being a student in a POS class. |
| Test Scores | Test scores are a lagging indicator of school growth, but because they potentially indicate a great deal of actual skill and knowledge development, they should improve as the school moves up the pathway. They are not a perfect indicator, but they offer some information. | Test scores can be temporarily improved by teaching to the test, but this strategy will result in a plateau effect and ultimately limit the ability to improve. The majority of what achievement scores measure will be the median overall X quality (see roadmap) at the school. So, every R and X at the school will contribute to the eventual test scores. |

| | | |
|---|---|---|
| **School's Perception** | Others' perception of the school is also a lagging indicator of movement up the pathway. This is an example of an O affecting our happiness in the job. It will be helpful to the improvement effort to encourage a perception (based in reality and an emerging vision) that the school is moving toward excellence, which results in more pride and community self-esteem. Success breeds success. So, an increasingly positive public perception *is* a meaningful improvement. | Actual improvement in R's and X's will be the best way to improve perceptions of a school internally and externally. But the leader X's related to PR are important too. Communicating success and improvement is valuable. And do not focus just on scores, also work to re-make or reinforce an excellence narrative with stories, testimonials, innovative X's, and putting your vision out there. But any "smoke and mirrors" will collapse eventually, so job one is to be truthful, sincere, and transparent. |
| **Student Interactions** | Students view one another as co-learners. They trust that in school open spaces students are kind and respectful of one another. Students learn to interact with all students – there is little cliquishness. Students are highly involved in after-school teams and clubs and side projects. Students learn to trust peer leaders and conflict mediators and to explore this role themselves. Students expect to solve their own problems and expect adults to act with integrity when it comes to enforcing policy. | High quality student interactions start with the consistent use of X's in the classroom creating the habits of collaboration, a culture of listening and respect, and solving problems in teams. This function starts with excellent technical management skills. Assessment is used to clarify what quality looks like and student regularly self-evaluate the quality of their cooperation, teamwork, process, and participation skills. Students are trained to be peer mediators. Class meetings are common. Adults act with integrity and hold students accountable to their commitments. |

| | | |
|---|---|---|
| **Motivation Level of Students.** | The trajectory is always toward more intrinsic motivation and self-responsibility, for both staff and students. We can see the effect as we give more and more responsibility to students, and we see them putting quality and creativity first and becoming less interested in grades. Students embrace being empowered as do teachers, and we see new grassroots initiatives. Students are free to put their energy into being innovative and taking risks as opposed to using their ingenuity to resist against a repressive structure. | Leadership is deliberate and conspicuous about empowering teachers and encouraging innovation and new initiatives. Classrooms commit to 1-Paradigm practice with self-direction as a goal. Students are trained to focus on the process and taught how to self-assess based on rubrics for quality. Remnants of 4-Paradigm X's are eliminated. Students are given ownership of their progress, growth, and assessment including leading their parent conferences. |
| **Habits of Students** | Students become accustomed to 1-Paradigm ways of being. As a result, they have replaced finding ways to meet their basic needs on their own and trust that the planned curriculum is needs satisfying. The students enjoy listening and being listened to. Teachers get used to a class of students who are all attentive and ready to engage in meaningful work. Students become accustomed to correcting peers who act in ways detrimental to the school. Pride becomes a bigger value than social Darwinism. | X's used in the classes promote the satisfaction of basic needs. Classroom management is characterized by POS X's and the principles of high functioning behavior. Creating a culture of listening and respect is intentionally grown. Work is meaningful. The qualities of excellence, creativity and inquiry are clarified and included in assessment criteria. Problems are viewed through the lens of basic needs issues first (see Figure 9.E below). Adults project a unified message that students need to strive to be self-directed and responsible to their agreements, and apply consequences when they are not, while refraining POF promoting X's. |

| Incidence of Wanted and Unwanted Outcomes | Goal of decreasing: office referrals, dropout rate bullying, verbal or physical violence rates, , tardy rates, parent complaints. | Every X will relate to every O. As the school moves up the roadmap and its X's are defined by improved R's and X's all of these O's will be |
|---|---|---|
| | Goal of Increasing: attendance rates number of students in after school activities, club membership, between class competition enthusiasm levels, sports team success, liter, graffiti, and others. | directly or indirectly affected. For example, in many cases, shifting all classroom management X's to 1-Paradigm will likely be more effective reducing Bullying than a formal Bullying program. Programs can be positive, but they are often dealing with the symptom (see below). A culture of care and respect shown to all by all reduces the need to displace aggression or passively resist an unloving institution. But at the same time the school (students and adults) takes on less and less tolerance for casual abuse, meanness, and acts of destruction. |

**Reflection 9.2:** Do we view our current state through a growth or fixed-ability orientation? Since our O's/outcomes are just information, then depending on how we choose to perceive them, we are in a position to use either a growth or fixed ability lens. The growth orientation asks "what can we learn about our X's from this data? And "How do my X's need to improve if I want to see improved O's in this area?" The fixed-ability orientation asks "How does this data compare to others? And "How does my ego feel about what this data implies about how our school rates?"

## Envisioning the Outcomes of Our Desired Roadmap Location

As Muhammad Ali once stated, "If my mind can conceive it, and my heart can believe it, then I can achieve it." There is great value to envisioning and operationalizing the outcomes defining where we are going on our journeys. It implies really getting to know the kinds of things that are normal and assumed at that location. A good way to get at the practical reality of that location will be to ask ourselves "what do we want our students' normal experience of school to be?"

In this desired location –

- What defines the students' classroom learning experience and why do they appreciate it?
- Why do people like working here?
- How do people talk to each other?
- How do they talk about the school?
- How do students feel during the day? And why do they feel that way?

When we ask our faculty and staff to conceive answers to these questions, we will need to expect there to be some debate about what is our "ideal normal." That is natural and healthy and keeps those who are most entrusted with the role of guiding the vision in touch and grounded. But as we examine the areas of data-driven decision making, and a vision-based strategic planning process later in the chapter, you will see that the success of these planning efforts will depend on our ability to operationalize our target.

In the formal vision-based strategic planning process described later, our success will depend to a great degree on our ability to define both where we want to go as well as where we are now. The better we can operationalize both the practical reality of where we want to go, including the micro level outcomes, as well as a clear-sighted assessment of our current practical reality, the more effectively our plan will be. Yet, before we discuss strategic planning, we need to make clear a distinction between solving symptoms versus real problems.

## Outcomes that Point to Problems – Solving Real Problems Not Symptoms

Frequently, when we examine a particular outcome at the school, it points to us some sort of problem condition or need. What any of us defines as problems is relative to the school and its priorities. We might broadly define a problem as the cause of something that is happening or continues to happen which we consider to be unacceptable, unwanted, and/or is leading us away from our vision. For any problem, we need to either act on it immediately, accept it for now, or intend future action to remedy it. Problems can be as small as why there was too much litter today, or as large as why there is a high dropout rate, or a lack of trust among the faculty.

As we engage in the process of identifying the key areas for change, we refer to as "priorities" and/or "problems," we need to distinguish between the real problem and the symptoms of those real problems (See Appendix 9.B). Symptoms are most often outcomes/O's (effects) and real problems are most often our R's and X's (causes). And we should be cautious about allowing others to define our problems, especially those without a clear sense of our vision.

A simple way to get at whether a problem is the true root problem or just a symptom is to ask ourselves the following questions, "Why is "this" the way it is?" and "What are we currently doing to contribute to it?" These questions can be asked in a faculty meeting, retreat, a committee meeting, and/or as a self-reflection. We might need to keep asking the question, and unpeeling the onion, until we get to something that is concrete and operational. At that point we will have something we can work with. Attempting to solve symptoms will inherently keep us stuck on our location on the roadmap. Solving real problems may require more care and intention, but they will lead to real movement.

**Case Study** – Mr. Smith is a Social Studies teacher in an urban high school. His personality could be described as friendly and supportive, but under-stated and business-like. He could be classified at a 1-Paradigm Style teacher given his heavy use of cooperative learning, projects, and inquiry. The school as a whole has a daily attendance rate of 75%, and constant issues with discipline. The fact that on average one student in 4 is missing each period could be defined as a "problem" at the school. In Mr. Smith's class the attendance is commonly 100% and on average well over 90%. He has no problems with discipline, in fact the students are cooperative with one another and focused from the beginning of the period until the end.

Examining this case, we can say that the school had an O of low attendance and poor discipline. So, what would conventional wisdom say to do? Those in the school could potentially address these symptoms with any number of perceived solutions. They could also take a fixed-ability view of their context and adopt the R assuming "this is the best you can do with "these" students." However, Mr. Smith's class shows that the students show up when they believe the class is worth it to them.

The school can implement an attendance incentive program (as an added X) to try to address their perceived "problem" directly. But it would have little effect if the typical X's did not improve. As the lesson from Mr. Smith's class shows, the "real problems" at this school are the X's, and the poor attendance is just a symptom. And those X's are the result of mis-guiding R's – which included "these kids don't show up to class and when they do they are unruly." Mr. Smith uses the R "these students want to be here and learn if there is something worth learning and they will act like self-responsible adults if they are treated like it." Therefore, he used X's consistent with those R's, and his resulting O's were students who were present, engaged and learning almost all of the time.

How many schools have tried to find a clever add on to address these kinds of symptoms, rather than looking at the real problems which are most often the quality of the common R's and X's at the school?

## The "Real Problem" with Trying to Solve "Symptoms"

When our assessment of an unwanted condition leads us to the conclusion that the symptom is the problem, we tend to try to fix the symptom directly or miss the opportunity to address the "real problem" (which is likely in the form of an under-examined problematic X). The results are (no pun intended) problematic (See Appendix 9.C). When we try to treat a symptom, it can lead to an effort to make direct, external, and/or controlling interventions – or what we often term a "band-aides". These can take the form of bribing, coercing, begging, manipulating, and/or conning students or our peers and ourselves into either doing more or less of something. Adding a novel isolated X into an existing system will require a great deal of maintenance because in most cases, it does not change the R's, so the result will be eventual regression to the mean X's. Neither our levels of capacity nor coherence are positively influenced. Appendices 9.B and 9.C at the end of the chapter further explore this area and include exercises that may be helpful in growth process.

# Meaningful Strategic Planning: Aligning Our Data Use with Our Vision

In many cases, schools engage in the process of formal strategic planning because it has been required or expected of them. Done well, the process has the potential to be powerful and highly useful to your overall improvement process. But, too often, it represents a somewhat disparate effort, disconnected from the more organic business of becoming a more effective school. The byproduct of this can be a great deal of effort resulting in a process that is not as meaningful as it could be and a product that is less impactful than it can be.

Our overall goal should be to align the practical elements and guiding references/R's of our large-scale ongoing administrative and organizational processes – strategic planning, vision development, teacher and staff evaluation, professional development, school promotion and school improvement generally. This starts with the expectation that coherence and integrity are priority R's. The next step will be to determine where these large processes are currently misaligned. Our guiding question might be "Does the way this process is being done today encourage the growth of the school as reflected in our vision and mission." Likewise, we might ask "Can we clearly see how this process or plan is moving us up to our desired destination on the roadmap?" Our ability to move up the roadmap will be related to our level of process *coherence* - the integrity of the fundamental school mechanism, and our level of *capacity* – the way in which these mechanisms function to promote our desired results and expand our ability to be successful.

Our strategic planning process should meet these five standards:

1.  It is aligned and integrated into our other essential processes and data-driven decision making.
2.  It acts to solve real problems in a meaningful way rather than just addressing symptoms.
3.  It acts to cultivate a more "living" mission and vision.
4.  It promotes a more meaningful use of data and understanding of what is actually occurring at the school.
5.  It supports our process of moving closer to our desired location on the school effectiveness roadmap.

There are several systems for developing strategic plans. They all have their benefits, but they can produce vastly different results. I recommend the four stage R->X->O process (See Figure 9.6). It is the most effective means of satisfying all five of the criteria above. Here it is contrasted to a more traditional model, and then explained in detail.

## Contrasting Two Different Approaches to Strategic Planning

We can contrast an R->X->O roadmap destination-based process with a more traditional O<-X approach. The traditional and commonly used approach to strategic planning begins with outcomes which are likely to take the form of symptoms. The starting point is a review of current outcome data, such as scores, rates, survey results, etc. Then, target or priority areas are selected based on data evidence that suggests a less than desirable condition. Next, goals are generated which imply solutions to the problems. Finally, action steps are outlined.

This approach is sensible and potentially effective but has a few potential problems.

- First, it can lend itself to solving symptoms rather than real problems as there is no mechanism to put data into a context that would differentiate the two ideas.
- Second, it can encourage direct (i.e., potentially mis-guided or incoherent) interventions to those outcomes/symptoms.
- Third it does not imply a broader vision or "meta" destination for the process.
- Fourth, it is by nature reactive rather than proactive.
- Fifth, it can lead to conceiving problems in isolation and solutions out of a larger context.

While models with these qualities are operationally practical, they seldom result in the encouraging of meaningful change.

Consider instead employing the vision-driven R->X->O four stage strategic planning process outlined in Figure 9.6. This process solves the five problems common with the traditional O<-X model and satisfies the five criteria for an effective process. By its nature it brings an increased level of clarity and depth to the effort. The R->X->O process consists of four stages:

1.  Articulate the desired roadmap location, using a wide range of data points representing a series of R's, X's, and O's.

2.  Assess the current roadmap location using a parallel set of data points.

3.  Determine the gap between the desired and current location that reflects the school's real problem areas, the priorities areas of focus, and key indicators of growth.

4.  Select a manageable number of the priority growth areas and translate them into macro goals. Then, for each macro goal, develop as many micro-operational objectives as necessary to represent the actions that would be necessary to bridge the gap in that area. Write micro-objectives in SMART goal format.

## Step One: Articulate the Desired School Effectiveness Roadmap Location

The place to start in our strategic planning process is to bring together a team of individuals who represent a broad set of perspectives and job descriptions, but all share a commitment to the school's vision, possess an interest in exploring data and accept their role as influencers/leaders. It is desirable if all or some of the members have previously or are currently also engaged in the vision, climate, or site governance processes/committees. If it is possible, you will want a team capable of carrying the effort through from its early to later life – brainstorming, data analysis, goal setting, facilitating the action plan, and then ultimately translating it into professional development. Done properly, the process represents a good deal of work and dedication. Therefore, members should be compensated for their time.

A critical frame of mind for the team is to recognize the scale and importance of the task, and not assume it can be done quickly or with short-cuts. The Chair of the committee needs to keep the team focused. A balance needs to be found to a) generate the necessary depth of analysis, b) representation of perspectives, and c) a productive pace, consensus, and tangible results.

The first task in the process will likely be the most time-consuming and challenging, but it will set the tone and define the capacity of the remaining steps. At this first stage, the team needs to articulate the desired school destination. This means the members of the team will need to be versed in the basics of the school effectiveness roadmap logic. The more concrete and operational this destination can be envisioned the better. Just as a teacher planning for the many aspects of a future class, the more that this ideal destination can be conceptualized in specific, measurable, behavioral, and practical terms the more likely it will be actualized. To facilitate the process of operationalizing our desired location, it will be useful to identify target qualities for each of the three levels of school phenomenon – R's, X's, and O's. Here we examine key considerations and guiding questions for each of these areas.

> **R's/References.** This activity will likely take the most amount of imagination. But it should be an energizing process. The group will want to inhabit the minds of those in the future - the teachers, staff, and students within the school when it has attained its goal location on the roadmap. The job will be to articulate the operating references at the school when it gets to this destination. It will work best to conceive and state these in the present tense – as if they have already occurred and are happening now. Be sure all members of the group are familiar with what you are talking about when the term R/reference is used. You can substitute the words values and beliefs, if need be, but the domain of references will include values, narratives, beliefs, conditioned patterns, mindsets, fears, desires, biases, and all other internal processes. Therefore, try to stick with references to capture it all. Here are a series of guiding questions to support your process of brainstorming:

- ✓ What are the guiding values at the school?
- ✓ What are the three main guiding internal questions that focus the actions at the school?
- ✓ What does it feel like to work at the school?
- ✓ What are the pervasive narratives (Chapter seven) and perceptions of the school?
- ✓ What can you say about the existence of the quality of trust at the school?
- ✓ What are some positive attitudes stakeholders take for granted?

Brainstorm as many ideas as you can for this area. Then pair your list down to 4-6 primary qualities. Next, include some evidence sources for how one would know these internal processes are occurring. Your evidence list for R's will likely be shorter than your list for X's and O's and will likely include what a perceptive person could infer, but can also include R related items on surveys, the internal thoughts which are communicated in various forms by the adults at the school and other sources. Place your lists of qualities and evidence into the Destination R's section of the plan.

**X's/Actions.** This will be the most important section in your entire plan. Here you will outline the kinds of X's - practices, policies, routines, activities, strategies, programs, processes, personal interactive patterns, etc. that will be common and normal in your desired destination. This will be a useful time to incorporate items from your "things you will see/things we do here" and "things you should not see/things we don't do here" lists (and/or the POS promoting practices or undermining practice list, See Chapter seven). The emphasis should be on what happens in the classrooms, but also include all other areas of the school, as well as leadership and decision-making practices. Review Chapter eight for all areas related to the X domain. Here are a few guiding questions to spur your brainstorming process for this area.

- ✓ What will students and visitors see when they walk into the school?
- ✓ What are the norms related to instructional methods?
- ✓ What are the norms related to assessment methods?
- ✓ What are the norms as far as classroom management and discipline?
- ✓ What kinds of pedagogy should be virtually absent?
- ✓ How will faculty and staff be using the professional development process?
- ✓ What policies will have been deemed no longer necessary? And which ones will replace them?
- ✓ What is happening in the area of student life, leadership, service learning, peer mediation, etc.?
- ✓ What is being done to promote social and emotional health within the school and why has it been embraced and appreciated?

Again, brainstorm as many ideas as you can here. The list may become extensive, but that is positive. Synthesize the list down to 5 to 7 items that best represent the desired X's at the new location. It is fine to refer to other reference documents or external sources. Next, list the sources of evidence which could be used to assess whether your desired X's are being demonstrated. There should be a substantial list of sources including, surveys, observations, self-report, formal evaluation data, student feedback, and your own anecdotal assessment. Place your lists of actions and evidence into the destination X's section of the working document.

**O's/Outcomes.** In the final section of step one of the process, the team will outline the outcomes which one would ideally see at the desired roadmap location. This section should be less difficult than the two sections for the R's and X's. This list should include quantitative measures such as test scores, but it will be useful to focus as well on the day-to-day experience of students, teachers, staff, and leaders - what is the personal experience in the school at this location? What do people experience that they may not be experiencing currently? Here are a series of questions to guide the exercise.

- ✓ What is the emotional state of a typical student on a typical day?
- ✓ What do students learn?
- ✓ What is the climate and culture like in the school?
- ✓ What is the public reputation of the school?
- ✓ What are the rates of your various reporting measures at this new location?
- ✓ How do students grow over their years at the school? and why do they?
- ✓ What are the indicators of achievement and successful generally?
- ✓ What don't you see at the school any longer (as a result of your efforts)?
- ✓ What makes you proud to work at this school?

Include all the outcome data measures that you see as meaningful indicators of your progress to this destination. You may want to focus on quantitative indicators, or you may want to use mostly qualitative evidence of success. But try to generate as much solid reliable evidence as you can. The SCAI is a very reliable way to judge progress and roadmap location for example. Then, as before, synthesize your list of desired location quality outcome indicators down to 4-6, and list all sound and meaningful sources of evidence you could use to assess those indicators (unless the evidence is the indicator itself, as it might be with test score levels, for example).

## Step Two: Articulate Your Current School Effectiveness Roadmap Location

In this stage of the process, you will articulate the current state of the school. The work product should be a side-by-side representation of what was created in stage one – outlining R, X, and O indictors, but in this column, it will characterize the current school reality. As with the first step related to conceiving the desired roadmap location, in this step, the team will identify indicators and support their assessment as much as possible with evidence in the form of multiple sources of existing data. This step can be done after or concurrently with the first step, depending on what makes the most sense for the team.

When the first two steps are complete, the team should have developed a parallel set of key-indicators for both the desired state and the current state at the school. Some variation is fine, but the goal is to represent a picture of before and after. The R, X, and O related questions offered in the previous section to spur the brainstorming process can be used for articulating the current state of the school as well. Also, it will likely be that members of the team will recognize items which they feel should be represented on one side when exploring the other side.

As with step one, open discussion and brainstorming should be encouraged early, but eventually the team will need to reduce the list of indictors down to a few, about 4-6 for each domain – R's, X's and O's. The before and after indicators should be reflective of one another but they do not need to be exactly parallel. Likewise, the data sources should be similar as well. But you may determine that you want to work with data sources in the future that are currently not something you collect, or that you want to cease collecting a source of data in the future. This process will be an excellent opportunity to reevaluate your data collection process and sources. The more meaningful your data use process becomes, the more discerning you will become related to the different advantages and disadvantages of various data sources – especially surveys.

Step two is complete when you have a side-by-side picture of where you are currently and what your school would be like at your desired destination – the R's, X's, and O's with evidence for each. Assume that coming to consensus will require commitment to a process of democratic consensus. Yet, ultimately the most ambitious vision and destination conception should take precedence over ideas that do not represent meaningful progress. And assume the process will require a high degree of EQ, encouragement, boundary setting, and process facilitation. The best ideas should be elevated, not just those of the most senior members or those with the most assertive personalities. Moreover, it is likely that you will need to encourage members to persist in the effort when they do not get fully what they want – managing egos is an essential part of the process. But in the end, these two stages should have produced energy and excitement about the growth possibilities for the school. The content created in these steps can be recycled with necessary modifications from year-to-year and will position the team for the work of the next stage of the process.

### Step Three: Assessing the Gap Between the Desires and Current Roadmap Location

In this stage of the process, the team will systematically assess the gap between the desired and current roadmap location indicators and evidence that were articulated in steps one and two previously. The job of the team at this stage is to identify the disparity related to the indicators for where you are and where you want to be and reduce them to a manageable set of priority goals. The number of goals will vary from school to school depending on the current capacity for making improvements and other factors. It should be noted that the work done in steps one, two and three will be useful generally in the various improvement initiatives the school is undertaking. But for this specific exercise in strategic planning, goals should reflect 1) priority values and areas of focus, 2) real problems as well as symptoms, and 3) highlight points of substantive disparity between the two columns representing areas of critical concern.

- **Priorities**. The team members should focus on what is most essential for becoming the school that has been conceived in step one. The data comparison may point to the critical priorities, but not always. Therefore, the mindset should be to spotlight what is most important and evokes the most passion among those on the team. Recall our earlier discussion, the goal of this process is to be vision-driven, meaningful and to translate into a document that inspires and spurs action.

- **Real Problems**. There can be a tendency to focus on data disparity as the primary take away from the gap analysis. Yet, the result of that can be to place too much attention on outcomes and symptoms of problems. Therefore, first, be steadfast in your effort to try to recognize the "real problems" implied by the gap. We might simply ask "Why is there a gap?" and then "Why is that?" repeatedly, as many times as necessary until we get to the root cause. One strategy for avoiding reductionism and too much attention on symptoms will be to select target goals from each domain list – R's, X's, O's. Focusing primarily on improving X's will tend to support the solving of real problems.

- **Substantive Disparity**. Identify those areas where there is a clear gap. The likelihood is that engaging the process will clarify both the conceptual picture as well as the practical realities at the school represented in the data. You will likely better appreciate some areas of profound disparity between where you are and where you want to be.

From this process of gap analysis, you will want to identify a series of priority goal areas. Every element of the gap you have identified is relatively meaningful and should be considered as you move forward in your individual and collective work as leaders, teachers, committee members, PLC members, community partners, etc., but for the purpose of this exercise (and document) you will need to select a few elements to operationalize more fully and formally. It is okay if they are more general (i.e., we create student centered classrooms), or more specific or quantifiable (i.e., we have a 95% attendance rate). In either case, we will need to operationalize them further.

## Step Four: Setting Goals and SMART Objectives to Operationalize Our Action Planning

The final step of the process will be to operationalize our priority goals into actionable objectives, responsibilities, and evidence we have been successful. After identifying a few broad areas for improvement in our gap analysis we will want to translate the essence of those ideas into a set of macro-goals. These goals should be stated as present tense outcomes and can be general and include abstract terms.

Then, for each of these macro goals, we will want to identify sub micro-objectives which imply what would be required for the goal to be actualized. We can create as many of these micro- objectives as necessary. The goal here is to operationalize our growth process and make our movement toward desired location specific, practical, and actionable. Making a parallel to effective classroom planning is instructive here. For any lesson and/or unit, a teacher will have broad goals, but will be most successful if they are able to write a list of concrete, observable behavioral objectives that define what it will look like when students have been successful in their learning. In the same way, we will want to write our objectives in concrete, observable, and behavioral terms (i.e., what will people do? what will it look like?) Using strong action verbs is encouraged here – just as it is in the classroom. For each of the objectives you will want to use the SMART goal logic (See example goal in Appendix 9.D).

- **Specific** – Uses strong behavioral verbs and operationalize the task.
- **Measurable** – What can we use to know if the quality or the quantity has changed?
- **Attainable/Assessment Evidence** – What sources of data can we use to determine progress?
- **Responsible person and Resource** – Who owns this objective? And what will they need to support their facilitation?

- **Timeline** - What are the expected increments of progress and what kind of results should we see at each increment?

It is important to focus on observable evidence in these objectives, but a broad range of types of evidence can qualify as reliable, valid, and sound. Choose "meaningful" sources even if they may be less tangible (i.e., the way that teachers perceive faculty meetings, or students deal with conflict, etc.) over less meaningful sources which may be more quantifiable.

Figure 9.6: Four-Stage Vision-Driven R-X-O Strategic Planning Process Template

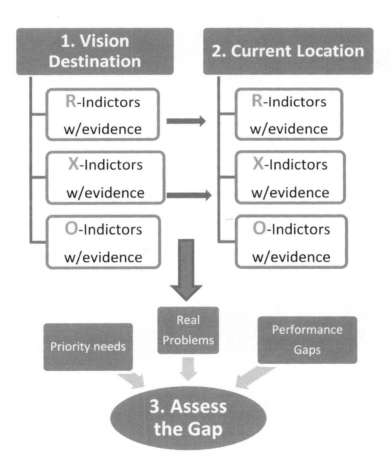

### 4. Action Planning with SMART Goals

| Macro Goals/ Micro Objectives | Description w/Evidence | Person(s) Responsible | Timeline | Resources & Roadblocks | Target Change Data/ Evidence |
|---|---|---|---|---|---|
| **A Coherence issue Goal 1** | | | | | |
| Micro Action Objective A1 | | | | | |
| Micro Action Objective A2 | | | | | |
| **B Capacity Issue Goal 1** | | | | | |
| Micro Action Objective B1 | | | | | |
| **C Reference Change Goal 1** | | | | | |
| Micro Action Objective C1 | | | | | |
| Micro Action Objective C2 | | | | | |

## Implementing Our Strategic Plan

Thoughtful completion of the four-step R->X->O strategic planning process will represent both a process as well as a product accomplishment. On the one hand, the process will represent an act of being and functioning as (intellectually and experientially) a 1-Paradigm institution. We will grow from the process itself – so will already have moved closer to our desired roadmap location. On the other hand, the work product will represent a valuable articulation of what our journey will ultimately entail. The components and the thinking done in process can be used for multiple other purposes from refining current systems, to clarifying our public relations messages.

Our success in executing the plan will be dependent on the commitment of all members of the school community. So, reflect upon why others (especially those who were not at the table) will buy in and care about the contents of a plan? We might reflect on our own experience here. Most of us commit to the extent that 1) the vision which guides the actions steps in the plan is aligned with our own, 2) we trust the leadership and their ability to facilitate results,

3) the work implied in the plan feels meaningful, valuable and coherent with the rest of our job duties, and 4) we trust that others will do their part as well.

The document and the execution process will become more alive when the ownership for its realization is disseminated to the many hands. Those who are in the best position to lead aspects of the process should be given that responsibility. Opportunities for progress updates should be built-in to the meeting schedule. Positive recognitions should be frequent – with the focus on effort not just results. The principles of cultivating trust and vision discussed previously should be applied faithfully. We will always need to keep the focus on the big picture. Any formal process in which we engage is an opportunity to embody the R's and X's of our desired location, so projecting a pervasive dissatisfaction and impatience with results (that are not meeting our expectation) will be counterproductive. Demanding can be empowering if the message is – we are better than we are showing (i.e., implying greater potential and a growth orientation), but not so empowering if the message is that we are not acting or achieving adequately (i.e., implies personal criticism, ego, comparison and that we *are* our results).

## Using Data Broadly to Encourage Growth

Outside of the strategic planning process, it will be effective to use data to ground our understanding of our needs and progress. First, it is useful to keep in mind that everything is data – all phenomena. So, on one hand, data is all around us. If we are perceptive, we can see where we are and areas in which we need to grow. On the other hand, we can have biases to our perceptions, or miss attending to important things. Therefore, finding high quality sources of data can ground our perceptions and increase their soundness and reliability.

As a school we need to be in the habit of using, sharing, and discussing our data. It breads transparency and trust. It will make the process more effective and less formidable if we view data as neutral and intended to give us benefit. We can learn to fear what the data may say – especially about us personally. Years of high-stakes and comparison-based data use has fueled much trepidation in many leaders where data is concerned. Therefore, one of the R's which we need to cultivate is a growth versus fixed-ability mindset toward data. In a fixed-ability approach to data, we fear it as it will lead to a potential unfavorable comparison – promoting a lot of self-defense and denial. In a growth-orientation, we see all information as a source of learning, and so we welcome it as useful to our growth. From top to bottom in the school/district organizational chart, we need to ask ourselves how we can promote the conditions in which individuals are comfortable taking on more of a growth orientation toward data of any kind.

---

**Caution: Beware of the term "evidence based,"** as in an "evidence-based program." In practical terms, there is no guarantee that the program in question would provide value to your process of becoming more functional or moving you up the higher levels on the effectiveness roadmap. What the phrase "evidence based" literally means is that in some cases there were schools which showed an overall statistical difference on some variable when the program was implemented. But it is essential to consider the context any program is introduced into before judging its efficacy. It can be the case that implement the same program (that will support a movement from a 2/10 level of function to a 4/10 temporarily) will not necessarily (or even very likely) get a school at a 6/10 level to a 7/10 level.

In many cases, there are programs, especially for classroom management that will move all schools toward the mean – i.e., a 5/10 level of function and performance, whether those schools were originally at a 3/10 or a 7/10 previously (See Shindler, 2018). This same analysis applies to the phrases "best practice" and "research-based."

---

## What Can Data Tell Us?

When judging the value of data, we need to examine it in terms of its soundness and its relevancy. All data will have value, but our job is to find the most meaningful sources. Data can be considered sound to the extent it is valid, reliable, and meaningful. Valid meaning that it answers the right question and leads us into investigating the essential phenomenon. Reliable meaning that it is accurate and could be confirmed by other sources. Data can take many forms. Below we examine some of the main sources which might serve us.

## What Can the Numbers Tell Us?

Test scores, pass rates, attendance rates, incidence of wanted or unwanted behaviors, student demographic data, etc. are good to know. They are informative. Yet, as discussed, 1) we can often over-emphasize norm-referenced measures where our performance is being compared to others, and 2) these kinds of numbers are lagging indicators of what we have done previously as well as countless other variables that we do not control. Therefore, it is best to first put these data into perspective, and then disaggregate them and make them available to the groups for which they would provide the most relevant information. For example, providing the standardized math scores to the math teachers, or the 3rd grade reading scores to the 3rd grade teachers. PLC meetings are a logical venue to process data. But there should be an objective for doing it, and the data should be related to a current initiative of the group.

**Case example**: **Test Score gains** – In CA, and many other states, schools were compared to one another by their API – Academic Performance Index. The intended goal was accountability, but the untended consequences include all the problems with an O<-X orientation to data use.

Once this comparison process became public and schools were given incentives and penalties to improve their API's, what often happened was that schools tried to deal with the test scores directly – they added the X's that could be characterized as "teaching to the test." Referring to our discussion above, these X's could best be described as clever, direct attempts to address a symptom of a perceived problem. The result, in the short-term, was slightly higher test scores. However, interventions which are by nature short-term fixes can only affect the scores so far (and introduce a new set of real problems, such as unengaging teaching practices/X's). Therefore, after a few years, these schools saw their API's plateauing or dropping back down. If the R's and common X's at the schools never changed, the improvement in the numbers was essentially only superficial. But during this era there were also schools that experienced improvement in their scores by making meaningful changes in what they did and incorporated more effective R's and X's. When their API's improved, it reflected sustainable growth. Take-away lessons include 1) we need time to see if any change is substantial or superficial, and 2) assessing what is done (i.e., the X's) in a school is a more reliable predictor of their performance over time than changes in numbers from year to year.

## What Can Surveys Tell Us?

Surveys are useful in illuminating common perceptions among those groups related to the items on the survey. Surveys can be effective at answering the "how many" and "how much" questions. But with surveys it is often difficult to interpret the "why" of a response. If 80% of the students are satisfied with their education at the school, what does that mean? Why or why not, and what are they satisfied with? Are our students just easier or more difficult to satisfy than the students in the next school? Therefore, it is almost always necessary to combine survey data with at least some amount of focus group data to contextualize it. In general, our effort should be to collect survey data that gets at the answer to our critical question and solves our pressing problems.

Not all surveys are designed the same way. Different surveys used for the same topic can include very different content. Therefore, shop and compare. As an example, the SCAI is designed in a way that supports reliability and interpretability by using a rubric structure, with a focus on identifying R's, X's, and O's not just perceptions of O's like many surveys. The result is its favorable predictive validity and more meaningful data. The item below (Figure 9.G) is from dimension five related to classroom management and provides insight into both the X's at the school as well as the underlying R's related to empowerment and student voice.

**Figure 9.7: Item 5.e. from the ASSC School Climate Assessment Instrument**

| 5.e.————O————————————O————————————O————————————O————————————O—————————— |
|---|
| I have had some say in making the rules in my class. | The teachers make the rules but consider our feelings. | The teachers resent it when we question why a rule exists. |

This item is very predictive of overall climate, function, and student achievement at any school. The data obtained from this item would be very predictive of the current location of the school on the roadmap.

## What Can Interviews, Focus Groups, Town halls, and Informal Conversations Tell Us?

Because survey percentages, scores, rates, and incident levels cannot tell us very much about causality, we will want to find efficient ways to get at the "why" and "the full story." I am always a little surprised that as educators we often feel hesitate to ask why. Yet, if we are to embrace our growth orientation mindset, and apply it to our data-driven assessment process we should be eager to learn from students and parents what they are thinking and feeling.

Moreover, when we engage in focus groups, town halls, informal conversations, it sends a message to everyone that our guiding R's include a culture of listening and *wanting to know*. Quite often it will not be possible to satisfy the request of a stakeholder. Yet, letting them know they were heard and that we care is a concrete action and meaningful in and of itself. However, so often when we ask, we learn so much. We can learn a great deal about that which was previously an unknown such as how parents feel about a particular policy. We find that when leaders sit down with a group of students or parents, what they learn is usually quite enlightening.

On a practical level, these input sessions can be done rather efficiently. We mostly need to ensure a representative sample of the population of focus. We might invite certain students to a meeting where we provide lunch, or give a few teachers a list of questions to ask their students during a designated point in the day. And it can be a useful habit to simply ask students on a regular basis about how things are going. Being able to say that "We hear you" and "We are sincerely interested in doing something about it" is a powerful X that will lead any school up the pathway. It projects trust, growth, and improvement-oriented R's.

---

**Reflection 9.4** – What would you say is your school's general approach to ascertaining what various stakeholders are thinking and feeling? What message have you been sending as a result?

---

## CONCLUSION

The use of data should have an important place in our process of actualizing the potential of our school. Outcomes are a useful reflection of what we have done previously and identifying where we are in our journey. Engaging strategic planning in a meaningful way using an R->X->O logic will support quality planning outcomes and deepen our thinking related to our school improvement work. We need to be sure to use data in meaningful ways and always in the service of our vision.

In the next chapter, we will briefly examine eight areas of school climate and function and consider useful guiding questions to focus our action within each domain.

## REFERENCES

Shindler, J (2009) *Transformative Classroom Management*, Wiley Press.

Shindler, J (2018) *Exploring the Limiting Influence of PBIS in the Growth of Students and Schools*. www.transformativeclassroom.com.

## Appendix 9.1: Re-Examining If We Are Addressing Symptoms or Real Problems

It is useful to explore the current state of your common X's to locate where there are potential band-aides, and where direct symptom interventions have become systematized into regular and ongoing practices. We could compare it to de-mining a mine field. First, we need to agree to the R that we do not want to have mines, i.e., these low-quality X, and then we need to create a plan for removing them one by one. Like demining, we will need to be patient and purposeful. It is likely that people have gotten rather attached to their gimmicks. And sometimes it is difficult to know whether we have located a hubcap or a mine – an unhealthy manipulative strategy or just a clever strategy for doing getting something done more efficiently. The way that we can check is to ask ourselves the following questions:

1. What was the reason that we added this X into our school or classroom?

2. Was that reason related to a real problem or a symptom?

3. Was the new X intended to solve a real problem or a symptom?

4. How has the new X influenced the overall school or classroom? Would we say that it is moving us up to higher levels of function and effectiveness, or is it keeping us stuck?

## Appendix 9.2. A Closer look at what is at the heart of real problems and the symptoms they manifest: Exploring basic needs and psychology of success (POS) or failure (POF).

| Symptoms (O's) | Corresponding Possible "Real Problems" (X's) |
|---|---|
| **Low Student Achievement Levels**<br><br>**Low Levels of School Climate** | **Low climate/function producing practices** |
| **Resultant behaviors when basic needs are NOT being met.** | **Basic needs are NOT met in or out of the classroom, and therefore the student is forced to meet those needs in less healthy and functional ways.** |
| Power struggles, bullying, gaining attention, not doing work, helplessness, undermining the class, etc. | • Power – Students are not given sufficient opportunities for choice, voice, self-direction. |
| Need to make excuses, hyper-comparison, fear of failure, bragging, put downs, need to win, etc. | • Competence – Students are not encouraged to see their strengths and progress. Students are compared. |
| Acting out, clowning, need to socialize, competitiveness, need for praise, isolation, low self-esteem, etc. | • Belonging – Students don't feel safe. They don't work as functional teams. They feel in competition with others. They don't feel listened to or valued. |
| Resistance, trying to get around rules and expectations, questioning the teacher or the lesson, looking for opportunities to break free and express, tagging, and graffiti, etc. | • Freedom – Student are not given increased responsibility when they show they can handle it. They are not given opportunities to take things in creative directions. |

| | |
|---|---|
| Daydreaming, socializing, going off task, looking for weaknesses in the teacher, silliness, looking bored, etc. | • Fun – Classes to not provide enough places where students win in teams and are able to immerse themselves in tasks that they find pleasurable. Not feeling safe emotionally. |
| **Byproducts of a POF**<br><br>**(symptom behavior)** | **Psychology of Failure (POF) is promoted by the practices, values and policies at the school – X's that encourage a POF (See Chapter 4 and Appendix X for an explanation and a list).** |
| Low motivation, looking for the easy path, not doing work without a reward, not taking responsibility for actions, blaming others, etc. | • External Locus of Control promoting X's |
| Feeling disconnected from peers and adults, gang activity, cliques, low self-esteem, reckless behavior, drug use, low pride in self or school. | • Worthlessness and Alienation promoting X's |
| Fear of failure, quitting quickly and low persistence, Accepting low performance in some subjects, short-term focus and lack of trust in self and/or the process, etc. | • Fixed vs. Growth Orientation promoting X's |

## Exercise 9.1.

As a team, list some of the most pressing problem areas at the school. List these in one column. In a second column, list ideas for what might be the most fundamental "causes" for these problems. Try to focus your list on factors that the school controls or affects (rather than on externals). Review your two lists and draw conclusions. This activity is useful anytime but may be especially useful when done shortly before engaging in the process of strategic planning described in the chapter.

## Exercise 9.2:

As a group examine the Chart below. Which of the 2 columns best characterizes your attitude toward your context?

### Appendix 9.A: Healthy Versus Unhealthy Perspectives on One's School's Context.

| Healthy (Caring R) Approach to Our Context | Unhealthy (Toxic R) Approach to Our Context |
|---|---|
| INFORMATION<br><br>I have knowledge of many of my students' home situations, I understand the challenges that they face every day. I use that information as I relate to them and conceive how I will teach. | EXCUSES<br><br>The more I learn about how my students live, the more I see that many of them will never be able to learn or meet high expectations. So, I lower my expectations for myself and them. |
| UNDERSTANDING<br><br>I realize that there are limits to how fast I can move from where they were to where I want to get. But those limits imply that things will take longer and require more skill and commitment. | VICTIM MENTALITY<br><br>It seems like no matter what I try, others always resist growth because it is new and scary, so I have learned to give up and see things as unfair, and the deck is stacked against me. |

| KNOWING HISTORY | FIXED ABILITY |
|---|---|
| I understand how my students were taught in the past and how that would create certain expectations, habits, and comfort zones. I understand how the teachers at this school have been used to doing things. It all goes in the general category of people doing the best they can, given their level of understanding and their situation. | My students are so used to being told what to do, being given negative recognitions to stop misbehaving, only trying when they get something, or when thing are going to be on the test, and/or doing the minimum that I do not see how I am supposed to change that. Other teachers tell me that they try to do 1-Paradigm teaching and it is too unfamiliar to students so it does not work. |
| COMPASSION | LABELING/LIMITING |
| I do have empathy for my students. I try to be understanding and work with their challenges to find ways that they can succeed, especially eliminating needless policies that penalize students because of things they cannot control. | At this school, "these students" are not ready for what the students at school X are. That stuff won't work with "these students." "Let me tell you a story about one of them that I heard the other day…" |
| RECOGNITION | LOSING ATTITUDES |
| Teaching students who do not bring in as much cultural capital presents an added burden to the job of teaching. But all students represent challenges. And our job is to teach the students we are given, the best we can. | How can the teachers here succeed with the students at this school? I cannot blame them for their apathy and cynical attitude. It is a miracle when any of us just gets through the day. We all have to do whatever it takes to survive and cope. |

## Appendix 9.3. Why Solving Symptoms May Create a New Set of Real Problems.

As discussed earlier in the chapter, attempting to solve symptoms directly is often ineffective for a variety of reasons including a potential lack of coherence, and very often simply being misguided effort. The reader is encouraged to identify and then solve the school's real problems. Below is a list of the main problems with adding a new X to the current situation in an attempt to address the symptoms of a problematic condition/O.

1.  The real problem has not been identified. If the real problem does not change in the form of fundamentally better R's and X's, in the long-term, the symptom will not change. We use the phrase "rearranging the deck chairs on the titanic" to refer to situations in which there is a new X added into the overall situation to fix an isolated O that does not address the real problem. Superficial changes will not have much overall effect when the fundamentals (R's and X's) have not changed. Capacity is not improved.

2.  These interventions do not work very well to change behavior at the whole school or classroom level. "Implementing" programs (i.e., program level X's) into a school or classroom can make either a positive or negative difference. It will only be positive if it directly or indirectly leads to changes in the R's toward higher quality and level. And

---

**Legend: R-X-O**

**R's = References**
The inner thoughts and operations we use to inform our actions such as values, conditioning, beliefs, attitudes, assumptions, and mental processes.

**X's = Actions**
What we do each day as an educator such as practices, methods, strategies, policies, habits, and all behavior (verbal and non-verbal).

**O's = Outcomes**
The results from our actions such as effects on students, effects on colleagues, and resultant learning (measurable and unmeasurable).

only if the program reflects coherence and congruence with the guiding R's.

3. Addressing symptoms keeps us mired in the lower-quality thinking. They are driven more by "complicated" and programmatic forms of thinking, and less by principles and system thinking that reflects an appreciation for the inherent complexity of meaningful change.

4. When leaders add a new intervention into the system which is not driven by a shared reference/R and/or has been agreed to by the group, they send a message to the members of the community that their concerns do not matter, and in essence, the one in charge cares more about their own convenience or reputation than the growth needs of the collective as learners and as an entity which is evolving in a particular direction.

5. They not only do not solve the "real problems" but more often create a new set of real problems. Even if a new isolated X is relatively helpful it will take effort to implement. But very often the X we select to deal with the symptom is a step in the wrong direction. Consider the case of Mr. Smith above, if instead of changing the real problem (i.e., the quality of the teaching), we might simply try to bribe, coerce, gimmick, control, con, and/or threaten the students into being in attendance. These kinds of interventions create unhealthy byproducts and will in many ways affect the direction of the school down the pathway to greater levels of dysfunction. They are like trying to make a flower taller by pulling on it and stretching it. They will do little to make the flowers taller but will leave damage which will make encouraging the growth process more difficult.

## Exercise 9.3.

Reflect on previous efforts at the school to solve problems. Attempt to classify the problems you were addressing as mostly symptoms or mostly real problem (in retrospect).

In those cases, where your remedy could have been characterized as a direct effort to solve a symptom, reflect on the nature of the solutions that you attempted to implement. If may be useful to review the list of possible issues in the appendix above.

Reflect on the effects these efforts had on the school, both in the short term and in the long term. What can you conclude? Does that contrast between the O-X and R-X-O logic help inform your current thinking?

Finally, note a few recommendations to yourself for how you might address the area of problem remediation in the future.

### Appendix 9.D. Example Smart Goal

# Writing SMART Goals and Objectives

- Engage Steps 1, 2 and 3 of the R-X-O Strategic Planning Process
- Identify a "gap area" that implies the need for change.
- Create an overall Goal that reflects a priority need.
- Then provide more specific subbjectives that include elements of SMART goal development, i.e., responsibility, timeframe, resources, specific measurable outcomes For example

### Goal #1: Student leadership capacity will increase on campus

| Objectives | Measure | Account | Time | Resource |
|---|---|---|---|---|
| 1A: Students will meet and develop as a leadership organization. | Student attendance | Ms. Santos – coordinator | Once every 2 weeks | Room 203 $200 budget |
| 1B: One or Two students will be selected to be members of the school site council. | Elected and attend meetings | Chair of SC will invite, or select | Perpetual | none |
| 1C: Faculty will learn about, discuss and share ideas related to how to promote leadership skills in class. | More student leadership in classes after PD | I will run a PD on promoting leadership | May 6th Faculty meeting (40 min) | none |

# CHAPTER 10:

## Exploring the Eight Dimensions of School Climate and Function

In this chapter, we examine the eight dimensions of school climate and function. Each dimension reflects a vital, independent component of a school's effectiveness. Each domain is also inter-related. They operate interdependently to produce a whole school phenomenon. The goal of this chapter will be to gain greater insight into the current state of our school related to these eight dimensions:

1. **Appearance and Physical Plant**
2. **Faculty and Staff Relations**
3. **Student Interactions**
4. **Leadership/Decision-Making**
5. **Discipline Environment**
6. **Learning and Assessment**
7. **Social-Emotional Culture**
8. **School-Community Relations**

In the effort to move up the school effectiveness roadmap (Figure 10.1), it is helpful to engage in a process of assessment of the school's current level of climate and function. Assessing the climate enables us to a) know how we are performing in each of the specific domains of effectiveness, b) capture the "X-factor" pervading the school environment generally, c) locate where we are presently on the effectiveness roadmap, and d) better recognize our current strengths and weaknesses, and where to best focus our attention in the improvement process.

### Figure 10.1/1.1: Growth Pathway - SCAI School Climate Ratings, and Corresponding Predicted Achievement

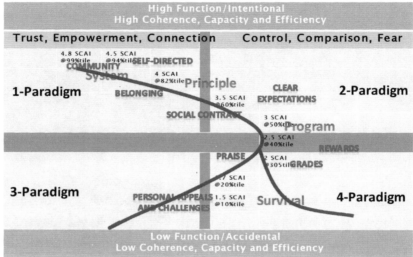

As discussed in Chapter two, the ASSC School Climate Assessment Instrument (SCAI) items are based in a theoretical construct related to the degree to which any school micro-phenomenon encourages or discourages a psychology of success/POS and higher levels of function. As a result, the rating of any individual SCAI item will relate generally to a location on the theoretical school effectiveness roadmap, just as will be the case for the overall dimension and overall aggregate means.

## Why are all Eight Dimensions Inter-Related?

For nearly every school for which we have SCAI data, we find the rating means for each of the eight dimensions tend to be very consistent with one another. For example, if the Dimension 3 mean related to student interactions was rated a 3.4, the great likelihood is that the mean for Dimension 5 related to classroom management and discipline (as well as the means for all the other dimensions), would be rated in that same middle 3-ish range. Why is this? There are three primary reasons, each providing useful insight in our improvement process.

**Reason #1: The Same Set of R's Inform All Eight Dimensions**: The main reason that phenomenon from each of the eight distinct areas of climate tend to be rated by participants similarly at a school is that the same DNA runs through all of what happens (See Figure 10.2). In other words, the practices/X's in each dimension are informed by the same set of collectively held references/R's.

## Figure 10.2: ASSC SCAI School Climate Levels

| | Level 3 | Level 2 | Level 1 |
|---|---|---|---|
| **System** | Intentional | Semi-intentional | Accidental |
| **Ethos** | Sound vision translated into effective practice | Good intentions translated into practices that "work." | Practices defined by the relative self interest of faculty and staff |
| **LOP Level** | System/Principle | Program | Reactive |
| **Effect on Students** | Liberating Experience changes students for the better | Perpetuating Experience has a mixed effect on students | Domesticating Experience has a net negative effect on students |
| **Staff relations** | Collaborative | Congenial | Competitive |
| **Psychological Outcome** | Promotes a Psychology of Success | Promotes a Mixed Psychology | Promotes a Psychology of Failure |
| **SCAI/Achieve Results** | Above 4.0/75%tile | 3.9 – 2.8/75 -30%tile | Below 2.7/30%tile |

**Reason #2: The Status Quo Will Seek to Maintain Itself.** The location of any school on the roadmap at any point in time implies a status quo. That status quo will be characterized by the collective/predominant R's and the typical X's at the school. The common X's employed in one area of the school will encourage those of the other areas to be at the same level. So, when we attempt to elevate a particular phenomenon in one domain of the school, the status quo of the other phenomena will act to hold that area down to its current level - much like the force of gravity. Likewise, if we affect improvement in one dimension, we can expect to see the other areas improve as a result.

**Reason #3: Students Acclimatize to the Common Level/Types of X's Used**. Students will become acclimatized to a level of X's – from our school as well as all others they have attended. Therefore, part of the status quo and the "normal" at the school will reflect practices to which students have become accustomed. Improvement will imply supporting a new level of expectations on the part of students. Correspondingly, the faculty and staff will need to be aware that they are recalibrating the students' expectations which will require persistence, patience, and a steadfast commitment to the higher quality X's necessary to make it happen.

In the following sections, we examine each of the eight dimensions of school climate and function as operationalized in the SCAI. Development of each dimension will include four elements.

1.  A general definition of the dimension.
2.  Key questions for leaders to consider.
3.  Some of the references/R's that are fundamental to the domain. These questions will be useful as you conceive your improvement "intentions."
4.  Some of the practices/X's implied in moving up the roadmap. These questions will be useful as you conceive your improvement "means."

## Dimension One: Appearance and Physical Plant

Examines the relationship between the physical characteristics and environment of a school and the climate it promotes. This dimension includes the degree to which intentional efforts have been made related to how outsiders perceive the school.

## Some Key Questions:

- Is student ownership evident?
- Is care for the space/place by school community members' evident?
- Is there intention evident in how things look?

## Values and R Alignment level Considerations

What does the school's appearance say to those in and out of the school community? Does it speak of care and pride? Is it important that things work? Does one see an intentional sense of an aesthetic purpose or use of school colors? Is the value of student ownership and sense of "a home" in evidence as one walks through the school? Is there a sense of the identity of the school exhibited in the physical plant? Is the custodial staff valued and appreciated?

## Practical and X Alignment level Considerations

Is there a pro-active policy for ensuring repairs get made? Is there a formal or informal policy about what is displayed on the walls? Is current student work encouraged? Are display cases maintained? Is graffiti and litter dealt with immediately? Is there someone with the responsibility for thinking about how the physical aspects of the school could be improved?

# Dimension Two: Faculty and Staff Relations

Examines the relationship between how faculty members relate to one another and the effects on the climate of the school. This dimension includes the degree to which collaboration, respect, capacity to interact, and a sense of collective purpose exist among the faculty. It also includes the explicit and explicit expectations among faculty as to how decisions are made, and duties are delegated and performed.

**Some Key Questions:**

- Do teachers have the time and desire to collaborate (i.e., time to connect skill/process-based references)?
- Do teachers/staff have opportunities to bond (i.e., connect personal R's and become a "we.")
- Is teacher leadership encouraged?

**Values and R Alignment level Considerations**

Do we hear a "We" in our narratives? Is there a sense that what we do each day is a team effort? Do we seek a collective ownership of our vision? Do we aspire to cultivating trust in one another? Do we assume a 1-Paradigm way of being in our interactions and discussions about teaching and learning? Do faculty and staff members expect to be given power over matters which affect them?

**Practical and X Alignment level Considerations**

Do faculty members have assigned time to collaborate, plan, and innovate? Does the school embrace both symbolically as well as practically the idea of being a professional learning community that embodies a growth orientation? Is an effort made by someone to encourage and plan celebrations, gatherings, time to share school and non-school related experiences? Is true emotional sharing encouraged? Do faculty and staff members care enough about serving students and being excellent that they feel some obligation to hold one another accountable for their R's and X's? Do faculty members feel comfortable taking on roles in which they have a heightened level of responsibility?

# Dimension Three: Student Interactions

Examines the relationships among student expectations, peer interactions, and their place in the school and the climate that exists. This dimension includes the degree to which students' interactions are governed by intention vs. accidental qualities.

## Some Key Questions:

- Do students feel safe from abuse – both verbal and physical?

- Is there an intention by staff to meet the students' basic needs?

- Do the structures in place (or absence of them) knowingly or unknowingly promote the advantage of the advantaged?

### Values and R Alignment level Considerations

Do students trust that the adults have a plan for their safety and personal growth? Or is the implicit assumption that students' interactions are outside of the control of the adults? Do students expect to learn in a consistent and student-centered environment? Or do they feel like every situation and classroom implies a separate set of assumptions and expectations? Do adults embrace being good role models for students? Do adults agree on absolutes including forms of student interaction which are unacceptable and trust that others will act if those kinds of interactions are observed?

### Practical and X Alignment level Considerations

What do adults do - in our classrooms, open spaces, gym, fields, assemblies, and offices – to promote the dispositions, skills, and understandings in students to interact in an effective, healthy, and respectful manner? Do we teach and assess cooperation in our classes? How do we create structures encouraging safety, and habits of human consideration? Are the students who are currently in the position of being the "advantaged" encouraged to be servants and role models rather than assume entitlement? Is student voice encouraged within classrooms? And is it reflected in an empowered student governance and/or peer mediation structure?

# Dimension Four: Leadership and Decisions

Examines the relationship among the decision-making mechanisms, how leadership authority is manifested, and the school climate. This dimension includes the degree to which the collective possesses a shared sense of values and an operational vision. It also explores the ways in which the quality of leadership affects school life.

## Some Key Questions:

- Is there an understood and shared vision?
- Are decisions made by those who are most knowledgeable and best situated?
- Are the principles which guide the school evident and conspicuous?
- Are there efficient democratic mechanisms in place to make decisions and process information?

## Values and R Alignment level Considerations

What level paradigm embodies the R's? Is the school about empowerment or control from the top down? Does each school leader see herself/himself as representing something bigger than themselves? Is leadership a pervasive quality at the school or is it just in the hands of the administration – i.e., Is shared leadership a priority? Does the school seek to embody democratic quality?

## Practical and X Alignment level Considerations

*This paragraph essentially relates to the purpose and content of this book generally. The practical considerations which apply are vast. Here are a few essential questions.* Are the R's clarified and cultivated at the school, or are they left to chance? Is a conspicuous and continuous effort made to align the X's at the school with the desired R's and the intended location on the roadmap? Is outcome/O data used primarily for self-assessment of the degree of progress toward the destination? Are there inclusive and functional shared leadership bodies? Is there a functioning mechanism for operating as a professional learning community?

# Dimension Five: Discipline Environment

Examines the relationship between the classroom management and discipline approaches used within the school and the climate created as a result. This dimension includes the degree to which management strategies promote higher levels of self-responsibility and self-motivation. It also examines teacher-student interactions as a source of management and motivation.

## Some Key Questions:

- Is there a consistent policy and set of R's/principles that guide action?
- Do practices promote increased "POS/ psychology of success" over time?
- Do practices promote more self-direction and self-discipline over time?

## Values and R Alignment level Considerations

Do adults see classroom management as a part of the overall learning and growth development process at the school, (or is it seen as merely a means to getting students ready to learn)? Is there an intention to create empowering, transformative 1-Paradigm classrooms?

## Practical and X Alignment level Considerations

Does leadership actively encourage consistent school-wide policy and expectations? Does the school have processes and policies (including performance evaluation) in place which encourage teachers and staff members to self-reflect on their current classroom management and discipline related X's? Do the adults in the building have opportunities to share expertise and discuss the complexities of creating the 1-Paradogm, self-directed, classroom community?

Given its fundamental importance, the entire next chapter is devoted to exploring the means for moving up the roadmap in this domain.

# Dimension Six: Instruction and Assessment

Examines the relationships between the instructional strategies and the assessment methods used and the learning and psychological climate created as a result. Instruction is explored as it relates to its level of engagement, student empowerment, and authenticity. Higher quality instruction and assessment methods are contrasted to less effective methods by the degree to which they promote a psychology of success rather than a psychology of failure, deep learning rather than surface learning, and critical thinking skills rather than just information processing.

## Some Key Questions:

- Is assessment used to promote growth rather than comparison?
- Is learning engaging and student-centered?
- Do students learn to function effectively in collectives?

## Values and R Alignment level Considerations

Are assessment practices (i.e., X) viewed as a concrete representation of the school's values (i.e., R) related to what is important and what it defined as "quality" and "success?" Is there an intention to find ways to assess the most essential learnings? Are the qualities of "highly effective learner" defined and operationalized? Is there a value for collaborative teaching? Is there an agreed upon conception of what an observer "should see" or "should not see" if they observed a class? Is there an intention for regular education and special education faculty and staff to collaborate for the highest good of all students in the class?

## Practical and X Alignment level Considerations

Do teachers have an intentional system for determining and considering students' learning styles and using necessary modifications for learning disabilities? Do teachers look for every opportunity to process content within an inquiry model or a hands-on manner? Is purposeful cooperative learning a regular practice? Do teachers create high quality in-depth rubrics for both process and product outcomes and have students regularly self-reflect on their progress? Is an effort made by teachers to differentiate instruction and assessment where it would benefit students? Are students given an opportunity to make choices and take ownership for some aspects of what they are doing and producing? Are student led-conferences or an equivalent process incorporated? Does the curriculum encourage student leadership and an orientation toward socially conscious engagement in the world? Do instructional and assessment related X's promote more psychology of success and less psychology of failure?

## Dimension Seven: Social and Emotional Culture

Examines the pervasive attitudes and social-emotional cultures which operate within the school and their relationship to the resulting climate. This dimension explores the degree to which social and/or communal bonds are present, the attitudes and narratives that the stakeholders possess, and the level of pride and ownership they hold. It includes the degree to which efforts in this area are made intentionally or left to chance.

### Some Key Questions:

- Are there traditions and rituals which help the students feel connected?
- Do students feel supported and listened to by adults?
- Do students feel a sense of voice and power?

### Values and R Alignment level Considerations

Do the educators in the school express an R of school pride which extends to their students and community? Are rituals and traditions maintained that symbolize the R's of continuity, identity, and a value for joy at school? Can the adults say in honesty that it is "the students' school" and they are there to serve? Is the emotional life and basic needs of the student considered when decisions are made?

## Practical and X Alignment level Considerations

Do the adults like the students and project an openness listen to their concerns and needs? Are traditions maintained which bond classes, grade levels, and/or the larger school community? Are there opportunities for students to engage in leadership roles, and a voice in the school? Are there vibrant student activities such as clubs, groups, intramurals, etc.? Is an effort made by adults to attend and promote school activities? Is there a committee or group responsible for planning for ways to encourage positive student life and school culture? If one was to ask students if they can see evidence of adults making a deliberate effort to promote each student's POS, would they say yes? Do the adults in the school make some level of effort to use their words (especially about the students as well as one another) carefully and purposefully when they were in private spaces? Are systematic mechanisms such as peer mediation and restorative practices in place to encourage student ownership of problems and conflict?

# Dimension Eight: Community Relations

Examines the relationship between the way the school is perceived externally and projects itself outward to the parents and community. This dimension includes the degree to which the school is welcoming, provides quality communication and resource tools, and takes advantage of the resources in the local community, including parents, and acts intentionally as a center of community life.

## Some Key Questions:

- Is the school welcoming to parents and community members?
- Do students have opportunities to serve and connect to their community?
- Does the school's vision extend to all aspects of the school experience?

## Values and R Alignment level Considerations

Is there a shared R that the school is an integral member (if not a hub) of its community? Does the school have an intention of using its local and global communities as part of the educational process for students? Do we value access and transparency? Are the highest-level R's reflected in the school athletics and other public events? Does the school seek the most effective means for providing school activity and student progress information to parents?

## Practical and X Alignment level Considerations

Does the school have systematic means of sharing information with parents and the local community? Do representatives take part in local events to stay connected and informed? Does the school promote its fine arts and athletics programs to support student participants? Are service-learning activities incorporated on a regular basis? Are community volunteers utilized? Does the school have a process by which volunteers can be educated in the "X's we do" and "X's we don't do" lists to encourage consistency and quality among all adults in the building? Do the teachers at the school take the opportunity to get to know the community?

## CONCLUSION

After exploring the nature of each of the eight domains of school climate, you are likely more skilled at assessing how each is currently functioning at your school, as well as what would be required to affect improvement in any of the dimensions. Within any school improvement effort, each area will require adequate attention if the school intends to experience movement up the pathway. As discussed, they will tend to move together and exist at a similar location on the theoretical roadmap. One encouraging aspect of recognizing the interdependence the domains is that we can trust our improvement efforts in one area will influence the growth process generally.

SCAI ratings will be a valid reflection of both the operating intentions/R's and the means/X's occurring at the school, and therefore, accurately represent the level of climate and function.

In the next three chapters, practical steps for moving our school up the pathway to higher levels of effectiveness, climate, and function are outlined. The next chapter explores what is required to improve in the dimension of classroom management and discipline. In Chapter twelve, we examine the growth needs of the school that is currently operating in the lower quadrants, and in Chapter thirteen we investigate the needs of the school currently operating in the middle region which seeks to move more fully into the 1-Paradigm location.

**Exercise 10.1:** As a group on individually, complete the ASSC School Climate Assessment Instrument (SCAI)

**Exercise 10.2:** As a group or individually, complete the form below (Handout D), by rating where you would assess your school to be on each dimension using the 3 levels of function provided? You may want to review Figure 10.2 for a fuller sense of the nature of each of the levels. In this exercise, participants are asked to rate each domain as being currently best characterized as either level 1, 2 or 3. Share and discuss your ratings as a group. You will likely find that these ratings confirm other means you have used to assess where your school is currently located on the effectiveness roadmap (Figure 10.1).

Handout D - Evaluating Current Practice Levels:
Rate the practices at your school across each category

| Dimension | Level 1 | Level 2 | Level 3 |
|---|---|---|---|
| | Accidental/POF | Semi-Intentional | Intentional/POS |
| | Sensory | Program | Principle/System |
| Physical Environment | | | |
| Teacher Relations | | | |
| Student Interactions | | | |
| Leadership and Decision | | | |
| Management/Discipline | | | |
| Learning and Assessment | | | |
| Attitude and Culture | | | |
| Community | | | |

# CHAPTER 11:

## Moving to the Next Level in the Area of Classroom Management and School Discipline.

This chapter is devoted to one area of the overall school improvement effort – classroom management and discipline. The reasons for this are:

- This domain is the most predictive of the overall school climate and most defining of each school's location on the roadmap,

- Our ability to move up the roadmap will be largely predicated by what we do in this dimension, and

- It is the area that most defines the emotional climate and our experience of happiness with our school and its inhabitants.

We will engage this area from three respective roadmap starting point locations – low, middle, and high. The recommendation would be that the reader start from the bottom as the requirements for moving to the next level are cumulative and built upon one another. Generally, the most basic elements for improvement will relate to moving up the vertical axis – so imply improving the level of function by way of trust, capacity, and coherence. Moving to the highest levels of the roadmap will involve the requisite levels of function, but also involve a movement toward the empowering 1-Paradigm quadrant of the roadmap and imply promoting more connection, empowerment, self-direction, and a sense of community.

# Growth "Pathway" on the School Effectiveness Roadmap

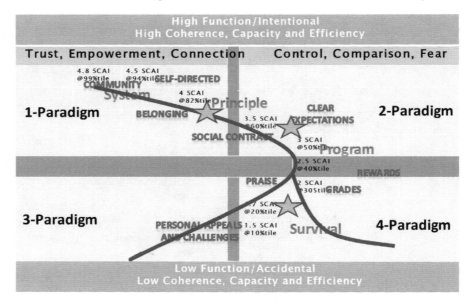

## Stage 1: Building Function: Trust, Capacity, and Coherence

Ascending to higher levels of function begins with stepping back and objectively examining the values/R's and practices/X's at the school. In most cases, what is currently taking place involves years of history, reactive programs, and patterns of action. Coping and game playing have become normal and the status quo. Improvement will require something of a reset. Much will need to be surrendered and replaced with a commitment to the use of only solid practices which create clarity and sanity. We all need to own some part of what has kept us at our current location, and vow to embody a more functional world in which teachers feel like the ground is solid, and students feel safe, clear, and trusting.

Most schools in the lower levels of the pathway deal with issues related to trust, coherence, and capacity. This is true of all areas of the school, but it is especially true when examining classroom management and discipline. Our desire is to live in a world defined by trust, capacity, and coherence. However, if our school is located at a lower level on the roadmap, we are likely experiencing less of those qualities, and as a result feeling frustration, resentment of others and like our problems are intractable. Yet, as we begin to unpack the problems at the school systematically, we will better recognize that our situation is both explainable and largely fixable.

# Vertical Axis

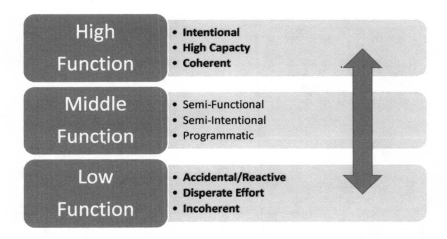

| High Function | • Intentional<br>• High Capacty<br>• Coherent |
| Middle Function | • Semi-Functional<br>• Semi-Intentional<br>• Programmatic |
| Low Function | • Accidental/Reactive<br>• Disperate Effort<br>• Incoherent |

A useful place to start in our self-examination is to identify what we desire, in the domain of classroom management and discipline, and compare that to what we would assess to be our current state. Figure 11.1 may provide some useful insight to that exploration process.

Figure 11.1: Exploring the Dimensions of Trust, Coherence, and Capacity in the Lower-Level School – What We Want and What We Likely Have

| Area | What we likely want | What we may have |
|------|---------------------|------------------|
| **Trust** | • A sane place to teach and learn.<br>• Adults trust students know the rules and will follow them.<br>• Administration supports the teachers when justified.<br>• Be able to trust our peers to do support the collective goals.<br>• Trust students to not need constant supervision.<br>• Trust that students want to learn and enjoy engaging in quality activities. | • A daily struggle with behavior issues<br>• Students don't trust that teachers can gain order in many classrooms.<br>• We don't trust one another to do what we have decided upon.<br>• We feel the need to maintain constant supervision or students will take advantage.<br>• We don't trust students' internal capacity, so we resort to extrinsic bribes.<br>• Teachers don't trust administration to support them (i.e., when they attempt ambitious practices or follow through with consequences). |
| **Coherence** | • A consistent discipline policy.<br>• All programs and initiatives work together and in service of the school's mission.<br>• Use only practices which are ethically sound and feel right. | • Inconsistent policies.<br>• Added disparate programs to address problem symptoms that are often incongruent or unhealthy.<br>• Control becomes the guiding value rather than human growth and development.<br>• Anything that "works" is acceptable. |

| Capacity | • Ability to move past a simply compliance-based paradigm. <br> • Have students support the function level in the class in conjunction with the teacher. <br> • Be able to include instructional models requiring student self-direction and cooperation. <br> • A process where teachers can share and grow in this area together. | • Feel limited in what we can teach because too many students lack self-regulation or good intentions. <br> • Have resorted to manipulative strategies, like bribes, praise, comparisons, card charts, that keep us stuck in our rut. <br> • Teachers get addicted to reactive and manipulative strategies, and students become more dependent on extrinsic incentives (and less mature) over time. <br> • Limited growth trajectory because there are no common goals and/or process values that we are striving for. |
|---|---|---|

As we examine the dimensions of trust, coherence, and capacity, we will likely recognize that much of what is keeping us from moving forward is within our control – both individually and collectively. It is natural to look at the students as the reason for our circumstances, and we may have many students who bring great and varied challenges to our work. But we can only control what *we* do. As we examine what we have done to this point, we will recognize that, to a great extent, our current X's have been keeping our problematic conditions in place. When we change our actions and reactions, eventually, the quality of the behavior at the school will change as well.

To help ground the process of moving up in the area of classroom management and discipline, it is useful to inform our vision of "better" with a series of "basic conditions" necessary to cultivate a solid overall strategy. If we begin our process of attempting to fix what we have, we can easily run into the trap of solving *symptoms* or implementing reactive and/or coping strategies. Therefore, using a series of fundamental conditions defining quality target outcomes will support the effectiveness of our process.

## Eight Fundamental Conditions Required for Moving Up in the Area of Classroom Management and Discipline

- Condition One: A Vision of Quality
- Condition Two: Clear Expectations
- Condition Three: Expert Technical Management
- Condition Four: A Social Contract
- Condition Five: Systems Promoting Growth and Reflection
- Condition Six: Meet Needs of Challenging Students
- Condition Seven: Use Only Quality Practices
- Condition Eight: Ensure Coherence Across Practices and Policies

### Basic level

The eight conditions listed above characterize the basic qualities which would be evident at a school experiencing a high level of coherence and function related to its classroom management and discipline practices. A high level is defined by the existence of clarity, positivity, a sense of fairness and faith in and among the adults in the building, and an ever-increasing level of function and ease. Each of these qualities is explained here briefly. Identified for each quality are, a) its basic goal, b) what ensues in situations when the condition is missing, and c) its key benefits.

**Basic Condition One - A Vision of Quality**: The practices used in the classroom and/or school have their basis in principles that create increased function and promote more human potential, self-responsibility, collective good will, and community over time. For a system to be considered complete, coherent, and excellent, it must *only* include those strategies/

practices which can be defended as healthy and promoting the long-term growth for the students, the adults, and the school as a community.

**Goal:** A clear picture of what excellent looks like and a long-term focus.

**If Missing:** Haphazard practices that may or may not be contributing to a healthy and functional classroom. Best case is a set of practices that is perceived to "work." But more often the result is a set of practices which are misguided, incongruent and/or unknowingly undermine the goals of the school.

**Key Benefits:** Coherence and a clear set of guiding principles which can be used to evaluate the fitness and efficacy of any practice or set of practices.

**Basic Condition Two - Clear Expectations:** The highest priority in any classroom would be a consistent and expert use of strategies providing the highest possible level of clarity. Clarity promotes the understanding of how to succeed in the school or classroom, contribute to the collective, meet one's responsibilities, and achieve one's personal goals. A complete approach to classroom management begins with promoting clear and positive expectations, agreements, norms, and boundaries. In a high-quality classroom these concepts are soundly developed with practical strategies, concept development, and modeling. Negative strategies of any kind become unnecessary when this goal is met. The result is classrooms in which students can feel solid, supported, sane, and empowered to meet their personal goals and those of the group.

**Goal:** Clarity for how to be excellent, successful and a positive contributor.

**If Missing:** Students feel confused. Their efforts may be tentative or misguided. The group does not work well as a collective or improve over time.

**Key Benefits:** Clarity breeds sanity. The path to success is made more accessible. Students can count on one another more readily. Trust is promoted.

**Basic Condition Three - Expert Technical Management**: An effective classroom requires systems in place which promote efficient interactions, routines, attention levels and activities. There must be effective "technical management" to support the other components of the system. On a fundamental level, this promotes the ease and smoothness of the class for both the teacher and the students. Yet, over time, it is the necessary groundwork for such things as a classroom culture of listening and respect, and a faith in the students' ability to function in whole school level situations that require orderly behavior.

> **Goal:** Smooth and easy interactions without negativity or the need for coercion.

> **If Missing:** Lots of wasted time. A perpetual issue with attention and most likely the un-necessary use of short-term based clever strategies to remediate the dysfunction. A pervasive feeling in the room of struggle and failure. Growth is limited.

> **Key Benefits:** Efficiency. Emotional ease and a feeling that there is order. Provides a building block for higher levels of collective function.

## Operational Support for Meeting Conditions 1-3

Many times, the biggest problems in this area are the easiest to remedy. Changing a student's mindset which is stuck in a fixed-ability orientation can require immense skill and persistence over months or years yet helping a class of students learn to be attentive to one another can be accomplished in a few days or weeks – if we approach it as a practical/technical task. Too often we mischaracterize the job and misplace attention and energy onto things which will not help the group grow. This is often the case with promoting technical management – attention, cues, procedures, and directions. When we observe a teacher at our school or another that is an expert at technical management and whose class is attentive without the need for any coercion, threats, bribes, and power plays, we will notice what they do appears to be a) quite simple, and b) similar to most other teachers who have success in this area. Therefore, we can conclude that it is not about personality, cleverness, or requiring of any special talent. However, it does require a system, being 100% consistent, situating this part of our job in the realm of pedagogy, and reducing the tendency to take things personally. A potential downfall in the effort to move up the roadmap in this area will come from the need to feel one's authority is being respected rather than simply encouraging an environment which promotes emotional ease and transparency. Respect tends to follow results. Therefore, for best results focus on your own level of clarity and consistency not their level of respect.

The skills of technical management are fully explained in detail in the book *Transformative Classroom Management (Shindler, 2009)*. The essential skills for success described in the book are outlined below. These techniques do not require special effort or training. They are simply practical. The intention should be to eliminate negativity in any form and use positive practical action instead.

- **Effective use of cues.** Simple audible or visual cue are used to gain/ shift attention from a state where students are working and not expected to be attentive to being attentive to directions or input. These can include clapping, call and response, words, bells/sounds, whistles, hand/body gestures, or phrases. The effectiveness of a cue will be the extent to which it is used with 100% consistency, the teacher waits for 100% attention before speaking, and uses simple emotion-free consequences when not receiving 100% attention for all students (such as starting over, stopping, using a simple redirect such as "we all have our eyes on X right now," or speaking privately with students who do not respond to the subtle clues).
- **Practicing Procedures and Transitions**. When students' actions reflect something less than what we think is adequate, we have

a lot of ineffective options (i.e., complaining, disappointment, resentment, warnings, lectures, apathy). However, if our goal is to create more long-term function, there is a more effective option, practice doing the procedure, routine or transition until the students can do it well. It may take time initially, but it is a positive activity, builds their confidence in one another and you, qualifies as a "team win," and saves much more time in the long run. No need to add any negative emotion or language to the situation. Choose active positive over passive negative.

- **Effective Directions**. Follow this sequence faithfully and students will ultimately learn to make asking questions and following directions natural, rewarding, and painless habits.

  - Begin with a **cue** and wait for 100% attention.
  - Provide a **finish word** like "when I say "Go!"
  - Be clear in your **directions**.
  - Call for **questions**. Here it is essential to encourage students get in the habit of asking clarifying questions. So, you need to make this a high-intention focus. Many students in low function schools refrain from asking when they do not understand (while most students in high performing schools do). Therefore, support the mindset and habit of your students to fearlessly ask questions until they and their peers are clear and ready.
  - Make random **checks for accountability**. This practice needs to be positive and low threat, but students need to understand that they need to understand the directions or keep asking questions.
  - Provide the **finish word**.

(It will be important to keep reminding students that our collective goal is a place where we feel empowered to ask until we get it, and that we are developing a culture of listening and respect. We need to help them recognize, in the big picture, it is all going in the direction of more accountability, focus, self-responsibility, and collective function).

- **Providing written descriptions.** Independently, by grade level, department, or as a school, guidelines for situational behavior contexts should be spelled out in detail. What constitutes quality for tasks such as a role in a group effort, lab work, and other every-day tasks should be spelled out in writing and made conspicuous. It is even more effective to construct the definition of quality in the form of a rubric. The rubric format encourages students to see a task can be completed within a range of quality. When teachers and students shift from conceiving success as "being on task" to success being "a quality effort" the result is a significant impact on your movement up. It will be useful in our effort generally to reflect upon why the goal of having students on task is fundamentally different from the goal of having them engage in a quality effort.

Moving up the levels of the roadmap will require an examination of what we do to promote the clarity of the expectations at the school. In all classrooms, the teacher is using strategies to encourage students' understanding of "the expectations." Yet, the quality and effectiveness of those strategies varies greatly. In practice, we can desire clear expectations but use strategies that encourage dysfunction and ultimately apathy toward our expectations (See Appendix 11.A: Ten practices that promote dysfunction). Producing sanity and efficiency is a matter of understanding and committing to high quality practices and refraining from lower quality practices (See Figures 11.2). Creating well-understood and appreciated expectations will result from using practices that a) create clarity and b) a positive personal asso-ciation with the expected behavior. Therefore, it is useful to frequently ask ourselves, a couple of questions 1) "Is the desired action I want from my students clear in their minds in practical terms?" and 2) "Is what I am asking them to do something that is good for them, or that they appreciate as valuable?"

Figure 11.2 outlines several popular strategies for promoting expectations. Each strategy is classified by its effect on the movement of your school/classroom on the roadmap.

**Figure 11.2: Approximate rating of common management practices related to their ability to create clarity of expectations and a positive association with the expected behavior, from most (four stars) to least effective (no stars).**

| Practice/Strategy | Clarity rating | Affect rating | Overall | How each level of strategies affects the location of the school on the effectiveness roadmap | |
|---|---|---|---|---|---|
| Purposeful Action<br>• Consistency<br>• Follow-through<br>Positive Recognition<br>Clarifying Statements/Mantras<br>Clarifying Questions<br>Expectation Cues<br>Debriefing<br>Written Expectations | +<br><br>+<br>+<br>+<br>+<br>+<br><br>+ | +<br><br>+<br>N+<br>N+<br>N+<br>+<br>N | ****<br><br>****<br>***<br>***<br>***<br>****<br>**½ | Strategies which effectively create cause and effect clarity and positive associations related to expectations Use promotes movement up the effectiveness continuum | ↑ |
| Personal Recognition/Praise<br>Warnings<br>Requests<br>"I like the way…" | N<br>N+<br>-<br>- | N+<br>N<br>N-<br>N- | *<br>*<br>½*<br>* | Strategies which have a marginal influence on promoting positive expectations and create inconsequential or confusing emotional climates Use promotes little movement up or down continuum | ↔ |
| Negative recognitions<br>Irrational or Negative Actions<br>Threats and Put Downs | N-<br>-<br>- | -<br>-<br>- | ½ *<br>0<br>0 | Strategies which do very little to promote clarity and do a great deal to create negative associations with the desired behavior Use promotes mostly movement down the effectiveness continuum | ↓ |

*From Transformative Classroom Management (Shindler, 2009)
+        demonstrates high levels of effectiveness in this area
N+      demonstrates some effectiveness
N        is neutral or inconsequential
N-       does a bit more harm than good but has an effect
-         does mostly harm

As we assess the strategies we are currently using, we will likely recognize the relationship between the current level of function in our class

(O/outcome) and the practices (X's) that we are using. Much of what is encouraged in the field at the time of this writing is termed "positive." However, in practice many of these stimulus and response-based strategies are essentially manipulative student-to-student comparisons and intended to obtain compliance rather than promote sanity and clarity. Some of these practices are outlined in Appendix 11.A of this chapter. If we do not accept that we need to give up the use of manipulative, external LOC promoting, disempowering, and subtly shaming practices we will struggle to move out of the lower quadrants of the roadmap.

## Leader's Role

As a leader, we can use the list in Figure 11.2 to assess the progress of any teacher's growth to a great extent. When we are in a teacher's classroom and we hear a lot of the lower-level practices like negative recognitions (i.e., I told you two to stop doing that ...) and personal statements (i.e., What is it with this class. . .?), it will be evident that the teacher is in substantive need of growth support. If we hear a teacher using strategies, such as "I like the way. . .," personal praise and/or a lot of warnings, we will be able to locate that teacher's practice at the middle level on the growth pathway. And if we observe a teacher who can demonstrate the higher level of expectation promoting strategies effectively, we know that they are probably someone we want sharing what they do with others at the school.

As a school our conversations (i.e., professional development, department, or PLC meetings, and among leadership teams) needs to keep the focus on the goals and the vision rather than on the current circumstances. If our guiding question is "what are we going to do to fix our problems?" all manner of ideas will seek to fill that vacuum. We may be tempted to enlist the kinds of coping, manipulative, short-term fix forms of practices which will limit our growth up the roadmap. However, if our guiding question is "How can we create clear and healthy targets for students and reduce the need for any negativity or manipulation?" we will find ways to create ever more function in the classrooms and sanity for all. A daily struggle to keep students on task and engaged is demoralizing and it leads to a loss of hope.

Therefore, finding a positive path to a better function and classroom clarity is a requisite for building the hope required for moving up.

**Basic Condition Four – A Social Contract**: A social contract implies collective agreements accepted and maintained by any group. For a school, that means an operating concept (defined by its specific examples and non-examples) needs to be developed for "who we are" and therefore, "what we do" and "what we don't do," both for the students and the adults in the school, and then spelled out in both general and specific terms.

Our social contract needs to include logical and reasonable consequences - ways in which those who violate their agreements can fix, repair, be held to account, lose an opportunity, or reflect on what they did so they can learn and move forward more responsibly. It also needs to include ways in which those who seek to make a positive contribution will benefit and be appreciated. Having the students involved in creating the social contract encourages more ownership and understanding.

**Goal:** Strong and just social bonds and faith in the system

**If Missing:** Students become mistrustful of why discipline is used or not used. The perception things in the class are not fair or reasonable. Student can grow to resent those who disrupt the class without consequences and the teacher for not being a leader. If the teacher acts outside of the legitimacy of a social contract, students will feel as if the discipline is subjective and personal and by extension illegitimate.

**Key Benefits:** Students feel as if they live in a fair and just world. When they make an effort, they can count on being recognized and appreciated for making good choices. Those who make choices to violate their agreements learn there is cause and effect operating to help them develop a sense of responsibility, self-discipline, and accountability to the collective.

**Basic Condition Five - System Promotes Growth and Reflection:** We need to build in systems for all students to reflect on their choices and how those choices affect the collective as well as their own personal welfare. This process can involve engaging the whole class, for example, where the teacher asks the students to reflect on their current actions in relation to how those actions may be helping or not helping the class meet its goal. Or it can happen in private interactions in which the teacher asks an individual to reflect on their actions and/or take responsibility for their choices.

**Goal:** More student ownership, responsibility, and use of cause-and-effect reasoning.

**If Missing:** Students can maintain a passive relationship to their learning and/or an external locus of control and foster immature ways of processing why things happen.

**Key Benefits:** When students reflect and recognize the cause and effect in their choices, they develop more self-responsibility. The result is growth in the critical orientations of growth mindset and internal locus of control.

**Basic Condition Six - Meets Needs of Challenging Students:** Some students bring to the class deeply conditioned problematic behavior patterns, mal-adjustments, negative identity patterns, or experiences from past schools that make theirs' and others' lives more challenging. Therefore, we should also create systems to support these students who have organic or deeply conditioned patterns that make such things as self-regulation, attention, and emotional composure difficult. Even in well-run, positive environments these patterns can emerge. These students need specific interventions that help support their ability to function in a classroom and lead to greater growth, ease, and well-being.

**Goal:** Student is integrated without undermining the outcomes of class as a collective. Teacher has a clear set of strategies, a plan, and support which offers them a productive path to success. Student grows and thrives.

**If Missing:** The student can make the teacher's job much more difficult. Other students may feel unfairly put upon or penalized by the student's presence. Student does not make progress.

**Key Benefits:** Everyone feels like things are getting better with time. They feel hopeful. Effort is put into actions that are promoting growth or at least effective maintenance, and not into reactive actions or strategies that result in short-term fixes and/or perpetuate or contribute to the problem. The students grow in confidence, positive identity, and learning, transcending their past patterns.

## Sequence of Cause in an Organization/School

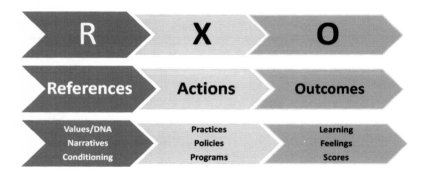

### Operational Support for Meeting Conditions 4-6

### Social Contract

Fundamental to any functional social structure is an operational social contract. A social contract implies a two-way relationship, responsibilities, and operating agreements between two sides – the school employees and the students. We could call it our social contract, or a more intimate term like a covenant, or agreements, or "Our Puma Pride." But in essence the social contract operates to make everyone feel sane, safe, secure, and solid. When the contract is not sound or is missing there will inevitably be problems. Many of the issues described above in Figure 11.1 such as insecurity, loss of trust, resentment, retaliation, passive resistance, confusion, low quality instructional environment and a generally depressed school climate are symptoms of a dysfunctional social contract.

Everyone in the school has a role in maintaining the social contract. The quality of and faith in the contract rely on everyone both actively doing their job to cultivate it, and to refrain from doing things that infringe upon it. Unfortunately, violations are much more impactful as our perception tends to process and recall negative events more readily.

Recall the R->X->O sequence. The most important part of our job when it comes to developing the social contract will be to hold it up as an essential value and intention – commit to it as an R. Therefore, we need to understand the tenet, appreciate why it is vital to our success, and expect it to be an ongoing challenge and require work. That may take the form of encouraging less committed peers, or students who have not as yet developed the appreciation, maturity, or skills to fulfill their side. As we have discussed, values/R's and practices/X's tend to be inter-dependent. In the role of leader, we will need to help all members of the school appreciate the value of having a sound social contract in place to facilitate the growth of those R's and X's.

Facilitating a more-sound social contract over time will mean evolving both our R's and X's. It will not come from common sense alone, or from faithfully implementing policy, or by simplifying it into "we need to do a better job of discipline." If common sense were the solution, our problems would have been fixed long ago. And it is not about rewarding outcomes. It is about changing processes. Rewards for either teachers or students will shift the focus away from the high-quality value/mindset (i.e., "we all do our job well and our world becomes increasingly more enjoyable") to a lower-quality value/mindset (i.e., "be better than others and you will get something").

In a practical sense, the social contract takes a few forms. First, there is a *default* social contract that everyone will use to navigate their interactive experience within the school – it is what is actual and based on current reality and can imply anything from a dystopia to a utopia. Second, the concept of social contract is fundamental to what we want to implement *schoolwide*. It includes our formal policies, but also all the large and small interactions happening within the walls and grounds of the school. Finally, a formal process for cultivating each *classroom's* social contract or classroom agreements is strongly encouraged (this process is outlined in detail in the book *Transformative Classroom Management*). Engaging in the development process faithfully and sincerely will send an empowering and caring message to students and help support the operationalization of what it takes to be a contributing member of a functional collective.

The formally and informally operating social contracts at the school should be conceived and applied related to a series of levels – from most base to most aspirational. For the school to successfully move up the roadmap, we will need to ensure that the basic levels are solid while aspiring to leverage the social bonds for a greater source of well-being and growth. The basic level will involve mostly things that need to happen or cannot happen if people in the school are to feel safe, solid, and sane. We might consider these as issues of "survival" in terms of Maslow's (1954) hierarchy of needs. We will struggle to aspire to higher levels of concern when these issues keep our attention on coping, self-protection and struggling to understand "the rules."

However, the social contract also implies many levels above this basic level. As we become more solid and trusting, we are able to operate in our situation with more ease and access the enjoyment of being good to others, thinking about the needs of the collective, find ways to contribute, and count on others to be helpful and supportive of us. These qualities are all part of the give and take of the social contract. We learn to give and receive and count on others because we know they can count on us.

Figure 11.3 outlines the references and actions required from teachers to ensure the basic levels of a functional social contract. In later sections of this chapter, more actualized levels of the teacher's role in the social contract will be explored. When a school is in a lower roadmap location currently, giving sufficient attention to professional development in this area will be essential for moving up.

Figure 11.3 Reference and Actions from Teachers to Encourage a Solid Social Contract.

| | Promote the Social Contract (SC) | Undermine the Social Contract (SC) |
|---|---|---|
| **R's or** <br><br> **References** <br><br> (values, thinking, beliefs, conditioning, biases, | • I serve the greater good (the SC) and don't take things personally. <br> • Take ownership of the quality and function of the social contract – "I take full responsibility for my role in making the contract solid, viable, and alive." <br> • It does not matter what students know or how they act today, our job is to help them grow into who they can become. <br> • Assume all students have a need for fairness. <br> • Focus on the future picture of what the class will be able to do, and trust it is possible. <br> • Think about how your actions affect others – what lessons are you teaching everyone by your words and deeds. <br> • Choose actions/X's based on what is better for tomorrow first, and today second. | • I need students to show me respect or there is a problem. <br> • Find ways to favor the students you like. <br> • Wish students were different. <br> • Feel sorry for yourself. Be a victim. <br> • Assume problems will fix themselves <br> • Allow yourself (or your students) to talk yourself out of being consistent or following through. <br> • Assume being negative or disappointed will get good results at some point. <br> • Make it about you. |

| X's or Actions (practices, strategies, methods, | • Keep your word, and do your job as defined by SC.<br>• Promote clarity in every aspect of your teaching and expectations or accept accountability for its absence.<br>• Use language which helps students recognize that they are all in it together, and a SC is collective agreement that only works with everyone doing their part.<br>• Apply consequences when students violate their agreements – without adding unnecessary lectures or guilt.<br>• Listen carefully to students who made a mistake. Show you care, but act based on the needs of the collective.<br>• Eliminate passive and negative actions. | • React to the situation with evasive cleverness or hostility.<br>• Allow students to cross the line without acting – enabling the student and abdicating responsibility.<br>• Don't follow through if you don't feel like it.<br>• Maintain vagueness as a means of holding power over students.<br>• React personally or defensively to students' immaturity or lack of outward respect.<br>• Make empty threats when you see something you don't like.<br>• Try to make students feel bad when they do something wrong or make it personal.<br>• Look for ways to passive aggressively get back at students who are disruptive. |
| --- | --- | --- |

Often students' disruptive, apathetic, disrespectful, or displaced aggressive (bullying) behavior is in response to what they perceive as teachers not doing their job within the social contract. Therefore, it is critical for teachers to evaluate behavioral problems first in terms of how well they met their side of the agreement, and then secondly from how well students' actions reflected their commitment to the social contract. Issues related to the demonstration of respect given to the teacher, display of attitude or affect, historical patterns, and etiquette should be put aside, as much as possible, when considering whether a student's actions really did violate the social contract. The teacher needs to be bigger than the situation. Our guiding questions should revolve around what is best for the individuals and the collective moving forward.

As the adults in the equation, our essential job is to cultivate the sense within the collective that the social contract is solid. That means that there is a sanctity and integrity to it, and we trust adults and students to do their part. And the contract exists to promote the growth or all individuals and the collective.

In Figure 11.4 below we examine the students' side of the equation. We can think of the students' role on two levels. First a basic (minimum) level – characterized by actions that demonstrate either a minimum commitment to or a violation of the contract. Second, a level of actions that represent choices that either contribute to the "common good," or hinder it. This second level has an infinite ceiling. When it comes to supporting the growth of the collective as it relates to the social contract, we will want to place most of our attention on the second level. However, without making sure that the first level is solid, we undercut our capacity for sanity, safety, and a solid platform to grow the second level.

Figure 11.4: Minimum Requirements and Desirable Contribution of Students to the School and Classroom Social Contract

| Basic: Minimum Required Do's | Basic: Unacceptable Don'ts |
|---|---|
| • Committing verbally to what you agreed to explicitly and/or implicitly in the SC.<br>• Showing an interest in your learning.<br>• Taking responsibility for your actions.<br>• Complying with reasonable requests or explain grounds for a refusal in writing, and/or to a review committee, if necessary.<br>• Accepting consequences and/or alternative remedies when violating your agreements. | • Saying no to your commitment.<br>• Refusing to do what you have agreed to do, without explanation and just cause.<br>• Harming others.<br>• Threatening others.<br>• Refusing a legitimate request without cause.<br>• Refusing a consequence.<br>• Lying about what you or others did |
| **Desirable Do's**<br>**(Positive Contribution)** | **Undesirable Don'ts**<br>**(Growth Limiting)** |
| • Being a great team/group member<br>• Asking when you don't understand<br>• Being Prepared<br>• Being attentive and respectful<br>• Doing your best<br>• Adopting a positive attitude<br>• Embracing a growth mindset | • Being Selfish.<br>• Letting others down.<br>• Being passive about your learning.<br>• Acting like a victim.<br>• Making a poor effort.<br>• Being intentionally unpleasant to others.<br>• Abusing or Bullying. |

Our job is to make the social contract clear, positive, conspicuous, and implemented automatically, consistently and without any needs for shame, guilt, or punishment. It should be about growth, maturity and development, not personal judgment. Our model should be nature. Nature does not have inherently positive or negative contexts. It teaches us to respect it, make good choices, and learn about ourselves whenever we engage with it.

Therefore, we will need to develop a set of logical consequences for violations of the social contract. The more natural and/or logical the better. For most students, a clearly articulated and implemented social contract will be a source of sanity and security. But for some students, learning to operate within it, will require learning and growth. All students have excuses for why they are not able to be their best selves, and sometimes those circumstances are profound. However, in most cases, if the teacher or staff member's action were not a contributor to the problem, following through with a consequence (not punishment), is the most powerful way to accomplish the following:

1. Make the social contract valid and alive.

2. Send a message to those who have demonstrated responsible behavior that their commitment is valued.

3. Promote the growth and maturity level of the student who is being asked to accept the consequence.

4. Demonstrate that we are doing the job that others have entrusted us to do.

If students struggle with being responsible by choice, assisting them to reflect on their choices is an effective way to encourage growth. Progressively harsher punishments will not likely serve the growth trajectory of the school or encourage more responsible behavior from the student. Instead, supporting the teachers' and staffs' use of high-quality self-evaluation strategies will be more effective. Some effective practices in this area include behavioral contracts, reality therapy conversations, reflective conversations, and restorative repair sessions. Yet, whatever techniques and strategies that are used must support the bottom line – we all trust that we are doing our jobs, or something happens to encourage and/or repair the integrity of the social contract.

It may be the case that a few students want to find a place in-between doing their job and/or accepting responsibility for changing their behavior, fixing what they did, or being accountable and honest with themselves and others. They may have excuses for being this way, but the bottom line is still the bottom line. They are part of a whole. Therefore, our message to them needs to be that "it is not a game," there is no way to wiggle out of being responsible. Moreover, in the end, it is not in anyone's interest to allow this student to continue to operate with this personally dysfunctional pattern. In these cases, removal from the collective context, a lost opportunity, or the requirement to devise a plan to fix the problem are typically sound consequences. These are not punishments but logical consequence. They imply the if-then social frame - if you cannot fulfill the minimum required for your privileged status, then you will temporarily lose that status. And that message should be projected with the sub-text that we believe in this person, trust they can do better, and have faith they will when they come back (from their time out, detention, suspension, opportunity to repair what they did, or reflective process). When there are clear boundaries and the parameters of the social contract are explicit, there is no need to add negativity and shame, or to feel guilty for doing our job (upholding the social contract). It may be tough love, but it is love.

## Leader's Role

The principles and practices of the basic level of the social contract should be clear in our language. And while, our focus should be on the desired destination, we need to be sure that the basic elements of the social contract are solid. It will be useful to describe policy and the recommended practices at the school within the lens of developing our solid social contract (as well as concepts like psychology of success, and 1-Paradigm practices) rather than just rules and punishments for dealing with behavioral issues. When we talk in terms of 'student behavior issues," most often the result is that we shift over to the adult side of the equation and lose the student perspective. This can breed a lack of personal accountability and an external locus of control. We need all adults to exhaust all contributory responsibility that their actions, lesson plans, classroom set ups, and classroom climates have to do with the behavioral issues occurring in their classrooms. For some teachers this is second nature, for others it may require some skill-building in problem analysis to help shift their perception. But in many ways our school's social contract will be as sound as these teachers' internal accountability R's.

The message to students is a sincere effort will be made to ensure a platform to share concerns. They need power in the equation. The teachers have the power of their position. Students need to know they have the power of due process. Moving up on the roadmap means embracing student feedback and needs whether it is pleasing or unpleasing. Repression will exacerbate behavioral issues. Empowerment will reduce them for adults with enough courage to listen to how things are for those they serve.

In cases where a student clearly violated the basic level of the social contract, our job should be to support the teacher and the policy. In most cases, it will be best to support the teacher when there is greyness involved as well. However, teachers need to know that those representing the school (counselors, administration, directors, deans, head teachers, coaches, etc.) will also listen to the student's side of the story, and potentially go to bat for the student. And your school policy may include restorative justice practices to solve transgressions. This process can be powerful but keep the bottom line in mind or the social contract will deteriorate. If the school or classroom has a policy that students need to meet and agree on a way to repair what they did in lieu of a consequence like detention, those accountable for that process taking place need to actually hold that meeting and complete the procedure. Restorative practices do not change the mechanics of a social contract. At the end of the day, we can tell if we are getting healthier if we see more commitment, sincerity, and genuine self-reflection from students as well as fewer acts of passive or displaced aggression, classroom arguments, and students who are stuck at low levels of maturity.

## Assessing Process Quality – An Underused but Exceptionally Powerful Tool for Moving Up to the Next Level

An effective strategy for promoting the more aspirational levels of behavior within the social contract is to clarify, systematize, and assess high quality process and participation. This practice cannot replace the foundational levels of the social contract related to accountability and dealing with contract violations. But added to the overall classroom level system, it will make everything clearer and more meaningful for both students and teachers and so will have a substantive effect on improving the quality of behavior and reducing misbehavior as well. This process is spelled out in detail at www.transformative-classroom.com. In essence, this strategy involves selecting and operationalizing a few essential classroom qualities such as effort, attention, cooperation, preparedness, process quality, or others which are judged vital to the effectiveness of the class. Qualities must be explained in practical, behavioral terms and then structured into a rubric format (See example in Figure 11.5). Students are regularly given feedback from the teacher as well as being asked to self-reflect the quality of their own choices and behavior. Group and/or individual systems can be used for one or more classroom contexts. These systems when done well, can be especially effective promoting increasing levels of all three areas of a psychology of success as they assess only choices and action over which students have 100% control.

**Figure 11.5: Ascending Levels of Quality Rubric for Membership in a Cooperative Learning Group**

| | Cooperation | Attitude | Effort |
|---|---|---|---|
| **Level 4** | Cooperates consistently with the other group members. Shares ideas and materials. Consistently takes her/his turn talking. Listens to others and expects to be listened to. Takes constructive criticism well. Performs his/her role in the group. | Approaches the task with a consistently positive expectation. Brings others in the group up, not down. Consistently says only positive things to their classmates and themselves. Looks for ways to solve problems cooperatively and does not blame or quit. | Makes his/her best effort when things are going well and when they are not. Works hard regardless of the situation or the behavior of the other members of the group. Effort is consistent from the beginning of the period until the end. |
| **Level 3** | Cooperates with the other group members. Usually takes her/his turn talking. Usually performs his/her role in the group. | Approaches the task with a positive expectation. Looks for ways to solve problems cooperatively and does not blame or quit. | Makes his/her best effort. Works hard regardless of the situation or the behavior of the other members of the group. |
| **Level 2** | Cooperates with the other group members. Usually takes her/his turn talking. | Mostly approaches the task with a positive expectation. Recognizes need to solve problems cooperatively. | Makes a sincere effort most of the time. |
| **Level 1** | Made an effort to be cooperative. | Refrains from negative language or destructive behavior. | Makes an inconsistent effort. |
| **Level 0** | Did not make the effort to be cooperative this day. | Was unable to refrain from negative language or destructive behavior. | Did not make a sincere effort on this day. |

Note: The unit of analysis in this scale is the individual within the collective context.

## Leader's Role

As a school, integrating the concept of "4 level" performance or behavior can be useful. It can be a shorthand representation for what happens in a classroom, field, or hallway which characterizes student who are choosing excellence. Using a classroom participation assessment system provides one venue for encouraging a "4-level' mindset to become the aspirational standard at the school. As leaders the question we are asking is "what are we doing to support more students in making "4-level" behavior their norm?"

On a practical level, leadership may use a faculty meeting to create a rubric to use school wide. Likewise, teachers can be given time to share the systems they are using in their respective classrooms. Instructional leaders will want to become expert in what constitutes a high-quality system, from the instruments created, to the way they are communicated, to how they are used. They should be able to support the positive evolution of the systems in each classroom. For teachers or any other school staff the daily participation ratings can be used in conferences with parents, or by the student in their student-led conference. They are an excellent indicator of the growth trajectory of a student, so can be used in a formal or informal reflection process.

---
### Personal Experience
---

My first experience with this process was as a new teacher in a small school. When I arrived, the climate of the school was not as good as it could have been. Over the course of my first year, using a system for assessing process/participation, what I experienced was that the quantity of 4-level behavior grew progressively until it became the norm. You can imagine the difference in the climate at the school, going from a place where only a few students innately embodied the qualities of the "4-level," to a school where nearly all students had internalized the personal and collective benefits of making 4-level choices and investment natural and normal. As you might guess it was dramatic and effected every other area of school life.

---

Recognition to students who have gotten primarily 4's can be motivating. But be clear about the intent. When we recognize and reward 100% student-owned behavior, we send the message that what is important at the school is *investment in the process*, not innate ability. However, when the recognition is perceived as being about "specialness," status, or "favoritism," it will have a counter-productive impact. As we better recognize the types of practices that have the capacity to raise our collective R's, we will increasingly appreciate the use of assessing process formally, and why it qualifies as a "plateau-free" improvement practice.

**Basic Condition Seven - Use Only Quality Practices**: Reaching the goal of coherence requires refraining from the use of classroom management or instructional practices which undermine the level of function in the classroom. Many classroom management or discipline practices are used with the rationale that they "work," or have been recommended by an experienced teacher or expert. But when examined more closely many common and popular classroom management practices have the overall net result of leading the classroom function level downward or limiting its capacity to grow (See Appendix 11.A). These include many practices which ultimately encourage an external locus of control, are based in shame, student-student comparison, seek compliance rather than responsibility, or have a short-term desired effect, but in the long-term promote unwanted outcomes.

**Goal:** The use of ONLY classroom and school practices that promote more function, responsibility, and growth over time.

**If Missing:** Frequently teachers work against their own interest as they implement unhealthy practices which counter the positive effects of the healthy practices they may be using. On a whole-school level, when teachers rely on unhealthy short-term practices, they make the work of their peers who are trying to encourage long-term growth outcomes more difficult.

**Key Benefits:** Teacher effort is coherent and efficient. Students are not confused and/or forced to process mixed messages. Behavior and learning improve in the long-term.

**Basic Condition Eight - Ensure Coherence Across Practices and Policies:** Coherence must include consistency across teachers, policies, and the many sources of information existing in the school or district. People work best when they are on the same page. Some of the critical areas which must reflect integrity with one another include; teacher evaluation criteria and processes, professional development, the school and/or district's mission statement, and the messages placed around the school. The recommendations of administration, teacher leaders, and educational specialists must match the stated goals related to management and discipline. This requires a conscious articulation of what kinds of practices are consistent with the guiding values and which ones are not.

**Goal:** Execution of the stated policy feels coherent and reliable school wide.

**If Missing:** Depending on the areas of dis-integrity, the result of mixed messages and incoherence could be teachers' lack of trust in one another or the administration, students experiencing confusion, and over time, a lack of faith and commitment from both adults and students.

**Key Benefits:** All policies work toward improvement and growth. When there is congruence and consistency across classrooms and other areas of the school it allows for a greater expression of commitment and confidence of movement toward the target.

## Leaders' Role – Building Trust, Capacity and Coherence

Moving up from a lower level of function will require a focus on the basics - building trust, capacity, and coherence, and resisting the temptation to put too much focus on outcomes such as rates of referrals, suspensions, and those in the school who have yet to appreciate a 1-Paradigm mode of action. The focus should be the process.

Almost any set of practices done with consistency and sincerity will operate to move us up to or maintain us a middle level of function. However, some practices which may obtain results in the short-term can have incoherence and capacity limitations built-in to them. Eventually those practices lead to a growth plateau usually around the middle level on the roadmap. Therefore, if that level is an acceptable destination implementing gimmicky, extrinsic, behaviorist, and manipulative strategies may get us there. However, if your goal is to develop sound fundamentals in your school-wide behavior system, it will be important to understand the difference between a) building responsibility and a psychology of success or b) gaining compliance using extrinsic motivators, comparisons, and emotional manipulation. In essence, when we cast our lot in with this second agenda, we make the "left hand turn" to the higher regions of the roadmap basically impossible.

To build a sound system we will want to stay true to the core fundamentals of human growth and collective function development. In operation, that will mean strengthening the social contract, dropping ineffective strategies, replacing them with effective ones, and supporting the growth process with what is helpful to that cause. All adults in the school need to learn to accept the expectation - we are trying to bring out the best in one another. Therefore, the use of toxic narratives, a fixed-mindset and victim thinking are discouraged. But also, they need to know that the administration has their back when they are being sincere and committed to their use of quality processes. Especially if those quality processes are new to them.

Students need to know that the adult goal is to give them power, and voice and that adults are listening to them and are there for their benefit. But also, that coming to school means making a commitment to being part of something bigger. The job of leader is to support the sincerity and faith within the process, and to fight against cynicism, apathy, and selfishness. We will be much more effective doing that if we are promoting principles and processes rather than programs and outcomes - in other words, embodying a vision.

## Stage 2: Moving Up from Middle to High Levels – Building Self-Direction, Ownership, Connection and Positivity

Moving the behavioral and disciplinary domain quality to the next level for the middle function school will mean shifting the paradigm. Whereas moving from lower to middle level is about building capacity in a concerted manner, moving up from the middle location will require a change in our guiding intention. But while changing attitudes represents an inherent challenge, the R's that characterize our target destination represent a more natural, healthy, and enjoyable reality. In this section, we will explore some of the useful practices, strategies, and X's for moving up and over on the roadmap. The key to success will come from using the more natural 1-Paradigm R's to choose essential actions. Those R's in the form of guiding questions include:

- How can we encourage ever increasing levels of empowerment and self-direction?
- How can we increase the level of connection among students and between adults and students?
- How do we create sound conditions for growth mindset to take hold and flourish?
- How do we encourage students to develop deeper levels of inter and intrapersonal skill development?

- How can my class become a more effective 1-Paradigm environment?

## Horizontal Axis

If our X's are guided by 1-Paradigm R's, our practices will grow and the develop. Failure to embrace the R's reflecting the 1-Paradigm will inevitably lead us to other locations on the roadmap – manifesting as other X's and O's. Figure 11.6 highlights a few of the vast number of examples of where the same type of practice takes on a different nature and effect when it is undertaken with either a 2- or 1-Paradigm intent.

Figure 11.6 Contrasting the Same General Practice within a 1-Paradigm or 2-Paradigm

| General Strategy | 2-Paradigm Form | 1-Paradigm Form |
|---|---|---|
| Positive Feedback | Personal Praise – about student as a person and the teacher's goals. | Positive Recognition – about the action and the student's goals. |
| Class Participation | Colored Card Chart. A system of student–student comparison and public shaming. | Process Assessment System. A system of helping students grow into the highest levels of quality behavior. |
| Gaining attention | Students show respect and listen to the teacher because he/she is the authority in the room. | Students become good listeners, develop a culture of listening to one another, because it is a necessary skill. |

| Expectations | What the teacher says goes. | What needs to exist for everyone to feel happy, sane, safe and effective. |
|---|---|---|
| Consequences | Punishments and ways to give students discomfort | Logical and/or natural ways to respond to a student breaking their agreement. |

Our effort to move up the roadmap will require more than just explaining and expecting certain practices. An appreciation/R on the part of all members of the school community is required as to *why* a 1-Paradigm world is more satisfying, productive, healthy, and rewarding than a 2-Paradigm world. And as with all things related to moving to our desired location, it will be more about becoming and modelling a 1-Paradigm than imposing it. So, it starts with us and what our actions/X's say about our values/R's.

### Advanced Conditions Necessary for the Shift Over and Movement Up.

To become solidly located in at least the middle location, the first eight basic conditions for a sound discipline system to exist needed to be put in place. For movement from the middle locations upward to the highest locations on the roadmap a few additional "advanced" conditions are required for this next level of growth.

- Advanced Condition One - Building Community
- Advanced Condition Two - Student Leadership and Voice
- Advanced Condition Three - Social and Emotional Health

These advanced conditions build on the essential qualities of function while encouraging additional possibilities for the school. When these qualities are in place, there is an increased likelihood of a pervasive positive feeling in the school, trust and respect among the faculty, and a sense that the environment contributes to students realizing their personal and academic potential. The collective/entity becomes increasingly capable of self-growth and actualization.

**Advanced Condition One - Building Community:** A system for building community and a sense of belonging should be cultivated. To move to a higher level of function, coherence and effectiveness, the school needs to encourage communal bonds as well as the societal bonds characterized in the basic level. When the school and the classrooms encourage students to feel like they are part of something larger and are important members of the collective, there is a different feeling in the school, and the capacity to appeal to each students' pride in being a member of the "We"/team. Creating identity, encouraging sharing, building team skills, and having students work collaboratively all encourage these communal bonds.

> **Goal:** Students feeling as if they belong to and are accepted by the collective.

> **If Missing:** Students can still function with only social bonds, but without the communal bonds they do not feel the same level of connectedness and feeling of family.

> **Key Benefits:** Students' needs for belonging are met. Students feel more ownership of the school. Classroom management can incorporate an appeal for being a good team player, contributing to the common good, and recognizing the positive experience and joyful bonds that exist.

**Advanced Condition Two - Student Leadership and Voice:** A fundamental goal of the 1-Paradgm is to encourage student voice and choice in all aspects of school life. As that value becomes increasingly normalized, it is useful to incorporate systems of peer mediation, student leadership, and conflict resolution leadership to help promote the capacity of the school for less conflict, positive role models, and more positive student-student interactions. Student leaders operate as models to encourage positive behaviors in others and shift the locus of power from the adults to students (which is more prevalent in higher functioning schools). Peer mediators can support the conflict resolution processes in and out of the classroom. The more leaders and peer mediators who are trained, the higher the number of students who are walking the halls with those skills and dispositions.

**Goal:** Students helping other students solve their own issues and encouraging each other toward positive goals and actions.

**If Missing:** Teachers and staff are forced be the sole sources of conflict resolution. Students maintain an irresponsible and immature demeanor. Many students see discipline as the game of avoiding adults. The leadership potential of students is left unrealized.

**Key Benefits:** Less conflict and more students contributing at the school. Systems are put in place to build capacity of leadership and conflict resolution, becoming self-perpetuating.

**Advanced Condition Three - Social and Emotional Health**: With a system for encouraging mindfulness and social and emotional learning (SEL), teachers and students can benefit from both formal and informal opportunities to become more centered and conscious during a busy school day. A formal systematic and intentional process/program for promoting social and emotional health is usually necessary if a school expects to promote positive outcomes in that area. In addition, approaching social and emotional health and mindfulness as an ongoing value influencing all teaching will be even more critical to success in this area. A good starting point is the recognition that everything that happens at the school is affecting the social and emotional world of the students. Therefore, both an additive as well as a fundamental approach should be considered.

**Goals**: Students grow in social and emotional health as a result of spending time at the school. Students know they will be encouraged to approach work, conflict, and choices with mindfulness.

**If Missing:** Without seeing how everything is connected, schools often add SEL programs over the top of a set of daily classroom practices which are having the effect of undermining the mental health. The correlation between the level of a student's mental health and his/her academic achievement is very high, so to neglect mental health is to neglect learning. In an absolute sense, most conflict and crisis are the result of a lack of mindfulness.

**Key Benefits:** Students trust that teachers have the intention and skills to encourage their growth. Teachers and student are aware of how students' actions are guided by thoughtfulness, high quality decision making, and a higher level of intentionality.

## Operational Support for Creating Advanced Conditions and Shifting to 1-Paradigm

As a leader, we need to recognize that moving over on the roadmap will require some stretching on everyone's part beginning with leadership. Our mindset should be to grow the intrinsic 1-Paradim nature/R's of the institution and not try to impose a "left hand turn" externally. Therefore, it will be useful to continually nurture the conversation about why the 1-Paradigm classroom is beneficial for both teachers and students. In addition, we will need to make sure that the elements necessary for trust to exist are in place (see Chapter six). Central to cultivating trust will be to focus on process vs outcome, and "failing forward" when necessary. Commitment to moving into the less comfortable and learning from both what worked and what did not is essential. As the change agent, the team looks for your commitment to be solid. There may be challenges and resistance. But if we believe in the destination and the quality of the process we will persist. Therefore, a vision of a great 1-Paradigm classroom is what guides our choices and actions each day. It is not so much about what happened today; it is about how tomorrow can be better and more aligned with our vision.

Below are nine classroom management and discipline practices to support our movement toward the 1-Paradigm and up to the higher levels of the roadmap. There are many more practices we could list, but these are a useful start. Each is explained here briefly (and explained in detail in *Transformative Classroom Management*).

1.  **Encourage a Vision of a 1-Paradigm Classroom.** For many students, what it means to exist in an empowering, connected world where self-direction is the norm will require some adjustment. It is helpful to use purposeful actions, concept attainment and clarifications to elucidate what it will mean to exist in this environment. Starting the year engaging student input into the social contract is a great place to begin. But it will require the teacher to continually point out where it is all going (i.e., "get used to this... eventually you will all be expected to.. it may not have been what you did in other classes, but in this class...") Another useful tool are mantras that reinforce and clarify the picture (i.e., "in this class, we... what is great about us is that we are able to...look what we are able to do now....we may not be there yet, but we will eventually be able to....") The message to students is that they have limitless potential: today we are using some of it, tomorrow we will use more of it, and eventually we will do things we did not know were possible. The belief is being held strongly by the teacher and students are increasingly buying into the possibility of the teacher's picture. See Appendix 11.B for examples of two teachers emerging into the 1-Paradigm.

2.  **Use exclusively POS promoting practices** and refrain entirely from POF promoting practices. After engaging in the POS/POF classification exercise (or alternately, using the descriptions in Chapter 4 or TCM ch.7), systematically grow all practices that encourage – internal locus of control, belonging and acceptance, and a growth orientation, and eliminate those practices which undermine them.

3.  **Promote student self-direction.** Increasingly allow students to set their own goals, to assess their own progress and quality, work without the perceived need for supervision or adult approval. Expect students to hold one another accountable for quality and effort levels. This process is part of the (if) responsibility- (then) freedom social frame. Students need to be aware that when they demonstrate the ability to work in increasingly

more self-directed ways, more opportunities will follow. Conversely, when students do not show this capacity, it is noted, and their freedom is temporarily reduced. Teachers progressively ween students off approval and use self-assessment questions to help students learn to become more self-referential.

4. **Commit to developing cooperative/team skill experts**. Teachers commit to a process of building cooperation and team skills. The starting point is to provide high structure cooperative tasks where roles are clear and quality behavior, processes, and outcomes are assessed with great clarity and detail. Over time students are asked to self-evaluate their process and products, becoming expert in group dynamics and function. Students are encouraged to take pride in their ability to work on teams and depend on one another. As the students become more skilled, tasks can become more creative, and students can take more ownership over defining quality and efficacy over products.

5. **Shift from the "what" to the "why" over time.** All classes need to start with the experience of being functional so students can learn to trust one another and the teacher. Early management efforts will likely require extensive explanation of *what* is appropriate, what good looks like, and what happens if conduct meets the standard. But once the students gain comfort with being functional – listening, following directions, engaging in activities efficiently and with a sense of purpose, internalizing the social contract, and expecting the same from their peers, it is time to encourage a shift. The teacher should then help the students appreciate *why* it is valuable to maintain a functional classroom. Eventually, the goal is to have students own the comfort, ease, and efficiency of a well-organized class.

6. **Encourage student leadership.** Initially, there may be few students who are ready to be entrusted with duties usually done by adults. But over time, all students should all take on duties and leadership roles in the classroom. A useful rule is – if a

student can do it, they should be doing it. The kinds of roles will vary depending on the grade level and subject. For younger grades, students should rotate a set of classroom jobs including such tasks as dismissals and determining whether the group is "ready" and other executive functions. At the secondary level, students can manage materials, and act as monitors. But in no case should students be the judge related to formal grades, disciplinary or social contract violations.

7. **Create classroom identities.** There are several ways this can be accomplished and use of multiple strategies is recommended. Students can be asked to name their groups by some category (i.e., college, country, team, animal, cartoon character, etc.), or characterize themselves as a collective such as songs, slogans, logos, etc. Teacher can use mantras related to positive classroom characteristics (i.e., this class is awesome at innovation, or being funny, or asking incisive questions, etc.) Activities can promote collective accomplishments – i.e., team wins where everyone feels like they did it together. Fun, healthy, low stakes competitions can be set up between groups, classes, or grade levels. But be sure to make the focus the fun and the teamwork, and not the outcome (Shindler, 2009).

8. **Use classroom meetings effectively.** Class meetings are a potentially powerful tool, but they need to be approached with skillful intention. If done poorly, students can increasingly appraise them to be wastes of time, not safe, or primarily devoted to complaining. Therefore, it is best to start with short meetings where there is a time frame, a minor problem to solve, and a strict adherence to the rules of class meetings. Once students learn to trust the process, gain comfort with the protocol, and experience results, they will develop a positive association with the meetings. Meetings are a powerful venue to processing emotional issues, but this should only be done if the leader is confident in maintaining an environment of active and respectful listening, honest sharing, and achieving an acceptable

resolution. A process for conflict resolution should be introduced before any real conflict is processed in a group venue. Once the students become expert at the procedures and trust one another, some of the more emotionally intelligent members of the class can begin to lead ever increasingly intimate and vital meetings.

9. **Encourage conditions for intrinsic motivation to grow.** The starting point for promoting more intrinsic motivation is to recognize that disempowering practices, extrinsic reinforcements, manipulative strategies, incongruent communication, and psychology of failure promoting practices will undermine our efforts. Next, we need to build a basic-needs (i.e., power, love, belonging, freedom, fun, competence, safety) satisfying environment. When basic needs are met, inner sources of inspiration and agency are nurtured. Helping students appreciate the process of inquiry, working through challenges, and trusting their creative gifts will support a deeper trust in inner sources. Assessing process rather than the product will support this goal as well. We need to place value on the process, or the student will always feel stilted and conflicted when they have creative urges. Finally, we want to assist students in ways to share and show pride in what they have done so they can experience that joyful emotional aspect of the creative process. Ultimately, we want to help them experience the acts of creating, learning, and listening to their inspired thoughts as the reward, rather than a means to a secondary reward.

## Leadership

Supporting the growth of practice at the school toward higher locations on the roadmap will entail making the picture of a 1-Paradigm very concrete, operational, and the norm. It will help if we have concretized it in various forms including (or expanding upon) our "things we do" and "things we don't do" list, or our psychology of success classification exercise. To effectively encourage our growth, it will also require a continuous focus on what it means to produce the high function, empowered, and connected classroom where students grow in their ability for self-direction. Leading that process of growth includes encouraging all strategies that we know to be empowering, consistent with 1-Paradigm leadership, and grounded in sustainable and meaningful human development. These are a few professional development (PD) ideas to consider as we seek to expand the use of these effective practices.

- Encourage a clear aim at the 1-Paradigm when teachers are asked to set goals for the year. This can be encouraged by using questions such as those listed at the start of this section (i.e., self-direction, connection, etc.) as support prompts in the process. Keep the focus on the essential question "how do I need to grow and change and what do I need to do to create the class in which I would love to teach?"

- Have high performing teachers, those who have internalized/R's and operationalized practically/X's the 1-Paradigm share what they do in professional development, or act as teacher leaders in the area of classroom management.

- Model high quality group development and team building skills in meetings and PD.

- Provide resources for how to create 1-Paradigm classrooms.

- Encourage teachers to include classroom management in their discussions related to their peer observations and instructional rounds.

- Focus on the destination of the journey – an increasing more trusting, empowering, and human-centered school. Expect this to be a values/R's adjustment for many. And a major adjustment for some. Therefore, include in the discussion both the target, but also allow folks to share their personal challenges and issues related to the process of becoming a more empowering educator. What does it take to look at students not so much for who they are now, but who they can be?

## Growth Pathway - SCAI School Climate Ratings, and Corresponding Predicted Achievement

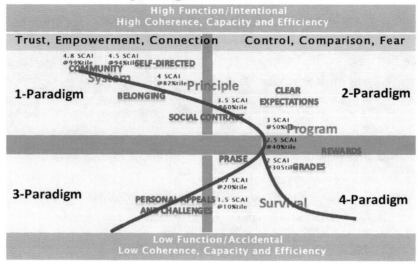

For the teachers who are struggling to embrace the "left hand turn," the process needs to both hold out the expectation that they can get there, as well as the security of a safety net. The safety net in this case includes the need to reduce as much as possible the perceived fear that if things go badly there will be a penalty. Making a growth orientation a school-wide R/DNA strand, means helping everyone feel safe making mistakes and trying, even when they do not feel 100% confident. We promote a fixed-ability orientation in the classroom or with insecure educators when we are critical of how things are going in the short-term as they are attempting practices that are new to them. The focus needs to be on the process. That means a continuous analysis of what one is trying to do and then reflecting on what the results could tell them about what they did. For these teachers, they will also likely need the safety net of outside support for their students who challenge them the most. The goal of a 1-Paradigm classroom is that very few students will ever need to be removed or pulled out of this highly effective learning context. But for some teachers, getting traction toward this goal may mean occasionally needing help with students who they have not yet learned to connect with, and who may derail their lesson momentum and confidence to embody an empowering and facilitative role. We will need to support their long-term goal of find ways to connect with these students (who in most cases connect well with other teachers) and integrate them into the class organically.

Above all else leadership needs to keep in mind the nature of changing R's and X's and embody the essence of the left-hand turn – trust, empowerment, connection, and growth. Therefore, trying to prematurely impose a picture of a 1-Paradigm kind of classroom management to those to whom it is too unfamiliar and threatening can be a mistake and incongruent with what is required to move to that higher location. Change will move as fast as is possible, if we are effective in our role and model and embody the 1-Paradigm. The collective needs someone to pull them toward the vision even when it is not comfortable. So, what message do they get from us? Is it (implicitly or explicitly), "you are inadequate and if you can do more 1-Paradigm classroom management you will be more adequate in my eyes and I will be happy with you, and I am not happy until you get there?" Or is it "we are all on a journey to find the most satisfying ways to encourage classroom function, learning, student growth, and fulfilling more of the potential of all at the school, so let's keep trying and asking the right questions, and sharing what we learn and celebrating our growth?" Achieving 1-Paradigm classroom results will be much more likely with 1-Paradigm leadership.

## Stage 3: Moving Up to the Highest Levels – Building Community and Selfless Contribution

Our movement to the highest locations on the roadmap related to classroom function and discipline will vary a little related our specific mission and vision. But we can identify a few common denominators of the highest roadmap locations and some potentially useful practices for getting us there. For some schools, the R focus will be more individual - reflected in the goals of self-understanding, empathy, and working effectively with others. For other schools, the R focus may be more collective - emphasizing a sense of community, contribution, collective success, and the school as the unit.

Both locations represent upper levels of the 1-Paradigm of the roadmap, and so can be synthesized in any manner that supports the school's vision. In this section, we will examine some of the practical strategies a school might consider in their growth process and the implications for leaders in that process.

### Selected Practices to Encourage a Schools' Movement to the Highest Levels:

- Students are taught, practice, and reflect on their skill development related to conflict, sharing, working past issues with others, and being self-aware and mindful of their inner processing. This needs to be approached from a holistic lens – so needs to include formal instruction, exist as a pervasive expectation, and be supported by the adults and the environment.

- Students should be increasingly enlisted and skilled in the role of peer mediator and peer conflict resolution agents. This process implies formal training and being selective of who is given the role. But over time, it can be something that all students could be expected to do and a function that everyone in the school assumes to be in place.

- At any location on the roadmap, it will support our process to have formal ways students assess the quality of their actions, behavior, process, group dynamics, etc. At the lowest levels this works best when it is mostly teacher-led, and the picture of quality is given to students. When moving up from the middle levels, it works best to have students as active as possible in the self-assessment of their process. At the highest levels, students should be encouraged to consider self-assessing the quality of their contribution to the task, the group dynamics and the procedural choices that were used as fundamental to any task evaluation process. Guiding questions from the teacher are helpful to focus the analysis, but as much as possible students should own their post-game diagnosis and prescription for the next iteration.

- Group meetings should be used very efficiently and when needed to process deeper issues. Eventually, students should be able to run simple meetings, but as discussed earlier, we need to make sure we do not break this process by putting students in a situation for which they are not ready. Simple exercises in making a classroom choice are useful ways to hone this process. At the highest levels of the roadmap, our social contract should be very intentional and alive. Therefore, when there is a perception that something about our agreements, a procedure, a policy, or the way it is playing out is not serving the collective effectively, the class meeting is a useful way to democratically make a change and hopefully solve the problem. Informal student circles should be encouraged as well, as means of processing conflict, social dynamics, a student who is feeling in need of support, or something else in the social emotional domain. Those circles might be more effective in a small group, or be something the whole class needs to be engaged in. There are an infinite number of ways this process can go wrong but many ways it can be invaluable. So skillful leadership and a clear intention is essential.

- For schools at all levels, the essence of the empowerment process will be the if-then relationship - if you are able to, then you can. Yet, to build the highest levels of student empowerment, that principle needs to be maintained in everyone's consciousness or we can slide toward the 3-Paradigm domain. Therefore, students need to get used to suggesting ways which they can accomplish more and stretch themselves, while assuming with great trust comes faith which needs to be earned. Therefore, our intention and messaging are that we want to say "yes." One 1-Paradigm leader put it this way — "Around here, there is a lot of yes."

- 1-Paradigm teachers and leaders recognize that community and team building exercises are worth the time and have multiple benefits. Therefore, to get to the next level, they need to be intentional and regular. It is best to start them at the beginning of the school year to set the tone. Competition has a precarious place at the highest levels of the roadmap. On the one hand, it can undermine our goals and encourage hierarchies, fear of failure, social Darwinism, and a "us vs them" mindset. On the other hand, if it is done with fun and low stakes it can be fun, bring energy, and help students learn how to put things in perspective. Competitions with other schools can be a way to show excellence and showcase effort and can foster the vital ingredient of team successes. So, be intentional and keep the perspective of John Wooden (See Chapter six) in mind – making it always about the process and striving for excellence rather than the outcome even when the stakes are high. Or just make it about a silly way to have fun, where it does not really matter who wins – the goal is fun – real winning is being at a school where we love to be and love what we get to do and learn.

## Leadership for Moving the School to This Higher Level

Supporting a school's movement to this highest level will start with keeping our guiding questions in the collective consciousness. One 1-Paradigm leader described it as making (the 1-Paradigm) part of the DNA of the school. Providing practical ideas and supporting growth in practice will be essential, but most importantly, our job is to encourage all adults at the school to ask, "is this practice expected to promote the highest levels of growth, and do I see evidence that it is?" As a 1-Paradigm community of learners, the adults in the school should become ever more comfortable and trusting of the processes of self-inquiry and vision-based decision making. Therefore, our input should be more in the form of modelling, highlighting, and providing resources which encourage growth.

Our process with adults (and students) will in many respects mirror the teacher's process of moving the students to the next level of self-direction and connection. Therefore, the process of evaluation should shift as much as possible to self-assessment based on the qualities of a 1-Paradigm classroom. The learning process should shift from input of ideas to inquiry within the PLC format, peer observation format, mentor counseling, and/or the instructional rounds process. However, growth in practice requires growth in one's knowledge base. Therefore, having the site leadership team select good sources (i.e., books, articles, videos, websites, etc.) that could be used to expand the conversation is encouraged. Too much reading can be a burden, so more is not better. Our guiding question might be, "what would make the teachers feel more supported?" If you feel like certain information is critical for everyone to know, have it presented professionally to everyone with the opportunity to discuss, process, and accommodate the ideas as part of the event.

## CONCLUSION

Your progress in area of classroom management and school discipline will be the most determinant of your overall ability to move up to the next level on the school effectiveness roadmap – thus the need for an entire chapter for this area. For best results, our improvement efforts in this domain should be concurrent with the efforts in the other areas. But it needs to be given a priority level of attention. After reading the chapter, you should be better able to recognize the necessary conditions, practices and leadership facilitation related to each of three levels of school function. Basic conditions and practices need to be in place to move to each successive level. In the next two chapters, we will examine how to integrate these ideas into the larger effort in moving schools from lower roadmap locations (Chapter twelve) and moving across from middle levels (Chapter thirteen).

## REFERENCES

Maslow, A. H. (1943). A theory of human motivation. *Psychological Review, 50*(4), 370–396

Shindler, J (2009) *Transformative Classroom Management*, Wiley Press.

Shindler, J (2016) *In Search of a Complete and Coherent School Discipline System* www.transformativeclassroom.com.

Shindler, J (2018) *Exploring the Limiting Influence of PBIS in the Growth of Students and Schools*. www.transformativeclassroom.com.

## Appendix 11.1: Seven Classroom Management Practices to Avoid and More Sound and Effective Alternatives

| Strategy | Why it Can Be Counter-productive | A Move Sound Alternative Practice |
|---|---|---|
| **Negative Recognitions**<br><br>"Brian, I told you to put that away." | When we remind a student to stop doing something that he/she already knows not to do ("Brian!" or "We are waiting for Brian"), we essentially train him/her to 1) keep doing it, and 2) wait for us to remind them to stop, and 3) assume that all he/she needs to do is to tolerate occasional reminders, yet is never required to actually change their behavior. These interventions also add a negative energy into the climate of the room and send the implicit message that the teacher is struggling to promote order in the class. | First, become an expert in technical management, and stop trying to be clever and tricky. Learn to use a clear cue for 100% attention, expect 100% attention, and stop whenever you don't have it, until it is the norm. When a student or a few of them do not understand that expectation, you will likely need to work with them to help them see that they need to find a way to self-regulate asap. And when it is the whole class, such things as clarifying statements (i.e., "We are all giving Maria our 100% attention, and she will wait until she has it.") are useful for bringing positive clarity for what needs to be happening. (See Ch. 4 and 5 of TCM). |

| | | |
|---|---|---|
| **"Proximity Control"**<br><br>Standing nearer the Students who are off Task | Much like negative recognitions, using our physical proximity to try to modify student behavior essentially trains students to assume they only need to be on task when we are standing near them and intimidating them with our presence. We make the implicit deal that we need to be close to them or we cannot assume or trust anything good will happen. It is a lose-lose for us and the students. Over time students remain irresponsible and we are never able to feel confident and trusting. | Being among our students is a great idea. Interact, and be involved, but not as a walking patroller, but a teacher. If students are off task, use expectation clarifiers, or purposeful individual interventions. We should be making constant comments related to what quality process investment should look like at any point (i.e., Ask yourself, are you executing your role in a way that is working to the benefit of your group?) If a group is off task, we need to help them self-evaluate and find solutions for being on task |
| **Using Colored Card Chart Behavior Systems** | Simply put, this is using public shame to try to coerce students into compliance. It does not deal with the real problems – either related to the student or what is happening in the classroom. So will not lead to real solutions. It focuses primarily on the negative, but in a global and non-specific way, so is not instructive in any way. And in the end, it actually tends to encourage students to stay stuck and comfortable at their color level, especially those at the bottom levels. | It is wise to avoiding any public student-student comparisons in all areas but especially with behavior. It only makes everything else in the class worse. However, using an intentional well-constructed system for assessing quality student effort, investment, cooperation, and/or participation can be really effective. Done correctly, it can help clarify what "good" looks like for students in a concrete and specific manner. And it can be used by the teacher to help clarify tasks, process quality, and what high quality behavior looks like for those who need it.<br><br>(See complete web-article at www.transformative-classroom.com) |

| | | |
|---|---|---|
| **Saying "I like the way __ is __ing" to modify those who are not ___ing.** | Manipulative strategies almost always back-fire. When we try to modify one students' behavior by publicly praising another student, we are being insincere and deceptive. It leads to confused emotions in the students and undermines the sense of acceptance and belonging in the class. When students hear us referring to one group and seeming to direct our attention to another, they might ask themselves "Who were we talking to?" "Have they just been compared?" And if so, "Do they care?" Avoiding using the words "I like" unless you are talking about your sincere personal preferences. | The clean clear positive non-personal alternative is a positive recognition. Instead of making it personal, simply help the class see what the quality behavior that you want looks like. A phrase such as "I see groups who have all their equipment out and are determining …" help everyone better see what good looks. Or we can use clarifying statements or questions (i.e., "I might be asking myself or those in my group …. Right now.") to help make a quality task more clear (See Ch 4 in TCM) |
| **Praising desired behavior with personal compliments** | When we give personal praise, we are giving the student something extrinsic (our approval and affection) for something they most likely see as part of who they are. This creates a shift away from their own sense of agency and intrinsic motivation, and over time makes them more dependent on external praise and promotes insecurity and a fear of failure. | Use positive recognitions, reflective questions, or refrain from saying anything. Rule 1 is do nothing to rob them of their intrinsic motivation and sense of internal locus of control. So often just asking a question about how it is going or finding something interesting about what they are doing shows that we are interested, without a thinly veiled agenda of giving our approval for what we want disguised as something positive. |

| Saying "thank you" as a way to reinforce wanted behavior | Why would we want to diminish the power of our sincere gratitude and the words "Thank You" by turning them into a knee jerk strategy given for compliance? If we are trying to create an authentic relationship with our students, we want to use our words to reinforce unconditional positive regard (love) and a sane and congruent message. Using caring messages to manipulate undermines that quality. | Say "Thank You" "I like that" or give praise when you are speaking as one authentic human being to another. In the role of the teacher, you need to make it about them, and their growth and how we can all produce quality outcomes, and not about you. So, a phrase like "We are getting there, cool" or just saying what is happening positive or negative is respectful. Let them know how they are doing relative to their goals and what is good for the collective. They need useful information, not our blessing. |
|---|---|---|
| Giving extrinsic rewards to bribe students into doing things | When we give students something extrinsic for doing something that we would want them to intrinsically value, we are killing their intrinsic motivation and training them to think that the primary reason they would want to do the task is because they are getting something non-educational for it in the end. If we set up this bargain in the form of a bribe, we are helping ensure that our students will do nothing without being given a bribe first. Study after study shows that giving rewards may get an initial response but eventually undermines motivational levels and decreases the likelihood that students display the desired behavior or performance level over time. | If we examine the top classrooms, we see engaging instruction and students who have a sense of internal locus of control and a growth orientation. Engaging learning is inherently motivational. Working with others and solving problems activates our intrinsic motivation. Sharing what we do gives us a sense of pride and self-efficacy. A sense of accomplishment that comes from reaching a goal and persisting through a challenge encourages an even greater level of motivation for the next task. Yet, when we introduce an extrinsic reward into the equation all those internal motivational instincts are suppressed to some degree. |

## Appendix 11.2: The Story of Two Teachers Who are Setting Out to Create 1-Paradigm Classrooms

To operationalize the practical task required for moving up the pathway and creating the 1-Style classroom, it may be useful to go on a journey with two teachers at a school which has committed to moving up the pathway. Follow the teachers' experiences as they engage the process of conceiving and then creating 1-Style classrooms.

The process of creating the 1-Style classroom for any new teacher will typically play out in stages. Each stage will be pre-requisite for the next. This three-stage process is explained in more detail in the book *Transformative Classroom Management*. The first stage is setting the *foundation*. In this stage we are teaching and cultivating the skills, expectation, and processes that are required for students to be able to begin to function in a more self-directed manner and feel safe emotionally. The second stage involves helping the students *transition* into a more self-directed pattern and democratic community culture. In this stage, we need to be very intentional about giving them more power and encouraging them to learn to trust their intrinsic motivational forces and the joy of winning as a collective. In the third stage, we try to help them fly on their own – our job is to mostly *encourage*. This may not be a stage that all classes can realize fully, but we can look for ways to help students take collective ownership of their school and their learning.

### Stage 1 – Building the Foundation

- Management Goals - Clarity and Intention
- Community Development Goals – Safety and Belonging
- Pedagogical Goal – Learning Skill Development

Jen and Carlos begin the year with a clear intention and commitment to moving their students up the pathway to higher levels of function. Even though the entire faculty created a vision statement that described a very 1-Paradigm goal for the school, Carlos and Jen are not exactly sure where their other colleagues are in terms of their will or skill to make it happen.

Therefore, Jen in her English class and Carlos in his Math class are expecting that they will have to change the paradigm for the students in their classes on their own, if need be. If they are supported by the rest of the faculty, that will be a bonus. But they do feel supported by one another and share ideas, experiences, and challenges whenever they can.

What strikes Jen when she begins the year is how much external and dependent language she hears out of her students. She did not notice it so much in the past, but now that she better understands the nature of the 1-paradigm location on the pathway, she better recognizes that her students are most comfortable being told what to do and have a lot of external LOC patterns. So, she takes the opportunity to let them know that while she appreciates that they need support, and there will always be instructional support, she is not going to enable them. She begins to use a few mantras with her classes to help them feel into the new way things are going to be. One of them is "We are ALL going to be self-motivated writing stars." What strikes Carlos is, while some of his students whine that they do not like to show their work and others do not like that he now assesses the quality of their group interactions, what he sees is that they are getting over their resistant mindset rather quickly and are getting used to the new policies. Correspondingly, he notices the quality of their math work, investment level and group processing are already much better than this time last the year before.

Both Carlos and Jen are seeing the foundation being built for a functional class. They know if their students do not have the skills to operate in a 1-Paradigm the expectation of a self-directed class will break down. So, they have both implemented a few essential elements. First, each engages the students in a social contract creation process. They ask the students to define what it would mean to be a high functioning class, and how students in such a class would talk and act. They included examples of rules and consequences and put the results on large paper and put it on the wall. A copy was sent home so the parents could see what was developed. As the semester will go on, they will revise it occasionally using the same democratic process.

Next, each teacher implements a substantial degree of process assessment. For Jen that focuses on skill building in her writers' workshop and cooperative learning processes. She assesses the students on how effectively they work with one another and excel as peer-reviewers in the writing assessment process. She has found her rubrics needed to become very specific and detailed. She also found herself debriefing after each workshop and cooperative event asking the students, "what did you or your partner (or group members) do, that you thought make the process more effective?" And she makes sure to have them self-reflect related to multiple aspects of their effort – task, collaboration, process. Carlos did much the same thing and found his students began to use one another much more effectively in the group process when he taught, analyzed, and assessed the skills related to how to process the content within a group context. Both spent a lot of the first month making very specific positive recognitions of what students in each group did that was effective and took every opportunity to help the groups see how much progress they were making in their many areas of process skill and application growth.

At the start of the year, Carlos and Jen also noticed they would hear some casual abuse between students. They had always viewed the students as nice kids and had not really noticed how they talked to one another. Now as they were attempting to be very deliberate about creating an emotionally safe classroom climate, they realized that many students did not feel as safe as they had assumed in the past. Therefore, they started with making sure that they talked to students in a respectful manner and encouraging the students to feel safe asking questions, sharing their thoughts, and giving answers. They made it clear that in the room it was good to make mistakes, but it was not OK to stay silent if one had questions. All questions were encouraged and even celebrated. Alternate opinions were given respect. The teachers found that while their demeanor was the most important variable, they had to spend sufficient attention on making sure all the students were on the same page. There was a zero-tolerance policy in each class for put downs. And both teachers found that it took about a month for their students to get used to the expectation that when someone was talking, in an all-class discussion, or direction giving episode, EVERYONE is listening. At the start of the year, they would need to many times stop a student who was sharing and then ask them to start over until everyone's 100% attention was obtained. Yet, over time, those reminders became less necessary, and after about a month, the students became used to the expectation that they were respectful active listeners and embraced a "culture of listening."

Initially, Carlos heard several students speaking with what he interpreted to be a fixed-ability orientation and helplessness around their ability in math. As a result, he became very deliberate about letting them know that if they invested, they would do well, and part of what they could control (and was included in their grade) was their effort level and how much they took advantage of the resources in the room. He was very careful not to be enabling toward students when they were projecting helplessness, yet he was very supportive of them in general and projected a belief in each students' abilities. Also, at this point, he gradually introduced an increased expectation of them being responsible for one another's success.

Among Jen's initial challenges was that her students were very used to going through the motions in their work and were not overly interested in its quality. In addition, they seemed hesitant to express themselves. She knew this was not going to change overnight, but she started by making sure that they knew that their ideas would not be criticized, she would allow them multiple modes to express themselves, and she would find literature that was culturally relevant and interesting to 7th graders. But she made it clear that there was a high bar in the class for the use of imagination and being committed to the process of peer and self-assessment of writing. She found that in free-writing journals she could provide feedback that encouraged their self-expression.

Both Jen and Carlos heard their students say things such as 'what do we get if we do that?" Or "what is our reward?" So, they would politely tell the students that becoming excellent was their reward. And they even laminated a saying and put it on their classroom walls. It read *"Your Reward at this School is that We Don't Use Rewards"*

During this first month, Carlos and Jen talked to the teachers in the PE class and advisory period who shared their students and coordinated some cooperative and community building activities that were incorporated into those classes as well.

## Stage 2 – Transitioning to the 1-Paradigm

- Management Goals - Shifting Locus of Ownership and Cultivating Intrinsic Motivation
- Community Development Goals - Creating Identity and Group Accomplishment
- Pedagogical Goal – Shift to Self-Reflection and Self-Assessment of Work Quality

Over time, the students in Carlos and Jen's classes adjusted to the "new normal." They accepted the idea that they were going to be a group of self-directed learners operating as a supportive community, and that was just the way it was. Students would test the new expectations with such behavior as acting helpless, disrespectful, or selfish, but that behavior began to stand out as inconsistent with the culture that was developing in the rooms. Between the creation of a few behavior contracts, conferences with students, and a regular process for feedback about the participation assessment grades, students who were most attached to their old patterns of mediocrity and immaturity began to become increasingly receptive to the benefits of a "psychology of success" (POS) pattern rather than an ego-safety and fear-based pattern.

For the first weeks, it required both teacher's substantial self-control to stick to their commitment of no negative recognitions (i.e., "Johnny and Freddy stop playing around, or . . .") They only used clarifying statements, and active consequences, when there was a minor problem. Eventually, they recognized that they did not miss them at all. In fact, they found that using a negative recognition would sound odd and ineffective coming out of their mouths now. Their students at first expected to be reminded personally with a negative recognition to be get back on task, but stopped assuming they would hear them, so have now become accustomed to self-regulating and as a result appreciate living with the assumption that are capable of a higher personal standard. It makes them feel empowered.

Jen and Carlos are seeing evidence that there is a good foundation for self-direction and self-responsibility that has been set. A lot of it has been that the students are getting used to what is not going to happen in these teacher's classes such as boring lessons, negative recognitions, enabling, nagging, acceptance of poor effort levels, acceptance of excuse making, or other students encouraging disruptive behavior to gain power or have fun. They are also getting used to what does happen such as debriefing the quality of the last activity, the teacher taking an interest in their ideas, freedom to make mistakes and take risks, grades which are related in part to investment and process commitment levels, and trust that the teacher is a true leader.

All of this makes the students feel less stressed. They did not realize they were dealing with so much fear and apprehension until they compare how they feel now - lighter more energetic and liberated to how they felt previously. They are not always able to put it into words, but they look forward to coming into these classes, and find that what they are looking forward to is more related to what they will be able to learn and contribute and less about what goofy entertaining event might occur that would break the monotony of a typical class.

With this foundation in place Jen and Carlos begin to discuss how to get to the next level. Given that they do not really worry about things like the students' investment level, attention level, or engagement level, they can start a) shifting the steering wheel over to the students, and b) creating a class identity. They start with some basics. Is there anything in the social contract that needs changing to reflect the emergent maturity of the group? They begin to ask themselves, are there ways the class can feel more like a community? As they hear the class bonding organically, they find positive or endearing qualities that distinguish them as a collective. One of Jen's classes self-referred as the "freedom writers" and another as the "hip hop poets" so she makes sure to use those labels regularly to make the class feel bonded. Carlos frequently turns the class's attention to celebrating the student projects on the walls of the room to remind them of something that makes them proud of their successful team efforts. Both teachers have student work on the walls and allow students to bring things for the walls that are voted on by the others as acceptable.

Neither teacher had previously appreciated how positively it would affect students to be part of a collective success large or small. They saw it on the athletic teams and in the drama performances, but now they could see it had the same powerful potential to unite and build the mutual admiration and collective trust within their classes. Therefore, they looked for every opportunity to have students win as collectives. This took many forms including group presentations in class, making sure there was sincere applause after each presentation, projects, class to class friendly competitions (with no real prize, and focus on the fun and process not the outcome), and anything else they could think of that made the class feel like they were a necessary and valued part of something bigger than themselves.

In the area of classroom management, they both tried to help students recognize the personal intrinsic value of being part of a class defined by a culture of listening and respect where they were listened to and were safe from abuse or put-downs. So, while they needed to make sure that the student still felt like there was a strong leader in the class, the main reason students trusted what was going on was that they could count on their peers. They would ask their students "how does it feel to be part of a class where you are listened to and supported by your peers? Don't take it for granted."

What that shift looked like in academics was each teacher helping the students trust their own authority, voice, self-discipline, skills, and judgment. Jen needed to be persistent with many of the students who wanted her validation of whether their writing was good. She gave them feedback but put much more emphasis on self-evaluation than teacher evaluation. In the same way, Carlos learned that he could make it through class some days with almost nothing but questions "So how did you get to this point?"

"Maria used this process to get to the answer (on the board), would you have used the same process?" "If I got stuck here, what did I do to run into that problem?" At first, students would complain that he asked too many questions, now he finds that when he starts to go into long explanations, the students tell him to go away and let them "figure it out on their own." Last year, he would have felt a little insulted if they had said this, now he sees it as a sign of success.

By Halloween, students get used to Carlos and Jen seeming unconcerned with some of the things their teachers in the past had seemed very attentive to, such as their mistakes, students asking for alternative pathways to the learning target, and students laughing in their groups. And Carlos and Jen are very adamant about quality and fidelity to the process, and self-reflection and how the students talk to one another. In the past, a lot of attention would have been given to who got the highest test score, now these teachers find themselves minimally concerned with who did the best.

Both Carlos and Jen try to show authentic joy when any class member or group demonstrate a breakthrough such as a new level of self-direction, a new level of care for one another, an appreciation for the beauty of the subject matter. At the end of one day, a few weeks into the year, Jen and Carlos talk and compare how they feel now versus last year. What they realize is that they feel much more like cheerleaders or coaches than policemen. They are getting used to using their energy to help students feel empowered and capable, and less trying to gain compliance and respect or domesticate them. They notice it feels more emotionally authentic and enjoyable to empower others, rather than the exhausting process of trying to use clever ways to be in control, corral and sell the content.

**Stage 3 – Encouragement of Self-Direction and Community**

- Management Goals – Facilitating Vision and Self Direction
- Community Development Goals - Fostering a Cause Beyond Self and a Sense of Tribe
- Pedagogical Goal – Integration and Self-Expression of knowledge and Skills

By the end of the year other teachers and administrators who were encouraged to observe what was going on in Jen's and Carlos's class, were influenced by what was possible to improve their own contexts. As a result, the school felt like it could take another step down the pathway. Teachers and administrators asked the students for ideas about how the school could be better. Included in the ideas generated were service-learning projects, integrating project across the classes, fieldtrips to places where students could use their knowledge or at least see knowledge applied in a real-world setting, and a conflict resolution/peer mediation program. The student recognized the difference between certain classes that felt safe and empowered, and those in which that feeling of safety was not present.

As a result, the school vision/climate team started the new year by asking a committee of students who had been elected by their peers to meet regularly with faculty and administration to address some of the ideas that were most pressing to students. In that committee, it was clear that the growth and vision process was an unpredictable and even messy thing. In one case, students from various sub-groups at the school had a heated discussion. Students had been given the school's SCAI climate data from the year before, and items 3b related to different groups getting along and 3e related to how the popular students acted, were rated relatively low at the school. The more popular students on the committee felt like the results were not that significant, but two students who were not from the "leadership/popular group" at the school took the opportunity to share their very different perspective. The process was emotional, but the result was a new level of understanding. The teachers present were able to share that what they witnessed at the meeting was similar to the adult process of trying to work together to create a collective vision and some of the issues and emotions that it raised. But as the committee chair reminded all the students, they were chosen to be leaders and servants and their job was to use their position on the committee to make the school better, not just represent the interests of themselves or their friends.

In Jen's class, one assignment involved the students videoing their acted-out adaptations of a type of persuasive technique used in advertising.

The students created advertisements for various activities at the school using the technique. The students loved seeing themselves on the video. Therefore, it became a more regular part of the class as the year went on. When the same students were in the 8th grade class the next year, they suggested that Jen show the videos at lunch. The idea worked and students from outside the class looked forward to Ms. (Jen) Rose's video day. As part of the exhibition, she had the students explain to the audience what they were trying to accomplish after the video was shown. At the beginning of the earlier year Jen would not have though to do this, but it just evolved as her students gained skills, confidence, and a sense of power and pride.

Carlos adopted the idea of students presenting to the whole school and started a "math fair" where his 8th graders would work in groups to create a project. He invited all the 6th and 7th grade classes to do a quick gallery walk of all the projects. He reminded the younger visitors that they would be doing the same thing when they were in 8th grade.

As the year went on the peer mediators became very skilled at their jobs. They learned how to talk to their peers like young counselors and found that more and more students came to them for a listening ear. Every few months, a new group of peer mediators was selected. The veterans played an essential role in mentoring the new group. All captains of athletic teams and clubs were required to be trained as school peer mediators/leaders. The 1-Paradigm that was expected in the classrooms became part of all school related activities, and aspects of school life.

# PART III:

# Integrating Leadership Processes into School-Wide Change

---

- Leadership for Moving Up from Lower Quadrants to Higher Function

- Making the "Left-Hand Turn" and Actualizing Your Potential

- Leader Personal Vision Creation and Growth Development

Note: Chapters twelve and thirteen are intended to synthesize the contents of the previous eleven chapters into condensed processes for school improvement. While readers will likely gain much from each chapter, they are each intended to serve essentially the same function – yet for schools at unique locations on the roadmap. If your school is already well on the way up the roadmap, you may want to skip to Chapter thirteen. However, if your school is currently near the middle of the roadmap or lower, you will want to begin with Chapter twelve.

All readers may find that Chapter fourteen related to the development of your own personal vision may be useful at any point in your exploration of this book.

# CHAPTER 12:

## Leadership for Moving Up from Lower Quadrants to Higher Function

> "If anyone on the verge of action should judge himself according to the outcome, he would never begin."
> — *Søren Kierkegaard*

In this chapter, we will provide a framework and practical guidance for the process of moving up from lower to higher locations on the roadmap. The nature of this growth process will reflect both the need to apply universal principals, as well as considerations unique to the demands and challenges of schools in this relative location. The primary focus of your efforts in this process will be to successfully progress up the vertical axis or the pathway defined by increased intention, capacity, and coherence.

Most efforts to significantly improve lower performing schools fail – about 95%. Therefore, we need to approach our work with clear sight and a necessary respect for the mountain we are set to climb. Without courage, an embrace of the challenge, and an appreciation of the rules of the process, we can assume as with efforts within most schools like ours the status quo will remain intact at the end of the day.

To begin, we need to set our intention and purpose. Our level of commitment will be much more powerful if that purpose is based in a service mindset, and we have vivid and concrete sense of who and why we are serving. Our actions and choices will affect the life trajectory of each of the students in the school. Our actions and choices will define the way that the adults in the school do their work and feel about their jobs and have a lasting impact on the way the school is perceived within the community. We need to believe in the value of the higher location on the roadmap for everyone – especially the students. It is not an abstract process or about a personal accomplishment, it is about real lives.

## Moving Up From Lower to Higher Locations on the Roadmap Pathway

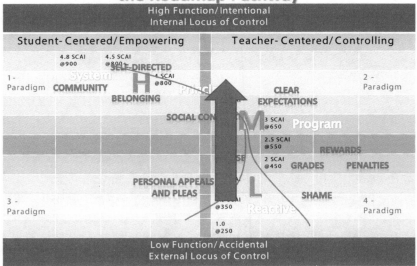

To engage our work with confidence we need to be able to see our desired roadmap location clearly. This chapter (and the book as a whole) is designed to be helpful in clarifying the macro picture of that location and operationalizing it into micro-phenomenon. Feeling confident in our purpose and our direction will keep the process focused where it needs to be: the common good and an emergent realization of the highest potential of the school. It will be best to leave egos at the door. Being grounded in purpose and vision will translate into being able to act with confidence and without the need to over-sell or over promise, or to lose faith in the process in the face of challenges.

With the common good as the goal and the team as the unit, trust and honest conversation are encouraged. The higher truth is that progress up the roadmap will be valuable on many levels for everyone. The day-to-day truth will be that there are endless challenges, sources of discontentment, things going wrong, messiness, and ultimately reasons to veer into a safer direction, so leadership needs to embrace and embody that higher value and project a solid core vision and a depth of humanity to best facilitate the journey.

The structure of this chapter is based on a series of essential considerations for your collective work. Each contributes a vital element to the process and builds upon the last. They represent a synthesis of the book (but are not intended to be a substitute to reading the earlier chapters) related to the specific needs of schools who are presently in a lower location on the roadmap and seek to move up effectively. Practical suggestions for promoting growth in each area are included. Each of the seven essential considerations are introduced here.

1. **Cultivate the core element of trust**. As you engage the process of moving your school up the roadmap, it will be essential to maintain awareness on the level of trust present within the process. In Chapter six, we explored how moving up requires a solid set of social bonds to ensure a sense of safety and fairness, a focus on the process rather than the outcome, and clear vision of the desired destination.

## Sequence of Cause in an Organization/School

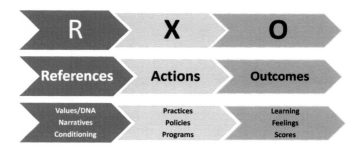

2.  **A guiding vision is essential**. Your success will be defined by the clarity and quality of the vision that is pulling the process forward. With the R->X->O sequence in mind, we need to define our desired R's in a formal sense as well as in an organic and operational sense (i.e., "The all is in the small"). Our personal and collective guiding questions moving forward need to be defined by our desired location more than our current situation.

3.  **Moving up will be defined primarily by the elements of the vertical axis – intention, capacity, coherence, and efficiency.** Conceiving what is needed to move up will be necessary first, no matter our ultimately desired destination on the roadmap. A thoughtful approach to building structural and human capacity within the teachers, staff and students is necessary for the process to be effective. Using our vision and guiding R's to judge the coherence and alignment of what we do all day (i.e., X's) will help reduce the dissonant, redundant, and incoherent effort that is likely in place currently.

4.  **Assessing the current location and state of affairs at the school will be valuable.** Collecting quality data will be highly useful to the process of understanding where we are currently and to help identify our real problems. Effective leaders want to know and are not afraid to look in the mirror. Multiple forms of data including informal input from teachers and students should be part of our expectation as an "effective leader." To know where we are going it is essential to have a full diagnosis of where we are currently.

5.  **Efforts should focus on solving the "real problems" identified by the assessment process and not just the symptoms of those problems**. Solving symptoms with direct interventions will have the effective of limiting the growth of your movement. Therefore, resist the temptation to define your change effort by an O<-X mentality – i.e., we have poor outcomes indicators, so what should we do to address them? Our real problems will be

defined by what we are doing currently. Solutions, therefore, will imply what we need to stop doing as well as what kinds of new practices/X's will we need to develop more fully. Quality data sources are necessary to best identify the real problems.

6. **Instructional leadership is necessary to promote higher quality X's.** Facilitating the change process will mean systematically encouraging higher quality practice, policy, and programs. This will require countless micro-processes encouraging growth, professional development, coherence, teacher empowerment, trust, and relationship building. Short sighted thinking that has resulted in symptom-solving, incongruence, and implementing disconnected add-on programs into the current ecosystem needs to be replaced with a coherent and thoughtful R->X->O mindset.

7. **A broad recognition by members of the school community of the value of reducing low quality, unhealthy and counterproductive X's.** Throughout the improvement process, stakeholders should be encouraged to examine their current practice and become more skilled at recognizing those which are counter-productive to the effort – i.e., are unhealthy for students, promote failure psychology, limit their peers' ability to raise their games, or limit the trajectory of the school's growth. These practices are often challenging to discard, letting go of them may need to occur gradually with the sensitivity that old habits are hard to break.

As you explore each of the seven areas of consideration for moving up in more detail, you will recognize that some of the suggestions offered imply actions which can be taken immediately and others you will want to wait to address until you feel the circumstances are sufficiently receptive. We cannot force change. However, we can act with a sense of purpose, and signal to others that change is part of the new normal. Change starts with an attitude of positive, optimistic belief in the potential within the school, starting with our own demeanor. It is encouraged that you share your personal insights, frustrations, excitements, and ideas for action with others.

While we will be invigorated by being pulled by a picture of a better future, we need to stay grounded and in the moment. We are here now, and we can only control ourselves. Yet, in very real sense we can also appreciate that our true self and our school's destiny is more consistent with our desired location than the current one. It would not excite us if it were not better aligned to our true nature and where we were meant to go.

## 1. Cultivating core elements of trust

One can readily appreciate that without the essential quality of trust being sufficiently present, progress will be limited. We might recall reform efforts we have observed or been part of in the past and consider how the relative existence of trust played a role. Therefore, our effort in this section will be to operationalize trust as much as possible relative to the kinds of challenges and situations that we are likely facing at our school. For that purpose, it will be useful to consider the five trust elements discussed in chapter six.

- Leader being personally trustworthy
- Trust in the vision (desired roadmap) location
- Focus on the process vs the outcome
- Social (contract) bonds are strong and promote sanity and fairness
- Communal bonds are strong and promote care, teamwork, and heart

Research shows us once trust is lost it is difficult to restore. And that an administrative team may have one best chance to set out the journey on the right foot and with the necessary hope and faith in toe. As we examine some of the considerations in this area, you will recognize the places where it will be necessary to focus requisite attention so as to build a solid foundation of trust to ensure that your growth journey is on sound footing.

### Integrity

A good place to start in the process of building trust is to commit to personal integrity. Can we speak honestly, from the heart, and avoid indirect and passive ways of getting things done? In the long-run, the sense of trust we develop from "being real" will be more valuable than other helpful, but less grounded qualities such as enthusiasm, blind-optimism, and "everything is great." At the heart of the sense of trust will be the level of commitment. That will start with our being able to look in the mirror and know that we are committed to the process. If we are sincere in our commitment, others will come to know it too without much need to explicitly state it. Commitment is a quality/R which needs to be built organically much like the vision. We might think of it as a contagious quality that comes from recognition – of the value of the effort, the commitment of the leaders, and eventually the efficacy of the process.

## Listening

An essential quality to building trust (as well as vision) is listening. People value being heard – teachers, staff and even students. We need to find formal and informal ways to get input. Transformative leaders recognize that listening is both a symbolic as well as practical act. Symbolically it says that the process is "our process" and the school is "our school." We are in this together to make this place a great place to work and learn. On a practical level, listening is one of the best ways to discover what is happening, how people are feeling, and what is going well and not so well. Transformative leaders make a commitment to being available and having systematic means of getting fresh and frequent input. Here are a few case examples.

- John is a transformative leader in a new school. He sent out an email to all teachers, staff and students inviting them to schedule a 30-minute meeting to share their thoughts and experiences of both what they thought was going well and not so well at the school.

- Joel, a transformative leader at an independent school, held regular community forums with parents and faculty. Even though he had been at the school for decades, he still encouraged everyone to give their input yearly. Joel was honest about how much he could respond to anyone's specific concern as concerns often imply conflicting solutions.

- Sue, the Director of a charter school, went to each of the 8th grade classes at her school and spent a period having students brainstorm solutions to series of problem areas identified in their SCAI data.

## Consistency, Clarity, and No Mixed Messages

The quality of trust is built over many iterations of action. Others at the school learn that there is a consistent commitment to certain values displayed in actions, plans, policies, words, and non-verbal communication. If we put ourselves in the shoes of the teachers at our school, we will recognize that a) there have been many initiatives which have come and gone and b) there have likely been several examples of mixed messages at the school over the years. When we examine SCAI data from schools in the lower-middle and middle range, we find this to be consistently the case. Teachers report low levels of trust in what administrators say because they have heard several cases of "this is the new thing" only to have a next "new thing" follow. So, first leadership needs to be able to honestly tell faculty that what we are all engaged in is a collective process of growth, not the implementation of a program (even if programs are eventually part of that process). Moreover, people need to feel confident that the rules are not going to change. Real change will require an intentional, persistent, and collective journey to an emergent destination.

Essential to maintaining trust is to be absolutely consistent with messages and actions related to focusing more on processes and less on outcomes. This is fundamental to cultivating a growth-orientation and mindset within the effort. Process focus and growth mindset need to be part of our language and emphasized regularly. Therefore, messages implying a need for R's and X's defined by a fear of failure, avoidance of mistakes, and/or an acceptance of using poor process (low quality X's) in the service of achieving short-term outcomes need to be essentially eliminated. When these attitudes are expressed by teachers and staff, it may be instructive to raise them to the level of awareness and talk about why they feel compelled to employ them. Why do some teachers feel the need to focus on outcomes and use failure psychology practices? Is it in response to past or present standards given to them by leadership? Changing old patterns will usually involve a multi-faceted effort, but if it can often be accomplished by simply clarifying a new normal.

Thriving transformative leaders don't' send out mixed messages. Their goal is high quality processes in the service of the vision of the school and the growth of the students. There is no "but." Therefore, be careful not to send the conflicting message that fundamental value is commitment to high quality process, and then later express the need to put outcome measures as the priority. If our sub-text is interpreted as "but you better get results," what others will hear is, "go ahead and abandon any of the processes that we have committed to and just do "whatever works" that you deem will get results (in the near-term)."

We can value the outcome measures, but they must be seen as only indicators of what we are doing. The quality of our X's will define our location on the roadmap. We will need to be understanding and patient with some of the members of the faculties' accommodation of the target processes. Trust will come from the target being clear and standing still (just like in the classroom). Examine examples of value consistency from other leaders.

- John was committed to having classroom X's defined by student empowerment. After a year of this new focus, the students' reading scores did not change. There were several members of the school that hinted there should be more focus on direct instruction of those skills. He reflected on what he was asking the teachers to do and concluded that it was sound. They stuck to their target vision. The next year the scores went up by 20%. The lessons here are a) usually a good idea is a good idea and b) outcome/O improvement will lag behind new practices/X's, and c) sometimes the X's need to be fully integrated into the school's R's before one sees solid implementation of the new X's.

- Debra works with several teachers who are used to using 2-Paradigm practices. She encourages them to employ 1-Paradigm practices. Because she doesn't talk about test scores, but instead asks clarifying questions such as "if we want our students to feel more ownership of their learning, what would we do more of?" the teachers gradually learn that the focus is on the process and not the outcome. It takes time for these teachers to trust the paradigm shift, but eventually most of them do.

- Sharon struggles to get her school out of the middle location. While she is positive, articulate and visionary, many of the school policies and goals that she verbally encourages are contradicted by a lack of follow-through, support, and/or competing policies. As a result of the mixed messages and lack of accountability, there is a low level of trust at the school and the growth capacity is limited.

## Active Trust Building

The emotional quality of trust is fragile, so it will be useful to put in place active measures to ensure trust, respect, and vulnerability are encouraged during collective gatherings. Being shut down, disrespected, marginalized, or minimized can cause a member of the school community to withdraw and/or resent the collective. Effective leadership includes putting mechanisms in place to ensure emotional safety and encourage ever greater qualities of sharing and intimacy to the conversations related to the school's journey. Developing basic meeting norms is an essential foundation to build a trusting team. Along with basic levels of respect, norms can also imply values such as honesty, active listening, expression of feelings and emotions, and getting to know one another.

- Linda Inlay, a transformative educator, leads faculties through a formal process of building "trust agreements." Ideas are solicited from the group defining the ways they would like to feel, be treated, and how they would like the group to operate. Much like the process used to create a social contract, ideas are listed on chart paper, organized into common themes, and then formalized into a list. Thereafter, this list of trust agreements is used regularly to guide meetings and maintain the norms.

## Social Contract Bonds and Cultivating a Sense of Fairness

In all collectives there are social bonds that operate to define what members need to give and what they can expect in return. In Chapter eleven, we examined how a highly functional social contract between leaders, teachers, and students related to classroom management and discipline was a fundamental ingredient to moving a school up the pathway. And in chapter six we examined what it looks like at both the school and classroom levels. In essence, the social contract operates to encourage a sense of fairness, job clarity, and peace of mind.

When there is a clear sense of what is expected of us and what we can expect from the other members of the collective, trust has a forum to grow. When these social bonds are missing or weak, we lose trust not only in the efficacy of the social contract, but in the collective as a whole and its ability to act and move forward together with purpose.

In the classroom between teacher and student, or in the school between leaders and teachers and staff, the social contract begins with agreements as to what is expected of a member of the community. It is encouraged that this process be conducted formally. A formal social contract is just a starting point, but it is grounding. At the end of the process, the collective will have developed a) a list of ways that teachers and staff demonstrate responsible action and b) a list of ways leadership demonstrates supportive action. In any context, those facilitating the process will need to assess the intentions of the group and the quality of the content being generated. It will be necessary to guide and direct the content of the social contract to ensure that the thinking reflects a desire to promote the common interest defined by responsibility and the highest good.

Some of the ways transformative leaders encourage a living social contract include:

- Be transparent about their actions and decisions.
- Have teachers set goals for themselves (implying how they are going to contribute, See chapter eight).

- Build consequences into the system (i.e., the evaluation rubric should imply target X's and non-target X's, give leadership roles to those who show more commitment, etc.)
- Ask the various stakeholder groups within the school what they think should change and what you need to do better to support the process?

In the end, we will know trust is present when we feel it. We might want to regularly put our finger on the pulse and assess the quality of trust. Often it is as simple as asking. A powerful tool will be to ask students how much they trust their teachers and why. Then we can apply the same logic at the school level by periodically checking in with colleagues. Moreover, what you will most likely find is that the qualities of trust, liking, and learning/effectiveness will be related. As we build any of those qualities the others will be influenced as well. And as the vision within the school becomes clearer the capacity for each will be expanded.

## 2. A Guiding Vision is Essential.

The nature of vision within the process at a school moving from lower levels will usually need to be a little different than a school which is starting at a higher location on the roadmap. Since there is more gravitational force holding the conditions at the school toward the status quo, the lower our current location, the more effort and willpower the movement up will require. In general, it will be useful to keep the ideal (R's, X's, and O's) in mind as we encourage an emergent collective recognition of what is good and healthy. This goal should be encouraged to be the reality as much as is possible. However, our current reality likely includes conscious or unconscious acceptance of many low-quality R's, habitual use of low-level X's, toxic narratives, and guiding questions defined by coping and doing "what works." Therefore, the job of leadership is to help pull the operating vision up out of its current state in the most effective means possible. This section will provide targeted ideas for doing this, expanding on the ideas presented in chapter seven where the process of cultivating a school-wide vision was explored in detail.

We might recall the story of the hounds and the fox from chapter seven. The hounds that saw the fox were much more likely to persist in their pursuit. In essence, our job is to grow the numbers at the school who have seen the fox – i.e., the vision of what is possible. This recognition will likely be unique to each individual. For some, the idea of engaging in a process of growth into something more satisfying, effective, and excellent will be exciting in itself. For others, it will mean a long process defined by seeing evidence and lived experience of something different than the current reality. The answer to our periodic self-reflection question "how many people have bought in?" will probably be a good indicator of our success overall.

## Launch Event

Depending on the current political climate at the school, it will make sense to use your judgment as to the timing of events. In a climate of mistrust, opposition or where many feel wounded, it may be better not to plan for a broad-based or whole-school launch event until the environment is more conducive. But within a year, leadership will want to find an occasion such as a day-long meeting or a retreat to engage all teachers and staff in setting a vision and formalizing a vision statement. The event is symbolic as well as practical. Symbolically, it represents a new beginning and a heightening of hope and receptivity. Practically, it is a chance to cultivate collective buy-in and define the target destination, and new normal in practical and operational terms. Very soon after, evidence of the vision-building event should be found around the school. Even in this age of electronic communication, the most effective institutions put their school-wide documents into poster form and strategically place them around the building.

## Conspiracy of the Infected

Anything is possible once we formally birth the process of moving up. It will be great (and it does happen) if the majority of teachers and staff feel inspired and liberated by the initial process and that energy persists. However, it is also likely that once the optimistic energy of the launch event wanes, a reversion back toward the status quo may take place. This can be expected.

But at this point we will have a better sense of who is on board. This is often called the "coalition of the willing" and might be better termed the "conspiracy of the infected" in this case. Those who have felt an internal connection with evolving to a better place will feel the desire for an opportunity to a) talk to one another and gain energy and clarity of purpose and b) share that passion and insight with everyone else. In most cases, these folks are those who have already been attracted to a 1-Paradigm mentality or feel very confident as teachers. It can also be the case that you have teachers who have felt dissatisfied and want to transform and be among those who exhibit the positive and aspiration energy at the school. And it is also likely that you will have teachers who want to take on the role of change leader mainly because they want to be seen as the authorities in the effort, even though they may not have really caught the vision. Working with the political and personal realities will require care and intention. Our goal will be to grow the quality and quantity of the contribution, by raising up some voices and politely muting others as gracefully as possible.

## Guiding Questions

The school's vision is an idea – a conceptual reality in need of human hands to become actuality. No matter how well this vision was captured in birthing events, or in subsequent meetings, connecting concept to practice will be a continuous process. And out of sight, out of mind. Actualizing the vision needs to be part of everything or else the status quo will fill the void.

What is the status quo? Coming out of the lower quadrants, the normal R's will be principally defined by the assumptions that a) we need to do "what works," given our circumstances, and b) we need to solve problems directly with interventions. In essence, we have largely been trying to solve our problems on the same level of consciousness at which they were created. Therefore, an essential job of leadership and the growing ranks of the conspiracy of the infected is to find ways to define a more conscious and well-conceived "better" as the target location, and therefore redefine "normal." This can take countless forms, but one area that will be both powerful and efficient is to help change the guiding questions/R's which are used to inform practices/X's throughout the day. We can do this as a formal exercise when we feel the team is ready, but starting right away, representing a higher quality of written and spoken guiding questions for the school is essential to the work of leadership. Empowering higher quality guiding questions have been highlighted throughout the book. Figure 12.1 lists a few salient guiding questions for the task of shifting the vision/R's up the roadmap from this location.

Figure 12.1 Examples of Guiding Questions Leading to Either Movement Up the Roadmap or Maintenance of the Status Quo

| R-X-O Focus | Guiding Questions that will Support Movement Up | Guiding Questions that will Keep Us in Our Lower Quadrant Status Quo |
|---|---|---|
| **R's/References** (values, beliefs, conditioning, narratives, vision, mindset) | • What gifts do have that I can contribute to the school's effort to improve?<br>• How do I need to grow as a professional and a person to be able to embody the change?<br>• How can I encourage more of a psychology of success in my classroom and the school?<br>   o Internal locus of control<br>   o Growth orientation/mindset<br>   o Self-Acceptance and Belonging | • What are the flaws within the process and the leaders that I can use to justify being resistant?<br>• What are all the ways the students and the parents at the school are deficient?<br>• How can I obtain acceptable levels of the following in my class?<br>   o Control<br>   o Compliance<br>   o Respect for me<br>   o Recognition that they are below standard |
| **X's/Actions** (practices, policies, programs, communication, non-verbal messages) | • What can we as a class do to grow and make tomorrow more effective?<br>• How can I encourage more student ownership, voice, agency, and self-responsibility?<br>• What skills do my students need to get to the next level and what is the best system to help them acquire those skills? | • From my previous experience, what "works" to get my students to be on task and complete their work?<br>• What can I give my students to motivate them?<br>• Shouldn't my students already know how to do that by now? |
| **O's/Outcomes** (scores, learning, feelings, rates, etc. experience, climate) | • What information could I collect to better understand my students' needs and perceptions?<br>• What do our various sources of data say about what we have done to this point and how we could do better? | • Whose idea was this survey? Are all these items necessary?<br>• What is the administration doing to fix some of the weak results in our data? |

The job of leadership is to infuse our dialogue with these empowering higher level guiding questions and help everyone recognize when they are asking disempowering questions. Once the concept of empowering vs. limiting guiding questions has been introduced, we can ask or at least imply the question "would you call that an empowering or limiting guiding question?" in a sensitive and thoughtful manner.

## Mirror Classroom and School Level Visions

Everyone in the school has a vision. To encourage growth, leadership needs to support the process of the teachers, coaches, staff, coordinators, counselors, and teacher leaders to develop a vision of the next level for their particular context. The ingredients of a more empowering and functional classroom are much the same as those for a school. Therefore, it will be useful to keep the notion of a mirror phenomenon in mind – we are moving our school up the roadmap which will encourage classrooms that reflect higher quality R's and X's, which will result in the school moving up, which will encourage better classrooms, ad infinitum.

# School-Wide Orientation Matrix

| | Empowerment Connection Trust | Control Comparison Fear |
|---|---|---|
| **High Function Intentional Leadership** | 1-Paradigm School - Empowering<br>• Vision-Driven Facilitative Leadership<br>• Student-Centered Classrooms<br>• Community Climate<br>• Mostly 1-style teaching | 2-Paradigm School - Managed<br>• Efficiency-Driven Top-Down Leadership<br>• Teacher-Centered Classrooms<br>• Institutional Climate<br>• Mostly 2-style teaching |
| **Low Function Accidental Leadership** | 3-Paradigm School - Amorphous<br>• Enabling Passive Leadership<br>• Unstructured learning<br>• Insecure Climate<br>• Lots of 3-style teaching (but also a random combo of others) | 4-Paradigm School -Bossy<br>• Dominating and Self-serving Leadership<br>• Lecture and Test Teaching<br>• Domesticating Climate<br>• Mostly 4-style teaching |

We cannot use entirely 2-Paradigm leadership practices (or any 4-Paradigm practices at all) to encourage more 1-Paradigm classroom practice. We also need to make sure that our empowering 1-Paradigm process does not leave so much undefined that the result is a high quantity of 2/4-Paradigm practices are still being chosen. 1-Paradigm is not a 3-paradigm vacuum for anything. If we do not create a clear conception of the 1-Paradigm classroom, we can find that the autonomy without clarity can result in many teachers continuing to judge coping and compliance-based teaching as desirable and/or at least comfortable.

Clarifying our higher function vision and asking empowering guiding questions helps pull folks out of their comfort zones. 3-Paradigm leadership will not result in progress toward your desired location from this location. As mentioned previously, the lower we are on the roadmap currently, the more the clarity of the vision and the projection of solidness of the process will need to come from leaders. As we move up, leadership can give away increasingly more ownership. But we will need to focus on moving up to make moving over more possible.

## Resistance and Addressing Misconceptions

Where there is the prospect of change there will be resistance. How much is difficult to expect. There are schools where there is very little due to all the trust elements that are developed and the innate desire of those in the school to move to something better. Yet, as discussed throughout the book, supporting new R's (values, beliefs, patterns of thought, assumptions, attitudes about the ability of students) and a restructuring of X's (adding some practices, developing new skills, ceasing some practices, etc.) will require a well-intended and multifaceted job on the part of leadership. No matter the degree of resistance, it is best not to give it energy by confronting it or use up our limited energy focused on who is not on board. It is best to focus the energy of leadership on growing the ranks of those that appreciate the vision. We do need to listen and recognize the concerns of the cynics and sceptics. In the same way that a teacher will work with a student who seeks to engage in a power struggle, leadership will not want to validate the person's ego need to be right or to hook them in. Instead, those leading will want to be clear about what they are doing and treat the resistant colleagues professionally.

Often skepticism is fear manifested as cleverness and apparent logic. We need to ask ourselves frequently, is this person's skepticism valid and warranted? It may be. They could be right. But if the leadership team regularly ask itself what is best for all staff, students, and the community, it will likely be able to recognize if the various complaints coming from the sources of resistance are valid or mostly based in fear or misconceptions.

At the end of the chapter, Exercise 12.A examines a series of misconceptions which typically operate as R's in schools at lower levels on the roadmap. As you explore each, you will likely recognize when you have heard them expressed by members of the school. At minimum, leadership will want to help teachers and staff members recognize the assumptions they are using when they espouse one of these myths (and appreciate what could be called the "actual reality" related to each). If leadership recognizes that limiting misconceptions are substantially dragging the process down, the team might address the topic directly and engage the faculty and staff in a small group reflection/discussion of a) the misconceptions and working assumptions that exist at the school, b) why they exist, c) how they affect what happens at the school, and d) how to raise the level of working assumptions/R's in the future.

## Toxic Narratives and Changing the Narratives

How we talk about our school has a powerful impact on our capacity for growth and improvement. A good rule to embrace is "We don't say anything about the school, our students, or ourselves that we don't wish to be true." This is an ambitious standard, but if we successfully embrace its intent, it will help promote our movement up. What we will likely find as we start listening to the operating narratives – the way we talk about ourselves, is that much of it is limiting our growth potential. In Chapter seven, we identified a series of life affirming vs. toxic narratives. These toxic narratives

- entitlement, victimization, guilt, cynicism, and inadequacy are common in all walks of life, and tend to find their way into schools because of the enormous demands and burdens of being an educator.

The starting point is always to model and presume life affirming narratives. But, if we feel that the prevalence of toxic narratives is a significant problem, we may want to address it formally. The goal will be to produce a set of "We are…." statements. If we see value in engaging this process, we will want to be prepared with solid preparatory thinking before we begin. The leadership team will want to run through the exercise first. Creating a seminal product with the whole faculty that misses the mark will be problematic. Alternately, if the outcome is simply a thoughtful discussion, the content resulting from the exercise is less permanent. Therefore, if the team is not sure how such an exercise would turn out, maybe wait to produce a formal product until the energy is right.

Along with other documents formalizing the R's and X's of the "target location," a document that formalizes "who we are as a school community" can be helpful and act as the antidote to the toxic narratives that live in the school currently. In essence, you are stating narratives that are true in an aspirational sense. With any aspirational vision, language, or conceptualization, we are in fact intending to become more consistent with our potential, and on a deeper level, more consistent with who we really are. When developing the "who we are" statements try to state them as processes – what we can be and do. Avoid outcome statements such as "all students…" because we cannot control student outcomes. When stakeholders see a statement that implies an unrealistic outcome goal their minds naturally start to tear it down and conceive of all the reasons it is deluded. Therefore, instead of 'we help all students get accepted to college" we might include statements such as "we nurture the growth of all students" or "we encourage all students to be leaders" or "we embody and encourage a growth mindset." Here leadership is working with a delicate balance (much like enlisting students in defining their own classroom agreements), we want a quality outcome which functions successfully, and we also want everyone to feel heard, to contribute, and to walk away with a sense of ownership.

### 3. Moving up Will be Defined Primarily by the Elements of the Vertical Axis – Intention, Capacity, Coherence and Efficiency.

If our school is currently functioning at a lower location on the pathway, no matter our ultimate target destination, it will make sense to conceive our effort as primarily one of moving up the vertical axis of the roadmap. Maintaining the 1-Paradigm as our target will always serve to pull the process forward in a sound manner. But function is requisite to making most elements of our success possible. Therefore, taking practical steps to build intention, capacity, coherence, and efficiency should define our primary effort at this stage. In this section we examine some ideas for building function.

## Vertical Axis

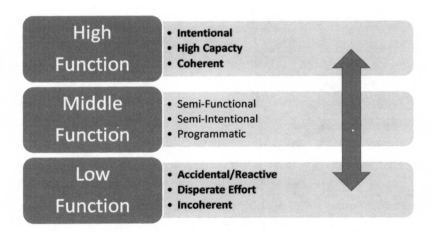

| High Function | • Intentional<br>• High Capacty<br>• Coherent |
| Middle Function | • Semi-Functional<br>• Semi-Intentional<br>• Programmatic |
| Low Function | • Accidental/Reactive<br>• Disperate Effort<br>• Incoherent |

Much has been said about the idea of intention throughout the book. But we might boil it down to the simple concept of making decisions with our vision and target destination in mind (and as our criteria for making choices). When we use these criteria faithfully, we will recognize that many of ideas that would have previously made sense, when viewed through this lens can be revealed as not as sound as they may have seemed. For instance, policies that lack clarity can lead us into the 3-Paradigm. Moreover, some practices/X's that may have seemed "positive" on the surface, can be better recognized as disempowering, and limiting to our trajectory. Steps that obtain short-term gains in function may be helpful initially, but they can also be ultimately limiting, if they put in place X's that have long-term side effects. As with all things, we will need to use our judgement, but with recognition of the long-term implications.

## Building Capacity

In a broad sense, capacity is defined by the structural elements within the school that make possible the degree to which certain qualities and practices can manifest. More capacity means more ability for qualities such as leadership, collaboration, and communication to flow. So, building more capacity will involve an infinite number of large and small actions. The job of leadership will be to consider and promote capacity in those things which make the most sense for all. For schools moving up from lower locations, the following areas of focus often represent places where there is high need and therefore great potential for growth.

- **Site-Based Leadership Team**. First, if there is not a team at the school functioning as a site leadership team, it will be essential to put one together in short order. The team should include the school's best teachers and those who at least appreciate what a 1-Paradigm classroom is about. If you have teachers who have created 1-Paradigm classrooms or who are primarily student-centered in their orientation, enlist them. The team should have staff representation, as well as student representative if possible. Like any team, this group will have to grow and mature. Initially the team should be responsible for meeting and representing the interests of the school as a whole. This team will be the most efficient group for synthesizing language and ideas for policy and school documents. The whole school may be the vehicle for generating the ideas, but this team will need to develop the skills of synthesizing and representing their colleagues' views and ideas. Ultimately, the group should be given the time to be integral in the processing of data, strategic planning, and leading professional development.

- **Student Leadership Development**. High function schools take advantage of students' ability to support one another and the goals of the school. A tendency for schools that conceive their students within tiers is that they can fall into a mindset defined by the question – how much support do students need (because of their dependence on adult interventions)? For some aspects of student learning support this logic is justified. But when it comes to decision-making, dealing with conflict, the process of self-reflection, student activism, student agency and voice, our focus needs to come from the question – how can we give students the skills and opportunities to be leaders and self-responsible? Stakeholders should view it as their obligation to encourage students who could be solving their own problems, planning their own events, providing peer mentoring and mediation of conflict, and speaking for their needs. It should be viewed as unacceptable when it is not taking place, especially as a result of existing structures and policies, or low expectations on the part of the faculty. The value of student compliance will not lead the school up the roadmap. Responsible students are those who have the skills and dispositions to assess what is going on and speak up and/or take action to make things better.

- **Classroom Management and Discipline**. Chapter eleven explores this area in detail. Your school will not move up without moving up in the domain of classroom management and discipline. In essence, all 3- and 4-Paradigm practices need to be eliminated. Building structures at the school which build on clarity and responsibility to one's commitments need to replace structures built on obedience, compliance, fear of shame or punishment, and dependence on the use of extrinsic methods to obtain short-term results.

- **PLC Structure and Intent**. Moving up to higher levels of function will require greater structural capacity for teachers to collaborate, share practices and ideas, plan together, observe one another, and process new information and resources. The school can term this mechanism anything that makes sense, but in essence here the school is developing capacity around becoming an ever more effective professional learning community (PLC). Even if everyone is not fully prepared to take advantage of a structure that provides so much opportunity, it is best to put the structure into place and then support the growth into it.

- ○ To illustrate the impact of the structural element, it is helpful here to reflect upon the experience of PLCs at two schools. Both schools were performing in the 2.7/30%tile middle/low range. Both had similar student populations and teachers reflecting a wide range of skills and commitment levels. But one school had installed a PLC planning period for teams at each grade level. The other school did not. While each school struggled with similar issues, the capacity of the school with the PLC structure to process new ideas, collaborate, implement new practices, and share resources was significantly improved. The result was a school that was a year or two ahead of the other in terms of its overall ability to move up to a higher location on the roadmap.

- **Scheduling should reflect the Vision and Mission of the School.** After visiting and communicating with many higher performing vision-driven schools, a common theme emerged – create a schedule which serves your vision. In many cases, this took a little imagination and a lot of courage. As one leader put it, "form follows function." If you build it, the capacity will be reflected in what it makes possible. Here are some recommendations for schools looking to move up.

  - ○ Build in a time for students to process non-academic issues. Many schools have advisory period. This is a good start, but there needs to be a broad purpose to this time and input from teachers as to how best to use it.

- ○ Build in time for teacher collaboration and PLCs.

- ○ Ask the teachers what they would like to see? Include all those who need to be consulted such as specialists, and staff. Begin the process with the parameters which need to be met within a schedule to meet compliance. Then engage a brainstorming exercise intending to generate suggestions that align the schedule to a school that is meeting its potential most effectively.

- ○ Consider block schedules to encourage deeper learning and more creative instruction. Each class meets for two blocks per week plus one normal period. One school using block scheduling effectively found that making Monday the day that all periods met was preferable to Friday (as many schools tend to default to for some reason) because teachers knew they would see all of their students and could get organized and set the course for the coming week.

## Coherence

No matter how effective we are as educators, our jobs will be inherently demanding and require substantial effort. When the focus of that effort is not coherent, we can expend substantial energy and find ourselves stuck in a rut. This is demoralizing. Most schools scoring in the 3.0SCAI/30-50%tile achievement tend to have climate and achievement ratings that stay fixed in the same location. The problem is usually not the level of effort expended or the sincerity of the intentions but the level of coherence and the nature of the intentions. Coherence is defined by a) an alignment of the school's practices/X's with its vision and targeted roadmap location and b) the congruence of those X's with one another.

Much of our success in this area will come from vetting new or existing policies, practices, or initiatives through guiding questions or another assessment lens (i.e., psychology of success, our mission, things we do or don't do list, higher values, "we are. . list," etc.). What we often find is that much of what is taking place at the school currently both instructionally (by teachers who have not yet developed the skills/X's or references/R's to do better) or administratively (policies, programs, accepted practices that are endorsed) are not congruent with the school's desired references and/ or intended targets. Many of the likely incongruent X's will become more evident as we examine some of the X's to eliminate later in this chapter. What is required to improve instructional practices school-wide will have an arc of years and involve expert instructional leadership, while changing policy and recommended practices can be achieved much sooner.

Most schools at the lower-middle locations tend to have adopted a whole series of programs to solve perceived needs over the years (O<-X). All of these programs have justifications, so on some level, were logical responses to problems. Yet, if one examines some of these programs from the lens of their coherence with one another and/or the target school reality, they will recognize that they are often incongruent. Adding new programs can foster improvement but can also introduce counterproductive elements into your improvement efforts.

It may be useful to distinguish formal external program adoptions from internal programmatic goal X's. Project-based learning, class meetings, inquiry instruction, transformative classroom management, and critical thinking are all broad initiatives that have a basic idea at their core and can be executed in many ways. Expertise in these initiatives can grow over many years of application. These types of initiatives have their efficacy in internal sharing of expertise and adaption to school needs. An external program adoption on the other hand is typically characterized by a standardized set of particulars and applications which are spelled out by a vendor. Schools at the highest points on the roadmap adopt few if any programs of this kind, whereas the schools at the lowest end commonly adopt many.

When practitioners have a clearly defined set of guiding principles, goals, and "why's" for a school-wide X, leadership has an increased ability to ensure that any practical implementation is sound and aligned with the desired R's (i.e., R->X->O). Typically, the externally developed program a school might consider adopting will provide the "how," of the specifics but may lack the "why's." Too often the guiding values which were used to create the specifics of that program may not be apparent to the user (and/or be sound or coherent). Therefore, in the end, it is best be a meticulous and skeptical consumer when it comes to any external program adoption.

## Efficiency

Efficiency will not be the sole cause of moving up, but the lack of it can significantly limit the movement. When leadership makes efficiency a priority (i.e., things work, systems create flow, processes are logical, intuitive and have a speedy turn around and meetings are well run), it has both symbolic and practical value. Symbolically, it shows leadership cares and are concerned about others' welfare and quality in general. On a practical level, it enables the big values to manifest without being constrained by the little things. One school leader put it this way, "doing a good job with the little things becomes a big thing."

Some specific areas of efficiency to prioritize include:

- How visitors and guests are treated and processed when they enter the school. We find an almost perfect correlation between how one is treated at the front desk and the location of the school on the roadmap.
- How meetings are run. A school's SCAI item related to how teachers and staff rate the quality of meetings is strongly correlated to its climate score overall. It might be useful to have a default process for meetings that includes:
  - An agenda
  - A minimum of bureaucratic reporting out (put that in an email) unless it is consequential content.

- An activity where faculty and staff process in small groups. Have a system for mixing up the groups and promoting heterogeneous composition at tables.

- A PowerPoint presentation with key information, such as task directions, key data, graphic depictions of ideas, and inspirational quotes.

- A process for making sure input is democratic and representative.

- Someone taking notes and disseminating them later.

- Walk around the school and look at all the fixtures and structures. What do you see? When a student sees a drinking fountain that does not work, or a net on a basketball hoop that is ripped off, or a broken window, or dumpy equipment it sends a message to that student about how much the leadership of the school values them. Would a student at the most desirable school in town see something similar?

- Have adults gotten in the habit of nagging students to demonstrate a school-wide expectation? Can you conceive of ways to reduce the need for nagging and adult monitoring and bribing, and build more student sense of accountability and clarity of the expectation? (See Chapter eleven related to technical management for ideas).

- Does the school have an efficient way for parents to access student progress?

- Does the school have an efficient way to manage attendance?

- Does the school have an efficient way to send out communication?

- What are the ways the school could use social media effectively to improve communication?

## 4. Assessing the Current Location and State of Affairs at the School

The school's improvement process will be greatly facilitated by including the insight from various sources of assessment data. The nature of that data use will say a great deal about the efficacy of our process. What we find is that a) the kinds of data schools collect will define what they value and put energy into and b) schools wanting to change want to know. Schools which want to appear proactive related to data use tend to collect a lot of data but do not process it with the kind of care, sincerity, and broad participation necessary for it to have an impact. In many cases, there is a lot of data being collected that ultimately informs little action.

The first step will be to explore the various assessment options and select a limited number of quality data sources. Your state or accrediting agency will probably have given you some input related to progress indicators for which you will need to be responsive. But you will want to reflect on the school's stated values, the kinds of changes you want to see, and then identify effective indicators of those outcomes (R->X->O). It is best to collect data from a broad range of domains of school operations – indicators of student achievement, student attendance and discipline, teacher working conditions, parent perceptions, and others. Chapter nine explores these options in more detail.

The school leadership team may want to take some time to identify what would ideally be accomplished from the process of data collection and a meaningful analysis. Quality data should provide insight and quantifiable benchmarks into how the school is doing across various dimensions. As we will discuss in the next section, the focus will need to be on avenues for growth and the "real problems" and real needs at the school. Focusing simply on symptoms will limit the efficacy of the data use, and ultimately your overall progress.

Some of the most vital reasons to collect data include:

- To produce a solid sense of the school's current location. Moreover, each subsequent iteration of data collection will reveal potential evidence of growth and the efficacy of various changes in the X's.

- To be able to drill down into smaller micro level data to see more specific needs, areas of concern or interest.
- To confirm accurate levels of perceptions among teachers, staff, parents, and students (as opposed to subjective perceptions). Trust requires accurate data.
- To be able to discern the real problems from the data source, not only the symptoms.

The following SCAI data table (Figure 12.2) comes from a low-middle function school (School A). The SCAI scale is 1 (low) - 5 (high), where average is about 3.2. Examining the SCAI ratings from school A for the teachers/staff and students, one will quickly recognize areas of relative strength or need. Dimension scores at nearly every school from the hundreds surveyed tend to gravitate in a narrow range. The reason (as discussed in Chapters two and ten) is that the same R's inform the X's in each of the eight areas. So overall, what one can infer from this school is that it is about a 3.0 function school and a little under the middle range location on the roadmap.

**Figure 12.2 SCAI Ratings for School A.**

| | Dimensions | Student Ratings | Teacher and Staff Ratings |
|---|---|---|---|
| D1 | **Physical Environment** | 2.69 | 2.82 |
| D2 | **Teacher Relations** | | 3.40 |
| D3 | **Student Interactions** | 3.04 | 3.57 |
| D4 | **Leadership** | | 3.36 |
| D5 | **Management Discipline** | 3.03 | 3.56 |
| D6 | **Learning / Assessment** | 2.91 | 3.84 |
| D7 | **Social-Emotional Culture** | 2.69 | 3.39 |
| D8 | **Community** | 3.16 | 3.28 |
| | **Overall School Climate Rating** | **2.92** | **3.28** |

Like many schools at this location on the roadmap, a distinct discrepancy between the perceptions/experiences of the teachers and the students exists at school A. This is not uncommon, but it is more common in schools which rely heavily on behaviorist discipline systems (Shindler, 2018), and on direct instruction as the primary mode of teaching. Exploring all eight dimensions of the SCAI data together is useful in the process of determining the general level of the school climate and the school's current location on the roadmap. Broad areas of need can be inferred in the School A ratings, especially where we see a lower number relative to the others. Therefore, at school A, they could assume the social-emotional culture, learning and classroom management practices, reflected in the student ratings would imply areas of attention. Those domains represent long-term issues, whereas the issues related to the school's appearance can be addressed much more immediately and directly. In the next section, we will examine ratings from one dimension that will provide a deeper sense of the climate and function level at school A.

Assessment methods tend to define what is important and therefore the direction of the attention and the nature of the intention. So, as one trans-formative leader said, "Assessment should be in the service of your vision and mission." Our question should be in essence - given what we want to do, what will we want to know, and given that, what are the best ways to gather that knowledge?

## 5. Focus Efforts on Solving the Real Problems Identified by the Assessment Process and not just Symptoms of Problems.

Simply put, most schools currently functioning at the lower-middle range on the roadmap pathway tend to a) focus on the symptoms of their problems and b) attempt to solve those symptoms with direct interventions. Those schools that persist in that logic will stay stationary in their location on the roadmap. There are justifications for taking this route. It is safe. It is defensible. It is easy to explain publicly. It sounds sensible. It appears proactive. It is not likely to send up red-flags and jeopardize our jobs. However, a true interest in moving your school up the roadmap will require addressing your real problems with meaningful and systemic solutions. In Chapter nine, this concept is explored in more detail.

In most cases, the "real problems" at the school relate to what we do (our X's) and why (our R's). As discussed, it is normal to focus on the outcome, but in most cases the outcome is the evidence or a byproduct of our activity. Recalling a presentation from an assistant principal at a low performing school, they shared with the audience that after seeing their data they realized that "they needed to do something" to address a problem area. This reaction was heartfelt, sincere, and well-intended, but what was not raised was that the school was doing something, all day, every day. What they had done up to this point was why they were in the state they were in. And while any direct interventions to a problem symptom at the school might potentially improve a particular area, unless there is a systemic change at the school toward improved overall better X's, the school will perpetually experience their "real problems" in that area down the road. Direct interventions to symptoms tend to miss the mark. They can often simply add a superficial remedy over the top of a dysfunctional condition.

As one examines the SCAI data in Figure 12.3 from school A related to Dimension 5: Classroom Management and Discipline, it is possible to dig a little deeper into the realm of the X's and the real problems at the school. Within the data one can see evidence of perceptions, but also the R's that inform the practices/X's as well as something about the quality and efficacy of the practices themselves.

**Figure 12. 3 School A: SCAI Dimension Five – Management and Discipline Ratings from Teachers/Staff and Students**

| D5 | Management Discipline | Teacher and Staff Ratings | Student Ratings |
|----|----------------------|---------------------------|-----------------|
| 5a | consistency of discipline-policy | 3.00 | 3.61 |
| 5b | clear expectations of discipline policy | 3.34 | 3.43 |
| 5c | effective discipline | 3.79 | 3.05 |
| 5d | student-generated ideas for rules | 3.13 | 2.65 |
| 5e | discipline effect on functionality | 3.84 | 2.84 |
| 5f | teacher-student supportive interactions | 3.65 | 3.07 |
| 5g | promotion of student self-direction | 3.58 | 2.77 |
| 5h | promotion of community in class | 3.68 | 2.84 |
| | Dimension 5 Ratings - Means | **3.56** | **3.03** |

If one were on the school climate leadership team of School A, these data would tell us a great deal about the current state of the school. School A, like many schools currently operating at this location, reflects a series of classic "real problems." However, before examining this data, teachers at the school would have quite likely defined their real problems as:

- Students are unmotivated.
- Students are frequently off-task.
- Other teachers are not consistent with the reward system or calling home.
- Some students disrupt the learning of others.

However, as one explores the SCAI data and does some reading between the lines, the actual "real problems" could be more accurately characterized as the following:

- Teachers feel as if there is a lack of vision and consistency in the policies.
- Students feel little voice, choice, or empowerment. Students' need for power is not met.
- Discipline and management methods are intended to promote primarily compliance, so students respond with apathy, rebellion, stunted maturation, and irresponsibility.
- Students do not feel a sense of community because little effort is made to encourage it.
- Students recognize the methods used are not very effective in creating a high function classroom, so they are not surprised at the level of classroom order.
- There is a disconnect between how teachers and students characterize the notion of "positive." For teachers, it is giving rewards for desired behavior. For students being given "positive reinforcements" is not perceived as positive. It is manipulative. For them, positive would be a functional nurturing environment.

School B is an example of another school functioning in the low-middle range. As one examines the SCAI ratings for Dimension four related to the leadership and decision-making patterns at the school (See Figure 12.4), it is evident that the school lacks vision and connected R's.

**Figure 12.4 School B: SCAI Ratings for Dimension 4 Related to Leadership and Decisions – Teachers and Staff Survey**

| D4 | Leadership and Decisions | Teachers and Staff Ratings |
|---|---|---|
| 4a | clear mission | 2.77 |
| 4b | presence of vision for the school | 2.86 |
| 4c | decisions based on mission | 3.00 |
| 4d | recognition of staff | 2.95 |
| 4e | shared values | 2.64 |
| 4f | representative decision making | 2.95 |
| 4g | faculty trust in leadership | 3.05 |
| 4h | success of leadership | 3.38 |
| 4i | staff responsibility for leadership | 3.09 |
| 4j | leadership sync. with student/ community | 3.27 |
| 4k | leadership sync. school climate | 3.09 |
| | Dimension 4 Ratings - Mean | **3.01** |

Data such as these represent the need for leadership to take ownership of some of the "real problems" at the school. Without the benefit of these data, if one were to ask the principal what the problems at the school were, he/she might rate the top problems as:

- The home life of the students.
- Teachers who are not on board with the school's policies.
- A lack of loyalty among many of the staff.

However, as one examines the SCAI ratings and talks to the teachers at school B, what becomes more evident is that much of what needs to improve is related to the leadership. As leaders we need to own a disproportionate part of the responsibility for the roadmap location of our school. Given the data above, if school B we were to identify their most pressing real problems in the domain of leadership and decision-making they would include:

- A need to cultivate a clearer and more positive student-centered vision.

- The need to cultivate an instructional value system with priority practices as well as the identification of those practices inconsistent with the desired values to be avoided.

- More trust in teacher leaders to facilitate professional development.

Historically, both School A and School B showed little improvement in their SCAI data over time. In each case, we can speculate the cause of that stagnation to be a result of a) a tendency to place attention primarily on their circumstances rather than on their own actions and policies, b) focus on symptoms of problems rather than their true problems, and c) an unwillingness of leadership to embrace elements of the 1-Paradigm concept necessary to promote growth at the school. In each case, the potential for steady improvement existed. But the recommended X's were informed by mostly 2/4-Paradigm R's. Given these R's, the predicted location of the schools would be about where they both were – in the lower 2-Paradigm region of the roadmap. Change can occur wherein there is an adopting of an alternate set of guiding DNA/R's implying a different destination on the roadmap.

Fortunately, we do not have to conceive the work of addressing our real problems as discrete efforts. In many cases our real problems will be best improved with a holistic focus. We can take a cue from the country of Finland (Morgan, 2014). In this country, they were able to improve their test scores in reading, math, and science, virtually eliminate the use of tracking, and realize a much-improved experience for students and teachers related to school life. The key was an overall shift in their guiding R's. Fundamental in that shift was a goal to make schools "happier" places.

Setting the aim in the direction of the 1-Paradigm will lead to remediation of a lot of your current issues. A rising tide lifts all boats and a rising school climate and function level lifts all areas of a school. Everything is connected. One example of this phenomenon is how it plays out related to (the justifiable national concern for) the disproportionate suspension rates for minority boys. Efforts to address this problem have brought helpful attention to some of the historic R's that have been greatly responsible for its existence. But direct remedies have had mixed results at best. However, what the ASSC meta-data tell us, confirming the findings of others, is that the problem is related mostly to the kinds of classrooms into which these students attend. What we find is that in a 4-Paradigm classroom the ratio of suspensions is about 6 (minority boys) to 1 (general population student) with many boys being suspended. In a 2-Paradigm classroom, the ratio is about 3-1 (with fewer being suspended) and in a 1-Paradigm classroom the ratio is close to 1-1 with very few suspensions. This is just one of countless examples of how the solution to what is often conceived as a discrete challenging issue is remedied by shifting the broad aim toward more 1-Paradigm R's and X's.

Moving up on the roadmap will have reliably positive influence on student achievement as well. As explained in Chapter two, SCAI scores, location on the roadmap, and student achievement measures are all strongly correlated (@0.7). When a school succeeds in improving its climate and function levels, we are likely to see improvement in test scores as well. As one leader, who saw significant achievement gains at her school, said, "We set out to improve our reading scores, and realized we needed to change everything else as we went along."

Engaging in the process of strategic planning outlined in Chapter nine will be useful at any point in our process to align our data use with our vision. As we explore the idea of practices to expand and those to decrease in the next section, you will likely recognize how your true problems are related mostly to the X's being used in the various classrooms, as well as the policies and systems within the school.

## 6. Instructional Leadership is Necessary to Promote Higher Quality and Function X's, and

## 7. A Broad Intention of all Members of the School Community should be to Recognize and Reduce Low Function X's.

The best overall indicator of the current roadmap location of school will be the average quality level of the classroom X's — practices, methods, strategies, policies, interaction patterns, communication, systems, procedures, and experiences in general. However, it is essential to keep in mind the inter-dependent relationship between what is taking place in each classroom and the overall school realities. Cultivating the kinds of R's to promote growth on both dimensions simultaneously should be the goal. Therefore, a clear conception of the target R's and X's for classrooms will need to be built into a) the vision development process, b) systems within the school, and c) be central to all professional development.

Moving up related to classroom X's will imply growing certain practices and reducing other practices. Both components of the process are necessary. To anchor this process of restructuring, a shift in R's will be important. Some of the descriptors for that shift include moving away from cleverness-based thinking to insight and wisdom-based thinking, away from defaulting to coping and embracing a more courageous approach to challenges, and away from convenience as the top priority to growth and quality. Most teachers do not explicitly endorse these lower quality R's, but these R's become common in an environment that feels overwhelming, un-motivating, unsupported, or where those R's are normalized.

A powerful change force is to encourage individuals and the collective to reflect upon the kinds of R's that are informing their instructional choices. Confronting the idea that our thinking has been defined to a great extent by mediocrity-based R's can be a powerful source of growth and self-improvement. But challenging others on the quality of their references is likely to produce defensiveness. Therefore, explorations into guiding personal references should be done by way of self-reflection exercises. But as a school, the vision and target R's, X's, and roadmap location should be implied in all we do. Increasingly teachers should be able to classify their practices within the school lens of "things we do" and "things we don't do." This can be related to any quality taxonomy which effectively defines the nature of your target location (i.e., psychology of success, basic needs, nature of the 1-Paradigm classroom, etc.).

In a broad sense, we will want to use the 1-Paradigm classroom as our target destination. If teachers have become positive and engaging 2-Paradigm teachers, they are probably on balance supporting the school's growth upward, but they will still want to reconsider some of their more compliance-based practices as time goes on. For those who find themselves operating in the 3- and 4-Paradigm quadrants, they will want to engage deeply in a process of restructuring their practice. As discussed in Chapter eight, instructional leadership is a complex process that may require months and years to effect results. The bottom line is that any of us act (i.e., X) because it somehow makes sense or works for us (i.e., it fits our R's). Nonetheless, the first responsibility of every educator in the building is to the students (i.e., our O's) who deserve to go to a school defined by the highest quality classroom X's possible.

In the following sections, we will examine classroom X's within four domains – a) instruction, b) assessment, c) classroom management and d) other important practices to consider. And for each domain we will examine those practices that will tend to move us up the roadmap from where we are, so will want to encourage, and those that are keeping us stuck or limiting our growth and so will want to reduce as much as possible.

## Instructional Practices

Moving up the vertical axis of the roadmap to higher locations in the domain of classroom instructional practices will require much of the same focus as it does relative to the overall school. We will want to build the qualities of capacity, coherence, and intention in each classroom. The essence of building capacity is developing students' core skills. Those skills will depend on the mission of the school, but will likely need to include teamwork and collaboration, concept development and use of abstract patterns, inquiry and use of evidence, and information organization and presentation, including technology. When these skills are accessible, the capacity exists to engage in high quality learning activity; when they are not, classrooms tend to default to lower quality instructional pursuits.

As we conceive the process of moving up, we can think of it as a progressive development of skills, strategies, and methods toward an aspirational target destination. This section operationalizes that aspirational instructional growth trajectory. Here we examine a) a series of aspirational instructional target destinations, b) the basic skills needed to progress toward them, c) reasonable intermediate steps toward the ideal target, and d) what it might look like in practice.

## A. Target – Self-Directed Individual and Team Project-Based Learning

**Base skills** – perform cooperative roles, work from a rubric for quality process and product, apply content-related skills, conflict and problem solving, and presentation skills.

**Intermediate step** – high functioning cooperative learning exercises which are highly structured giving students a clear sense of the quality process and product expectations.

**What it looks like** – Time and practice is required to support students' understanding of how to execute their role in their group, what high quality process and products look like (and how they are being assessed), and how to solve problems. During and after each iteration of the task students are encouraged to debrief and reflect on their process and self-evaluate. Students learn to become more comfortable and expert in developing and presenting the product of their effort.

**Observation** – We regularly walk into lower performing schools where one or more teachers have made a devoted commitment to creating high functioning cooperative groups. After about 3 months the level of function and capacity in these rooms reflects a roadmap location many levels above what is happening in other classrooms at these schools. They possess high levels of order, ease, enjoyment, and no sign of behavioral issues. Conclusion – it's the teaching not the students.

## B. Target – Self-Directed Inquiry or Laboratory Investigation

**Base skills** – processing data, concept attainment, cooperative learning, following directions and safety rules, displaying abstract concepts in figures, computation, presentation.

**Intermediate steps** – 1) concept attainment exercises, 2) having students show evidence for making conclusions 3) engaging in lessons where there is a purposeful movement through the C-R-A process (concrete to representational to abstract).

**What it looks like** – Building inquiry skills requires the development of both procedural as well as cognitive skills. Procedurally, students will work in teams to process data and implement a procedure for investigation. Students develop their confidence approaching the concrete phenomenon and working with it systematically. Cognitively, they will see the C-R-A pattern in their work, - what is the nature of the data/material they are examining? How would they describe and classify it? What conclusions or generalizations can they make and share with others? Each step is essential. Over multiple iterations students become expert in the procedural as well as the cognitive processes necessary.

**Observation –** We often witness classrooms where the students are experts in working with concepts, doing abstract classifications, and readily apply effective strategies to abstract problems, in schools where the common narrative is that the students are not capable of executing these tasks.

We observed a group of 3rd graders who were expert in their use of concepts and abstract patterning. Across the street on the same day at the Middle School (where these same students would attend) we observed that the teachers did little concept attainment and when they did the students did so poorly with it that most teachers gave up on the idea and rarely tried again. The 3rd grade teacher had simply made a commitment that his students would be excellent at this skill and eventually they were. The Middle School teachers made no such commitment.

C. **Target – Students can research, organize, and write a quality research paper**

**Base skills** – writing skills, research skills, outlining information, peer editing, recognizing and classifying the nature and quality of source evidence, word processing, creating graphics, nature of facts, and inferences and opinions.

**Intermediate steps** – 1) writing well-structured essays, 2) concept attainment, 3) evaluating the quality of sources and supporting conclusions with evidence, 4) group investigations which are presented.

**What it looks like** – Students get used to evaluating the quality of evidence using criteria. They do frequent processing of their investigations using an organizational format. They write frequently and engage in peer editing which supports their growth as writers but also editors. They are expected to support their conclusions with sound evidence.

**Observation** – Middle School X had been underperforming for years, as a result the school was forced to significantly restructure. Upon reopening, one of its early initiates was to commit school-wide to having students learn to support their thinking and conclusions with evidence. At first it was unfamiliar to how students had operated previously, and many resisted. However, after a few months, the skill became natural and expected. The level of dialogue in the classes reflected care and precision.

As you can see, for each target, the key is building the capacity through skill development. It should be noted that skill development is not a) programmatic and b) does not have a time frame. Growth happens because there is a plan and systematic focus on developing the skill. In most cases, the driver is an individual or small group of teachers simply having an R that "my students are going to have this skill, because I think it is important." The implication for leadership is to elevate the appreciation of that value and the capacity for it to grow. Where can we create professional growth venues for teacher leaders to share their practical understanding of how to support a valuable new skill or other X (i.e., PD, PLC's, peer collaboration, instructional supports)? And how can we communicate the relationships among a) the growth of the particular skill or other X, b) the collaborative process of sharing collective expertise among the staff, and c) the overall growth trajectory of the school toward a higher location on the roadmap?

## A Reflection on Creativity

There may be a reader or two who is asking — "what about creativity?" Simply put, we should encourage everyone to tap into their creative sources and celebrate creativity. But here are some thoughts on the topic.

- Helping students develop their voice, an appreciation of their gifts, and ways that they can make a unique contribution is a great place to start. All students can access these qualities if they are encouraged to and practice listening to their inner voices and resources. We can all make a difference and feel like we are doing what we are meant to do, no matter what anyone else calls creative or interesting

- When we examine the most beautiful and inspiring creative accomplishments, they are most often the product of a lot of skill. And the development of that skill took a lot of intentional effort and practice to cultivate and probably involved teachers who were highly skilled. When we have skills, we have so much more to work with in our creative expressions. Therefore, if we want students or teachers to feel empowered to be creative, we need to help them feel confident in the skills which are useful in that creative exercise.

- Not everyone loves to be creative, so make sure the process does not subtly shame those who are less creative by making it the highest value. For some, a blank piece of paper and the instructions to "just be creative" is their worst nightmare. Focusing upon or assessing the process tends to relieve this issue.

## Instructional X's to Decrease

When examining the idea of identifying instructional practices to reduce, the question is not so much which ones, but how much of any of them. Unless one is teaching incorrect, unethical, or culturally insensitive material, anything that leads to learning has some relative value. However, moving up the pathway requires using more of some practices and less of others. The more authentic and engaging the X is the better. Some of the X's to consider limiting would include:

- **Whole class lectures**. Some lecture is acceptable, but it is not very engaging.
- **Single model instructional planning**. Learning requires different kinds of experiences. Concepts are best taught with some form of concept attainment model. Effective inquiry requires a structure and a thoughtful use of concrete material for students to examine. Skills require a sequence of modeling, practicing, and independent work. Discussions and processing information requires an intentional means for making connections. Using a single model to teach these distinctly different forms of knowledge will lead to less learning and more frustration.

- **Computer-assisted modules**. Filling in missing information with a computer program can have value, but it is not a long-term substitute for taking part in authentic and engage learning.

- **Focusing on completion as the value rather than quality**. When observing classrooms in low vs. high performing schools, one of the noticeable differences is how both teachers and students perceive the task in the two settings. In low performing schools, very often the students rush through their work and are excited to tell the teacher they are done, and the teacher gives them praise for being done – the value is on completion. In the high performing school, the student engages the task for understanding and with recognition of what quality work implies. The teacher gives feedback on the quality of the work, ideas, innovations, and creative effort.

Using the concept of coherence can assist in think about what to do more or less of in the classroom. If I am a student, do I generally find myself trusting that the learning I will engage in during the day will be consistently – Authentic to real life? Fit the ways my brain works to process the content or reach the outcome? Encourage me to stretch and grow? Activate a wide range of my humanity and intelligence? If it does, I learn to lean in and embrace learning situations and trust myself and my teachers. If it does not, I learn to cope and compensate (i.e., low motivation, disruptive behavior, boredom, resistance, negative self-image, etc.)

## Assessment

What and how we assess will represent what we value and how we define student success. It is a very concrete indicator of the DNA/guiding R's of the school. So, it is essential for our ability to move up the pathway to align our assessment practices with the values of our desired location. When considering an assessment practice, educators can simply ask "Would I characterize this practice as something that will promote (value) X?" If so, employ it, if not, consider reducing the practice (even if it is something that has become common and fundamental to the way the school has done things historically).

The accountability movement in the early part of the century encouraged a view of assessment that was competitive, comparative and based on indirect measures; measures that were often indicators of things that students did not control and did not reflect what they had learned or their growth. In many cases, our process of moving up will mean reconciling various competing interests. If the last two decades have taught us anything it is that the best way to stay stuck in a low level of function and performance is to focus on trying to improve test scores. What we better understand now is that test score improvement follows when we improve our school performance and function generally.

Using the lens of a psychology of success (POS) – internal locus of control, belonging and acceptance, and growth mindset is a high-quality rubric for judging the effectiveness of any assessment practice. As recommended earlier, the exercise of having teachers classify their practices by whether they would promote the qualities of POS, or its opposite, can be a powerful way for them to recognize which practices would be the most beneficial and sound (See book Appendix A). And just because a practice seems to "work," it can be counter-productive to the larger goals of learning and creating healthy and productive students.

Moving up to a higher roadmap location means making some shifts. First, we need to focus more on the process rather than the product. Second, we need to give more ownership of the assessment process to the student. And third, we need to shift from a focus on summative to formative assessment practices. The job of leader is to reinforce those intentions, build the capacity within the system to make them actualized, and to encourage coherent messages to students and adults.

Expanded use of the following assessment practices are encouraged as they have been shown to promote movement up the school effectiveness pathway.

- **Effective Cognitive/Behavioral Learning Objectives**. This may sound like a basic skill, but if one were to examine the written or mental lesson plans of most teachers, a great deal of what characterizes their lesson goals and objective are "task related" outcomes. High quality teaching starts with a clear sense of the cognitive operations we want to see in action as well as necessary skill and dispositional growth outcomes for the lesson (using Bloom's taxonomy is still a helpful tool here). A focus on task objectives leads to completion as the primary goal. A focus on cognitive learning outcomes provides the teacher a means to engage in formative assessment, lesson modification, and meaningful interventions.

- **Clear Criteria and Systems for Assessing the Process**. The reasons to assess the process are countless – it encourages internal locus of control, growth orientation, encourages higher quality process investment leads to better quality outcomes (Shindler, 2009). The reasons not to assess process are usually related to a) a lack of skill and ingenuity related to creating rubrics, and b) misconceptions and faulty R's often encouraged at the building level. Resources and in-depth explanations for how to do this are available at the TCM website.

  ○ One school, engaged in a long-term process of school improvement, presenting at a school climate conference shared that after three years of their effort, what became clear to them was that an essential key to their success was going to be assessing the process in the classroom. After three years of inquiry and self-examination the result was a shift in their R's. Like many schools, given the opportunity to deeply explore their goals, experiences, and available means, they came to the realization that meaningful change would need to include changing how they assessed.

  ○ Ralph had been teaching middle school for ten years and had not considered assessing process previously. After learning the practical aspects of how to assess quality process, participation, and investment in a graduate course, he tested it out in his most challenging class of the day. After collecting before and after data, he found that students in his process assessment class had made a collective shift of one or two levels (related to the quality of their participation) in two months. In his words, the class improved from "his worst class to his best" in those two months because he implemented a system for assessing the quality of their participation and process investment.

- **Clear Criteria for Assessing Products.** When surveying the quality and quantity of the rubrics that are used in our classrooms, what do we see? Simply put, the better and more purposeful the rubrics in the classes are, the more clarity to the learning task. Therefore, the higher the quality of the learning, the more POS being cultivated, and the faster we move up the pathway. Leadership can encourage this trend by providing PD specifically devoted to creating process and product rubrics, encouraging teachers to share and/or create them collaboratively, and when possible, create space for student involvement.

  - School Z made a purposeful commitment to project-based learning (PBL). It was fundamental to how they conceived and marketed their school's mission and program. But over the years while the school did engage in many PBL activities, their SCAI and student achievement ratings remained stagnant in the 40%tile range. Upon closer examination, what was evident was that they had done a relatively poor job of assessing either the desired target process or product quality within the PBL activities. The result was students who were mostly going through the motions. The lesson here is that it was not the intentions/R's that were the limiting element, but the execution of the necessary X's, especially related to the use of assessment.

- **Student Peer and Self-Assessment.** When students assess their own work or that of their peers, they look at the work with the lens of a teacher. Instead of thinking simply in terms of adequacy or inadequacy, they are encouraged to recognize the elements of quality and purpose. Over time, this builds not just agency and POS, but a value for quality. Self-assessment is empowering, pulls students out of a passive mindset, and teaches a valuable real world skill set. However, like any other form of increased requirement of responsibility, it means teaching the skills and procedures purposefully, and making a commitment to doing it well. We can expect resistance from both students and adults to raising their game. But like all movement up, once the higher location becomes the norm, few will desire a return to a lower form of experience.

- **Student-Led Conferences**. If the goals of our assessment include promoting growth, self-reflection, internal LOC and agency, self-responsibility for learning and assessing progress among other values, the choice of where to put the ownership during a student conference is pretty clear. Including opportunities for teachers and parents to exchange information is still a valuable component of the process, but purposefully shifting the onus to the student is the best way to actualize the benefits listed above. As with all X's, our question is, "given our values, and desired outcomes, what is the structure that will best translate those values into action?"

  ◦ If we ask those who have made the transition from teachers-led to student-led conference formats, we will likely encounter the following themes. First, that the shift took a substantial amount of preparation, especially related to the need for students to learn a new role and new skills. Second, the first iteration was usually clumsy and disappointing. And third, once these schools had made the transition, and experienced the benefits, they would not consider returning to the previous format.

## Assessment X's to Decrease

In general, the process of moving up will imply encouraging more active, responsible, growth-oriented, and quality-focused students. Therefore, as leadership examines the common assessment practices at the school, the team will want to encourage a minimum of those that encourage passive learning, a focus on completion, norm-referenced grading and student-to-student competition. The logic for employing practices with these qualities was born in time when a central job of the school was to sort students into various hierarchical life paths. Not only is this logic unethical today, putting it into practice leads to poor results across the board.

Assessment practices to keep to a minimum would include.

- **Grading on a Curve**. It may be historically accepted, but if we examine its nature, we see that it is based on a fixed-ability view and a belief that comparisons are motivational. Using a criterion reference system is just as easy to construct, is more honest, creates a clearer sense of the learning targets and is motivation to all students (rather than the few whose fear of failure motivates to them to great levels of effort).

- **Student-Student Comparisons**. If we ask ourselves a simple question "what does student A's learning progress have to do with Student B's learning progress?" we will likely draw a blank. Comparison leads to all manner of psychologically dysfunctional thinking and motivations. Reflecting on quality, contribution, innovation, growth, progress lead in the opposite and infinitely healthier direction.

- **Too Much Reliance on Objective Tests and Quizzes**. Tests and quizzes are useful tools as part of a broader assessment system. But we find that schools or teachers who don't incorporate them don't really miss them. As a rule, teachers should derive less than 50% of the students' grades from objective selected-response tests.

- **Unsystematic and Subjective Grading**. While assessing process can be a powerful tool to promote POS, giving a percentage of the grade for an undefined quantity like "participation" or "behavior" or "citizenship" is unsound, unless it is done systematically. If assessment targets are clear and stationary, students will learn to hit them. If assessment targets represent undefined vague concepts existing in the teacher's mind (e.g., how I want people to act and be in "my class," or acting lively, etc.) the target is typically unclear, manipulative, creates insecurity, and in the end operates essentially as a power-play. So, the bottom line is that if you are going to assess something like participation, do it soundly or don't do it at all (Shindler, 2009). But it is best if teachers do in fact learn to do it soundly – purposefully, objectively, systematically, and in a way that is empowering rather than manipulative.

## Classroom Management and Discipline

The place to begin in our exploration of classroom management is with our first principle of change – everything is connected. We can also state this as "everything is contextual." Therefore, our effort will be to build a healthy, sane, and productive eco-system. That will mean encouraging classroom management X's – practices, policies, and programmatic initiatives which promote congruence with our target destination. It also means recognizing that all the X's in the school will affect the eco-system and thus each student's level of motivation, interest in being a contributor or a disruptor, sense that things are fair, conception of the ways students should treat one another, and perceptions in general. Simply put, a healthy eco-system translates into fewer problems and more growth of the qualities desired. The examination here will be brief as you are encouraged to read and apply the deeper discussion of classroom management in Chapter eleven. For more information *Transformative Classroom Management* offers a richer treatment of this topic and will integrate well with the content in this book.

In many cases, schools currently functioning at the lower-middle levels on the roadmap tend to view discipline with a situation-response (i.e., O<-X) mindset. While this may have relative use, as much as possible, we will want to make a shift to an R->X->O mindset. The starting point is getting clear on the guiding R's – values, expectations, knowledge base, habits of heart and mind, and guiding questions and assumptions. We must accept that most of our problems in this area are rooted in our current R's. Therefore, supporting the shift from lower to higher function R's will be as important as any job leadership will take on. Next, all adults in the building need to grow in their recognition that some X's – practices, strategies, policies, communication patterns, systems, and non-verbal messages will support movement up the roadmap and others will affect movement down, or at least limit growth upward. The assumption of leadership needs to be that supporting this process will need to be systematic and that human nature is to hold on to what we have been doing and resist change. Outcomes in the form of student behavioral issues or anything else will be mostly a product of what we are doing all day throughout the school.

## Shifting Our References

The essence of progress upward is making a shift away from 3 and 4-paradigm/style R's and X's toward a more solid and consistent use of 2 and 1-Paradigm R's and X's (See Chapter eleven and TCM). Therefore, the objective is to eliminate coercive, aggressive, punitive 4-Style ways of managing as well as the chaotic, enabling, and passive ways of the 3-Style, and replace them with healthy, sanity-building, coherent and empowering ways of approaching the task. In many cases, the reasons educators cling to 3 and 4-Style ways is out of fear and a lack of confidence (even if there is an appearance of outward confidence). However, the movement up is toward a more satisfying natural condition that produces more mental health for everyone. Therefore, even though fear may keep some from readily stepping out of their comfort zones, there is a part of everyone that knows on some level what they and the school need to do to move up and that it is fundamentally right and good.

As discussed, the reasons why we change our attitude about something varies from persons to person and context to context (See Chapter seven). The teachers in our school have not lacked for people telling them what they should do. Therefore, we need to accept the limited value of simply telling. Instead, leadership must engage teachers and staff in a long-term conversation about where the school is going related to classroom management and discipline and listen and appreciate the fundamental difficulty of the job and why few of us successfully present as who we would like to be in this area. Here are a few practical ideas for supporting that shift.

- Have teachers engage in a classification exercise of classroom management practices into those that promote or undermine the core values of the school. It is recommended to use the POS elements as described in book Appendix A. The goal is a self-evaluation that provides a clear conceptual framework for future action.
- Have teachers observe the 1-Paradigm teachers in the building and include time in the process to share and discuss specifics.
- Have teachers set meaningful goals in this area.
- Support the grand "team win" - we are all working together to create a school that is a great place to be a student and an educator. We are a team that is getting better every day (not a group of individuals in competition who need to protect their egos from unfavorable comparisons).

As we conceive the necessary areas of shift, it is useful to consider the operational implications of our intentions. For example, we will need to strive to move away from negativity (i.e., punishments, shaming, nagging, put-downs, etc.) toward more positive practices. But in practical terms, the opposite of negativity is not so much positive reinforcement, as it is clarity. An analogy can be helpful. Let us imagine that we are searching in the dark for an apple tree (struggling to learn and contribute). Now imagine that we are given negative feedback related to how inadequate we are and how we are not going in the right direction. Understandably, we appreciate this feedback to be demoralizing and unhelpful. However, consider two alternatives to what we could term negative feedback. One, the "positive" alternative might be to provide encouragement and tell us "We can do it," or promise a reward for finding the tree. Two, the clarity-based alternative would be to illuminate the scene with lights and point us toward the path to the tree with signs. In practice, conceiving our role as one who is encouraging clarity and a clear path to the goal can be much more empowering and ultimately effective than the role of providing positive vs. negative feedback.

## Creating the Conditions for Success

Collectively, the aim is to shift away from being reactive to proactively building the conditions for success. It can be helpful in our process to ask ourselves aspirational questions such as, "At our target location on the roadmap, what do people do differently? How do students feel? Why are they motivated? What do teachers focus on mostly? Conceiving our desired set of conditions will encourage the quality of the thinking in the process and help keep it out of the small and petty level (i.e., "that won't work because…", "I tried that before and…," "this is working for me and I hear others are struggling with ___ which I don't because I do ___," etc.). Vision-based conversation pulls us up, historical conversation keeps us in place.

In figure 12.5 we examine some of the essential conditions for success, as well as some unhelpful elements that will limit our progress.

Figure 12.5 Essential Conditions and Unhelpful Elements to Moving Up

| Essential Conditions/ What we need | Unhelpful Elements/ What we don't need |
|---|---|
| • A solid sense of social contract bonds among all members of the school community.<br>• A high level of skill in the technical and mechanical classroom management practices required for simple levels of order and function.<br>• A commonly accepted effective process for dealing with extreme behavioral issues – understood and implemented by teachers, supported by administration, and clarified to students.<br>• Engaging instruction for meeting students' basic needs or sense of power and competence.<br>• Active practices for promoting classroom and school community, identity, and pride.<br>• A POS disposition within and among adults in which they take ownership of their actions.<br>• A POS disposition among students where they have multiple opportunities to reflect on how to become more self-directed, connected to their peers, mature, and positive contributors to the collective.<br>• All personal energy exchanges are for something positive and affirming. Problems and conflicts are dealt with practically and with well-established norms. | • 3 and 4-Style teaching<br>• An excessive concern by adults with being respected and student obedience. Respect is earned and is not the point. The point is whether the student is doing what they have committed to.<br>• Clinging to clever, manipulative practices that get results in the short-term, but in the long-term will limit success.<br>• The "it works" "or "that won't work with these students" mentalities. Everything works, by definition. Ask – "Is this practice creating more of the positive qualities that I desire in the long-term without unhealthy side effects?"<br>• Frustration, disappointments, and resentment playing out as Xs' in and out of the classroom. Using strategies for pay-back or passive aggressiveness just magnifies the quantity of pain in the equation. |

The process of shifting toward the conditions characterizing our desired destination and away from limiting elements will need to be continuous and non-linear. As discussed previously, it may take months or years for some adults to recognize the unhelpful nature of their patterns of thought or practices. And our progress personally and collectively will always be more effective when we set our sight on becoming the vision of a better self rather than putting too much energy into dwelling on who we do not want to be. Our job as leader is to make the need for the fear, mistrust, and control less necessary so everyone can be more open to growth.

## Practices/X's to Add or Increase

The following list is a brief explanation of some of the X's which we will want to expand and cultivate. The list is ordered from most fundamental to more ambitious

- **Social Contract**. The foundation of any classroom, school or society for that matter is its social contract – what we can all expect from one another. If we are conceiving this as rules and punishments, we are missing the point and its essential value. The social contract is based in the agreements and commitments we make to one another. Our undertaking as a school is to make these agreements and commitments as explicit as possible. The social contract is made real and meaningful in action. Those in the school learn what it is by watching how adults talk and act, and what happens when students live up to and/or violate their agreements. When students trust the social contract, they feel safe and like things are right. When students do not, they feel like they cannot trust adults and need to protect themselves. Here are a few ways to make the social contracts within the school more actualized.

  ○ Have teachers and students create a social contract together at the start of the year.

  ○ Support teachers when students violate the social contract.

  ○ Use logical and related consequences for contract violations.

- ◦ Focus on the positive nature of the contract – the benefits including how nice it is to feel safe and trusting.

- ◦ Be consistent.

- ◦ Use behavioral contracts for students who struggle to make responsible choices. Personal contracts help the student reflect on how they can grow and hold themselves to agreements and goals they set for themselves.

- ◦ Incorporate a maximum amount of student input in refining and revising the agreements and policies defining the contract. It should represent a democratic process – by the students for the students.

- **Expert Use of Strategies Which Make Life Easy and Smooth**. The aim is for all personal energy exchanges to be neutral or positive. Toxic energy makes classroom management seem difficult. Simple practices such as gaining attention can be easy and free of all personal implications such as respect, compliance, and obedience. The experience of the emotional state of disappointment is mostly the result of poor technical management skills. TCM (see also Chapter eleven) explains in detail how all classes can be places where full attention, a culture of listening and respect, following directions, smooth transitions and procedures are the norm. Many teachers in lower-middle function level schools seldom realize how difficult they are making this aspect of the job until they practice the effective strategies and recognize that their job just got much easier. When we are unable to experience 100% attention (or do not believe it is possible), it is difficult to trust the possibility of a more evolved classroom. Yet, when we feel solid in this basic element of function, imagining creating a solid 1-Paradigm classroom seems more attainable.

  - ◦ **Case Example**. Maria is one of dozens of former students who have had essentially the same experience. She attended a graduate classroom management class while in her first year of teaching. She started the term with a belief that getting attention was a challenge and that some students were *never* going to be good listeners, and that was just the nature of the job. After learned how to use effective technical management strategies and to trust an expectation for 100% attention, she returned to class the next week and shared her discovery, saying, "I did not believe you at first, but now I just expect 100% attention from my students, and I have 100% attention."

- ◦ **Case Example**. We see so many great examples of teachers who make technical management something that is fun and positive (like a team practicing). We also see many teachers who struggle each day. The difference is that the effective teachers a) see it as a practical challenge related to patterns of action and not something personal, b) they challenge the students to be great at it, c) they find ways to make routine and procedures fun (i.e., think "team wins"), d) when execution is not to the group's standard, these teachers have students practice it until it is to standard, and e) and they focus on the emotion of pride in excellence rather than disappointment for lack of success.

- **Increased Use of Student Involvement and Ownership**. Your movement up the roadmap will be directly correlated to the school's ratings on SCAI items related to student ownership and voice.

  - ◦ Are students involved in creating the classroom agreements?
  - ◦ Are students engaging in leadership roles in the classroom and school?
  - ◦ Is there a student leadership committee and program?
  - ◦ Do students take ownership over solving their own problems?
  - ◦ Is there a peer mediation and/or conflict resolution program at the school?

- **Case example**. We have observed many first and second grade classrooms (often in urban public schools) where the students were integral to developing the social contract, ran the practical operations of the class, and had systems in place to deal with conflict without the need for teacher involvement. And when these classes have a substitute, the students are capable of self-managing their day without much direction. Considering this is possible with very young students, if follows that it is possible with students at any grade level.

- **Expert Use of Expectation Clarifying language and Strategies.** As discussed in Chapter eleven, few teachers in lower-middle function level schools use precision in their language intended to cultivate a clear classroom vision of quality. Techniques such as positive recognitions, debriefing, expectation cues, clarifying questions, and other high-quality practices are powerful tools in support of this effort, and reduce the need for lower-quality practices such as reminders, warnings, negative recognitions, threats, disappointment, proximity control, and manipulative and comparative strategies.

- **High functioning Collectives and Team Wins**. High functioning classrooms take much clarity of intention and practice. Effective teachers learn to help students recognize the impact of their good choices. Simply asking students the question "Isn't it nice when we can all relax and learn, and you can trust one another?" is a powerful way to help students recognize a grand "team win" – they are a functional group. The greater the number of small team wins we can structure and recognize the better. Winning breeds trust and liking, and liking and trust breed winning (i.e., learning, collaboration, motivation, persistence, grit, enjoyment, and bonding)

- **Assessing Process Systematically**. (See Chapter eleven and Shindler, 2009).

## X's to Reduce or to Keep at a Minimum

As we take stock of what we have and want at our school, it will be helpful to become increasingly clear and specific about what will serve us and not serve us on our journey upward. As discussed previously, it is best if this realization occurs organically and is internalized within the individual adults at the school. But it will also be helpful for the school to systematically endorse the growth of some practices and the reduction of others. We might think of the practices to reduce as baggage that was perceived to be necessary in the past but will need to be released as we move forward. That baggage might be divided into two categories, a) things most of us agree are not healthy, and b) things we might really like, but as we look at their effects more closely, we see they have a substantially limiting effect on the growth of students, classrooms, and the school. Examples from each category are outlined below.

## X's to Reduce ASAP (most teachers will generally agree they are not healthy)

- **Negative recognitions**. This is the strategy of publicly calling out unwanted student actions. If teachers develop effective skills for technical management, and commit to using only strategies that promote clarity, they readily recognize they can lose the need for negative recognitions. Assume about a third of your teachers will embrace the idea of resisting the temptation to use negative recognitions, a third will need a lot of support, and a third will think the idea of giving them up is crazy. Leadership support will need to build the will and skills necessary to trust in the wisdom of letting go of the limiting practices. Encouragement and positive recognitions as well as supportive mentors will likely be necessary for those who are currently lacking the will to grow beyond their comfort zones.

- **Personally Attacking, Pain-Based and Punitive Actions.** The place to start is to help those who are attracted to punitive discipline to understand that it is not very effective (even if they believe it is). Showing the entire faculty and staff the roadmap and pointing out that 4-Paradigm practices correlate to low function and achievement will support this realization. TCM and ASSC includes an online chapter exploring moving up from 4-Style (paradigm) practice.

## Questionable X's for Which One Should Make an Informed Judgement

Many schools seeking improved student behavior are tempted to adopt programs rooted in applied behavioral modification. These programs usually recommend a series of strategies that are termed "positive," yet, in essence, rely on extrinsic modification and manipulation to affect student behavior. When compared to most 4-Paradigm practices, they are an upgrade. Yet, over time, they will have the effect of discouraging student POS in the long-term. They will be attractive to many teachers and will be sold as healthy and positive. But adopting them at your school will create a plateau to your growth potential at about the 3.5/60%tile level (Shindler, 2018). If your school vision is defined fundamentally by students "being on task" these strategies may be a good fit, but if your vision is about healthy, empowered, POS, classroom communities, extrinsic behavioral modification techniques will be largely counterproductive. These practices are explained in more detail in Chapter eleven and on the website transformativeclassroom.com. Common but limiting practices are briefly outlined below.

- **Extrinsic rewards**. In the short-term, promote wanted behavior. In the long-term undermine student intrinsic motivation, shift focus from quality to the reward, create reward addition.

- **Colored-Card Charts**. (See Shindler 2009 at TCM website). Public shame-based systems erode relationships between teacher and student, marginalize students and promote poorer levels of classroom community. And can exacerbate negative behavior patterns in many students.

- **Manipulative Phrases and Praise**. See Chapter eleven for a comparison of these strategies to more healthy and effective alternatives. Example, "I like the way (student X) is (acting appropriately)" – in an attempt to modify the behavior of Student Y. These statements represent incongruent communication that sends a hostile message to student Y with the guise of being positive. Over time they create a classroom climate of insecurity and mistrust.

- **Proximity Control**. Standing by students to intimidate them into being on task. This is a lose-lose bargain. Students become dependent on the intervention, while the teacher is forced to engage this strategy each time he/she wants compliance.

- **Win-Lose Competitions**. Competition can be healthy and fun. But it can also be a source of pain, socially and emotionally destructive, and encourage dysfunctional values. Healthier competitions are defined by a) essentially meaningless or intangible rewards (we do it for the fun of it, b) focus on the process and the teamwork (so how you play is more important than who wins), c) teams are redistributed regularly, and d) results are not left to linger, we get on to the next thing.

## Other X's to Support Movement Up the Pathway

In addition to promoting higher quality instruction, assessment, and classroom management consider other X's which will encourage our movement upward. In examining your school climate data and/or exploring the reflection questions in Chapter ten related to the eight areas of school, you will likely recognize areas for targeted improvement. Schools that make the most progress tend to be the most creative in the process of identifying and then tapping unmet possibilities and thinking outside of the box. Here are some ideas that you might consider.

- **School Pride Promoting Activities**. Class-class competitions for fun. Assemblies that engage students in fun. Talent shows. Marketing and encouragement to attend Athletic and Fine Arts events. Dress up days. Spirit posters.

- **Student Work on the Walls**. It is the students' school. Placing student work of all kinds on the walls makes a statement of ownership, value of who is there, and shows an intention related to the school's appearance.

- **Use of Social Media to Promote Successes and the Events Calendar**. Parents and students want to see photos of events in which school members were involved. And be able to share positive comments to participants.

- **Intentional After-School Programs**. Designing afterschool programs that are aligned with the goals and mission of the school adds value on many levels.

- **Student-Led Clubs and Gatherings.** A strong indicator of our movement up will be a) the sense of empowerment students feel toward suggesting to leadership that a new club would be a valuable idea, and b) the number and quality of those clubs.

- **Support Groups**. For some schools, there is a perceived or as yet unrecognized need for students within a sub-group at the school to meet, share their concerns and bond as a community. Our job is to support it with staff, provide a stable location, and above all let students know we have a willingness to make it happen.

- **Physical Education is a Gold Mine of Possibilities**. PE class can be a place where students learn powerful lessons not readily learnable in the academic classroom – how to challenge various aspects of themselves, integrating mind, body, emotions, and relationships, connections between effort, commitment, and results, and many others. Conversely, it can also be a place where students learn to protect themselves from shame, comparison, and boredom as they engage in activities which they perceive to have little value to their futures. A great PE program will be an invaluable asset to your school's process of moving up, a poor one will keep in place a lot of the unwanted old DNA that you are trying to replace.

- **Take Advantage of Your Athletic Programs.** For many students, what will primarily define their educational experience will take place on the field, in the gym, or on a court. Those leading these teams and programs must share the same commitment to human development, a growth-focus, and social and emotional development as we would expect from all adults in the building. A list of things we should see and not see in the realm of athletics at the school should be at least assumed if not explicitly developed for all coaches and coordinators. Proactive Coaching is an excellent resource in this area.

## CONCLUSION

In this chapter we explored the essence of what is required for moving our school from lower to middle/higher locations on the roadmap. On a macro level that movement will be facilitated by shifting references/R's from lower to higher quality and building the conditions necessary for an eco-system out of which improvement can emerge. Conceiving the effort within the lens of moving up the vertical axis of the roadmap will be useful. Encouraging the qualities of trust, intention, capacity, coherence, and efficiency will be valuable guiding principles. On a micro level, we want to engage effective instructional leadership and vision development to encourage the adults within the school to reflect upon and improve on their X's; expanding some, developing new skills for others, and learning to reduce the use of others. In the next chapter, we will examine the process of facilitating the movement of a school at a middle location up and across (the horizontal axis) on the pathway to the higher realms of the roadmap.

## REFERENCES

Morgan, H. (2014) Review of the Research. The Education System in Finland: A Success Story other Countries can Emulate. Childhood Education, v.90, issue 6.

Shindler, J. (2009) *Transformative Classroom Management*. Jossey-Bass, San Francisco, CA

Shindler, J. (2009) Assessing Process and Participation. Retrieved from www.transformativeclassroom.com.

Shindler, J. (2018) Limiting Influence of Behavioral Practices on Students and Schools. Retrieved from www.transformativeclassroom.com.

Shindler, J. (2009) How to Move up to Move Functional Practices from 4-Style Classroom Management. Retrieved from www.transformativeclassroom.com.

Shindler, J. (2009) The Problems with Colored Cards and other Shame-Based Behavioral Systems. Retrieved from www.transformativeclassroom.com.

## Exercise 12.1: Exploring Misconceptions Limit our Growth

The following is a list of misconceptions commonly maintained by some teachers in schools currently functioning in the lower quadrants of the roadmap. They are commonly raised as counter arguments to suggestions to adopt higher function R's and X's. As a faculty and staff, explore these assumptions/misconceptions and how they apply to the current dialogue and common practices at the school presently. For each, you are offered alternate conception which could be considered a more reality-based way of thinking about the topic. The goal of the exercise is to raise awareness about the realities related to each of these ideas. Judgment and condemnation of those who hold these misconceptions is counterproductive. This exercise is intended to promote a dialogue.

- What is the source of these assumptions?
- Does the alternate reality hold up in your analysis? Why or why not?
- What are the implications for practice?
- What are the implications for leadership?
- What have you found to be effective in supporting growth in R's?

### Misconception: "This (higher function X) stuff "won't work" with these students at this school"

Reality: First, as we have discussed, usually when we hear that something won't work, we can read between the lines "I am afraid, or feeling threatened, shamed, or inadequate, so it is easier to say that it won't work than to say I don't understand or feel confident in my abilities." So, no need to psychoanalyze. We just need to focus on how it *is* working somewhere. Because the reality is that the high-quality practice is being used with students just like those at your school with good results. It may even be by a teacher at your school. All sounds practices work everywhere.

Second, what does the statement assume about the students at the school? Who are "these students?" Are they a different species, or inherently inferior? Why are they so different than the students somewhere else? When we actually try to answer these questions, we find that the R's behind these assumptions are pretty difficult to defend or at least take pride in.

## Misconception: What I do has worked for me in the past and it gets results

Reality: The X's that we have used have gotten us our O's. Look at where your O's are on the roadmap. What do your current O's say about the efficacy of the current X's? As discussed, we need to get in the habit of questioning the phrase "it works" every time it comes out of someone's mouth. We may even want to make a rule that we can't use that phrase in our faculty discussions, or when we do we have to rephrase what we just said. When our O's (and an external observation) would indicate that we are operating using a mixture of POS and POF X's, and/or our climate score says we are at a 2.7 out of 5 (in one or more areas), we have to re-evaluate what we are doing, and even why we might have previously characterized it as "working." Engaging the X classification exercise is a useful process to opening up some defensive minds and support the rethinking of current practices.

## Misconception: Sometimes you just have to use ... (POF promoting) strategies

Reality: Sadly, if students have become accustomed to being taught with Psychology of Failure (POF) X's, they will become accustomed to them. And like junk food even desire them over time. But that is a short-sighted view. First, no matter how much an addict is asking for an unhealthy additive item, it is not usually a favor to give it to them. So, we cannot justify the use of POF practices because student respond to them. Even if they are the only way you feel like you can get your class under control, or on task, or motivated. The long-term reality is that every use is making your class worse and making it more difficult to use more POS and positive O promoting X's. POF promoting X's are not making your job easier. They are keeping you from growing, experiencing a more satisfying reality as a teacher, and keeping you captive to their use.

## Misconception: If I try cooperative learning, or inquiry they will just socialize and play around

Reality: This may be your valid experience. But it implies a less than excellent application of this strategy. The reality is that someone who has students much like yours conducts cooperative groups that are functioning like well-orchestrated teams - students who lose track of time because they are so engrossed in their learning. In those classes, every use of these X's leads to ever more effective applications as the skills and procedures necessary become more systematized. Cooperative learning, collaborative inquiry and project-based learning all possess potential learning and growth capacities that independent learning does not.

## Misconception: If I give them freedom and ownership, they just will take advantage of it.

Reality: Creating responsibility is not easy. The 1-style classroom is not a 3-style classroom. Students need to be trained in how to be self-responsible. But with intentional development including - a clear sense of collective pur-pose, consequences for being irresponsible, engaging work, self-reflection in cause and effect, and the faith of the teacher, most groups will exceed our expectations for self-direction and internal motivation. It is a win-win proposition. We lose nothing meaningful when we give them as much power as they can handle, and we gain a few steps up the pathway.

## Misconception: Our students are not even at grade level, they are not equipped to do project-based learning

Reality: it is true that we cannot teach some content if students do not have prerequisite content. But to extend that logic to the kind of pedagogical X's we use is fundamentally flawed reasoning. With a commitment to certain X's (that were discussed in this chapter) a first-grade class can become highly skilled at being a self-directed, project-based, cooperative learning, and inquiry using class. Of course, we could only expect them to process first grade level content, but as far as pedagogy, the possibilities are vast.

Withholding quality learning processes from students because we need to wait until they have all the content is a formula for waiting forever. That thinking leads us into a perpetual mentality of remediation that just digs us deeper in our hole – and further downward on the pathway.

# CHAPTER 13:

## Making the "Left-Hand Turn" and Actualizing Your Potential

> "Never doubt that a small group of thoughtful, committed, citizens can change the world. Indeed, it is the only thing that ever has."
> — *Margaret Mead*
>
> "Non est ad astra mollis e terris via" - "There is no easy way from the earth to the stars"
> — *Senecac*

In this chapter, we explore the process of facilitating the movement of a school to the highest regions of the effectiveness roadmap. For most schools that will require making an intentional "left hand turn" toward the more empowering, connected, growth-oriented and trusting top left corner of the roadmap and the 1-Paradigm quadrant. This process will imply recognizing and then actualizing the highest potential for the adults and students. In practical terms, we are discovering an emergent, but self-evident future for our school, rather than forcing it into a mold. We are being pulled by a vision of what our school can be at its best that represents a place in which we will most enjoy working and learning, is consistent with the laws of human development, and is defined by quality and excellence.

## Growth Pathway - SCAI School Climate Ratings, and Corresponding Predicted Achievement

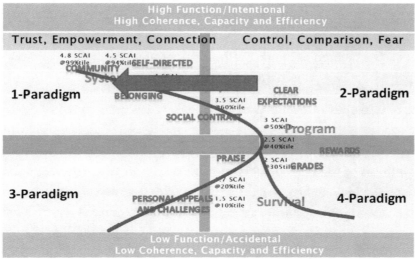

Keep in mind that the nature of movement up the "pathway" will be similar at all units of size - individuals, classrooms, and campus communities. Therefore, our starting point will be to appreciate that our effectiveness as a leader in the school's process of growth and emergence, we be strongly related to the extent to which we embrace our own personal growth journey. In many ways the school's effort will mirror our own. Likewise, our efforts will be best served by adults who are willing to embody that growth and improvement mindset, at the same time they work to make the school's vision a reality.

Each school on this journey will need to define the practical qualities of their target destination for itself. Our school may be committed to a wide variety of missions or "what's" – PBL, leadership, STEM, SEL, the arts, college prep, Montessori, Waldorf, or general education, etc., but the nature of the, "why's" and "how's" that will lead to reaching your highest potential will have a common set of qualities. In this book, I offer the 1-Paradigm region of the roadmap as that universal target, and an attempt to capture that self-evident aspirational roadmap location. There are many ways to actualize lower quality or more modest levels of effectiveness, but as we examine what is required for the highest levels, the gate narrows. We find that the pathway to a high-quality learning environment reflecting coherence with the needs of human learners, lands at a largely explainable target location. That destination has a nature, and therefore what it is as well as what it is not can be defined both practically and operationally. In this chapter, we explore what will get us there and what will not.

The nature of the movement to the highest levels is both up and over on the roadmap. Each chapter of the book so far has offered some insight into the process of moving to the target destination. In this chapter, we explore a synthesis of the essential ideas for the job of moving our organization from the middle to high regions of the roadmap pathway. The content of this chapter is organized into seven sections representing a progressive set of considerations for our necessary work, which are summarized below.

1.  **Trust and Cultivating the Soil.** The foundation of an effective process up the growth pathway will imply a quality of trust that pervades the effort – both in leadership and among all stake-holders. This will include setting a course for where the effort is going and embodying a commitment to what it will take to get there. Most notable that will imply putting in place core process values that can be refined and executed with ever greater levels of expertise and innovation.

2.  **Vision and Taking Aim toward Our Destination**. The school's success will largely be a function of its ability to create a shared vision of a more actualized version of itself. That vision will be fundamental to all decision-making and what is played out as action. As one transformative leader put it, the goal is everyone in one canoe going in one direction.

3.  **Promoting Social Bonds and Effective Structures**. The social agreements and bonds necessary for feelings of safety, fair-ness, and accountability need to be cultivated and maintained systematically. Without an ongoing focus of promoting the level of function (i.e., the vertical axis on the roadmap – capacity,

coherence, intention, and efficiency) the effort can potentially descend and take on qualities of the 3-Paradigm.

4. **Promoting Connection and Community Bonds**. Efforts to move toward the 1-Paradigm location will naturally encourage greater degrees of connection and community. However, moving up the pathway will also require intentional effort toward cultivating practices, routines, rituals, and ways of being which promote connection among the adults, students, and their families.

5. **Empowerment and Distribution of Voice and Leadership.** The goal in the 1-Paradigm is to empower adults and students to contribute and express their sense of agency in the ways which make the most sense for the individual and collective good. Therefore, we need to be intentional about the process of empowerment and encouraging shared ownership and voice. We will need to leave some 2-Paradigm baggage behind and accept some level of discomfort as we make the left-hand turn.

6. **Effective Use of Data, Evidence, and Planning.** Knowing where we are on the roadmap and being able to recognize how we can best focus energy for change is useful in our process of moving forward on the journey. Conceiving the process using the R->X->O logic will be helpful here. Outcomes are evidence of our progress, not the primary driver. Our vision drives us, and outcome data explain how we can make our X's more effective.

7. **Promoting Congruence and High Quality among the Pedagogical Practices**. As the vision of an actualized school emerges, we will progressively recognize the practices, policies, and programs that will support our movement upward as well as those we will want to leave behind. For schools needing to make a significant left-hand turn, appreciating that even well-executed 2-Paradigm practices will not lead to 1-Paradigm results is important. For all schools, it will be useful to engage the process of examining current and prospective practices from the lens of coherence and long-term influence.

# 1. Trust and Cultivating the Soil.

As we begin our collective development of the "how" to move into quadrant 1, we need to start with the quality of trust. Reflecting on the improvement efforts with which we have been involved, in any capacity, we can ask the simple question "if there was trust in the equation, how did it go, and conversely, if there was not, what happened to the effort over time?" Our likely answers to these questions are why we lead off this chapter examining trust, even before we discuss the equally critical quality of vision. In Chapter six. we explored the essential qualities for creating the quality of trust within the process. All five of those elements are needed to be sufficiently present if we expect to realize sustained progress.

1. Trust in the Commitment Level and the Qualities of the Leaders as People

2. A Clear Sense of Destination for the Journey

3. Process Values are Primary, Outcome Values are Secondary

4. Social Bonds and Sanity Promoting Structures are Sufficiently Cultivated

5. Communal Bonds and a Sense of Team are Sufficiently Cultivated

## Leaders as People – Personal Trust Qualities

We are asking others to venture into uncharted territory. Why would they trust the process? One effective 1-Paradigm leader suggested his goal was everyone in one canoe rowing together. Using that analogy, why would others trust us to steer the canoe effectively? Simply reflecting on that question should prove instructive, and here are a few areas for consideration.

- **Honesty and Integrity.** If we are going to take a risk, we need to trust that the one leading us into the unfamiliar is being honest with us. Therefore, seek to be transparent and sincere and avoid being unrealistic and optimistic in ways that insult others' intelligence. Be a paragon of integrity. Say what you mean and mean what you say and avoid the temptation to agree in public and then act in very different ways in private and when it is time to create policy. We need to walk our talk.

- **Commitment.** Before engaging in a journey implying a long-term effort, assurance needs to exist that those in the role of visionary will be in place for the duration. And we want to know that those who are articulating the vision are passionate about it themselves.

- **Having a Winner Attitude.** We all have a winner within us. We can define a winner as "someone who does what it takes to reach the goal." Trust is crucial throughout the organization, so we need to know that when the going gets tough the ones leading the effort will rise to the occasion. Winners believe in themselves and have a grounded confidence. Winning energy is comforting and contagious.

- **A Yes Mindset.** Transformative leaders share the inclination to find a way to "make it happen" – to find the "yes." That does not mean they are agreeable necessarily. It means that they see and get excited about possibilities.

- **Appreciate the Little Things and what is Important to Others.** Embodying a sense of grand purpose is essential, but on the ground level of the effort, we need to appreciate that the little things matter – no matter whether we judge that they should or not. This growth effort will disrupt the status quo on many levels. We may not be able to make everyone happy, but by being considerate and respectful (and not dismissive) of other's challenges, we may lessen the level of frustration and the urge of some to quit on the process.

## Setting Out the Course of Our Destination

Before we set out on an implicitly long and challenging journey, we want to know where we are going, why it is a good idea, what it will take to get there, and why it is better than where we are now. When members have questions, doubts, confusions, and misunderstandings we will have to provide satisfying answers/clarifications in multiple forms on a continuous basis. As we will explore in the next section, when others share the vision of the destination, everything works more effectively.

But we will need to conceive of our destination as both an emergent idea (that is self-evident and can be recognized by those who adopt a clear-sighted perception) and a concrete phenomenon that can be operationalized into minute detail (given the time and will to do so). The 1-Paradigm location implies a collective journey, a shared vision (conception), and a collaborative and distributed process for creating the specifics. As leaders, we need to have a sufficient conception of various practicalities characterizing a picture of success. Yet, being too attached to a desired image of the specifics can lead to unhelpful rigidity. While conversely, being too relativistic can lead to the effort taking on 3-Paradigm qualities.

> **Power of Yet.**
>
> In a classroom in a 1-Paradigm school, the teacher created a poster with the Heading "The Power of YET." On one side of the poster was a list of phrases such as I can't, or it is not done, or I don't know. On the other side was the same list, but with "yet" added to each phrase to make them for example, I don't know yet.
>
> In the 1-Paradigm world, it is about the process, so all of us can use the power of yet to stay in a growth mindset rather than a fixed ability mindset.

## School-Wide Orientation Matrix

| | Empowerment Connection Trust | Control Comparison Fear |
|---|---|---|
| **High Function Intentional Leadership** | 1-Paradigm School - Empowering<br>• Vision-Driven Facilitative Leadership<br>• Student-Centered Classrooms<br>• Community Climate<br>• Mostly 1-style teaching | 2-Paradigm School - Managed<br>• Efficiency-Driven Top-Down Leadership<br>• Teacher-Centered Classrooms<br>• Institutional Climate<br>• Mostly 2-style teaching |
| **Low Function Accidental Leadership** | 3-Paradigm School - Amorphous<br>• Enabling Passive Leadership<br>• Unstructured learning<br>• Insecure Climate<br>• Lots of 3-style teaching (but also a random combo of others) | 4-Paradigm School -Bossy<br>• Dominating and Self-serving Leadership<br>• Lecture and Test Teaching<br>• Domesticating Climate<br>• Mostly 4-style teaching |

In figure 13.1 below, the 1-Paradigm "what's" and "how's" are contrasted to those of the 2- and 3-Paradigms. It is helpful to know where we aren't going and what won't get us there as well as better understanding the 1-Paradigm by way of contrast to other potential roadmap locations. First, we need to recognize that we cannot move up the pathway into the 1-Paradigm location using 2-Paradigm R's and X's. What our research tells us (Shindler, 2016), is that schools at different points on the pathway are both doing and trying to do different things (and experiencing different outcomes). Therefore, doing a great job of being a 2-Paradigm school will only help us move within the confines of the 2-Paradigm region of the roadmap. We need to make a left-hand turn to access the 1-Paradigm. That will mean a potentially substantive adjustment in the R's of both adults and students. However, the recommendation here is not to exchange standardization and control for unbridled freedom and relativism. Doing this will land us in the 3-Paradigm region of the map. While in the mind of some, the logic of the 3-Paradigm may be appealing (i.e., we all get to do what we feel like) - in practice, the lack of coherence, function, and shared intention leads to both unhappy as well as unproductive results. The goal will be for all members in the school community to grow in their understanding and appreciation of the 1-Paradigm target destination and how it differs from the more limiting paradigms outlined here in Figure 13.1.

## Figure 13.1: Classification of 1-Paradigm Destination vs. the 2 and 3-Paradigm

| Area | 1-Paradigm | 2-Paradigm | 3-Paradigm |
|---|---|---|---|
| Goal/Our Why | To grow and evolve as a collective into an environment where the most authentic learning occurs in the most fundamentally sound environment for promoting human actualization and collective and individual growth. | To create a safe, positive, and orderly environment where students learn fundamental knowledge and social skills to be competent and contributing citizens. | To create an individualized learning environment allowing students the freedom to do what they like, (but in actuality the experience is defined to a great extent by each students' subjective experience and each teacher) |
| Guiding Ethos /Value | Quality Processes | Desirable Outcomes | Freedom of Choice |
| Long-Term Results | High performance, a healthy climate and an ever stronger and connected sense of community. | Adequate performance, a safe climate, an overall experience which is familiar to most parents and students. | Mixed levels of ability depending on subjective experiences, mixed social experiences depending on the situation. |
| Students' Needs | To be, live, and learn in an environment where students can reach their true potential, feel a sense of belonging to the community, and gain a sense of contribution and sharing and discovery of their gifts. | To be given a well-rounded curriculum, caring teachers and supports when students have special needs to achieve success and enjoy school. | To be given rich learning opportunities providing them with stimulation and a chance to explore. (yet, in actuality this is too difficult to execute, and students experience the accidental nature of this learning environment.) |
| Common R's | Community, Respect for Difference, Inquiry, Internal motivation, Critical thinking, Self-Reflection, Belonging and Acceptance, Growth Mindset, Social and Emotional Development., Creativity, Empowerment and Everyone is a Leader. | Positive Reinforcement, Character, Grit, Persistence, Following the Rules, Respecting Authority, Doing Quality Work, Being Prepared for College, Completive Competence. | Self-expression, Creativity, Freedom, Novelty, Unconventional Choices, Individualism. Something good happens just by being at school. |
| Common X's | Team Projects, Inquiry, Labs, Creative Projects, Process-focused tasks, Direct Instruction of foundational skills, Socratic discussions, games, Open play or non-directed social time, Process focused assessment, Authentic Research, Service Learning. Peer assessment. | Direct Instruction, Interactive presentation, Cooperative learning, Computer-assisted instruction, Selected Response Assessment, Worksheets, Labs, Expository writing, Text and Program- Based Curriculum. | Student-Design-Projects. Unsystematic Tasks where tasks are active but lack purpose. Students doing things of interest. Minimal Assessment and/or Subjective grading, Busy work. Discussions. Teachers telling stories. |
| Motivation | Build intrinsic motivation and self-direction with clear boundaries, recognition of the satisfaction in work, and working collaboratively to accomplish things. | Provide extrinsic rewards for desired behavior, encourage students to see what appropriate behavior looks like with comparisons. | Provide each student opportunities to engage in tasks to satisfy their interests. But in practice, the motivation level can be low, and a lot of time is spent idly. |
| Adult Relationships | Collaborative community defined by a sense of share purpose. | Collegial professionals | Caring community; congenial, but random. |
| Use of Data | Recognition/Evidence for how to grow and assess the gap between the current state and the desired state. | Address symptoms of problems reflected in data to meet standards of performance. | Used unsystematically and as it interests those at the school or is required. |
| The Problem | Anything we can do better to become more of the school we desire to be. | Indicators of performance and behavior that are below the set standards. | It is not going the way we intended. |

## Process Values

In most cases, making the "left-hand turn" toward the 1-Paradigm from the 2-Paradigm will imply shifting the emphasis from outcomes to processes as the primary value and driver. As discussed in Chapter six, when we take a systematic approach to refining and improving the quality of our processes, several things happen, including the following:

- Those in the school become more proficient at executing those processes which leads to better quality outcomes in the long-term.

- It provides a forum for a shared growth process which bonds the adults and encourages an efficient way to reflect, receive feedback, innovate, and move toward excellence.

- It encourages a growth vs. a fear of failure mindset.

- The flaws, undesirable side-effects, and limiting qualities of 2/4-Paradigm practices are revealed as they are given closer examination within the process.

- It encourages persistence and trust in the target destination for the school.

As discussed in Chapter six, giving a prominent emphasis to outcomes will limit our growth. If teachers are made overly concerned about delivering on a bottom line (such as test scores, referral rates, looking good to others, etc.) there is a justifiable assumption that they are encouraged to do "whatever it takes" to obtain those outcomes. They hear — "you told me to value this outcome,

so I am doing whatever I can find to effect it, no matter if it is congruent, healthy, or is aligned with my values or the vision of the school." The effect of raising the priority of outcome values shifts us toward a 2-Paradigm mentality. In the 2-Paradigm logic, a doing "what works" approach fits well. On some level, we all do this in our day. But a focus on "doing what it takes" usually leads to a shift away from a commitment to the process and a growth-orientation and leads to limited results in the long-term.

Transformative leaders recognize that momentum, trust, confidence moving forward, persistence, and peace of mind require an environment which is free of mixed messages. Therefore, we need to make our values explicit and demonstrate in our actions, policies, and words we are sincere. When basketball coaching legend John Wooden's teams won ten national championships in twelve years, he *never* told them he wanted them to win the game. Instead, he told them to execute the processes that the team valued, and they had practiced, and to make their best effort. When the outcome is the objective (e.g., winning in the sports metaphor), we will typically experience the anxiety that comes from fear of failure, and which breeds insecurity rather than trust. *When the process is the goal, we can put our energy into becoming excellent.* One leader put it this way "When we are all doing our best to make the school a great place for our students, by definition we can't fail - that is success!"

In schools which are already far along the pathway into the 1-Paradigm, their commitment to process values can be seen in the high quantity of words used to explain the various priority/valued processes at the school – both in terms of what the adults are committed to as well as what they want to develop in the students. Outcomes can be stated in a few words, but process values need to be explained and operationalized. In practical terms, as the school engages the growth process, members will need to be able to expand the vision from its concise and elegant macro level (a clear and powerful set of statements) to a vast operational explanation of how that would be applied on the micro level. The process of operationalizing the micro level is, by definition, infinite.

Where transformative leaders have led successful movement up on the roadmap, nearly every case is defined by a) a commitment to the process, b) no mixed messages undermining the vision and shared values, and c) walking the talk. All three are essential. The quality of trust is built over time. If we do not walk our talk, others will lose trust in the integrity of the process. Gerald, the transformative principal of an independent K-12 school, has been able to turn around a series of schools as a leader. Very quickly the teachers in each school he leads recognize that he is committed to the process of growing the quality at the school and is authentic and consistent in his actions and messaging. For him emphasizing process is not a game he is playing. It is the means to untapping the potential at the school. He is about helping teachers grow as individuals and as a collective. As a result, the energy moves effectively in that liberating (left-hand turn) direction with minimal hesitation, resistance, and fear of failure.

In the same way, John, who has inherited 2-Paradigm schools and moved them into 1-Paradigm levels of function, is a paragon of commitment to the process. He encourages teachers to fully be about what the school is about, and let the outcomes follow. He supports his faculty as they persist in implementing ideas and processes even when the secondary indicators don't show initial results. But he has faith in the efficacy of the process and projects that faith onto others. Eventually, the sound ideas have translated into measurable results others can appreciate. But the outcomes are not the goal. Research from ASSC (Shindler, 2016) supports this phenomenon. Change needs to start with the quality of the R's, transfer to the X's and eventually the O's will manifest the improvement. But the quality (i.e., roadmap location) of all three variables will inevitably reflect one another.

## A Trusting Worldview as a Fundamental R at the School

Each of us has a relatively complicated perception of trust given our life experiences. We can have reasons not to trust other adults or students. We have experienced that being trusting in some cases has led to undesirable results. Yet, building trust as a basic core value will be fundamental to our growth as a school.

Therefore, we will need to define what we mean by trust. To value trust is not to say that the goal is to trust that everything is fine, or that everyone will act in a trustworthy manner, that is naiveté, and will lead to – a lack of trust in our leadership. So, what does it mean to be committed to trust as a fundamental R at the school? We might begin with the following:

- The basic goodness in people and their innate ability and desire to find purpose and value in their work and contribute to the good of the whole. This desire may be masked by a great deal of fear and reactivity, but it is there somewhere wanting to express itself.

- Everyone functions best in an environment defined by certain qualities (e.g., psychology of success), therefore, work to create those qualities as primary concerns.

- People function best when they are trusted. Trust breeds more trust. More trust encourages more good things. Moreover, our experience in any group will support the reality that trusting promotes liking, liking breeds winning, and wining encourages more liking and trusting.

## 2. Vision and Taking Aim toward Our Destination

Success moving up the roadmap to the highest locations will be related to the strength and clarity of the vision that is pulling the process upward. A vision is an idea. It is abstract, but like any abstraction is exists in its practical manifestations. Where does it exist? This is an important question to ask ourselves early and often in the process. If we look to effective schools and other institutions in the process of improvement, we can see that the vision needs to exist in a) leaders' minds and hearts as a picture of quality, and b) in the collective within the school community as a shared picture and embraced and owned personally, and c) in documents which reflect and operationalize those shared values and ideals. Our vision needs to be in the DNA of the school. One may ask, how can the vision exist in all these places? On the surface this may seem complicated, but this multi-dimensional quality is in the nature of how a guiding abstraction will need to live and have efficacy to inspire the practical work of a collective.

Effectively leading will mean embracing the reality that one manifestation of the vision will require it to be concentrated (in one or a few) so that it can maintain coherence, integrity, and decisions can be made efficiently. If the vision is too diffuse, the effort can descend into the 3-Paradigm where things happen accidentally, randomly, and without a congruent intention. A popular phrase to describe this descent is "mission drift."

But if we do not cultivate a shared collective vision, we will never succeed in shifting out of the passive compliance-based ways of being that define the 2/4 side of the horizontal axis of the roadmap, no matter how pure and altruistic the vision of any individual. If we examine schools that we would characterize as being vision-driven, we will recognize both the influence of visionary leaders, as well as a shared collective vision, co-existing imperfectly with some tension and messiness, but still able to grow interdependently.

## Guiding Questions as the Essence of Our Ideas

To a great degree what takes place at our school is the results of the answers to a set of questions. If our actions are not informed by a process of self-reflection related to quality internal guiding questions/R's, we are likely just going through the motions. As discussed in Chapter seven, there are guiding questions that will raise the quality level of our actions and those that will limit them. Moving to the highest levels of the roadmap will require asking empowering guiding questions.

One of our initial guiding questions will need to be "what are we about?" The school that is about "school" will not find itself very high on the pathway. We need to be clear about our purpose. That purpose may be something which has defined the school for a hundred years or something still to be developed. But we need a "why." Then, subsequently, once we have determined that we are about, whether it is creating leaders, or scientists, or artists or well-rounded humans, that leads us to a next level of empowering questions such as – what do ____ do? And what qualities do ____ have? And what skills do experts in that area need to possess? With those answers leading us to another level of guiding question.

To grow effectively as a 1-Paradigm institution, our vision needs to be driven in large part by our "how" questions as well as our "who" and "why" questions.

How do people learn science best? How do excellent teachers approach their work? How do we want to feel each day when we come to work? How do our students think about themselves and others? Questions clarify our intentions and reduce the amount of time we act in an unreflective habitual manner - playing out our subjectively developed definition of "school." Questions force us to articulate answers that can be used to guide future action. Questions drive discussion and debate. They bring out practical realities and give us a window into one another's values and guiding R's. In 1-Paradigm schools there is an expectation that there are frequent discussions about the how. In schools lower on the pathway, these discussions are less frequent, because they tend to evoke conflict. One of the hallmarks of the 1-Paradigm, growth mindset school is that adults embrace the integrity and courage required to talk honestly to colleagues about practice.

## Cultivating Vision – Listening, Focusing Attention, and Articulating

In practical terms, promoting a sense of real-time vision involves leadership committed to an effective pattern of communication. The process of effective communication is as much art as science and will be driven by both a commitment to the process as well as the outcome of people feeling like things are sound and transparent. As discussed in Chapter seven, the practical act of promoting vision involves three main components – listening, clarifying, and articulating.

- **Listening**. Transformative leaders want to know. They find ways to get out of the office, talk to both adults and students, and learn what people are thinking. This is both a practical act of finding out what is really happening in the classrooms, hearts, and minds, as well as a symbolic act of showing we want to know and that we care what others are thinking and experiencing. Speaking of the value of getting out into classroom, one leader rephrased the familiar classroom adage (students don't care what you know until they know that you care) into his context as a leader, he said, "the teachers won't care about your vision for the school unless they believe you care about them."

- **Clarifying**. As leaders collect ongoing information about the experiences, practices, feelings, narratives, within the school, they will need to engage a process of making sense of it all for themselves and everyone else. In the 1-Paradigm classroom, the teacher does an effective job of helping students process and represent their data before making broad conclusions. In the same way, the 1-Paradigm leader takes what they have learned and the available data and processes it as honestly, transparently, and collaboratively as possible. Much like in the active listening process, we need to check in on what we are hearing and seeing. Do we have it right? We are acting as the eyes and ears of the collective. Therefore, we want perceptions to be accurate. Next, we need to make inferences about what is going on. Here we want to help the adults keep attention on the "real problems" and not the symptoms. What are the priority areas of attention in our growth? What is the next level of growth and what would it look like? The use of guiding questions throughout the process will be valuable. We are asking, not telling. And effective questions will pull the discourse up and keep it from focusing so much on what is lacking (which has its place but will not inspire as much movement up).

- **Articulating**. Vision needs to be centralized and synthesized to be actionable. That can range from one person to a committee. After listening and clarifying, the collective needs to hear from leadership the ideas, actions, initiatives, conclusions, and understandings that reflect what was clarified. We have all been to a listening session in which input was provided and then later heard how that input was interpreted and wondered how those inferences could have come from that input. When there is a disconnect in this process, no matter how innocent the reasons, the result will likely be the assigning of motives that will be potentially damaging - i.e., the leaders were not listening, they had their own preset agenda, they are insincere, etc. Therefore, maintaining a loop of feedback and/or gaining consensus on the big ideas and initiatives is essential. In a broad sense, we need to find opportunities to communicate - "This is what I heard", "This is what it means," "This is what it implies we should do, and why." And as much as possible, we will want to contextualize the process into terms of a) where we are currently, b) where we are going and c) given what we know, what make sense to get us to the next level on our journey.

When a leader engages in a continuous process of asking, clarifying, and articulating, those in the school learn to trust and feel a solid sense of the vision. Everyone may not like everything, but they will appreciate that a vision is being grounded in a desire for the collective good, and the leadership has the courage to be upfront about the what's, how's, and the why's.

## 3. Promoting Social Bonds and Structures

The essence of the 1-Paradigm school is vision-based decision-making – using R->X->O logic. Therefore, our guiding question need to be "does this X (policy, practice, structure, routine, etc.) serve our vision?" Building structures that promote the capacity to actualize our vision is vital. As one effective leader phrased it, "form follows function." Some of the areas requiring priority attention include:

- Does the daily schedule support the fulfillment of the vision?
- Are there effective processes in place for collaboration, innovation, and sharing process expertise?
- Are there strong and evident social bonds and agreements helping everyone feel safe, sane, and equitable?
- Are there communal bonds cultivated so the school day feels enjoyable, collaborative, and human?

### The Schedule

Often, we use a schedule because we have gotten used to it and changing it would be inconvenient. But, if we find our schedule limiting our capacity, we need to consider rethinking it. If we examine various 1-Paradigm schools that have made improvements to their schedules, we find the commitment to their Values/R's evident in their choices. In one newly designed middle school that had a commitment to integrated curriculum and PBL, there was a significant demand for collaborative planning time. As a result, two hours of teacher collaboration time was built in on both Tuesday and Thursday. The school found that to meet their goals/R's related to planning at least that much time was necessary. At a high performing K-8 school, the school director changed the schedule every year based on the needs and desires of the teachers. Given that each year goals and agenda change, it was determined that the schedule would adjust to reflect the individual and collective goals.

## Collaborative Planning

Moving up the pathway indicates becoming an increasingly more effective team. Conceiving structures to plan collaboratively are an essential part of growth and day-to-day effectiveness. We need time to process our X"s - to share, refine and improve them within a systemic and reliable forum. Teachers also need time to conceive and plan quality lessons, often with others. Those outcomes require time and a quality system. Some of the models that schools have chosen to employ include:

- A systematic use of the professional learning community (PLC) format. Built into the schedule are times when members of a grade level, subject area or interdisciplinary team meet, plan and process new ideas.
- The "instructional rounds" approach from Yale University (AITSL, 2018). In this process teams a) identify a problem area, b) observe one another and collect data related to the problem, c) debrief in detail, and d) make recommendations for the future.
- The creation of "inquiry groups." These groups meet regularly and as needed to address areas of concern or growth.

Each of these models have unique benefits and are intended to solve real problems (what we do, i.e., our X's), in a collaborative, evidence based, systematic manner. Our school might consider adopting one of these models or synthesizing them to meet our needs. Whatever system we pursue, it should function to serve our needs. Some of those needs will likely include the following.

- Engage in a process of sharing and receiving feedback related one's growth. Ideally this process includes (non-evaluative) opportunities to observe one another's practice and provide feedback.

- An efficient forum for processing ideas, evaluating data, sharing new resources and information, solving problems, and any process requiring being in the same place at the same time.

- A team responsible for ensuring coherence across the curriculum and assessment process, which exists within the school's organizational structure for making decisions. Ideally, teams should have an elected leader who can represent the group at leadership committee meetings.

## Social Contract and School and Classroom Agreements

In every relationship, there is an underlying social contract, whether it is between two persons, between a teacher and his/her students, or the school administration and the teachers and staff. As we move up on the roadmap to higher destinations, the goal is to make these underlying agreements more solid, explicit, and needs satisfying. Issues of fairness and incongruence can undermine sanity, confidence, and morale. Here are ideas to consider in this area to encourage your growth up the pathway.

- Many 1-Paradigm schools have school-wide agreements. Often the same agreements can be used for adult and student interactions. Alternately, lists can be created for each group.

- As discussed in Chapter eleven, creating classroom social contracts and/or agreements have an added benefit to any school-wide agreements. There is a greater opportunity for them to be created and owned by students. Agreements are more empowering, as well as effective, when conceived and committed to by the group which will ultimately use them.

- All those entrusted with facilitating a social contract need to weigh the needs of both the collective and the individual. For the collective, the primary need is for the leader/facilitator to follow through and do what the contract implies they should do. A contract is only valid and legitimate to the degree it does its job of encouraging accountability. For the individual, it is helpful to have members reflect on what they have agreed to. The goal is to promote growth and empowerment, so it may mean finding creative ways for individuals to fulfill their commitments to the collective as well as taking into account personal situations and needs.

- When a democratic decision is made to install a policy, it needs to be consistently applied. Everything is connected, and each of our actions effects every other member of the community. Therefore, members do not have to love a policy to execute it. They just need to appreciate that some policies (such as for tardiness, deadlines, discipline referrals, homework, etc.) only work if everyone applies them. Having no policy for a particular area is usually more desirable than having one that is not followed.

- One of the basic sources of stress and unhappiness occurs when an adult has an unspoken expectation of another and gets upset when the other person (adult or student) does not meet their expectation. Therefore, we need to cultivate a principle at the school that expectations and agreements are spelled out, and if they are not, it is on us when others do not do what we had expected.

- An agreement at one school states "We (students) find ways to solve problems ourselves, before we ask an adult for help." The students in this school are very effective doing this. In a 1-Paradigm school, the principle is that we solve problems directly and use an effective process for communication, and when the occasion arises, we rely on a process for conflict resolution. Effective communication strategies include:

  - The use of I-messages and speaking in specific and constructive terms.

- ◦ The knowledge that loaded conversations require a degree of conscious mindfulness and an awareness of the tendency for egos to take over.

- ◦ Going around others is seen as disrespectful and counter-productive. Instead, engage directly with those who are responsible for the concern.

- ◦ Gossip and excessive complaining are not welcome.

Occasionally complaints need to go to an administrator but should be reserved for cases where a) direct communication has been tried, b) we recognize the elevated emotional and political nature of the issue, and c) it is too important to leave be. How leaders respond to those who are inclined to solve problems passively will set the precedent. Putting in place a protocol for dealing with conflict and adhering to it will be essential in encouraging the norm for honest and direct forms of communication.

## 4. Promoting Connection and Communal Bonds

The nature of the 1-Paradigm location creates and is created by connection and communal bonds. If the school is actualizing its potential, the experience of both students and adults will be characterized by increased levels of feelings of family, team, school pride, shared identity, home, acceptance, and belonging to something larger. These bonds are created naturally in a quality learning environment. When we work together to create and learn, recognize one another's gifts, and learn to know each other more deeply, we connect. On one level, creating the 1-Paradigm teaching and learning environment will encourage that feeling of "team" connection, and the liking and trusting which goes along with it. If we reflect on groups with which we felt a lot of affection long after the experience, it was likely because of a common bond forged by experiences. Likewise, when we reflect on times when we would characterize our experience as being fun, it was likely related to a sense of satisfaction with what we were engaged in and/or being part of a collective group effort, rather than an activity that was assumed to be "fun." But we should recognize that everyone finds different things fun and satisfying. Some of us enjoy more intimate and thoughtful experiences. Some find more excitement in experiential activities. Some people love being part of a team and others would rather be more independent. Therefore, while we can generalize to a large degree what makes for a quality community environment, we do need to consider the variability of human needs and personalities.

While communal bonds are best cultivated organically as part of a quality environment, we can do much to nurture them as well. Without opportunities to really get to know one another, engage in team building, mix with a broader circle of members, and see each other as something other than a student, teacher, or administrator, our level of connection to others will be limited. Therefore, to promote greater levels of connection and communal bonds consider the following ideas:

- Attending a retreat together. The goal is to build connection, get to know one another, build collective agreements and cultural norms, and set the tone moving forward. Starting the term as connected humans, rather than isolated entities and roles within an institution is a powerful way to begin a school year together.

- Include collaborative time in faculty meetings where groups create something or process ideas in groups.

- For some faculty gatherings, systematically assign teachers and staff into mixed groupings for tasks. Encourage everyone to interact and get to know everyone else.

- Spend the first week or so with students building teamwork skills and a classroom culture.

- Use classroom meetings effectively to make decisions, check in emotionally, and process future plans as well as past events.

- Give students multiple ways to serve the school.

- Give classes and student groups multiple ways to serve the larger community or make a difference in the world.

- Conduct fun and low stakes competitions between classes (see principles of healthy competition in Chapter eleven and TCM website). The focus should be on the innovation, creativity, and shared effort of the class, not on an ultimate reward.

- Support and recognize those in extracurricular activities. These activities can be a powerful source of pride and community building.

- Include student work on the walls. Try to represent as many students as possible, and not just top-quality efforts.

- Teach students how to be effective peer tutors. One powerful idea is to have a systematic process in which students from an advanced grade work with students of a younger grade periodically.

- Connect members of the school with parents and community members.

- Traditional gatherings, as well as organic celebrations of meaningful events.

- Traditions that are unique to the school, even if they seem a little silly.

A final thought on building community. Keep in mind that certain practices will undermine our efforts to promote connection. These will include competitive and comparative structures, focusing too much on outcomes, public shaming, allowing cliques, and neglecting the social contract bonds. It is a lot easier to destroy community than it is to build it, so be mindful of those sources of toxicity that will limit the affective growth of the collective.

## 5. Empowerment, Voice, and Distribution of Leadership

Among the most fundamental shifts characterizing the "left hand turn" from the 2 to the 1-Paradigm will relate to who has the power. In the 1-Paradigm, the goal is to create maximum levels of internal locus of control, agency, voice, and self-direction. Therefore, the intention will be to maintain the explicit school R/value that leaders and teachers embrace opportunities to systematically empowering others and distribute leadership. Classroom efforts should mirror those for the school as a whole. When a student casually and confidently walks up to the principal in a 1-Paradigm school and makes a suggestion about how the school could be better (as is observed commonly in empowering schools), it is evidence of a thousand classroom X's from the past and an overall school environment which encourages that level of empowerment.

An empowering culture cannot come from a program or an initiative, it needs to be part of the DNA/fundamental R's at the school. In most cases, building more trust, voice, self-direction and distributed leadership is related to the will to do so. As Earnest Hemmingway said, "the best way to find out if you can trust someone is to trust them." Depending on our current roadmap location and what the adults and students have been used to, we will want to deliberately build the skills, expectations, and capacity to grow in the direction of more trust and self-responsibility.

## Teacher Leadership and Empowerment

In the book *Trusting Teachers with School Success,* authors Farris-Berg & Dirkswager (2013) describe the effectiveness of "teacher-powered schools." In these schools, teachers are given the primary responsibility for running the school, and the results are promising. When teachers were given the freedom to design their own systems and practices, the common outcomes of the process were a more intentional approach to self-improvement and more meaningful and constructivist curriculum for students. In general, the schools moved more toward 1-Paradigm function than the 3-Paradigm disorder some might expect. Among the take-away lessons from these teacher-powered schools is that when people have ownership over their own work and growth, most often they take advantage of it to produce a greater level of good for everyone.

The essence of empowerment in the 1-Paradigm school is for the leaders to inspire adults individually and collectively to embrace the vision of the school and then grow and express that vision in their own R's and X's. Fundamental to expressing that vision is to grow in their knowledge, skill, and confidence to empower students to become more self-directed and embrace their own growth process. Autonomy driven by a vision of empowerment and growth is a powerful force moving both the school and each classroom up the pathway. Autonomy without vision, or the intention for growth, is simply intellectual freedom. Promoting a more empowered faculty and staff starts with the intention to be so.

Our explicit/collective and implicit/internal guiding questions should include "How can we support ever more empowered and self-directed students?" "Will this practice, policy, or program promote more internal or external locus of control? And "How can we provide more power, ownership, and responsibility and find occasions for students to be leaders?" A teacher with those intentions will need only opportunities and structures to create, share and express them. Ideas and practices supporting this shift toward empowerment include:

- **Personal Goal Setting as the Basis for Professional Growth**. As discussed in Chapter eight, to encourage personal ownership and self-reflection, a school's performance assessment process should feature yearly personal goal setting. Goals should be specific, relate to one's own growth trajectory, and include clear, observable outcomes for various points in the year.

- **Autonomy over Choices**. The guiding principle here should be that members are expected to own the consequences of the choices that are made within their domains. That starts with being given autonomy over those choices. We might want to include some oversight, but faculty and staff should feel like they have ownership over what they teach, grade level or subject area decisions and coordination, the appearance of their rooms, and classroom-level management choices. But with autonomy comes accountability and the need to justify one's choices within the lens of the school vision.

- **Peer Coaching and Observation**. As discussed in Chapter eight, teachers benefit from opportunity to observe and learn from one another, provide feedback using agreed upon criteria for quality, and a chance to reflect and refine their practice with the insights and support of peers.

- **Teacher-Led Professional Development.** Teachers who have developed a model practice or have acquired information of benefit to the collective should be encouraged to lead professional developments for the whole.

- **Formal Teacher Leaders.** Those teachers who have demonstrated a high level of proficiency for demonstrating their own competency as well as being able to facilitate others understanding and skills related to creating the high function 1-Paradigm classroom (i.e., A level: Will and A level: Skill, See Chapter eight) should be given opportunities as teacher leaders. Teachers whose general expertise and/or specific skill set such as in a content area, reading, special education support, or social and emotional learning make them valuable vehicles of peer support should be provided compensated time to work with others.

- **Site Decision-Making/Vision Committee.** Democratic schools benefit from representative decision-making bodies and groups which can process data and create or advise on policy.

- **A Commitment to the Truth and Non-Defensiveness.** The expectation that constructive criticism or suggestions for improvement are desirable and welcome – especially when the suggestions come from students.

## Student Voice and Agency

Our move up and across on the roadmap will require a corresponding commitment to the empowerment of students as well as the adults. When observing empowering practices/X's, most often it is in the classroom of a teacher who possesses the value/R that empowerment is a priority goal for his/her students individually and collectively. And when we find a teacher committed to empowerment it is likely in a school that has made it a priority. So, as with most areas of the move over and across, cultivating more student empowerment will come from using empowering questions to guide our classroom and school wide X's.

As a teacher, if I am looking for ways to empower my students and cultivate empowering structures, I will find them. And as with the other essential qualities of the 1-Paradigm location, the more we empower students, the greater our capacity to empower them further grows. We might break down the broad domain of empowering practice into a few sub-categories.

- **Internal Locus of Control**. Students view their actions within the lens of cause (their thinking, choices, intentions) and effect (their circumstances), being the author of their own fate, and taking responsibility for their actions.

- **Self-Direction**. Students demonstrate the capacity to manage themselves and deal with problems related to organization, collaboration, conflict, and sharing, by using quality strategies without an over-dependence on adult direction.

- **Agency**. Students recognize that they are capable of achieving their goals and meeting the demands of given tasks.

- **Ownership.** Students take ownership control of those parts of their learning and relationships over which they are capable of managing. Teachers help them reflect on the those means as well as the effects of the choices made.

- **Voice.** Students are inspired to be co-creators of the class and are included in as many choices as possible: especially those affecting them most directly.

- **Contribution.** The reward in the 1-Paradigm school is that students learn that the greatest motivator/satisfier is the feeling of contribution and sharing one's gifts and being appreciated for it.

When we have the intention to cultivate the above qualities, we will find ways to share power and help our students learn to trust themselves and develop in their knowledge of how to take advantage of growth opportunities for themselves and the whole class. However, we need to keep this intention in perspective. Cultivating empowered students needs to be viewed as an incremental process and engaged in with great care. Growing the capacity for responsibility is necessarily built on the principle – when you show you are capable of being more responsible, you will be given more freedom and choice, and when you show you are not ready for a particular level of responsibility, you will need to lose some freedom until you can show you are ready. Giving away power to those who are not ready for it or tend to abuse it will nosedive us into the 3-Paradigm and lead to all manner of dysfunction and emotional distress. Practical forms empowerment can take in the classroom and school will include:

- **Student Involvement in Creating the Classroom Agreements/ Social Contract**. Engage in a process where students democratically develop the guiding principles for behavior and the consequences for violating those principles.

- **Students Roles in the Practical Management of the Class.** A series of classroom jobs and roles can be created. Anything that students can do, they should be doing. Roles and duties should be rotated regularly.

- **Student Led-Conferences**. Students prepare for the conference by representing their growth over a period of time with work samples. The student then presents the exhibits of their growth and performance to their teacher and parent(s)/guardians.

- **Students Develop Goals or Design Success Criteria for Projects**. As students become more expert in understanding the nature of quality in general, they can be given increasingly more ownership over creating their own criteria for judging the quality of their proposed work products.

- **Peer Editing and/or Evaluation**. Students learn how to apply quality criteria to the process of assessing one another and accepting feedback from peers.

- **Reduced Direction, Supervision and Critical Feedback by Teachers.** For some tasks, the teacher can send an implicit or explicit message to students that they trust the students to be engaged and pursuing excellence, by allowing students to self-direct and self-assessing for quality without the need for constant supervision by the teacher.

The teacher may be engaged with a few students, interacting informally with students, or even doing a similar task themselves and later sharing their own insights along with the students when they are done. But this context is only possible after the cultivation of a high level of capacity for self-direction, students have internalized criteria for quality, and when students perceive the greater level of freedom as an intentional gift rather than neglect.

- **Student Lead Class Meetings.** Once students learn what a well-run meeting looks like, they can be given more opportunities to lead meetings. The recommendation is that the meeting is short and has a narrow purpose and a well-established protocol. Start with students who are willing and able to lead, but eventually encourage more students to conduct the meetings. It is a recipe for disaster and can cause emotional damage to have anyone unqualified run a class meeting where students are asked to divulge emotionally, discuss delicate or sensitive information, or speak about being wronged publicly.

- **Student Run Clubs, Events, Teams, Committees.** Maximum responsibility should be given to those students who are ready for leadership roles on their committees and clubs. Students should be encouraged to create new clubs and intramural activities. Adults can support student leaders with resources, ensuring safety and coordination of spaces.

- **Students are Represented on Site Governance Committees.** Students provide an invaluable perspective to a school site council, and it sends a message to the students that the adults want to know what they think.

- **A Thousand Acts a Day.** In the 1-Paradigm classroom, teachers project the goal/R that every X is intended to support student growth, help students feel into their power, and generally cultivate each student's POS. Therefore, when students question "why," make suggestions for how things can be better, and advocate for themselves, the 1-Style teacher perceives it as progress and not a threat to their authority.

Considering data use as a form of empowerment is worthwhile. As discussed in the next section, data is power. When we ask a question (in a survey or another inquiry process) we empower others. The school-based leadership team should be empowered to process the various sources of assessment data collected at the school and be tasked with the data analysis, priority setting, and strategic planning, as well as data dissemination. When students are included to the data analysis process it adds a powerful perspective and valuable source of insight.

## 6. Effective Use of Evidence, Data and Strategic Planning

One of the most vital aspects of our move up the roadmap is how we conceive and use assessment evidence and data and incorporate it into our strategic planning. The goal will be to have our assessment data serve our vision-driven journey effectively. It is useful to contrast the idea of assessment within the lens of our destination – i.e., the more effective 1-Paradigm, with its common use in a 2-Paradigm structure. In the 1-Paradigm, data is used as evidence of progress toward the destination. In the 2-Paradigm the goal is to improve outcome measures. Therefore, in a 2-Paradigm approach there is a tendency to a) take the most direct and short-term action to improve indictors of low performance, and b) assume adequate indications of performance to signify things are on track. In this paradigm, there is also a counterproductive level of attention placed upon outcome comparisons – between the school and other schools, between teachers, and between students and external proficiency standards. As explored earlier in Chapter nine, when we place preeminent value on the outcome, it commonly leads to an effort to solve "symptoms" of the actual problems, with "whatever works." While this can lead to potentially more positive results when compared to an absence of data use to inform decision making (i.e., 3 and 4-Paradigm), it will limit the growth trajectory of the school and keep it stuck in the 2-Paradigm performance location.

Therefore, making the left-hand turn will necessarily involve transitioning to a more effective and evolved use of assessment data. As with most of the other aspects of the move up the pathway, the starting point to high quality data use will be a well-conceived vision and picture of our destination. Processing of assessment data is engaged in the service of the vision, and it functions as indirect evidence of success in the process of moving toward our vision-based destination. Therefore, we will need to identify those data indicators which will best help us validly, reliably, and meaningfully assess our progress and performance. This should involve a thoughtful process and include broad participation and expertise. Our guiding question will be "what assessment data will best help us know how well we are succeeding at what we most value?" The data use will be more meaningful and impactful if the teachers value the forms of data being collected and see its validity and usefulness.

In the 1-Paradigm mindset, the goal is to know the honest reality for the purpose of growth. There is, therefore, a de-emphasis as we move up the pathway on whether we are or are not meeting the standards – outcome thinking. We will want to shift to more process values. So, our assessment data needs to support that shift. As a teacher, my guiding questions are less related to , "are my students meeting the standards," and more related to, "am being most effective in the process of developing the skills which my students need to get to the next level?" When we focus on outcomes, we tend to look at the symptoms of the essential reality and think in terms of comparisons. These tendencies are limiting. They lead away from a focus on growth – our own and that of our students, and/or toward becoming expert in cultivating and implementing quality processes. In the 1-Paradigm, the use of assessment data needs to encourage a collective growth mindset. "Real problems" are related to what we are doing, and how we are doing it. Success is therefore related to how well the school is becoming an organization and community of individuals who move most effectively toward their desired destination. Data sources need to function to provide information as to how we are doing in our effort to develop ever more quality processes.

The most meaningful indicators of learning and academic progress will be those which are the most direct and authentic. For example, if our target outcome is for students to be able to think scientifically, the most authentic means of assessment will involve creating clear and specific criteria for quality performance in that area. And providing that criteria to students and having them practice it early and often. An indirect assessment of science knowledge may have its place in our overall plan, but only secondarily and should be considered a much less valid source of evidence of our success. 1-Paradigm teachers are experts in authentic assessment construction. And in the 1-Paradigm, teachers are expected to, and trusted to have a detailed knowledge of their students' levels of learning (i.e., skills, knowledge, dispositions, performance, and reasoning) progress. Moreover, in the 1-Paradigm, students are assumed to be the primary users of classroom assessment data and are expected to and trusted to take ownership of their learning progress. Therefore, a parent who leaves a student led conference should feel much more informed about their child's learning experiences and progress than they could from reading a report card. We may be required to or choose to still give the test, but it will not represent the students' success as well as the more authentic measures. It may be helpful to explore what other 1-Paradigm schools are doing in this area. Often, schools develop their own measures of academic progress to fit their goals and academic programs. Assessment defines success. So, whatever we measure will strongly influence what we do in practice.

As you determine the most essential indicators of your school's progress, in addition to student learning, it is likely that you find the need to assess other salient indicators such as the quality of student experiences, school operations, teacher experiences, social and emotional health, and other areas important to you. Thankfully, there has been a proliferation of excellent tools for assessing these areas. The ASSC School Climate Assessment Instrument (SCAI) is highly useful in capturing a broad range of quality indicators. A discussed throughout this book, and specifically in Chapter two, what has been discover is that success as measured by the eight factors of the SCAI is highly predictive of a school's success generally.

## School D: What Moving Up Would Imply

School D is a very successful school with a high level of function. We could place its roadmap location as somewhere between the 1- and 2-Paradigm in the high function level. Its performance rating is around 3.7 SCAI and 70%tile student achievement. In figure 13.2 are SCAI ratings from teachers/staff and students across the eight dimensions at the school. From the ratings we can ascertain that the school is well-run, students feel safe and happy, the academic program is solid, and behavioral issues are low.

### Figure 13.2: School D: Overall SCAI Mean Ratings for Each Dimension

| | Dimensions | Middle School Staff | Middle School Students |
|---|---|---|---|
| D1 | Physical Environment | 3.58 | 4.09 |
| D2 | Teacher Relations | 3.66 | |
| D3 | Student Interactions | 3.90 | 3.87 |
| D4 | Leadership | 3.53 | - |
| D5 | Management Discipline | 3.69 | 3.55 |
| D6 | Learning / Assessment | 3.89 | 3.76 |
| D7 | Social-Emotional Culture | 3.80 | 3.49 |
| D8 | Community | 4.19 | 4.17 |
| [ ] | **Overall Climate Rating** | **3.70** | **3.80** |

School D is much like other schools at its location on the roadmap. Students are learning. There is a clear intention to the procedures, and it runs smoothly. The adults are committed and have high expectations for students. Leadership is attentive and interested in guiding the school to excellence. But as one examines the SCAI ratings, it is evident that to move to up the pathway, the school will need to embody the left-hand turn more intentionally. On a practical level, this means making a greater commitment to empowering teachers and students and providing more voice and ownership. Examining SCAI dimension 7 ratings related to the social-emotional climate at the school, in Figure 13.3 below, one can see where the issues of empowerment are apparent. For example, item 7c represents a red flag. When students feel empowered, they rate this item highly, so for students to rate their level of school pride low, it indicates that they feel a little repressed. This is further confirmed by the low ratings for student voice (7d) and ease in approaching adults (7h) as well as the effect of adults on their levels of stress (7j) and their own level of stress (7k).

**Figure 13.3: School D: SCAI Dimension 7 (Social-Emotional Culture) Ratings for Teachers/Staff and Students**

| D7 | Social-Emotional Culture | Middle School Staff | Middle Sch⊂ Students |
|----|---------------------------|------|------|
| 7a | students feel part of a community | 4.25 | 3.92 |
| 7b | student's avoidance of abusive language | 3.74 | 3.43 |
| 7c | student's sense of school pride | 3.91 | 3.03 |
| 7d | students voice | 3.67 | 3.14 |
| 7e | student safety from violence | 3.92 | 4.19 |
| 7f | expectations for students | 4.35 | 3.49 |
| 7g | graduates leave with sense of gratitude | 4.12 | 4.15 |
| 7h | student comfort in adult conversations | 3.78 | 3.41 |
| 7i | maintenance of traditions | 4.21 | 4.08 |
| 7j | adult influence on student stress | 3.73 | 3.04 |
| 7k | stress resilience | 3.26 | 2.89 |
| 7l | students part of something larger | 3.84 | - |
| [] | Dimension - 7 - Ratings | 3.80 | 3.49 |

What we can conclude broadly from these data is that School D has done an excellent job of creating function, order, and a positive climate (moving up the vertical axis), but it has not given the same level of intention toward being an empowering place (moving across on the horizontal axis). The implication is that for School D to move to the next level on the roadmap it will need to embrace the challenge of becoming a more trusting, empowering and emotionally connected place. In this case, the leadership at school D is embracing that challenge. They are making a purposeful effort to encourage student voice and ownership. They are incorporating more project-based and inquiry-based instruction and are re-examining their classroom management approach.

School D is a positive example of a school that has embraced a POS and a growth mindset. Implementing more trusting and empowering X's will take time and require raising the level of the R's by way of becoming a more effective professional learning community. But they can see the higher destination and appreciate why it is worth doing what it will take to get there. They use their assessment data as evidence of their progress and are open-eyed and honest about what the data tell them – the epitome of a growth mindset. Therefore, their growth edge will mainly be defied by a process of clarifying and operationalizing the next level as a vision/R's as well as in practice/X's.

## Systematic Use of Your Assessment Evidence

Chapter nine outlined ideas for processing data and a strategic-planning framework. It is important to have both a school-wide and classroom-based logic for processing data effectively. In the next section, we will discuss ideas related to the classroom level – where the rubber meets the road and arguably the more important of the two levels. However, the school level is also vitally important and can be the difference between either spinning our wheels or feeling solid in the journey forward. On the school level, there are many essential considerations including:

- Is there a school-wide system for effectively using assessment data and translating it into strategic plans and actions?

- Is the assessment system serving our vision? Or does it serve less meaningful purposes like external accountability or to be able to say we are doing it?

- What do we learn from our data? Is it examined for meaning or as a formality?

- Do those at the school know what the data say? Is the process transparent and honest?

- Are those who are part of the team examining data the right ones to be doing it? And/or are they able to translate what they learned into useful information or action later?

- Is the collection of assessment data making the school better?

In the 1-Paradigm approach, school-wide assessment should be viewed within the lens of continuous improvement. We are always improving, and everything is data. If you are actively engaged in a process of school improvement and an effort to move up the pathway, it is highly recommended that you conceive your assessment system as the process of bridging the gap between your current location and your desired location. If not, you can find yourself in the situation of most schools where your data collection and strategic planning are largely formalities requiring a great deal of human capital yet providing little benefit. Therefore, it is worth the time and effort to define and articulate both the current location and the desired location, based on a broad set of data indicators (see strategic planning process in Chapter nine). Next you will want to engage a team in making sense of the gap between the two states based on the evidence. Here you will want to identify the school's a) real problems, b) excessive gap areas, and c) priority areas. And finally set SMART goals to address the priority needs. This process may require a substantial amount of time, reflection, and contemplation. But in the end, there is almost no way to fail if you engage the process sincerely, as both the process and the outcome will be inherently valuable.

There will be a place to engage all teachers and staff within the process, but at some point, deep analysis and visionary insights will be required. Typically, this is best accomplished with time and devotion to the task by a chosen few. Broad input should be encouraged, but eventually a few trusted members of the school community will need to synthesize that input into a coherent process, and eventually product. As you initiate the task, consider all the deep learning, insight and wisdom which will come from revisiting the school's vision and exploring the data. That insight is powerful. So, how it can be used subsequently to effect change? The better we can comprehend our ideal school clearly, the better we are able to recognize it as happening or not happening when we observe what is taking place around the school, as well as within our own practice. Therefore, linking the involvement/ responsibilities of those engaged in assessment data analysis, strategic planning, and delivery of professional development can be of great benefit.

## 7. Moving the Level of Pedagogy/X's Up the Pathway

The place to start when examining pedagogy is principle one – it's all connected. If the goal is to move the school up the roadmap and actualize the 1-Paradigm, it needs to happen in the classroom. But classrooms will reflect the R's at the school generally. Therefore, as a leader, if we want connected, empowered, trusting, rigorous, quality-driven, collaborative, and self-directed classroom communities, we will need to embed those values into everything at the school. And as with the R's and X's at the school broadly, each classroom will need to embrace a process of growth toward a vision of quality. Given that everything is connected, our collective results will reflect the average of the X's that were used that day. Each improved R and/or X from an individual represents a step further up the pathway.

The process of moving up requires a guiding vision of pedagogy and some form of process to operationalize that vision into practical execution. So, the starting point will be to articulate a clear vision/picture in the form of a conceptual framework or set of principles for classifying pedagogical practices/X's into levels of quality – i.e., 1) those which are target level, 2) those which are acceptable, 3) those for use in emergencies only, and 4) those which have no place in the school. This process can take the form of a) a formal document like a "things we do, and things we don't do list," b) ongoing activities where practices are classified into levels of desirability or c) be accomplished more organically within discussions and activities as part of the professional development and growth process. But no one should be held to expectations which have not been clarified and processed sufficiently (a principle that is also highly valuable in the classroom).

Moving up will imply both doing some X's better and reducing or removing other X's entirely. Therefore, we will examine each of the three domains of pedagogy – instruction, assessment and classroom management and explore each in terms of the kinds of practices that will move us up and those that will move us down or keep us stuck. If we were able to observe all practices/X's at the school on a given day and classified them into one of the four levels of desirability (above), and then averaged them, we could very accurately locate the school on the roadmap and infer its climate and academic performance. So, improvement will relate as much to X's we stop using and leave in the past as X's we add or do more effectively. That reality needs to be embraced as a school – growth implies changing unhelpful habits, which means some discomfort and growing pains. But what is lost is not so much a safety net as it is deadweight keeping us collectively and individually down. The leader's job is to cultivate an appreciation for all the opportunities within the challenge. Change will mean growing as individuals and as a collective. And the winners will be every member of the school community, the level of self-respect, the level of pride in the school and one another, and most importantly the lives of the students in the long-term.

**R's Encouraging Movement up the Pathway from 2 to 1-Paradigm**

- I have an intention to be excellent and grow every day.

- I have a POS and a growth-orientation – so I trust the process, and I am not afraid of making mistakes.

- I will not mistake clever ways of doing things for high quality, excellent practice.

- When I get the instinct to use a clever strategy, I will ask myself if this is helping me be more efficient, or if I am avoiding living up to the R's to which I have committed.

- I will look for ways to be more trusting of my students and my own potential.

- I will see the challenges that I face each day as useful information for ways I can better grow.

- I worry less every day about looking powerful and ask myself how I can create more power within the class by promoting and empowering learning context.

- I take care in the process aspects of my job to use clarification, instruction, reflection, and assessment to help my students individually and collectively grow in the skills they need to be excellent in all critical procedures and processes.

## *Classroom Instruction*

As the improvement agenda is conceived in the domain of classroom instructional practices, the analogy of exercise fits. Almost all forms of exercise have some benefit. Yet the kinds of exercise that will be best will depend on our fitness goals. If our school's mission is based in producing great scientists, leaders, artists, or career professionals, the pedagogical emphases will need to reflect the kinds of instructional models best suited to achieving our goals. It is a safe assumption that to produce great athletes will require an expert use of a wide range of exercise regimens. Likewise, to produce 1-Paradigm outcomes related to instruction a wide range of instructional models, practices, and strategies are needed to best promote our goals.

In the 1-Paragigm classroom, a thoughtful selection of instructional models is used to process knowledge, skills, concepts, products, performances, processes, and dispositions. Depending on the nature of the learning targets, teachers may use one or a combination of several learning models including direct instruction, concept attainment, inquiry, laboratories, discuss formats, cooperative structures, project-based learning, problem-based learning, viewing video content, web-based research, and group presentations. Most of these forms of instruction will be useful at some point.

An important aspect of the process of making the shift from the 2- to the 1-Paradigm is the need to transition from a value on the outcome to the process. When our message to students is to "score well on the test," "Complete your homework," "Get the right answer," we keep them concerned primarily with the outcome of their work. These messages are not so much harmful as they are limiting. When teachers and students are primarily concerned with being on task, following directions and how many answers they will get right in the end, learning takes on a domesticating and routinized quality. The implicit value/R in the room is for the teacher to do whatever it takes to get the students to the right answers and for the students to do whatever it takes to get a good score.

In the 1-Paradigm classroom, the implicit value/R is the quality of the work and approach to learning itself. Therefore, teachers need to become expert in leading process skill development. They recognize and implement those models, strategies, and practices/X's which will be most effective in any given situations to support the growth in those skills. 1-Paradigm teaching will include countless iterations of building facility with new processes, using some form of the following sequence:

- Introduce the new process or skill systematically and deliberately.
- Practice the new process with simple content and in a low-stakes context.
- Debrief and analyze the nature of the process and what is required to execute it well.
- Incorporate the process or skill into ever more challenging contexts
- Include formative self-assessment of the process aspects of the task during and after as appropriate.
- Use higher intensity applications of the process as summative assessments.

Some of the processes that are used in high functioning classrooms include: peer editing, cooperative learning, brainstorming, conflict resolution, inquiry, executing roles, scientific method, listening skills, and effective use of technological tools.

Regardless of the content emphasis at our school, the 1-Paradigm target location will imply a commitment to project based-learning (PBL), inquiry, and investigative learning processes. Quality application of each of these instructional models requires the development of many sub-skills. Often prerequisite support skills may need to taught using micro-direct instruction and concept attainment, such as how to function in groups, how to research, how to process evidence and sources, how to present, how to organize information, etc. Recalling our discussion above related to professional development, developing expertise in creating high quality PBL and inquiry in one's class is as complex as rocket science, and therefore, greatly supported by a PLC structure that allows sharing of ideas, rubrics, micro lessons, units, and work products.

Our guiding questions in the domain of instruction will include:

- What models of instruction will be the best fit given the learning targets for the lesson or unit?
- Are students developing the skills and processes expertise they will need to succeed in the next task?
- Are students growing in those skills and process applications defining a "successful graduate" of our school, based on our mission?
- Are the kinds of instructional contexts created in the classroom authentic and as close to real world applications as possible?
- How can we engage students in the process of design and assessment of their own learning tasks?

## The Place of Programs in the Process of Moving Toward Higher Levels of Function

Entities called "programs" have a precarious place in the authentic improvement process at any school. For those schools in the lowest levels of the function continuum, a program can provide greater consistency of both R's and X's, and as a result, a quality program usually leads to some improvement in O's for those schools – contingent on the fact that the program is a "quality" program, not just a gimmick and/or an effort to directly address a symptom rather than the real problem.

However, as we move up the function continuum, adding programs becomes less of a guarantee of a positive results. In fact, in many cases, they can make us less functional, or at least keep us stuck in lower road-map locations. We need to first ask, is any X – as small as a phrase used in classes, or as large as a school-wide math program – consistent with the R's that will lead us up the pathway? If the implied R's underpinning a program are 2-paradigm (teacher-centered and external), it may help the most dire school, but will not help the already functional school. Many schools are stuck in the location of school D, and they implicitly believe that more faithful implementation of a program will lead them to better results. The data suggest it will not (Shindler, 2016, 2018). If our school operates primarily at a program level of thinking (vs. principles and systems), it will be perpetually stuck in the middle of the pathway.

Therefore, as the need or desire for any particular program arises in our conversation, we will want to keep in mind four principles:

1.  Programs have the potential of leading a school either up or down. Program R's can vary in every extreme: the only constant is that can only function as "programs" and not principles or systems.

2.  Programs implying a set of R's which are lower quality than those at the school currently will lead down the continuum.

3. Programs which are consistent with 1-Paradigm R's and represent 1-Paradigm X's can encourage the movement up the pathway (for a relatively functional school), but only if they are used to service the values and system R's at the school. In other words, like any program, a purchased external program can be a useful tool in the service of the larger goal/R's of the teacher with their eyes on a location further up the pathway.

4. The term "evidence-based" is essentially meaningless to a school moving from the 2- to the 1-Paradigm. The fact that a program was shown to have an effect does not mean that it would have an effect that would be desirable for your school.

Therefore, a program can never be 'the answer." The answer is to change the way we collectively think about our jobs. However, some programs can be useful tools, once we have created a clear and systematic set of R's and recognize the kinds of X's which will get us to our target location.

### Classroom Assessment

How we choose to assess concretely defines "success" for our students and will greatly influence the motivational and affective climate at the school. Assessment at all levels should serve the school's vision. So, given our profile of a successful student, we might ask, "what is that student able to do (best case) after their years with at the school?" Then we will want to ask, "what is the best way to see those outcomes and processes (i.e., knowledge, skills, reasoning, products, performances, and dispositions) that is the most authentic to the real world, supports students in their learning process, and encourages the kinds of outcome we most want?" When we ask ourselves those questions, it encourages us to give the area of assessment its proper place, as well as to recognize that we likely have room to grow in this domain.

One of the essential areas of improvement on the journey up the pathway is cultivate expertise in process assessment across the school. The necessary development in students' process skills simply will not happen without the clarity, reinforcement, importance, and values encouraged from implementing quality authentic process assessment systems. In fact, they can make the difference in whether our left-hand turn trend ascends toward the top of the roadmap or dives into the 3-Paradigm. Without clear targets for assessment efficacy even the best intentions can ultimately translate into low quality work and poor motivational outcomes. Teachers who commit to mastering the skills related to formally and informally assessing the process aspects of their students' learning achieve a much higher level of student motivation and performance. When we assess process investment it promotes students' attention to the quality of their work and collaborating effectively, and as are result, outcomes tend to be of higher quality, Moreover, it increases students' level of internal locus of control, growth mindset and psychology of success (POS) generally.

Process assessment can be incorporated in these areas:

- Assessing the process aspect of a project
- Grading part or all of a task focusing on the process or investment level
- Evaluating procedural and lab execution
- Rubrics for independent micro-task quality (i.e., working at a station)
- Gauging the quality of cooperative group interactions
- Assessing peer-editing or revision procedures
- Grading the quality of the preparation

**Case Example** – Students at a high functioning 1-Paradigm school were engaged in a project-based task. One aspect of the assessment involved the teacher assessing the quality of the students' process and outcomes based on a rubric which included some standard elements as well as some elements created just for this task. In addition, students were also asked to self-assess using the "Core Elements" (which had been created by the grade level team at the school, were emphasized with students, and used for many assignments). These elements included growth, innovation, collaboration/teamwork, and quality) for use by students to assess their own processes and outcomes. Students considered each core element and how it applied to their efforts both during and after the task and ultimately produced an assessment summary incorporating the elements.

## Some of the Assessment X's that Will Lead Us Down or Limit Our Growth

Given that how we assess will define success in a very real and practical way for our students, we will want to make sure that our choice of practices/X's in this area cultivate the most desired orientations toward the work done in school and elsewhere in students' lives. Some of the practices that we will therefore want to discourage will include:

- **Student-to-Student Comparisons.** This usually takes the form of norm-referenced grading or a competitive grading logic, i.e., grading on a curve. Comparisons are motivation killers and promote a psychology of failure (POF) mindset.

- **Public Display of Performance.** Representing quality work can be useful yet consider whether a display of any kind (lists, rosters, awardees, etc.) implies winners and losers.

- **Using Objective Test Results as the Primary Measure of Success.** Indirect measures like objective tests can provide useful input, but in the 1-Paradigm, finding the most meaningful, direct, and authentic measures of learning is key.

- **Purely Subjective Grading.** Process assessment needs to be done systematically or not at all. Giving a subjective grade for undefined participation is not recommended (i.e., 10% participation at the end of the quarter defined by the teacher's personal criteria). When assessment criteria are undefined it disempowers the student.

Clear rubrics and regular feedback need to be part of the assessment process. (See TCM website for an article on this topic).

- **Disproportionate Use of Summative Assessment.**

In general, the move toward the 1-Paradigm will entail more focus on formative as opposed to summative assessment. Summative assessment leads to a "do what it takes" mindset rather than a focus on quality. W. James Popham in the book, *Transformative Assessment* (2008) outlines a useful protocol for implementing a process-based way of approaching teaching. In the book, the author helps teachers appreciate how having clear target outcomes and identifying learning process increments provides the capacity to make adjustment in their teaching. It also allows students to assess where they are at key points in the process.

As we transition our pedagogy from an outcome and comparison focus to a process and growth value structure, it will imply a commensurate adjustment for students. What we are transitioning toward is ultimately more natural, satisfying, enjoyable, growth promoting, and performance enhancing, but even so, it will take time for students to accommodate the new value emphasis and the changes in their world. As with all elements of the left-hand turn transition, it will require students to a) understand both the what's and the why's of X's that are new to them, b) trust that we are sincere and we will not pull the rug out from under them if they do in fact begin to trust us and the focus on quality over completion, and c) reflect on the benefits and advantages of the changes in how things are being done.

But if we need a concrete human reminder of why we are encouraging our students to make this adjustment, we might just locate a student who had become accustomed to an empowering, trusting, connected 1-Paradigm environment for a time and was then later placed into an outcome comparison and control-based 2-Paradigm environment. If we ask her/his about their experience in each context and how it feels to now be disempowered, their response may help clarify and motivate our thinking. Too often our students lack the perspective on what can be until they experience it first-hand.

Depending on what the adults in the school have been used to, they may voice impassioned rationale for why continued use of these dysfunction producing X's is necessary or that "they work." It will be difficult to prove that any one of the X's listed below is doing harm to a teacher's class when the net effect of the collective X's they are using seems relatively effective. But we need to gently encourage them to trust the reasoning behind why it will be better to remove these practices, the data showing their limiting influence, and the testimony of other educators who function much better without them. This process may take months to fundamentally change R's. But as we discussed in Chapters seven and eight, sometimes R's change when someone gains comfort using a new X and sees the results for themselves. Policy changes can speed up the process of altering the use of certain X's but supporting a shift in the underlying R's should be the priority.

## Social and Emotional Wellness Learning and Curriculum

Our efforts to move up the pathway will require a conscious intention related to promoting social and emotional health (SEL) and competency. School D described previously is a useful example of a school that is generally high functioning, yet to shift solidly into the 1-Paradigm roadmap location needs to be more intentional about cultivating social and emotional wellness. The question is often asked, "To create more SEL health, is it more about what we do during the day, or do we need to implement a program for it to achieve effective results?" To answer that question, we might examine those schools which are currently doing that aspect of school well. What we find is that it does start with what we do (our X's motivated by our R's) throughout the day. But we also find that adding an intentional element can increase the benefits and add more dimensionality to students' SEL learning.

The place to start is to remember that everything we do is connected and consequential. We are creating either more or less social and emotional health and well-being with each action. Using the lens of the POS sub-factors – internal locus of control/agency, self-acceptance and belonging, and growth mindset – is a helpful tool. If we are creating more POS, we are creating more social emotional health. Likewise, intentional efforts to promote more community, empowerment, and self-reflection will encourage students' development in this area. In addition, we will want to encourage teachers to take advantage of opportunities to cultivate mindfulness (i.e., achieving some distance from one's thoughts and emotions to better see one's mental activity with a more conscious perspective), the skills for conflict resolution and dealing with emotions related to interpersonal conflict, as well as empathy, generosity, and appreciating the power of approaching things with an attitude of gratitude rather than dissatisfaction.

There are a growing number of useful SEL curricula being developed which can enhance the efforts. They will not be a substitute for promoting SEL in the day-to-day practices. However, when students are given a formal task of taking one SEL idea at a time and to consider, they can often organize and conceive the ideas in a way that promotes the connection of terms and concepts with life applications. Learning *about* SEL can be a supportive tool for ultimately applying it in action later. And when we have all students engage in such lessons, we can know that we have common vocabulary which we can assume students can apply later at school and at home. Our overall success related to social and emotional health and wellness will come from approximately 70% indirect learning, reflective practices, and contextual application into our daily practice, and about 30% from direct instruction of concepts and skills. And if we had to identify one area which will most greatly determine our growth success related to SEL, it will be our goals, policies, and practices in the domain of classroom management.

### Classroom management

Our movement up the pathway will be vitally dependent on moving the classroom management R's and X's toward those of our desired location. What we intend and ultimately do related to classroom management will define our values related to human nature, relationships, motivation, power, growth, human basic needs, and more. Thus, why an entire chapter (11) was required to support the practical aspects of what it entails to move a school and each classroom up in this area. And as noted previously, we should assume that no matter how well we execute 2-Paradigm classroom management X's, they will not encourage 1-Paradigm outcomes (i.e., self-direction, responsibility, community, a psychology of success, trusting relationships, internal motivation, emotional ease and safety, and empowerment).

When contrasting the values/R's of 1-Paradigm with those of the 2-Paradigm, differences in the area of classroom management clearly emerge. In the 2-Paradigm, there is a tendency toward binary thinking – "that teacher has good classroom management or not," or "those students are on task or not." Embracing the 1-Paradigm requires a shift from binary thinking to a perspective defined by cause and effect and levels of quality. All adult actions/X's will have an influence on students. Our job is to choose and implement those which we have discerned to have the most desirable effect in the long-term. When looking out at a class, we should see a group of students who are being supported toward ever greater levels of function and human development as a collective and as individuals.

Exploring Chapter eleven, we should gain a reliable sense of where our school is in its progress up the pathway related to classroom management. The final sections of that chapter explain how to move a school to the highest levels in this domain. Any school's growth process will imply building a quality foundation for the move both up and across. That foundation will need to include the following:

- **Solid Set of Expectations and Agreements/Social Contract.** Both adults and students need to understand, own, and commit to school and classroom level agreements for all stakeholders to feel safe, sane, and solid. Both adults and students need to do their jobs related to those agreements to preserve trust and a sense of emotional safety.

- **Collaboration and Team Skills.** Students need to learn how to work together efficiently and in the spirit of true cooperation.

- **Easy and Efficient Technical Management.** Teachers need to use only humane and clarity building strategies to encourage order and efficiency.

- **Empowering and Emotionally Congruent Language**. Teachers need to learn how to promote clear and well-established expectations using only strategies supporting increased self-direction, clarity of the task, and that project emotionally congruent and supportive messaging and non-verbal energy.

Success in building this foundation is why students feel easy and safe at the school. Therefore, if they do not feel a basic sense of safety and sanity, then fostering the trust, connection and empowerment related to the left-hand turn on the roadmap will be virtually impossible. Next, we will need to undertake the process of eliminating negative, manipulative, coercive, extrinsic, pain-based, or comparison-based strategies and policies. These practices tend to require a great deal of energy to maintain and stunt students' growth. Facilitating a transition away from limiting practices will be accelerated by whole faculty activities such as classifying practices based on POS/POF, developing a "things we do" and "things we don't do" list, or using other high quality values clarification tools for classifying examples and non-examples of sound/desired practice. It will also require a process of individual teacher self-reflection and growth. Even effective teachers can collect some dysfunctional practices. As with any habit, poor classroom management practices are difficult to discard, especially when one perceives them to "work" or they were taught by an authority. So, leadership will want to support the process of weaning teachers off these limiting factors operating in their classes. Practices to reduce or eliminate during our progress up the pathway will include:

- **Extrinsic Rewards**. Even though extrinsic rewards can motivate in the short-term: over time, they lose their power and progressively extract intrinsic motivation and agency. Therefore, they are inconsistent with the goals of a 1-Paradigm classroom.

- **Incongruent and Manipulative Language and Strategies**. When we try to motivate students with subtle shame and comparisons ("I like the way ___ is sitting quietly), insecurity and unsafe relationship energy between the teacher and the students is created.

- **Behavior Charts and Names on the Board**. When we use public shame to motivate, a whole series of unwanted consequences are set in motion. Again, these systems have no place in the 1-Paradigm classroom.

- **Personal Praise for Compliance**. When a teacher gives students, who are being compliant, personal praise for doing what *they* want (i.e., "I like the way…," "It makes me happy when…," "You are so good for being…"), students become insecure, dependent on external praise or resentful, all of which are counterproductive to the goals of the 1-Paradigm classroom. See Chapter eleven and TCM website for the alternatives.

- **Negative Recognitions and Public Criticism of the Student**. Negative recognitions of unwanted behavior (i.e., "Billy, I told you to put that away.") train students to be passive and wait for the teacher to remind them to get on task. They act to reinforce the unwanted behavior which is publicly recognized. Public criticism encourages a fear of failure and undermines a growth orientation.

- **Use of Disappointment, Punishments and/or Shaming**. The use of these common strategies creates a POF by producing insecurity, a shift to an external LOC, and a breakdown of the relationships in the classroom.

- **Over-emphasis on Comparisons, Contests and Awards that reward the Best and Top Performers.** These encourage a fixed-ability orientation and promote the advantage of the advantaged. Conversely, rewarding outcomes over which all students control and have a relatively equal opportunity for success, such as effort, improvement, and persistence, used in moderation will have a slightly positive impact on function (see Chapter eleven and the online chapter on competition at the transformativeclassroom.com website).

As the foundation becomes more solid and limiting practices are eliminated, there is more capacity to incorporate more empowering and connecting practices. This shift will include the freeing up of a lot of creative energy that was spent maintaining the compliance-based practices.

The keys to supporting this shift will be a) the R's that come from leadership, and b) the R's of each teacher. If my guiding question is, "how can I create more self-directed students," my actions will become increasing consistent and effective in reaching my goal. When a teacher is committed to a quality outcome, he/she will find a way. But as we have discussed, beware of mixed messages. If we want empowerment, we cannot also place a high value on compliance and obedience. The 1-Paradigm classroom can achieve much higher levels of order than the average 2-Paradigm classroom. Yet that order will not arise from compliance but instead from students who have internalize the value and intrinsic rewards of being part of somethings satisfying and functional that encourages their growth and learning. Therefore, the messages from leadership should consistently support 1-Paradigm values without counterproductive (mixed) messages such as dissatisfaction with the level of compliance, focusing on what is not going right, or pleasure with order which has been achieved through manipulative, coercive, or compliance-based strategies.

For some teachers creating the self-directed connected community is inherently exciting. Leadership will want to encourage these members of the school to share their approaches with their teams as well as the collective. For many, transitioning to cultivating a more transformative environment will be appealing, but difficult to operationalize into practice, and so may engender feelings of insecurity. Giving those members support and encouragement and access to solid 1-Paradigm models will be helpful. The following is a list of core 1-Paradigm goals and practices that will be helpful as we try to operationalize this picture (taken from Chapter eleven and TCM).

- Use exclusively POS promoting practices and refrain entirely from POF promoting practices.
- Promote student self-direction.
- Commit to developing cooperative/team skill experts.
- Shift from the "what" to increasingly including the "why."

> "Problems cannot be solved at the same level of consciousness with which they were created."
> — *Albert Einstein*

- Systematically promote student leadership.

- Create classroom identities.

- Use classroom meetings effectively.

- Encourage conditions for intrinsic motivation to grow.

- Cultivate mindfulness skills related to conflict, difficult internal emotions, and challenging situations.

- Enlist students as conflict resolution leaders and peer mediators.

- Have students self-assess the quality of their participation (effort, attitude, cooperation, attention to quality) and make plans for ways to grow and improve.

- Assume rules, consequences, procedures, routines, and other practical aspects of the class are owned by the collective (teacher and students) serving the group and modified when changes are judged by the group to better serve its needs.

Explanations for implementing each of these ideas is available in TCM and elsewhere, but what one will find is that once teachers connect with the value/R of a practice or compelling goal they will become masters of its application and find sophisticated and creative ways of making it an excellent part of what they do.

While the goal of the 2-Paradigm is a fixed state (related to creating order and on-task behavior), the goal of the 1-Paradigm is perpetual improvement and growth. The target is always moving ahead. If we succeed in encouraging a solid sense of self-direction within our class, what would the next level look like? If our students have learned to count on one another, how else can we take advantage of that quality to grow even more connected and coordinated as a collective? If we have developed a high level of care and respect among the members of the class, how can we encourage a greater sense of gratitude and appreciation for one another? In terms of Maslow's hierarchy of psychological needs (1954), the process of becoming a 1-Paradigm class is a movement toward self-actualization. Therefore, for the adults in the school, the journey will be characterized by a deepening appreciation of the basic goodness of the persons within the school community, and the pull toward a more satisfying destination. Bribes or manipulation are not needed to get there, just an effective process and frequent opportunities to recognize that growing toward this destination feels right.

## CONCLUSION

After considering all that is involved in moving one's school from the 2- to the 1-Paradigm location of the roadmap, the reader may feel a bit overwhelmed. But keep in mind that any quality action taken in the right direction will result in movement toward our goal. Even if a portion of what is outlined here is accomplished, our school will improve significantly. And, unlike improvement built on gimmicks and short-term interventions, applying the practices in this chapter will result in sustained change. Each improvement will act synergistically with the others. The hope is that all the members of the school community will feel empowered to set out on a course toward your desired destination on the school effectiveness roadmap, knowing that the path is clear, and success is a function of staying commitment to the vision. In the next and final chapter, we delve into the leader's journey of self-exploration. Moving up the pathway as a person and leader will greatly facilitate success as an agent of school transformation.

## REFERENCES

Australian Instutute for Technology and School Leadership *(2018) How to Guide to Instructional Rounds*. Retrieved from https://www.aitsl.edu.au/docs/default-source/default-document-library/how-to-guide---instructional-rounds.pdf?sfvrsn=72acec3c_2

Farris-Berg, K., Dirkswager, E., Jung, A. (2013) *Trusting Teachers with school success*. Rowan and Littlefield Education, Lanham, UK.

Maslow, A. (1954) *Motivation and Personality*. Harpers Psychological Series. New York.

Popham, J.W. (2008) *Transformative Classroom Assessment*. ASCD Press, Alexandria VA.

Shindler, J (2009) *Transformative Classroom Management*, Wiley Press.

Shindler, J. (2009) *Assessing Process and Participation*. Retrieved from www.transformativeclassroom.com.

Shindler, J. (2009) *The Problems with Colored Cards and other Shame-Based Behavioral Systems*. Retrieved from www.transformativeclassroom.com.

Shindler, J (2014) *Examining Healthy Versus Unhealthy Use of Competition in the Classroom*. Available at www.transformativeclassroom.com and published online at a academia.com.

Shindler, J., Jones, A., Williams, A. (2016) Examining the School Climate – Student Achievement Connection: And Making Sense of Why the First Precedes the Second. *Journal of School Administration Research and Development, Summer 2106 v.1*.n.1. pp7-16.

Shindler, J (2016) *In Search of a Complete and Coherent School Discipline System* www.transformativeclassroom.com.

Shindler, J (2018) *Exploring the Limiting Influence of PBIS in the Growth of Students and Schools*. www.transformativeclassroom.com.

# CHAPTER 14:

## Leader Personal Vision Creation and Growth Development

> "Be the change that you wish to see in the world."
> — *Mahatma Gandhi*
>
> "I wanted to change the world. But I have found that the only thing one can be sure of changing is oneself."
> — *Aldous Huxley, Point Counter Point*
>
> "We are addicted to our thoughts. We cannot change anything if we cannot change our thinking."
> — *Santosh Kalwar, Quote Me Everyday*

Our job performance and our ability to lead will be a direct reflection of who we are and how we think. And it is highly likely that the quality and trajectory of our school's growth and improvement process will mirror our own ongoing personal growth process. We lead who we R. And our R's will be continually projected onto our school and its day-to-day activities. This realization may seem intimidating yet is really a golden opportunity to stretch and grow as a person and gain a deeper insight into what it means to be a leader as we activate more of our personal potential.

If our school or organization is going to improve, it will be primarily a result of more evolved and improved R's. The same will be true for any of us as individuals. But because of the critical importance and consequential nature of our work, it will be especially important for those in the role of leader to have an intimate understanding of the nature of the growth and change process.

In this chapter, we will provide an opportunity for you to reflect on your own process of development as a leader and a person. We begin by outlining a step-by-step process for discovering your personal vision. Next, we examine the elements of personal vision and self-reflection within each of the two axes of the growth roadmap developed earlier in the book. First, we explore the horizontal axis related to one's guiding principles, ranging between empowerment and a psychology of success and/or fear and a psychology of failure. Second, we examine the vertical axis related to the level of function and quality of intentionality with which one operates.

## What is a Transformative mindset?

A transformative mindset is simply an intention to do away with the self-limiting R's being used currently and being receptive to discovering more of the potential within us, our colleagues, and the students at our school. Then finding and applying the X's that are most likely to make that shift happen.

## Your Personal Vision for Your Life and Work

As we begin the process of creating a working personal vision, it is useful to recall our earlier examination as it related to the school-wide vision creation process. When examining individuals or institutions which we could characterize as vision-driven, we will recognize that they tend to process experience with a R->X->O sequence of thinking - references to actions to outcomes. Who they are and what they value/R's drive their actions/X's.

On a personal level we could interchange R->X->O with the words Be-Do-Have. Yet, if we listen closely to many personal and institutional narratives we hear the reverse, that is – since we are/my life is/my situation is, so..., then I have no choice but to do, react, cope in the ways I do, so...., then I/

we can be OK/successful. However, when we examine the ultimate results of a O->X->R or Have-Do-Be mode of operation we find that it is most often a formula for mediocrity, low quality, and unhappiness.

The operating assumption being made here is that no matter how widely unique and varied each of us is and how each personality, set of finger-prints, and life's mission is distinctive to each of us, our true calling will include being excellent and sharing our gifts with others. The process of moving up the pathway to excellence is inherently defined by an R->X->O orientation in which we start with cultivating high quality values and vision. Therefore, we might begin by seeking to better recognizing the high-quality references that are seeking to emerge from within us. Figure 14.1 offers a set of five universally limiting R's/reference and five universally elevating R's for your consideration.

Figure 14.1: Five limiting R/references and the Five Elevating R/references Regarding our Personal Growth and Success.

| Five Limiters of our Growth and Success | Five Elevators of our Growth and Success |
|---|---|
| **#1 – Seeing Yourself as a Victim.** A victim mindset is the antithesis of a leader mindset. When you start hearing yourselves say, "why aren't things (the way they are supposed to be)" or "why do I always have such bad luck with. . ." you need to stop and hear the victim ego running the show. Recognize, in truth, the only thing against you is your perception. | **#1 – Giving Yourself Permission to be Excellent.** How many excuses do you have running in your head for why you can't be great? Why not lose all those agreements with mediocrity and accept that it is Ok to be excellent. That is not conceit, ambition or projecting superiority, it is just you accepting your true gifts and potential. |
| **#2 – Being Run by Toxic Narratives.** Listen to how you talk to yourself and others. How do you finish the phrases "the students at this school are . . ." and "the teachers at this school are. . ." Or "my life is . . ." What kind of narratives do you hear? Narratives are when we make something conceptually solid in our thinking/R's. What are the narratives that you would like to R/run you? | **#2 – Tapping into Your Personal Vision and Sense of Purpose.** Do you have a sense of purpose that is at the core of who you are and why you make the choices you do? What is your picture of you and your school meeting its full potential? The more vivid that vision, the stronger your commitment will be and consequently your level of passion, resilience, energy, and clarity as well. |
| **#3 – Defaulting to Lower LOPs such as Cleverness and Coping.** Sometimes cleverness is useful and supports efficiently moving through life. But if it is a substitute for living from principles and a vision, it will lead to mediocrity and existence in the lower locations on the roadmap. We all need to cope, but do we ultimately have our eyes on the prize? | **#3 – Using All Experience for Growth and Learning.** Do you embody a growth-mindset? Avoid getting caught up in calling events either good or bad. They just happened and there is something to learn from them that will serve your growth and betterment. A grateful attitude is a powerful transformer. |

| | |
|---|---|
| **#4 – Approaching Things with a Win-lose/Me-they Mentality.** Winning over another person or a situation is mostly an illusion of the ego. When we beat someone, that losing energy is added to the overall mix of the whole as more negativity. So, the question "how can I make this better," is a much better question than "how can I win?" | **#4 – Acceptance and Not Taking Things Personally.** Spend an hour in high judgment of others and yourself – how does it feel in your body? Now try to just allow and give up the judgment – how do you feel? Non-acceptance is paralyzing. Acting from an accepting mindset you not only feel more alive but experience more freedom, intuitive, and confidence. Cultivating the skill of not taking things personally is enormously liberating. |
| **#5 – Neglecting your Body and Health.** When we neglect our bodies we lose integrity and perspective as well as decrease our effectiveness. When we disregard our bodies need for exercise, quiet, and good nutrition we increase the need to look externally for satisfaction and coping. Instead, take a walk, give yourself time to pay attention to your body's needs. If you are required to be sitting, check in with your body and heart periodically and take intentional breaths. Good health and the 1-Paradigm are best friends. | **#5 – Feeding Your Spirit and Level of Mindfulness.** When we get out of our small thinking and pull back into the vast infinite intelligence and the wonder in life, we find perspective. For you, is that mindfulness found in moments of silence and stillness, nature, prayer, meditation, a community/institution, books, or unconditional loving others? When we bring mindfulness to our work, we see more clearly the answers for how to move up our pathway most effectively. |

The references listed in each column do not come from the same part of your being. The higher-quality references arise from a truer and more aware aspect of yourself. The limiting references come mostly from your ego and the aspects of your unconscious that exist to defend your self-image. We can learn to develop the capacity to listen to one voice over the other.

## Exercise 14.1: Creating Your Own Personal Vision

Here you begin the process of creating a personal vision. There are many systems for going through such a process, but they will all inevitably involve a similar sequence of steps as is outlined here. It will benefit you to engage in this process periodically, as your vision will evolve over time.

### Step 1: Preparation and Getting in the Right Frame of Heart and Mind

Begin by disconnecting from all external distractions. Give you thinking a chance to quiet down. This may take some time. A useful strategy to support focus is to sit in a chair alone and away from any electronics (no TV, cell phone, computer, music with words, etc.) and get comfortable being alone with your thoughts. Have a pad of paper and a pen ready to write down ideas that emerge.

### Step 2: Listening to Your Inner Vision

Begin this stage by letting your mind relax and avoid "trying" to think. It will help to tune into an accepting mental space and let your goals and life situation subside for the time being. Feel into the reality that in the big picture you are accepted and fine the way that you are, and that life is basically good. Attending to nothing or only items from nature will be more conducive than looking at the objects in your work environment.

Give yourself 10 to 20 minutes to let the most immediate thoughts process. After a while you will start to access more fundamental thoughts. A vision wants to emerge from you. You just need to listen from the right place. Be patient and don't force the process. Assume that the first few thoughts will be less valid than those that will come a little later which will arise from that deeper and truer source.

When you feel like you are settled, and as though life is supportive, then ask yourself some questions.

- What am I here on this planet to do? What is my mission?

- What are my unique gifts? How could I best use them?

- What would I be doing and how would I be doing it, if I did what my heart (and truest self) was telling me to do?

- What are the most worthwhile goals and desires that want to emerge from me?

## Step 3: Writing Down What Comes to You

Write down what comes to you as you contemplate these questions and listen internally for the emerging vision for your life. It may be useful at this stage of the process to write down what you would call your R/principles. What are the few principles that you will use to guide your life and leadership? You may get ideas from the remaining pages of this chapter or the others but try to make these guiding principles as personal and subjective to you as possible. You will live them to the extent that they come from your heart (or you catch them as realizations) rather than merely a sense they *should* be valuable to you.

## Step 4: Classifying Your X's.

Now, reflect on the X aspect of your life and work. X's are all the actions, behaviors, habits, routines, patterns, and practices in and out of work, and ways of acting in which you currently have or might potentially engage in the future. As you reflect on your vision and values, you will better recognize each of these X's as being more or less consistent with whom you are becoming and that which will support your growth.

On a blank sheet of paper, draw a line down the middle and at the top label the two columns a) things I plan to keep doing, do more of, or do better, and b) things I need to do less of or not at all. As with all lists generated within this process, this one is likely to grow over time as more insights come to you.

This step in your personal vision setting process is the most important to your own growth. It will be similar in kind to the collective X classification exercises explained in earlier chapters (i.e., things you should see vs. things you should not see, or POS vs. POF practices) engaged in support of your school's growth process. Creating principles and goals/R's is profoundly valuable and important, and may be challenging, but changing behavior/X's is where the rubber meets the road. For your faculty, this process is as difficult as anything they are asked to do, and for you personally, it will test your self-discipline and commitment to excellence daily. Similar to the school-level process, your greatest personal improvement will likely come from the X's that you recognize as having been holding you down and that you will want to stop doing, even more than the improvement related X's that you identify as valuable additions.

### Step 5: Putting Your Desired O's into Perspective

The last step in this process is to examine the O's/Outcomes you would expect to occur from living consistently with the R's and X's you have committed to in the earlier steps. In this step, you are enhancing your vision with a practical representation of some of the ways that your commitment to your process values may out-picture. How will it look and feel as your vision becomes a reality?

It is critical to keep in mind that in your personal process or in the one that you are leading at your school, becoming too emotionally and egoically attached to the outcome will be counter-productive and limit your success. Emotional attachment to the result typically leads to frustration, having your head in the future, fearing failure, taking short-cuts, seeing people as a means to the end, and being unfaithful to your R's when it is convenient in the short-term, among other drawbacks.

We might simply ask the question, "If I were to be faithful and committed to my stated vision (my guiding personal R's) and improved plan of action (more of some X's and less of others), what kinds of outcomes would I expect to see?" There are logical effects from the causes that we are attempting to create. So, while we will want to give up the need to control or be too attached to them, the O's that result from our actions will provide some data for our personal data-driven decision making. Allowing ourselves to be open to potentially positive outcomes can also support an abundance vs. scarcity mindset.

## Exercise 14.2: Creating Your Own Personal Pathway on the Roadmap

As with our school's overall vision, we could place our own personal vision on the theoretical function and effectiveness roadmap (see Figure 14.2). In the following sections, we will examine both the horizontal and vertical axes introduced earlier in the book and explore how each relates to the various R's and X's which run our day to day lives. Reflect on where you are and where you are intending to go on this roadmap (or any other roadmap), you might consider a couple of questions. First, do you see common characteristics between your own personal path and the path of your school? Second, into which of the four roadmap quadrant paradigms do you find your thoughts and actions typically fitting?

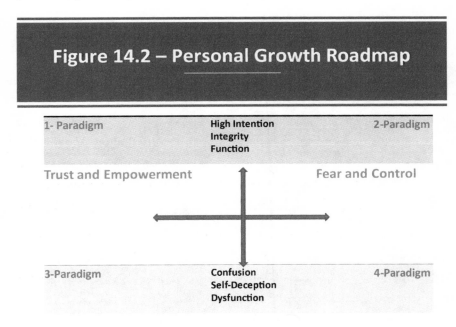

**Figure 14.2 – Personal Growth Roadmap**

| 1- Paradigm | High Intention Integrity Function | 2-Paradigm |

Trust and Empowerment — Fear and Control

| 3-Paradigm | Confusion Self-Deception Dysfunction | 4-Paradigm |

## Part I: Reflecting on the Horizontal Axis

In this activity, you are given the opportunity to examine your personal situation, your current R's and X's, and your intentions in life from the lens of the horizontal axis, defined as being either trust- or fear-driven. This exercise may feel the most emotionally challenging. It will be tempting to want to jump to judgment, denial, comparison and/or defensiveness. Avoid this pull and embrace the opportunity for honest self-exploration. It is said that our true selves are more consistent with who we want to be than who we are today. As you read and reflect try to listen to what your inner best self is telling you, and attempt to show self-acceptance of your current patterns of action.

Figure 14.3 revisits Figure 4.2, introduced in Chapter four. The content has been modified to reflect the focus of this chapter which is the personal rather than the institutional. For each of the various dimensions of this axis, questions are offered which characterize either end of the continuum. Reflect on each question and explore what your answers reveal about where your R's and X's are currently, and what they imply about moving forward.

Figure 14.3: The Elements of the Horizontal Axis: Personal Questions to Ask ourselves to determine our Current Location on this dimension at any Point

| | Toward Empowerment | Mixed Motivation | Toward Control |
|---|---|---|---|
| Ethic | Empowerment – Does my positive intention project outward toward others? | Am I aware of my intention or do I let the situation dictate? | Control – Do I mistrust others and feel as if I need to try to manipulate them into doing what I want? |
| Emotion | Trust – Do I feel open to possibility and trust myself and others? | Do I enter the room with a preconceived notion of how everyone will act? | Fear – Do I come into the room with a ready defense or a pervasive self-doubt? |
| Who is it about? | Those I serve – Do I see myself as a servant of the common good? | Do I try only when I feel the love and shut it down when I feel unsupported? | Me – Am I primarily in self-interest or self-preservation mode? |
| Relationships | Connection – When I look around, do I mostly see people seeking the same basic things I do? | Do I assume there are people who understand me and others who just don't? | Comparison – Is what I see mostly people who are inadequate by my standards? |
| Psychology promoted by R's and X's | Psychology of Success (POS) Am I guided by a mindset defined by an internal locus of control, a sense of belonging, and a growth-orientation? | Am I a mixture of both POS and POF R's and X's? | Psychology of Failure (POF) – Am I guided by a mindset defined by an external LOC, a sense of alienation, and a fixed-ability orientation? |

## Reflecting on Our Personal Psychology – POS or POF

In this section, we will explore each of the three components of the psychology of success (POS). You will be guided to reflect on each in terms of your current R's and X's as well as the R's and X's that define your personal vision and desired location on the roadmap. The key to deriving value from this process will be your ability to be honest with yourself. Most people will abstractly agree that having the qualities of a POS is more desirable than those of a POF. In one's intellect, one can readily appreciate that we want an internal locus of control (LOC), a sense of belonging, and a growth orientation. But as you examine the ideas and questions below, ask yourself, "What is the honest truth in my conscious and unconscious thinking related to these three areas?"

## I.A: Where is our Locus of Control (LOC)?

Do we feel like we are authoring our own lives, or is life happening to us? Our answer to this question is likely quite context specific. But we can ask, what are we cultivating as a habit? As we are well aware, we can only control ourselves. But do we take 100% responsible for the actions of that self? Do we have a friendly relationship with cause and effect, the natural laws that govern things, and do we experience life as basically supportive? Or do we feel like we spend a lot of time resisting and battling something outside of us?

In figure 14.1, a victim mindset was listed as the #1 limiting factor to our success for good reason. It not only defines an external LOC, it defines all elements of a POF. There is no need to feel shame when you recognize an external LOC arising within you. It happens to everyone and is the norm for most people. But as you become more skilled at identifying that victim voice arising in you, it will increasingly weaken its power. Start by holding a clear intention to a) not validate it or internally defend it, and b) just listening for the victim narrative and then c) when we hear it, acknowledge it for what it is, and then bring in an internal (truer) LOC message (see examples below). Moreover, it is useful to recognize that all external LOC thoughts are just perceptions we have created in our minds and do not reflect any true reality.

To build our internal LOC and cultivate a more accurate and true perspective, it is useful to take ownership of our internal narrative. Here are some useful (self-talk, affirmation, grounding) questions to help us support the development of our internal LOC.

- Am I taking 100% responsible for my thinking and action right now?
- What is important NOW?
- My thinking is making me feel the way I feel at this moment. Is it in need of an adjustment?
- If I want different O's, how do my R's and X's need to change?

**Reflection 14.1: Energy and Locus of Control**

It is logical to think of the level of effort and energy that we have to put into our lives as a fixed quantity. Reflecting on your own experience, you will recognize that it is not really the case. Considering how your LOC is involved is helpful. Think of how much effort it takes to make others happy, be concerned if you are liked, worrying about if what you are doing will be judged as adequate to others. Now think of how much effort it takes to get into a project that you like and care about, or sharing your gifts with others, or undertake an adventure. What did you notice as you compared the two types of conditions? When we are attempting to please, acting out of a sense of obligation, or proving our adequacy, it is depleting. When we are sharing our gifts, are in the flow of the game and/or creating, we feel more vital.

## Reflection 14.2: Don't Apologize for Speaking Honestly

Do you make excuses or spend a lot of time defending your actions, hemming and hawing, and apologizing for what you know to be true? Try this exercise. Pretend that you are listening to someone else who is doing one or more of those things. What would you say to them? That's right. You would tell them to stop apologizing. So, take your own advice. Being open, flexible, willing to change, and/or providing explanations for our reasoning behind an action is not the same as projecting guilt or the fear of rejection. So, the more we operate from a POS, the more we can express from honesty, confidence, and self-authority.

Embodying internal LOC is also related to our level of personal integrity, follow-through, and sticking to our word. It is important to recognize how we act when we are a) embodying a vision-driven leader, or b) acting out of a "pleaser" mindset. Feeling compelled to be nice is externally focused and repressive. Living from integrity and vision is internal and freeing.

When negativity arises within us and/or within our school, it is very often the result of inaction – in the form of procrastination, denial, not wanting to follow-through, fear of creating temporary unhappiness, rationalizing and the like. The result is often an unwanted condition that our inner voice recognized as needing to be addressed but was put off until later. The negative condition likely increased and was then compounded by our own sense of shame for not living up to our higher principles by acting when we knew we should have. Solution – be proactive and do not delay action if possible. Find the courage that is there in your best self to embody the transformative leader you are.

A final thought: As one observes the leaders that we tend to respect the most, we find that they are humble and honor the service of others. They readily take responsibility for failures and give away credit for successes. Logically this may not make complete sense, but in operational and socio-political terms, we find that doing those two things has the effect of projecting a POS and raising one's respect level.

## I.B: At What Level is Our Feeling of Acceptance and Belonging?

Success in and out of the leadership role starts with self-acceptance. Likewise, the ability to have a genuinely accepting attitude toward others is strongly inter-related and exceedingly valuable as well. Of course, cultivating this mindset is a challenging aspect of anyone's growth journey requiring constant attention. When feelings of self-judgment, inadequacy, and being in over our heads emerge, we need to work with them. Again, recognizing that they are just thoughts is a great place to start. In addition, we will want to avoid a few dysfunctional solutions, beginning with denial. Denial leads to personal dis-integration and to neglecting important physical and emotional needs and information. Likewise, conjuring favorable comparisons to less effective leaders may make us feel a little better temporarily, but in the end comparison is a losing battle. Similarly, seeking constant confirmation from others is rooted in insecurity and POF. External validation may be comforting for a short while, but in the end, it is no substitute for liking, trusting, and valuing ourselves.

Better and more solid sources of self-acceptance will arise from an appreciation of the following:

- The unique talents you bring to your job, commitments, friends, and family.
- Your sincere interest in the success of the school and the welfare of the students.
- Your commitment to being prepared and doing your best.
- The benefits to the school when it accomplishes the improvements that you envision.
- Your basic goodness, decency, and intention for the highest good.

It is helpful to recognize that all leaders have felt deep inadequacy at some time. We are human. We can by definition only do the best we can do. So, avoid perfectionism or getting caught up in winning. It will only lead to fear and stress. And stress is always a sign there is a lack of self-acceptance. So do not confuse your pursuit of excellence with the goal of perfection. Excellence is trusting, integrated, and process oriented. Perfection, based in a fear of failure, is a concept in our heads/egos, and is inherently outcome oriented.

Cultivating a sense of belonging is rarely easy. But a great place to start is to work on your ability to accept, like and feel compassion for others - your family, friends, colleagues, and students. Your attitudes about them will show and will define your ability to relax and enjoy your work. Another universally valuable orientation is gratitude. When we look out at our school with a sense of gratitude, our feelings of acceptance and belonging are heightened.

Our best results here will likely come from asking ourselves guiding questions such as the following:

- How can I be more accepting of those with whom I work?
- Can I see the best in others and be less judgmental?
- Can I see the whole school community as a unit and feel a sense of belonging and liking for everyone, and not just those with whom it is easy to work?
- Can I find reasons to be grateful right now? And can I feel grateful for no reason?

The life of a leader can be lonely. Few people outside the job understand the politics, the stresses, and the challenges involved. Moreover, in the role of leader, we need to make difficult decisions which can, at times, inevitably distance us from the teachers and staff. The more responsibility we obtain the fewer friends we might seem to have.

Leadership in a dynamic improvement effort represents distinct challenges when compared to contexts in which there is a status quo. In a static condition (a school, family, or any group that is comfortable staying in the same patterns over time), acceptance of the existing R's, X's and O's is less difficult. We can bond over anything which helps us feel commonality – complaining, small talk, sports, likes and dislikes, others who are not part of our group, etc. Belonging is relatively easier to cultivate. In contrast, within a condition defined by the goal of improvement and growth - where there is a transformative vision and an emerging definition of quality – sources of commonality can be more difficult to find, and sources of potential separation can increase. When change for the better is the order of the day, those leading that effort cannot, by definition, validate all the existing R's and X's. Decisions must be made which disrupt the status quo, producing perceived winners and losers, and as a result divisions and resentments. Those in the role of encouraging growth will often be called to acts of "tough love." There is never an easy answer when there are no absolutes involved, but it can be helpful in cases where we feel conflicted to ask ourselves the question, "what needs to be done for the long-term greater good of all?" We might also phrase it as, "What is the most loving action I can take in this situation?" And see what answers emerge.

Finally, when a leader is in the role of change agent, they need to find a delicate balance between creating a team of allies/advisors and minimizing the perception that it is a clique of insiders who have special privileges. But we do need a team, allies, and others with whom we can process ideas. We will also need to surround ourselves with positive energy.

Ask yourself, what has a grounding effect on you? Looking around at all the students who attend the school to pursue a better life? Engaging in genial conversations with the janitor? Appreciating a flower outside of your office window? Recognize the need to give yourself permission to keep boundaries between yourself and those who tend to have a toxic effect on you. You owe people your honesty and service, but not access to your inner-being, guilt strings, or dignity. Your sense of inner peace hinges on the quality of your thinking, so loving and respecting yourselves is job one.

## Reflection 14. 3: Recognizing Patterns of Resistance

It may seem like a paradox, but we can confirm in our experience that the life conditions that we resist, dislike, avoid, and complain about tend to persist. Oppositional energy tends to keep things in place. So, if we want to make a change, the place to start is to let go of the internal resistance to it. We still take action to make the change, but we can do that without making the situation or person "bad."

Can you think of any example of this from your experience?

## I.C: Are Our R's and X's in Life Defined more by a Fixed or Growth-Oriented Mindset?

We are confronted with the choice to use either a growth or fixed ability orientation dozens even hundreds of times each day. Leaders cannot model a growth mindset to those they lead if they do not have it deeply embedded in their own personal R's, just as the teachers at the school cannot model it to their students if it is lacking in them. So it starts with us. And that means it starts with our own self-examination.

A great first step is to recognize the difference between a growth and fixed-ability mindset. Then, we need to internalize a growth mindset into our being, unconscious R's, and day-to-day actions/X's. We need to conceive clearly what a growth mindset looks like operationally. No matter what we might assume we believe about ourselves, we can always learn what we genuinely believe by observing what we do (i.e., our R's, translated into X's).

Your honest answers to the questions below will help you recognize where you are solid as well as where you need to grow related to your level of growth mindset:

- Do you trust the quality processes to which you are committed, or do you bale out and take short-cuts when you feel threatened?

- Are you persistent when challenges arise, or do you start hearing a (fixed-ability) "I'm not good enough" voice coming in?

- Do you find yourself trusting that you are learning important lessons even if the path is not perfectly predicable, or do you find yourself fearing failure if things get a little uncharted?
- Do you learn from your mistakes and move on, or do you obsess about what you should have done differently?
- Are you driven by the desire for safety and the sure thing, or do you take risks that are likely to improve things (but not 100% assured)? Great leaders are risk takers.

Brian Tracy in his series the Psychology of Achievement (2002) provides wise perspective on worry and fear of failure. He suggests that if you find yourself fearing an undesirable outcome take the following three steps, 1) imagine the worst-case scenario, 2) resolve to accept it and recognize that you *could* live with it, and then 3) go about taking the actions necessary to ensure that a positive outcome becomes the ultimate result.

> "The desire for safety stands against every great and noble enterprise." —*Tacitus*

As you increasingly cultivate a POS and internalize it into the R's that guide your day-to-day actions you can expect to feel the resulting clarity, ease, and confidence of a person living in integrity. And, doing so will inevitably encourage your movement both over to the empowerment end of the horizontal continuum as well as to the more intentional levels of the vertical axis. Moreover, it is useful to keep in mind that the goal and the process to get there have the same nature. Just as with our school improvement effort, the essence of the destination and that of the process are consistent. When we do 1-Paradigm, we actualize the 1-Paradigm.

---

### Reflection 14.4: Dealing with Worst Case Scenarios

Think of a situation in which you currently fear something undesirable might happen. Engage Tracy's 3 steps and see if you feel less anxiety than before.

---

## Part II: Reflecting on the Vertical Axis and Dominant Use of the Levels of Perception (LOPs)

Recalling Chapter three, the vertical axis of the function and improvement roadmap deals with our level of intention, function and which of the levels of perception (LOPs) we operate from most regularly. As you engage in this reflective process, see if you can gain more clarity of your most essential intentions? Function will always follow high quality R's and X's, therefore, grounding ourselves in quality-promoting R's will be a valuable place to focus our attention. Consequently, engaging in the vision clarification process, described in part of this chapter, will be a powerful way to encourage your movement up this axis.

We might also periodically ask ourselves a few questions to explore what might be limiting our progress up our roadmap. They include:

- Where have I been holding back, instead of being true to the excellence that wants to emerge in me?

- What unnecessary baggage do I carry around that is holding me down?

- What would it take to be more receptive to the vision that wants to pull me up the pathway?

Figure 14.4

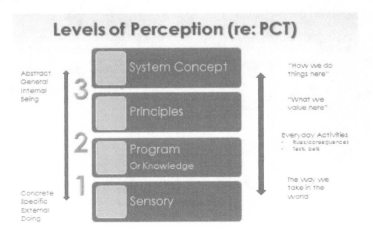

Using the concept of the levels of perception (LOPs; Powers, 1973) introduced in Chapter 5 (Figure 5.4), we can reflect on the kinds of thinking that are most prominent in our minds during the day (See Figure 14.4). The four LOP's are – starting from bottom to top – sensory/reactive, program, principle, and system and relate to what kinds of processes we are using to interpret and act in the world at any time. We are working with all LOPs all the time, but it is instructive to be aware of which levels are defining our thinking and action most of the time, or at any moment? When we use our higher levels of perception – system and principles, our lives reflect more intention and as a result higher quality. When we get too stuck in living from a routine (program) and operate in a reactive mode, we can lose touch with our vision and values. The more successful we are at operating from higher LOP's, the more expansive our awareness, and thus, the more capacity to be effective on multiple levels.

Let's examine each LOP from top to bottom, with the use of questions representing the concerns at each level. Your answers should offer some insight as to where you are operating most of the time.

**System level (What R's and X's are we systematizing into our lives?)**

- Am I being true to who I am and my sense of mission and purpose?
- Am I being true to what wants to emerge from me?
- How much do I feel like I am aligned and integrated and not having to compartmentalize?
- Do I trust my intuition and gut instincts?
- What are the narratives running my life?

**Principle level (What are the values guiding me?)**

- Are my highest values apparent in my personal vision and my work?
- Do I have a clear sense of my priorities?
- Do I find it easy to be honest?
- Do I live from more of a POS or POF?

Or

- Do I have trouble being honest with myself or others?

- Do I have trouble making decisions or keeping commitments?

- Do I have trouble clarifying my priorities?

**Program level (What has become routine and habitual?)**

- Do I find routines that keep me from getting lost in the minutia of life and the job?

- Do I create healthy habits which promote living from my principles?

- Am I disciplined in how I make my high-quality X's a seamless part of my day?

Or

- Do I find ways to rationalize not doing what I have committed to?

- Do I find that I have developed patterns that help me just get through the day and cope?

- Do I just do what "works" in the short-term without reflecting on the long-term implications or how it fits with my vision and values?

---

**Reflection 14.5 Where Are My LOPs?**

If your primary internal thought as you read this chapter is that it all seems overly difficult and you are looking for clever short-cuts requiring less actual growth, it is a good bet that your life and work will tend to hover at the program level. Instead of feeling judged and rejecting the opportunities presented in the chapter, consider starting with one or two ideas and working with those. Also, what is the voice of your "best self" telling you?

**Sensory/Reactive level (How do I interpret and respond to my physical and emotional sensations?)**

- Do I feel pretty relaxed and at ease during the day?
- Do I pay attention to how my body is feeling and what it is telling me?
- Do I find myself laughing some on most days?
- Do I see the positive as well as areas of potential improvement as I circulate the school?

Or

- Do I tend to ignore my body as it is inconvenient to listen to what it is telling me?
- Do I feel a lot of distress during the day?
- Do I feel overly serious at home or work?
- Do I eat or drink too much to make up for a lack of satisfaction in other areas?

As you reflect on these questions you will naturally elevate your position on this axis. Usually, you will not have to think too hard for an answer, just asking yourself the questions can lead to more clarity of intention, and as a result more effectiveness.

---

**Reflection 14.6: Sharing Insights with Allies**

What did you find as you reflected on the questions for each level? It might be useful to pick one or two areas at a time on which to focus. Sharing the areas you have committed to improving with is trustworthy colleague or friend can enhance and deepen the process. But only share with someone who respects the Importance of your journey shares your commitment to growth.

---

## Part III: Your Personal Pathway

The more clearly we see our current mental and emotional processing patterns the better we can appreciate that, like our school, we are on a journey on a pathway. The better we become at accessing (i.e., hearing or seeing) the personal vision that wants to emerge, the more we will find a clarity of intention. We are on our own pathway heading toward being more of our true self, guided by our vision.

Figure 14.5 outlines the concept of the four quadrants used throughout the book and relates them to one's personal narratives. While we all need to find the map that makes the most sense to us and functions best to encourage us, these quadrants offer a parallel framework to connect our personal assessment and improvement process to the one applied to our school's collective journey. Engaging our personal growth along a similar trajectory to the one that we are leading in our school has several benefits. These include, consistency of guiding R's/values, the ability to apply insights and breakthroughs across domains, and a well-conceived definition of "better" which works as both process as well as destination. And akin to our school's effort the movement up and over leads to a more natural and enjoyable condition.

As you examine Figure 14.5, reflect on where you would currently place your guiding R's. Where could you stretch yourself to better embody a 1-Paradigm leader?

## Figure 14.5 Quadrants Relating to One's Personal Experience

|  | Trust and Empowerment | Fear and Control |
|---|---|---|
| **Function, Intention and Effectiveness** | *1-Paradigm Personal R's*<br><br>*Pulled by a vision of Excellence*<br><br>I define success as emergent quality within the collective.<br><br>I trust the high-quality processes I have found. The more I trust and focus on refining the process the better the outcomes.<br><br>Others are basically good if I let myself see them clearly. Everyone is on their own journey and is trying to get their needs met.<br><br>I can feel a movement to a self-evident natural condition which feels internally right. Overall life is improving. | *2-Paradigm personal R's*<br><br>*Working hard to make it happen*<br><br>I need to do whatever it takes to win<br><br>I make it happen with effort, telling, selling, and policy. It mostly "works" for me.<br><br>Others tend to be helpful one moment and then let me down the next. If others were a little better, my life would be better.<br><br>I feel like I am having to work hard to keep everything together and working correctly, with moments of success and relief. |
| **Dysfunction, Accidentalness, and Ineffectiveness** | *3-Paradigm Personal R's*<br><br>*Letting life happen to me*<br><br>One can't ever really win in the end.<br><br>There is really not a lot anyone can do to make things better.<br><br>Others are doing their own thing. Who am I to judge? We all have to do what works for us.<br><br>I feel like I must rely on myself and can't really relate to any definition of universal good or "the right way." | *4-Paradigm Personal R's*<br><br>*In opposition to a resistant world*<br><br>I win and you lose<br><br>If you don't take to the offense, you will get run over by the system and all the predators out there.<br><br>Others tend to be mostly confused, brainwashed, prejudice, losers, etc. if they were smart, they would see how great I am and respect me.<br><br>I feel like life is a struggle against so many oppositional forces, and overall, the world seems to be getting progressively worse. |

To promote our personal and institutional growth processes, self-honesty must be a fundamental element/R. Pretending to be something we are not is stressful and requires a great deal of impression management. If we are not clear-sighted about our current patterns, and workings of our inner world, we can miss valuable opportunities for learning. Therefore, be patient and honest with yourself. Any moment defined by honest self-awareness is success. Place growth over appearances.

Embrace the vision of a better future for both yourself and your school. That vision exists not so much as a wish but a concrete reality that is wanting to actualize as the future. The potential is already loaded in the equation. But success requires will and a transformative mindset (and leadership) to active it.

## CONCLUSION

As an educational leader, you have been given a rare opportunity to both make a profound difference in the lives of others and to use that vehicle to grow into a more evolved and capable human being. In this chapter, we have examined a series of exercises to support your growth. You are encouraged to revisit the process of personal vision setting, and the other reflective activities on a regular basis. You will find that your vision and level of consciousness evolves and refines over time.

As you encourage the journey of growth at our school up the roadmap, keep in mind that a quality journey is the goal. In fact, a school which embraces a sincere, student-centered, growth process is, by definition, existing in the 1-Paradigm. Work inspired by the values of growth, empowerment and quality cannot fail, and will inevitably move up the roadmap. Skilled and self-aware transformative leadership can accelerate that process significantly.

## REFERENCES:

Dweck, C (2006) Mindset: A new psychology of success. New York, Random House.

Powers, William T. (1973). *Behavior: The control of perception.* Chicago: Aldine de Gruyter.

Shindler, J. (2009) Transformative Classroom Management: Positive Strategies to engage all learners and promote a psychology of success. Jossey Bass. San Francisco, CA.

Tracy, B (2002) *Psychology of Achievement*. Berrett-Koehler Publishers.

# APPENDIX A:

## Facilitating the POS/POF Classification Exercise

This appendix outlines the process of leading a group of educators through an activity in which they classify practices using the three factors of a psychology of success (POS). The activity is suitable at any time but is especially useful for clarifying the aims of the school related to aspirational practice, defining the 1-Paradigm, and what it means to use high quality X's. The activity is also available on the ASSC website as a PowerPoint presentation.

**Pre-Task:**

1. Prepare the following materials –

    a. chart paper with a adhesive back or tape if paper has no adhesive.

    b. packs of colored markets (see necessary colors)

    c. copies of a POS handout for each group

2. Create space on the walls to put up the posters being created.

3. Arrange tables or desks as group workstations.

4. Download the POS activity ppt slides from the ASSC website.

5. As the leader, you will want to have read Chapter four of TLR and have developed a solid understanding of the factors of a psychology of success.

### Step One: Explain the Task and each of Factors

To begin the process, explain to the group the purpose and the eventual product of the activity. The purpose will be to better recognize the relationship between teacher practices and the psychological orientations which are produced as a result. The product will be 6 posters reflecting the brainstorming efforts of the 6 group – one poster each for each of the 3 elements of a POS x 2, 1) for things teachers do that promote the quality and 2) for things teachers do that undermine the quality. Explain that the activity will take the form of a graffiti exercise in which the chart paper will move/transfer and the groups will stay in place. Provide each group with access to either a paper or electronic explanation of the three factors of POS.

Sub-factors for the Theoretical Construct of Psychology of Success (POS)

| Psychology of Success (POS) | Psychology of Failure (POF) |
|---|---|
| Internal Locus of Control | External Locus of Control |
| Belonging & Acceptance | Alienation and Worthlessness |
| Growth- Orientation | Fixed-Ability Orientation |

## Step Two: Place Participants into Six Groups

Six groups should be created numbering between 2 and 7 members. When possible, it is best to randomly assign participants into the 6 groups. If the overall number of participants is small (i.e., @12) two persons per group will create the correct arrangement. If the group is medium sized, simply numbering off by 6 will work best. But if the group is larger than 40, it will be necessary to create 12 or 18 groups (factors of 6) (with 3-7 members) so that sufficient involvement is possible for each member of each group. In that case, groups would have duplicate functions, which is fine (i.e., 2+ groups would take the role of group 1, for example).

1. Internal LOC – promoting (red)

2. Internal LOC – Undermining (blue)

3. Acceptance and Belonging (green)

4. Acceptance and Belonging–Undermining (orange)

5. Growth Orientation promoting (purple)

6. Fixed Orientation promoting (brown)

6 Groups: Starting Point

### Step Three: Give Directions

Once groups have been created, instruct one member from each group to collect a sheet of chart paper and a pen of the correct color (see slide above, for example, Group 1 would need to collect a red pen, Group 2 blue, etc.). Do this before giving the formal directions.

Group Exercise: Graffiti Model

▶ **Directions**
  ○ Random assignment
  ○ Everyone has same role
  ○ 3 minutes per station
  ○ Chart paper and pens (different color for each group)
  ○ Chart moves, groups stay
  ○ Groups present synthesis

Once everyone is settled in, give the directions very clearly one more time.

1. Instruct each group to place a heading on their chart paper corresponding to their initial task. For example, Group 1 will place the heading – Promotes Internal Locus of Control, Group 2 would write Undermines Internal Locus of Control, and so on. Be sure that members know that the ideas of 6 groups will be represented on each sheet of paper and so not to write too large, but large enough to read from a distance later.

2. All groups will stay in place.

3. You will always use the same pen color.

4. You will want to find a flat surface to write upon. Individual tables are best.

5. Brainstorm each idea for 3 minutes. And then pass your chart and get the next one.

6. You will be given a signal and a 30 second warning before you pass.

7. You will always pass to the same group – group 1 to group 2, group 2 to group 3, … group 6 back to group 1, etc.

8. Your job is to brainstorm as many ideas as you can which characterize the title on your paper. For example, group 1 will ask themselves, "What do teachers do that promotes his/her students' internal locus of control?" (As leader, help them appreciate that the brainstorming process gets easier as time goes on and they get into a flow mind).

## Steps Four: Engage Groups into 3 Minutes X 6 Iterations Task

Ask for questions, and then check the time. When everyone is ready let them get started on their first poster. Encourage them to talk within the group and try to keep your leader input to a minimum. The exception is if a group is struggling with the task, you will want to re-clarify the directions and potentially offer an initial idea for their chart. Be positive and encouraging. Allow the process to pick up momentum. Near the end of the 3 minutes (you may want to speed up or slow down the process depending on the needs and the energy in the room), provide the 30 second warning. Then, when the time is up, give a clear signal to stop. Restate the directions to pass posters to the correct next group (and stay in their spot). And remind them to keep their pen for all their posters. They will be able to see their contribution on each poster by color.

Repeat this process 5 more times.

When all groups have completed their last iteration (all groups have contributed to all posters), have them place their poster in order on the wall (it is best to line posters up by group number - 1, 2, 3, 4, 5 and 6, in order).

## Step Five: Groups Synthesize their original topic and share it with Whole Group

When all the posters have found their way to the wall, instruct the groups to find their original poster (the one they titled). Their task is to synthesize the contents of the poster and share it with the whole group in a one-minute presentation. Give the groups 3-5 minutes to discuss the essential content and identify key ideas to highlight from the poster they will be presenting.

## Step Six: Debrief the Process

Instruct each group in turn to present their synthesis of their poster and what they found to be key insights. Once all groups have presented, engage the whole group in a discussion. It does not need to be structured. However, these are helpful questions to illicit deeper reflection from the participants.

1. What are your initial thoughts as you examine each of the posters?

2. Is there anything on the psychology of failure posters that we need to do?

3. In other words, could we choose to do either all POS or all POF practices?

4.   If it is mostly (or all a choice), then why does anyone choose to use the POF practices that you have listed here?

5.   If there was a student whom you really loved, and you knew that they were either going into a) a class where the teacher used mostly POS practices, or b) a class where it was mostly POF practices, what would you do to influence the outcome? Why do you care?

6.   What if the POF teacher told you it was just their style, how would you react?

Also, you might point out some of the specific content and ask those who put it there to explain why they did so. This process can expand the time needed for the activity greatly.

## Appendix A.1: Psychology of Success - Terms Defined in more Detail.

**Growth vs. Fixed-Ability Orientation**. Carol Dweck (2000; 2006) and her colleagues in their research over the course of 30 years have developed a very useful paradigm with which to examine academic self-concept, achievement, and motivation. They have demonstrated in a series of studies with students that future success is not as much the result of talent (i.e., fixed-ability factors) or current level of ability, as it is the result of the orientation/cognitive strategy one uses to approach learning tasks (i.e., a growth mindset). Dweck offers a useful lens for distinguishing two contrasting cognitive strategies for feeling competent and how over time they have dramatically different results. When a student uses a growth orientation they view a situation as an opportunity to learn and grow. They do not see their performance within a situation as a measure of their innate ability as much as a measure of their investment – better results requires more practice. Students who approached tasks with a fixed-ability orientation viewed the context as a reflection of how much ability they innately possessed in that area. The result is a student who is looking for situations that will not challenge their fragile self-image or make them feel "dumb." Dweck found that students with a growth pattern were more likely to persist in the face of failure and experience higher levels of academic achievement.

In general, a growth orientation or growth R comes from being encouraged toward learning process goals vs. performance and outcome goals, getting recognition and feedback related to effort rather than ability, being encouraged to take risks and then recognizing that feeling challenged is a positive experience, and VIPs communicating a growth vs. fixed view of intelligence and ability.

**Acceptance and Belonging vs. Alienation and Worthlessness.** This second factor within the framework for a POS reflects the degree to which any member feels connected, wanted and part of the group and the degree to which one likes and accepts oneself. The more one feels connected, accepted and acceptable, the more one will be able to express oneself, act authentically, and be fully present to others (Osterman, 2000).

In general, a sense that we are accepted, acceptable and a valued part of the collective comes from non-competitive contexts in which comparisons are minimized, accepting messages from VIPs (including self-talk), practicing a positive approach and attitude, experiencing emotional safety, and feeling part of a community, being part of collective successes, and being recognized for making a unique contribution to the collective good.

**Internal vs. External Locus of Control.** The third factor in the construct of POS is defined by one's sense of internal causality and orientation toward personal responsibility. The more internal locus of control (LOC) we possess, the more we feel that our destiny is in our own hands. It could be contrasted to an external LOC or an orientation that views *cause* as an external factor and one in which life "happens to us." An internal locus of control can be defined as the belief that one is the author of his or her own fate. An internal locus of control comes from having a causal understanding of behavior and effect. Another term we could use for internal locus of control is "personal empowerment."

In general, the development of an internal LOC R comes from recognizing (on our own or with the assistance of others) that our actions result in consequences, seeing cause and effect relationships related to success and failure, being given freedom, power, and control with an expectation of using them responsibly, and being generally empowered and trusted.

# APPENDIX B:

# Contrasting the Four Roadmap Paradigms Across a Series of School Phenomena

| | School Paradigm | | | |
|---|---|---|---|---|
| | 1-Paradigm Empowering School Environment | 2-Paradigm Orderly, Predictable, Effective School Environment | 3-Paradigm Dysfunctional Amorphous School Environment | 4-Paradigm Dysfunctional Coercive School Environment |
| **Essential Questions** | Has a POS been consciously honored for all teachers and all students? Are discussions and decisions primarily made at the systemic and principle levels? | Have we successfully followed the directions we have been given? | Are the teachers happy and do they feel good about their work? | Did you do what the principal told you to do today? |
| **Principal** | The principal is a leader and facilitator rather than a manager. He/she is focused on empowering others to develop an internal locus of control. He/she refers to the school as "our school." | The principal is a manager and is focused on policies and procedures. He/she refers to the school as "my school." | The principal abdicates power and passively allows the teachers to do what they think is best. He/she refers to the school as "our school." | The principal retains all power, is autocratic, reactive and may direct unpredictably. He/she creates a hostile work environment. He/she refers to the school as "my school." |
| **Vision** | School is Vision-Driven based on references at the systemic and principle level; consideration is given to developing the whole child rather than just developing the intellect. | School is Driven by Programs the goal of which is to improve standardized testing scores | There is no school vision. | School is Driven by whatever the leader wants on any given day |
| **Strategic Planning** | The principal proactively leads the faculty and staff to articulate shared references, expected practices and intended outcomes. Use of R-X-O format | The principal and maybe a few teacher leaders create an action plan to include achievement targets and expected teacher practices. The principal directs its implementation. 0-X thinking. | There is no written action plan. | There is no written action plan. Do what the principal tells you to do today. Process is usually a formality for external accountability. |
| **Participation with Decision Making** | The principal proactively empowers all stakeholders to participate in school-level decision-making. | The principal and maybe a few teacher leaders control school-level decision-making. | There is no established process for school-wide decision-making. | The principal makes all decisions and expects obedience. |
| **Process for Deciding Instructional Implementation** | Problem solving for implementation is based on principles. Coherence among references, practices and outcomes is maintained. | Problem solving for implementation is based on practices which improve test scores. | Problem solving for implementation is individual by each teacher and reactionary and depends on what happens from day-to-day | Problem solving for implementation is non-existent. |

| | | | |
|---|---|---|---|
| Curriculum and Instruction | The principal creates the environment and sometimes facilitates the process of teachers designing instruction which includes strategies for a Psychology of Success. Teachers examine the underlying principles of their content. Often include are the higher levels of Bloom's Taxonomy, the design of authentic problems and student-led instruction. | Content and pedagogy are predetermined by the adopted program. Most, if not all, lessons are teacher-directed. | Content and pedagogy vary day-by-day determined by each individual teacher. | There is no plan for specific content and pedagogy, but without prior notice, the principal might direct the teacher to make changes to his/her instruction. |
| Supervision of Instruction | Leaders individualize their instructional supervision depending on the degree to which teachers have created a style-1 classroom. Supervision leads to an internal locus of control and growth orientation among all teachers and to skill making pedagogical decisions based on principles. | Leaders supervise well so that teachers implement programs as designed. | The leader does not supervise any implementation of instructional decisions since these are made individually by each teacher. | The principal supervises instruction through intimidation |
| Teacher Evaluations | The principal and teachers together design the evaluation system. It includes strong components of self and peer assessment. | Using the district designed evaluation system, the principal implements it with fidelity. | Teachers typically are formally not evaluated. | The principal may or may not decide to evaluate the teachers. The evaluation will reflect the opinion the principal has of the teachers and not be based on a predictable policy or procedure. |
| Trust & Communication | Administrators, faculty and staff trust one another; together they have created shared norms for communication. Communication is open and nonjudgmental and leads to innovations. All faculty and staff practice behaviors described in the Psychology of Success. Faculty members may have different references, but those differences are discussed and analyzed openly. | Communication might be about how best to implement. Faculty members trust one another to follow through on commitments. | Communication among the adults varies day to day. It may address educational issues randomly. | There is no trust between the leader and the faculty and communication is top-down and directive. The general feel at the school matches the Psychology of Failure. |

| | | | | |
|---|---|---|---|---|
| **Psychology of Success** | The principal understands the elements of POS and intentionally creates an environment reflective of it for all adults and children. | POS is not addressed. | A sense of belonging is in evidence. | The Psychology of Failure is very much in evidence. |
| **Professional Community** | Communal bonds exist among the adults; each one contributing to the benefit of the whole. | Staff members are willing to follow rules to benefit the whole but there is not a sense of contribution to the group. | Social bonds may exist among various staff members; there is no sense of professional group identity. | There is no professional group identity. There are minimal social bonds among staff members; there may be a group choosing to coalesce and rebel. |
| **Professional Development** | Administrators, faculty and staff members each take responsibility for knowing their own strengths and needs and seeking the best methods for their own growth. Group PD is needs-based and most often led by teachers but can be led by the administrator or outside consultant. | Administrators, faculty and staff members attend professional development as directed by school or district leadership. Teachers are well trained to implement adopted programs with fidelity. | Some teachers may choose to attend professional development but there is no overall plan or expectation. | Professional Development may take place depending on the direction of the principal. |

# APPENDIX C:

## Leadership Tendencies of Four Cognitive Style Combinations

| | Intuitive/Abstract | Sensate/Practical |
|---|---|---|
| **Judger/Sequential** | **NJ**<br><br>**Visionary Decision Makers**<br><br>The NJ combination of Abstraction with Sequential thinking tendencies produces a leader who is comfortable looking at the big picture and confident in their assessment of how it could best be improved. The NJ is at ease designing programs and procedure and setting out long range goals. They approach their goals with an inner vision and in most cases can present their vision in a compelling way to others. They can be highly determined when their goals are clear. They tend to dislike inconsistency and incongruity.<br><br>**Strengths**<br><br>• Visionary<br>• Integration of big picture with daily practices<br>• Analytical and Insightful<br>• Innovation<br><br>**Areas of Improvement**<br><br>• Can be over confidence of ideas<br>• Can put too much trust in long-term strategies<br>• Can appear disrespectful of status quo<br>• Can miss opportunities waiting for the perfect solution | **SJ**<br><br>**Realistic Decision Makers**<br><br>The SJ combination of Practical and Sequential thinking tendencies produces a leader who is comfortable with organization and managing institutions big or small. The SJ is at ease finding better ways to achieve practical goals and create higher levels of efficiency. The SJ leader is most often dependable and well informed and bases their decisions on past experience. They tend to dislike ambiguity and disorganization.<br><br>**Strengths**<br><br>• Organization<br>• Streamlining processes and operations<br>• Team oriented<br>• Institutional Respect<br><br>**Areas of Improvement**<br><br>• Can put too much faith in policy<br>• Can be uneasy about changing status quo<br>• Can rely too heavily on common sense<br>• Can be perceived as controlling or inflexible |
| **Perceiver/Random** | **NP**<br><br>**Adaptable innovators**<br><br>The combination of Abstraction and Random thinking tendencies produces a leader who is motivated to explore new possibilities and challenges. The NP tends to be a less conventional type of leader who is uncomfortable being confined by existing structures or expectations. The NP will typically value innovation over maintenance and the status quo.<br><br>**Strengths**<br><br>• Change oriented<br>• Connections and Ideas<br>• Spontaneous action<br>• Depth of analysis<br><br>**Areas of Improvement**<br><br>• Follow through and completion<br>• Unrealistic goals<br>• Comfort with Spontaneity and change in direction can appear capricious to others.<br>• Can be seen as being too independent and not enough team-oriented | **SP**<br><br>**Adaptable Realists**<br><br>The combination of Practical and Random thinking tendencies produces a leader who is the most adaptable, in the moment, and hands on. The SP values data, information and experiences and makes decisions based on things that they have found to work for them. They tend to trust theoretical or less tangible solutions to problem less than other types.<br><br>**Strengths**<br><br>• Practical solutions and common sense<br>• Trouble shooting<br>• Grounded in reality<br>• Flexible and Spontaneous<br><br>**Areas of Improvement**<br><br>• Can Lack global vision<br>• Actions can appear disintegrated<br>• Can miss deeper patterns<br>• Can be slow in making larger decisions |

# APPENDIX D:

# Classroom Management Tendencies of Each Teaching Style

| | Intuitive (N)/Abstract | Sensate (S)/Practical |
|---|---|---|
| **Perceiver (P)/Random** | **NPs - Creative - Spontaneous**<br><br>The Intuitive (N)/Perceiver (P) combination tends to be the most creative and free-thinking type. A good term for their classroom management style mentality is "global." They tend to incorporate a broad set of principles and are very comfortable making adjustments on the fly.<br><br>**Things to learn from the NP:**<br>• A dynamic approach to teaching<br>• How to use data/events to learn to evolve and change<br>• How expectations can be implicit but well-understood<br>• The benefits of reading the students and the situation and not being a slave to the plan<br><br>**Things the NP might need to work on:**<br>• Making the structure more explicit (especially for the SJ students)<br>• Keeping in mind that changing plans can create discomfort if it happens frequently<br>• Being sensitive that setting and keeping to time frames is helpful for many students<br>• Being very clear and concrete when giving directions | **SPs - Realistic and Spontaneous**<br><br>The sensate (S)/Perceiver (P) combination tends to be the most tuned-in to the present moment reality. Their classroom management can be the most subjective, in the sense that they interpret events on a student-by-student basis. They are the most likely to trust a strategy that has worked in the past, and they rely less on theory than experience.<br><br>**Things to learn from the SP:**<br>• How to appreciate the subjective nature of teaching and students<br>• How to adjust to the situation<br>• How to project an authentic and "here and now" affect<br>• Practical innovations to the job<br><br>Things the SP might need to work on:<br><br>• How to be more consistent and principle-driven<br>• How to be less personal and reactive with student misbehavior<br>• Thinking more in terms of long-term outcomes as opposed to what seems to work in the short-term<br>• Communicating a sense of vision and purpose to students |
| **Judger (J)/Sequential** | **NJs - Systematic - Rational**<br><br>The intuitive (N)/Judger (J) combination tends to be the most principle-driven of all the types. Their classroom management style mentality begins with a set of theoretical assumptions as the primary reality, which are then applied to practical situations as needed. They tend to have very strong ideas about what they want and desire all the aspects of their class to fit into an integrated whole.<br><br>**Things to learn from the NJ:**<br>• How to think more systemically<br>• How to attend to patterns below the surface rather than just what is apparent<br>• Innovative ideas they develop<br><br>**Things the NJ might need to work on:**<br>• Changing strategies when something is not working<br>• Allowing more flexibility in the day for some students<br>• Being tolerant of the diverse needs and approaches of students<br>• Being concrete when giving directions<br>• Not assuming that a good theoretical explanation will translate into "what to do" for most students. | **SJs - Realistic and Organized**<br><br>The sensate (S)/Judger (J) combination is the most common among teachers possibly for their natural affinity for order and structure, and their comfort with institutional settings. Practical system-thinking comes easily to them, so their classrooms usually reflect a high degree of efficiency. They typically find a set of effective routines and procedures and refine them over time.<br><br>**Things to learn from the SJ:**<br>• How to create efficient procedures<br>• Practical ideas that save time and energy<br>• Ways to visually display and manage ideas and materials to good advantage<br>• Consistency and Fairness<br><br>Things the SJ might need to work on:<br><br>• Changing patterns when there is evidence that a need is present<br>• Mistakenly interpreting an efficient practice as one that is inherently effective/healthy for students<br>• Putting more emphasis on promoting intrinsic types of motivation rather than relying on too many extrinsic forms<br>• Being more flexible and spontaneous when it would benefit the situation |

# APPENDIX E:

## Ten Practices that Encourage Movement Up And Ten Practices that Limit Growth or Lead Down

| Move a School Up | Limit Growth/Move Down |
|---|---|
| Positive Recognitions | Negative Recognitions |
| Assess Process Quality | Colored Card Charts |
| Clear Learning Targets | Extrinsic Rewards |
| Student Self-Evaluation | Personal Praise |
| Team Building/Cooperative Learning | Proximity Control |
| Clarifying Questions and Debriefing | "I like the way" Manipulation |
| Focus on Quality | Focus on task Completion |
| Student Leadership | Focus on Compliance and Obedience |
| Group Identity Building | Student-student Comparisons |
| Sound Social Contract | Incoherent Policy |

# Practices that Encourage Movement Up

| Effective Practice | Why it is Effective |
|---|---|
| **Positive Recognitions.** Providing feedback related to the task quality and student' goals for that task. | Empowers the student with information and helps them recognize what they chose to do that worked. |
| **Assess Process Quality.** Rubrics that define quality process to use in the process of growth a self reflection toward higher standards. | Promotes a picture of quality in practical and hierarchical terms. Encourages student agency over their own actions. |
| **Clear Learning Targets.** What is good is clearly spelled out in rubrics and guidelines and used throughout the learning process to guide actions | When the target is clear and standing still the student can trust what they are doing is worth persisting in. |
| **Student Self-Evaluation.** Questions are used to help students reflect on how their choices are playing out and what they could do differently. | Questions help students recognize the cause and effect within the phenomenon and support growth in responsible choices. |
| **Team Building/Cooperative Learning.** Students learn to work collaboratively with a ran roles and tasks and solve conflict and challenges democratically. | Helps build cooperation skills which are essential to every aspect of a high function class and personal success. |

# Practices that Encourage Movement Up Cont.

| Effective Practice | Why it is Effective |
|---|---|
| **Clarifying Questions and Debriefing.** During and after an activity have students examin what went well and what did not. | Debriefing helps encourage quality iterations and so is a powerful way to demonstrate a growth mindset. |
| **Focus on Quality.** Feedback and assessment criteria and grades in general support process qu and effort. | Students tend to want to focus on outcomes and how they compare. Shifting their focus promotes growth mindset. |
| **Student Leadership.** If students can lead it, or take ownership of it, they should. Including class meetings, conflict resolution, decision making, et | When students are given real power their level of responsibility, maturity, and desire to contribute grows. It's a basic need. |
| **Group identity building.** Find fun low stakes ways for students to bond together in ways wher they can accomplish a goal together or in a competition with another class. | When students can experience "team wins" it leads to liking, trust, and bonding. Bonding leads to many other benefits. |
| **Sound Social Contract.** Everyone at the school commits to doing what is best the common good and it is spelled out and formalized into clear language and actions. | For the school to feel safe, solid, and sane, we need to trust others to do their part and embrace our role in the democracy. |

# Practices that Limit the School's Growth

| Ineffective Practice | Why it is Limiting |
|---|---|
| **Negative Recognitions.** Pointing out all the cases when students do not do what they are supposed t | Students get addicted to the reminders, others are annoyed and lose trust in the teacher. They breed the need for more. |
| **Colored Card Charts.** Students behavioral levels are displayed on a chart as a form of public shamir | Do not encourage quality behavior or growth. They only promote avoidance-based obedience or resentment. |
| **Extrinsic Rewards.** Students are given stickers or prizes for "on task" behavior in an effort to reinforce that behavior. | Giving extrinsic reinforcement systematically reduces intrinsic motivation and makes students addicted to the rewards. |
| **Personal Praise.** Students are given personal praise related to how good they are being or how happy the teacher is with them. | Shifts the focus of the work externally to the teacher's value and away from the student's value. Creates dependency and insecurity. |
| **Proximity Control.** Teachers goes over and stands next to student who appear off task an effort to physically intimidate them into more positive beha | Promotes untrustworthy students, creates dependence on the teacher's proximity so ultimately reinforces the unwanted action. |

# Practices that Limit the School's Growth Cont.

| Ineffective Practice | Why it is Limiting |
|---|---|
| **"I like the way" manipulation.** Teacher points out students who are on task when another is not ; says to the whole class "I like the way this student sending the message to the off task student. | Students feel compared. The communication is incongruent and dishonest and so breeds resentment and unsafe feelings. |
| **Focus on task completion.** Teacher walks around and praises students for getting done with the task being so quick about their work. | Students learn that the point of the task is to get done (regardless of the quality) so that they can be praised and gain approval. |
| **Focus on compliance and obedience.** Teacher tells students how happy she/he is when the stude what they are supposed to do and how unhappy wh they are not on task. | Students learn that their job is to make the teachers happy. This breeds external locus of control, anxiety and insecurity. |
| **Student-student comparisons.** Teacher compares one student's grades or performance to another for the purpose of motivating the lower performing student. | It encourages a fixed-ability orientation and a fear of failure. Breeds student-student resentment and passive aggressiveness. |
| **Incoherent policy.** School puts in place policies and programs for various reasons, but they do not have a unifying vision or values so compete with one another. | Teachers work hard but don't see good results, few feel like their work is aligned. Students are frustrated by mixed messages. |

# APPENDIX F:

## School Frowth Pathway including SCAI School Climate Ratings and Corresponding Predicted Achievement

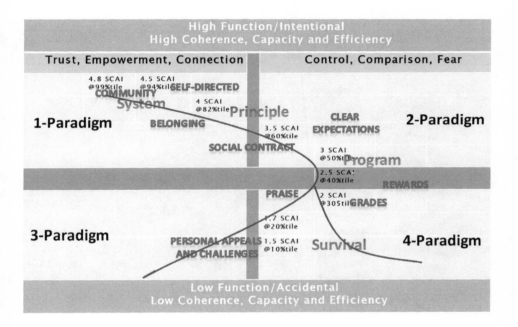

High Function/Intentional
High Coherence, Capacity and Efficiency

Trust, Empowerment, Connection | Control, Comparison, Fear

4.8 SCAI @99%tile    4.5 SCAI @94%tile    SELF-DIRECTED

COMMUNITY System

4 SCAI @82%tile    Principle

1-Paradigm    BELONGING    CLEAR EXPECTATIONS    2-Paradigm

3.5 SCAI @60%tile

SOCIAL CONTRAST

3 SCAI @50%tile    Program

2.5 SCAI @40%tile    REWARDS

PRAISE    2 SCAI @30%tile    GRADES

1.7 SCAI @20%tile

3-Paradigm    PERSONAL APPEALS AND CHALLENGES    1.5 SCAI @10%tile    Survival    4-Paradigm

Low Function/Accidental
Low Coherence, Capacity and Efficiency